# Give Us Each Day

Alice Dunbar-Nelson *(Ohio Historical Society)*

Also by Gloria T. Hull

*All the Women Are White,*
*All the Blacks Are Men,*
*But Some Of Us Are Brave:*
*Black Women's Studies*
(edited with Patricia Bell Scott
and Barbara Smith)

# Give Us Each Day

## The Diary of Alice Dunbar-Nelson

EDITED WITH A CRITICAL
INTRODUCTION AND NOTES
by Gloria T. Hull

W · W · NORTON & COMPANY

NEW YORK · LONDON

Published simultaneously in Canada by Stoddart, a subsidiary of General Publishing
Co. Ltd, Don Mills, Ontario.
Printed in the United States of America.

The text of this book is composed in Electra, with display type set in Baskerville.
Composition and Manufacturing by The Maple-Vail Book Manufacturing Group.

FIRST EDITION

Library of Congress Cataloging in Publication Data
Dunbar-Nelson, Alice Moore, 1875–1935.
    Give us each day.
    Includes index.
    1. Dunbar-Nelson, Alice Moore, 1875–1935—Diaries.
2. Authors, American—20th century—Biography. I. Hull,
Gloria T. II. Title.
PS3507.U6228Z465 1984      818'.5203 [B]      84–6055

ISBN 0-393-01893-8

W. W. Norton & Company, Inc., 500 Fifth Avenue, New York, N.Y. 10110
W. W. Norton & Company Ltd., 37 Great Russell Street, London WC1B 3NU

1 2 3 4 5 6 7 8 9 0

For Alice Dunbar-Nelson herself,
who lived these days of triumph,
years of pain

# Contents

# List of Illustrations

Note: In some cases, newspaper articles and other illustrative materials have been cropped or otherwise not reproduced in full because of space, readability, layout design, and the aim of focusing on Dunbar-Nelson. Except where otherwise noted in captions, all photographs and illustrations are courtesy of Pauline A. Young.

# Introduction

THIS DIARY OF ALICE DUNBAR-NELSON is only the second one by a Black woman that we have had the good fortune to see. Charlotte Forten's *Journal*—kept during the middle years of the nineteenth century and first published in 1953—has been the only book-length one available. It is the record of an aware and sensitive young Black woman during her schooldays in Salem, Massachusetts, and her adventures teaching with the Civil War Port Royal experiment. However, Forten, a proper, self-effacing New Englander, had a different life and personality, moved in a different world, and consequently produced a very different document than did Dunbar-Nelson, her later counterpart.

One wonders how many other publishable diaries by Black women have been written, but have not come to light. It is impossible, of course, to answer this intriguing question. It is not impossible, though, to understand why, until now, we have been able to lay hands on only these two. Alice Walker, in her essay "In Search of Our Mothers' Gardens," feelingly sets the perspective by explaining "the agony of the lives of [Black] women who might have been Poets, Novelists, Essayists, [Diarists] and Short Story writers . . . who died with their real gifts stifled within them" because of slavery, racism, sexism, sexual abuse, overwork, child-bearing and -rearing, prohibitions against reading and writing, and exclusion from every other recognized outlet for creative expression. *

Even those few Black women who have somehow managed to occupy positions where diary keeping might have been a possibility have been as hampered as their less fortunate sisters by subtler forms of prejudice. Bearing the burden of their relatively privileged status, they have thrown their energies into social reform and racial uplift, and, I suspect, they have also regarded the journal as an alien and uncongenial tradition in which to package their experiences. Clearly,

---

* Alice Walker, "In Search of Our Mothers' Gardens: The Creativity of Black Women in the South," *Ms.* (May 1974), 66–67.

then, diary keeping has not been compatible with the conditions of the lives of the vast majority of Black women. Furthermore, Black women and their writings have not been so valued that life documents by them have been preserved, sought, or published. It is, therefore, also not surprising that printed collections of letters by Black women do not exist.

However, Black women have chronicled their lives in other autobiographical forms; and it is to these that we must turn for a tradition-making body of work. This tradition includes the slave narratives of such figures as Harriet Brent Jacobs, Nancy Prince, Sojourner Truth, and Elizabeth Keckley. It also comprises the relatively large number of autobiographies that have been published by diverse Black women, such as Susie King Taylor, Daisy Bates, Billie Holiday, Mary Church Terrell, Ossie Guffy, and Ann Moody. (Note though that, among writers, only Zora Neale Hurston, Pauli Murray, Gwendolyn Brooks, Nikki Giovanni, and Maya Angelou have set down versions of their lives.) It is more than interesting that Black women prefer to show themselves in the form of traditional autobiography. Of course, the autobiographical impulse in Black writing is extremely strong (some would say dominant), but it almost appears as if Black women could not assume the luxury or run the risk of the spontaneous self-disclosure of diary writing. And, finally, there is the countervailing influence of the oral tradition that suffuses all of Black culture.

What was it, then, about Dunbar-Nelson and her life that impelled her to this strange form of self-expression? Perhaps looking at her background and her circumstances when she wrote the diary will provide some clues.

Dunbar-Nelson was born Alice Ruth Moore in New Orleans, Louisiana, July 19, 1875, her father a merchant marine and mother a seamstress. After attending public school and then graduating from Straight University in 1892, she began teaching in New Orleans and assumed a prominent place in its Black and Creole society, especially in musical and literary circles. She was president of the Whittier Club of her A.M.E. church and acted in dramas that it presented. Generally, she was considered a beautiful and talented young woman from whom much was expected. In 1896, she came northeast for further schooling, subsequently matriculating at Cornell, Columbia, and the University of Pennsylvania. Her areas of study included English literature, English educational measurements, and psychology. At Cornell in 1908, she produced a thesis on the influence of Milton on Wordsworth that was so insightful that scholars such as Professor Lane

Cooper wrote to her for information and an article based upon it was published in *Modern Language Notes* (April 1909).

Shortly after she began teaching at the White Rose Mission in New York City in 1897 (which later became the White Rose Home for Girls in Harlem), Alice began a storybook courtship with Paul Laurence Dunbar, America's first famous Black poet. He had seen a picture and poem of hers in a Boston magazine and initiated a decorous and romantic correspondence. After marrying on March 8, 1898, they set up house in Washington, D.C. Even though they sincerely, it seems, encouraged each other's writing ambitions, their marriage was tempestuous. Accusations of selfishness, infidelity, and cruelty cropped up between them, aggravated by gossip, the frequent separations necessitated by Paul's career, and his medically induced drinking. (Because of his tuberculosis, doctors had prescribed alcohol for him, to which he became addicted.) Moreover, Paul had always been extremely close to his protective mother, and Alice's family had exhibited some misgivings about his very dark skin color and his work with minstrel shows and musicals. After Alice left Paul in 1902, she refused to be reconciled with him. Therefore, they were estranged when he died at his home in Dayton, Ohio, on February 6, 1906. Yet the world gave respect to her as his wife, sending her numerous condolences, requests for information and souvenirs, and commercial propositions.

After the separation, Dunbar-Nelson (and her family) moved to Wilmington, Delaware, the place that remained her base for the next thirty years. From 1902 to 1920, she taught at Howard High School (then the only secondary school for Blacks in the state) and served as head of the English department. She executed her often tiresome duties well—teaching, supervising, procuring funds, directing class-night plays, writing the history of the school, assisting the administration, and so on. Though her quick tongue and near-white complexion sometimes inspired animosity, she maintained working friendships with her colleagues. For seven of these years at Howard, she also directed the summer sessions for in-service teachers at State College for Colored Students (later Delaware State College), Dover, and taught two years in the summer session at Hampton Insititute.

On April 20, 1916, Dunbar-Nelson made another marriage, to Robert J. Nelson (1873–1949), whom she called Bobo, Bob O, or Bobbo (pronounced Bob-O). A journalist and widower from Harrisburg, Pennsylvania, he had two children whose mother had died of tuberculosis. Because Dunbar-Nelson and Robert were both involved in politics and racial activities, theirs was a good professional union. They cooperated when that was in order and pursued their separate activities when that was necessary. Together, they edited and published a progressive Black newspaper, *The Wilmington Advocate*, from 1920 to 1922.

During this period, Dunbar-Nelson was also active in many civic, racial, and women's causes. She was an organizer for the Middle Atlantic states in the women's suffrage campaign (1915), a field representative in the South for the Woman's Committee of the Council of National Defense (1918), and the first Black woman to serve on the State Republican Committee of Delaware (1920). She was a working member of such groups as the National Federation of Colored Women's Clubs, the National Association of Colored Women, the League of Independent Political Action, and the Delta Sigma Theta Sorority. Furthermore, Dunbar-Nelson had already achieved some renown as a writer.

When she was only twenty years old, she had published *Violets and Other Tales* (1895), a collection of poems, tales, sketches, essays, and stories. Being a juvenile work, the book—with its diverse inclusions—evidences a beginning writer's experimentation with various tones and genres. The pieces are usually brief, slight, impressionistic—but some of them possess charm and interest. *Violets* was followed in 1898 by a volume of short stories, *The Goodness of St. Rocque*, published by Dodd, Mead, and Company. The stories here are longer, better developed, more polished. They are all set firmly in New Orleans and fully utilize the Creole history and distinctive culture of the city, usually in conjunction with themes of love. In addition to some earlier writing and editing for the *A.M.E. Church Review*, by the time she began her diary, Dunbar-Nelson had compiled two volumes of works suitable for platform and program delivery, *Masterpieces of Negro Eloquence* (1913) and *The Dunbar Speaker and Entertainer* (1920). Articles by her were appearing in print—such as her two part "People of Color in Louisiana" in *The Journal of Negro History* (1916–17)—and her poetry was being regularly published and anthologized.

Throughout her life, Dunbar-Nelson was regarded as the temperamental family genius, always having to be calmed down from one emotional peak or another. She was forceful, strong-willed, inquisitive, imaginative, and stubborn. Yet, in her own way, she was very much a "lady." She liked pretty things (and even luxury), flowers, dogs, and children. There was a romantic side to her nature, and she took art, piano, and cello lessons, did lacework, and frequented the theatre. Furthermore, she had a high regard for reputation, manners, and the proprieties. A tall, attractive, auburn-haired woman, she presented an imposing appearance. In her dress, she was elegant and fashionable.

This background, then, reveals Dunbar-Nelson to be an educated, culturally sophisticated Black woman writer. Being such, she was familiar with the form and tradition of English diary keeping. She did not find it alien, was, in fact, favorably predisposed toward it, and recognized its possibilities for herself. Ever so often within the diary, she reveals her knowledge of the tradition and sense of forming a part of it, as when she begins her July 19, 1929 birthday entry with "Does one have to record thoughts?" thus showing her awareness that it was almost *de rigueur* to do so in a journal. Yet Dunbar-Nelson's background and literary bent do not sufficiently explain why she kept a diary, while other Black women similar to her in education, discretionary leisure, and sense of personal importance and destiny did not. The question remains a puzzling one, especially on a group level; and even when answers are attempted on an individual basis, they too prove tentative and inconclusive.

During the periods when she kept the diary, Dunbar-Nelson's life was in flux or crisis. This supports the axiom that diaries are most often and most interestingly written in times of change and turmoil, or, as it is often put, in times of mobility—most often thought of as geographic, but just as plausibly psychic as well. When she first began her diary on July 29, 1921, Dunbar-Nelson was undergoing agonies of soul and spirit trying to adjust to the traumas of the previous year; and the work ends after 1931, just when Robert is given the appointment that frees them from debt and worry.

During these years of upheaval and personal change, Dunbar-Nelson used the diary as a place to vent her thoughts and emotions. There was not a person in her life with whom she could openly be all of the things that she was and with whom she could be totally unguarded (a classic case of female schizophrenia and isolation). Her good friend Bowse expressed horror at her socializing with boxer Jack Johnson and his wife; her sister Leila could not share her outgoing political and social enthusiasms; her husband Robert was unable to accept her romantic and physical interest in other women—to cite only three major unmeshings. And there were many times when Dunbar-Nelson's contemplations would have frightened and alienated those around her. A husband who could not stand to be told of her anxiety about money and a sister who became alarmed at an outburst of ranting certainly would not have known how to deal with her suicidal yearnings. Such things as these she confined to the pages of her diary. As with all frank diaries, one feels that the impulse for a full, true revelation of self (perhaps for posterity) was a strong operational motivation.

However, Dunbar-Nelson never directly indicates that she is conscious of employing the journal for venting purposes. When she started the diary, she wrote in its preface, "Had I had sense enough to keep a diary all these years that I have been traveling around, . . . there would be less confusion in my mind about lots of things." And even though she had an extremely good memory and naturally retained vivid impressions of long-ago events, Dunbar-Nelson persisted throughout in referring to the diary as a mnemonic device. What she does not make clear, though, is whether she intended for it to help her recall simple events or discern the more complex patterns of her life. Thus, many of her entries are mechanical or journalistic, while introspective thinking and deeper revelations break through in others. There are only two recorded instances of her rereading what she has earlier written (her 1931 birthday, and the anniversary of her 1930 trip to California). But, based on the fact that these are significant dates, and also considering the diary's general importance to her, one can probably assume that she read it over on other occasions as well.

It seems that Dunbar-Nelson also saw the dairy as a self-imposed disciplinary task and a private test of her constancy and character. She frequently voiced irritation and resentment at it (even once calling it a weight on her heart), but continued to keep it up in varying degrees. Clearly, the diary became for her a given, an unchanging focus in the midst of change and uncertainty. These attitudes accord well with her personality because she was basically orderly and precise and had very high expectations for herself, which prompted her to be self-disparaging about laziness. Finally, as is usually the case, the keeping of the diary became for her its own reward, a kind of end sufficient unto itself.

For some years, a day-by-day type of memorandum book served as the basic diary. Usually Dunbar-Nelson limited her entries to the one page per day allotted, even when she had to cramp her handwriting and disregard the lines to squeeze in everything that she wished to say. Sometimes she wrote or typed on other sheets too and pasted them in. These supplementary sheets often reflect her activities and whereabouts—for example, the letterhead of the Paramount Syndicate Company (her own, it seems) and the reverse side of programs from the National Negro Music Festival, one of her Inter-Racial Peace Committee projects. (A more detailed discussion of the original manuscript can be found in the Editorial Preface.)

Dunbar-Nelson wrote her diary, like most diarists, when the spirit moved her, and like most women diarists, when she could find the time. One pleasant morning she is sitting by the open kitchen window drinking a cup of tea and writing in the diary. Another time, she is upstairs, in bed, plugging away at 2:00 A.M. During the first years of the journal, she constantly vowed to write daily, but was never able to keep her resolves. Some lapses were five to ten days long; others lasted three or four weeks; and once she stopped writing altogether for two months. On this last occasion, she resumed by saying that she did not know why she stopped, suggesting, for one thing, that she did not clearly know why she kept it up. Finally, in 1930, she stopped making resolutions and simply let the words fall as they would.

Actually, Dunbar-Nelson's "blanket" entries are, in at least one way, preferable to her diurnal jottings because they are usually more discursive. The kinds of entries that she made also varied from year to year—ranging from the leisurely sentenced ones of 1921, to the choppy ones of 1926–27, to the intense and briefly reflective entries of 1930. Likewise, she writes in every one of her many moods, only confessing once, in 1931, that she deliberately refrained "when the misery and wretchedness and disappointment and worry were so close to me that to write it out was impossible, and not to write it out, foolish."

As fascinating as are the issues raised thus far, the heart of the diary lies in what it reveals, through Dunbar-Nelson's life, about the meaning of being a Black woman in twentieth-century America. These revelations include both the commonplace and the startling and add up to a picture whose cumulative impact is staggering.

First, one notices that during her entire career, Dunbar-Nelson received attention for being Paul Laurence Dunbar's wife and widow and not necessarily for her own individual achievement. When he was alive, she was thought of as his wife who incidentally "wrote a little herself," a secondary status that she sometimes buttressed by her deferent poses and feminine role-playing. She also chose to continue carrying his name, thus ensuring the linkage. However, upon reflection it becomes clear that Dunbar-Nelson did this partly because of her awareness that, in a racist, sexist society, it could be helpful and because of the certainly galling knowledge that, as a Black woman, she needed as much help as she could get. Ironically, sexism cuts both

ways. When she died—after twenty-nine years of widowhood, a sec-
ond husband, and many illustrious accomplishments of her own—the
Philadelphia *Afro-American* ran a banner story with this headline: "Alice
Ruth Moore's 2 Husbands / First, a Volatile Genius; Second, a Calm
Newsman / Washingtonians Recall Romance of the Dunbars / Mrs.
[Mary Church] Terrell Recalls When Wife of Poet Borrowed / an Ice
Cream Freezer."*

At the outset, it is apparent that Dunbar-Nelson's basic living situation is that of a female-centered household and strong woman-to-
woman family relationships. The core consisted of Alice, her sister
Leila, their mother Patricia, and Leila's four children, three of whom
were girls. They added on husbands and other children as their life
choices dictated, but always remained together. Dunbar-Nelson never
bore any children herself, but she acquired two—an elder daughter,
Elizabeth, and younger son, Bobby—when she married the widowed
Robert and helped to raise them as well as her sister's four. As different
as these women were, their personalities seem to have complemented
each other more often than they clashed, and they constituted an in-
house support system for one another. They often had fun together,
too, as when Dunbar-Nelson and Leila, a very exclusive, self-styled
club of two, treated Leila's daughter Pauline to a night out in Philadelphia.

Still, there were stresses between them in the home. Probably the
most acute ones were generated by mother Patricia's long, difficult
illness and lingering death. During this time, Dunbar-Nelson wrote
things in her diary like "home—to a muddling sort of kitchen full of
nervous overwrought Leila and Pauline, a diddling Miss Waters [the
nurse] and a glum Robert. I sometimes wonder why I come home at
all" (January 5, 1931). Money, being a scarce commodity, was also a
potential sore point and leads to the even more serious observation
that the household was an economic unit—albeit a marginal and precarious one, especially becasue its members were predominantly Black
women. They all worked—very hard—when they could find jobs and
until they could no longer do so because of age and health. To paraphrase Toni Morrison in *Sula*, these women had nobody / nothing
"either white or male" to fall back on;† hence they had to rely on
themselves. It was a constant struggle.

One might ask, "What about Dunbar-Nelson's husband?" His

* The Philadelphia *Afro-American*, September 28, 1935.
† Toni Morrison, *Sula* (New York, 1973; rpt. New York: Bantam Books, 1975), p. 44.

position as a *Black* man was far from the secure sufficiency that would have allowed her the luxury of leisure. He was making his way in the world as best he could, hanging on to teetering enterprises like the Black Elks' (the Improved Benevolent and Protective Order of Elks) Washington *Eagle* newspaper and hoping for political preferment. Page after page of the diary is filled with Dunbar-Nelson's financial plight. She helped to found organizations—such as the Industrial School for Colored Girls in Marshalltown, Delaware—to create employment, even if low-paying, for herself and grabbed at flimsy schemes that promised reward. Some of her most harrowing passages concern bounced checks, unpaid mortgages, humiliating inquisitions with finance companies, and the like. At her lowest point, during the height of the Depression, she seriously entertained the idea of selling encyclopedias and Spencer undergarments door-to-door.

Dunbar-Nelson's helping relationships with the women of her family were also part of a larger system of Black female support. She knew practically all of the active and prominent Black women of her time— Nannie Burroughs, Charlotte Hawkins Brown, Jessie Fauset, Laura Wheeler, Bessye Bearden, to name a few—and associated with them. As with her family, these associations were not without their jealousies and pettinesses. But, in a world that contrived to devalue them, these Black women were essential to each other's well-being.

Many of these leading women of the day were a part of the flourishing Black women's club movement, which became especially visible and effective with the 1896 founding of the National Association of Colored Women. Working first on a local level and then confederating in regional and national efforts, Black women of all classes united to combat negative stereotypes about themselves and to materially and spiritually aid in the overall betterment of the race. For a woman like Dunbar-Nelson, this work entailed such time-consuming activities as attending local executive and full membership meetings; cooperating with other clubwomen and the public to carry out official duties, tasks, and projects; planning and participating in state, regional, and national conventions. What they accomplished in housing, education, civil rights, women's suffrage, travel accomodations, health, cultural affairs, and so forth was impressive.

The beauty of the club movement was the opportunity it provided for like-minded Black women to work together. Dunbar-Nelson's relationships with three particular women in the diary reflect this kind of racial and sororal camaraderie. One is Edwina B. Kruse, founding principal of Howard High School, who gave her emotional sustenance and encouragement. Dunbar-Nelson's esteem for "Krusie" or "Ned" (as she was called) is best documented by the fact that she wrote an unpublished novel based on Kruse's life, entitled *This Lofty Oak*. Truly a labor of love, the original manuscript runs to 565 typewritten pages. Even after Kruse retired and became senile, Dunbar-Nelson continued to be dutifully attentive. The second is Georgia Douglas Johnson, the most popular Black woman poet of the 1920s. They shared womanly interactions (Dunbar-Nelson teaching her how to wear hats) and related to each other as sister artists. Johnson invited Dunbar-Nelson to be a special guest at one of her Washington, D.C. literary gatherings, and Dunbar-Nelson, in turn, kept up with what Johnson was producing and reviewed her work. They both benefited as women and as writers from their contact with one another.

Finally, there is Mary McLeod Bethune, who was not a close personal friend. It seems that she served certain role-model functions for Dunbar-Nelson. The diary presents a few scenes that are so pricelessly suggestive that a reader is moved to wish, "If only I could have been there." One of these is a picture of Dunbar-Nelson doing her hair while Bethune gets a pedicure at Bethune-Cookman College. It should be mentioned that Dunbar-Nelson spread her strength outward—for example, to the young women at the Industrial School. She bought them watches when they excelled in their studies, counseled abortions for them, and helped to see them through college.

The next issue of Dunbar-Nelson's life illuminated by the diary is the question of class, which becomes problematical when related to the ambiguous status of Black women. Even educated, "middle-class," professional Black women like Dunbar-Nelson almost always come from and / or have firsthand knowledge of working-class or poorer-class situations. In addition, being Black, they have no entrenched and comfortable security in even this achieved class status—and being women, their position is rendered doubly marginal and complicated. These facts foster many contradictions that the diary reveals, sometimes unwittingly. For instance, on March 28, 1927, Dunbar-Nelson writes very grimly about having to go to the pawnshop to raise twenty-five dollars on her rings and earrings to pay the water bill and then in the next paragraph details a "palatial" and "very fine" gathering of the Philadelphia Professional Woman's Club at which she spoke.

The white women ("*wives* of professional men") at this affair had no idea that they were being addressed by and were socializing with a woman who had just visited a pawnshop in order to pay her water bill. Nor was this anywhere uppermost in Dunbar-Nelson's consciousness.

Undoubtedly, she was dressed to look like "a certified check" (her phrase) and was comporting herself likewise. Dunbar-Nelson had the breeding, education, culture, looks, and manners of the "higher classes" (and thought of herself in this way)—but, as we have seen, none of the money to back it up. This is and was very often the case.

Related to this class issue is the notion of the "genteel tradition" in Black life and literature, with its special ramifications for Black women. When scholars of this period talk about cultural strains, they frequently identify two—the "genteel" and the "bohemian / realistic." Dunbar-Nelson—together with W. E. B. DuBois, novelist Jessie Fauset, scholar Alain Locke, and others—is put in the first group and considered to be "bourgie," conservative, stiff, uptight, and accomodationist. Of course, this stance was basically a part of the attempt to counter negative racial stereotypes and put the best racial foot forward. For Black *women*, extra burdens were added. They were always mindful of their need to be living refutations of the sexual slurs to which Black women were subjected and, at the same time, as much as white women, were also tyrannized by the still-prevalent Victorian cult of true womanhood.

Recalling facts like these aids in the understanding of why Dunbar-Nelson carried herself in a manner that one New York newspaper called "distinctively aristocratic."* It also provides perspective for some of her less flattering utterances and attitudes—her refusing to ride in a car with the printer's wife and "Taylor Street friends," her describing a poor Black high school graduation ceremony as "very monkey," and this November 6, 1929 characterization of the president of the National Federation of Colored Women:

> Sallie Stewart is a fine women. But she offends my aesthetics. Fine woman in the sense of achievement—but hopelessly, frightfully, common-place, provincial, middle class.

The truth of the matter (that is, the other truth of the matter) is that Dunbar-Nelson was a genuine, down-to-earth person who, when she allowed herself, enjoyed all types of activities and people. She drank blackmarket Italian red wine and bootleg whiskey, played the numbers, bought "hot" clothes, had friends whom she dubbed "rough-necky," went to Harlem dives and cabarets, and indulged what she called a "low taste" for underworld films and S. S. Van Dine novels. However, one would not have guessed any of this by her apperance.

---

*The New York *Inter-State Tattler*, December [?] 1928.

The same kind of complex duality also marks Dunbar-Nelson's life in the areas of love and sexuality. Her relationship with Robert seems to have been characterized by a strong sense of mutual self-respect and sober practicality typical of many Black heterosexual liaisons. Clearly, they were friends and partners in life. Robert's attitudes were conventionally male (he liked her to be at home when he ran in, and he scolded her for looking like a charwoman—even while she was scrubbing the house), and he was jealous and somewhat possessive (causing Dunbar-Nelson to write on one occasion that he "was cross, of course, as he always is, when I show any interest in any male or female . . ."— September 21, 1928). Nonetheless, he admired, respected, and encouraged her, and even once surprised her by giving support instead of an expected "snort of disgust" when she casually mentioned that she should study law (October 13, 1921). Regardless of whatever other people she may have involved herself with, Dunbar-Nelson appeared to always value their relationship, saying on Thanksgiving 1930: "And yet I have a lot to be thankful for. Bobbo, first, last and always, the best of all."

Before uniting with Robert, Dunbar-Nelson made a secret, short-lived marriage in 1910 with one Arthur Callis, a young Black man twelve years her junior who came fresh from Cornell to teach at Howard High School. She never publicly revealed it, clearly intended that it remain undisclosed, and spoke about it mysteriously even in the diary. Some imperatives of her position—perhaps her thinking about the differences in their age and / or social standing—bade her keep it secret. (Of course, for a man, this circumstance would not have been a problem.) Callis provides the occasion in the diary for Dunbar-Nelson to muse about her lifetime loves:

> [Leaving him] . . . I walked slowly home through the beautiful streets thinking after all, love and beautiful love has been mine from many men, but the great passion of at least four or five whose love for me transcended that for other women—and what more can any woman want? (June 4, 1931)

Apparently, she did want more. The woman-identification revealed in the diary encompassed at least two or three—and probably more—emotionally and physically intimate relationships with women. They were very important aspects of her inner life. But, of course, for her—given her personality, place, and time—it was absolutely essential that they remain hidden. Of the two such lesbian relationships explicitly recorded in the diary, the weightier was obviously with Fay Jackson

Robinson. Dunbar-Nelson was ecstatic about their touching, recording that she wrote a sonnet that began with the marvelously apt, female imagery of this first line: "I had not thought to ope that secret room." And, despite misunderstandings, miscommunications, and disappointments, Dunbar-Nelson could yet sigh in her diary on March 18, 1931: "Anniversary of My One Perfect Day . . . And still we cannot meet again."

Despite the cryptic and hesitant allusions, Dunbar-Nelson clearly reveals the existence and operation of an active Black lesbian network. Dunbar-Nelson mentions that a friend of hers tells her to "look over" a Betty Linford, and that a "heavy flirtation" between two clubwomen friends of hers puts her "nose sadly out of joint" (July 25, August 1, 1928). All of these women were prominent and professional, and most had husbands and / or children. Somehow, they contrived to be themselves and carry on these relationships in what most surely must have been an extremely repressive context—with even more layers of oppression piled on by the stringencies of their roles as Black women.

In the diary, Dunbar-Nelson refers to other affairs and flirtations. Generally speaking, she was a sensuous woman whose passion could not always find expression. Its strength is often revealed, however, as in this excerpt from a sexually charged description of a midnight swim that she enjoyed with a mixed company of friends shortly after her fifty-fourth birthday:

> . . . racing in under the pulsing water to the solitary light on shore. An experience worth having—a glorious, wonderful climax. Only equalled by the velvety luxuriousness of the times when swimming far out—we slipped off our bathing suits . . . and let the water caress our naked forms. (July 27, 1929)

Equally as crucial for Dunbar-Nelson were the conditions and struggles of the workplace. The first year of the diary dramatizes such *Advocate*-related traumas as her being coldly dismissed from magnate Irénée du Pont's office when she tried to sell him stock in the paper and her having to endure the patronizing attitude of a Wilmington political figure who helped to finance it. Perhaps the most graphic revelation of what it meant to be a Black woman on the job emerges from her work with the Inter-Racial Peace Committee. Here, her white male boss questioned her executive ability and even stooped to complain about her lipstick. The Quaker (Society of Friends) board that controlled her committee also gave her a hard time, receiving her reports in silence, failing to attend her functions, and begrudging the two thousand dollars it would have cost to keep her Black-oriented program in operation while squandering large sums of money on other projects (see February 26, 1931). And, of course, there were inescapable annoyances like the Quaker lady who came into the office and inveighed against Blacks in her presence (not knowing her race because of her light complexion), and the member of an audience of Black ministers who, when she "railed at them" for not answering her letters, "piped up" from the back of the room, "Sister, we didn't know how you look!" (February 16, 1931).

How work outside the home and work within it interface shows up clearly in the diary through such matter-of-fact statements as "Home by seven . . . Get some dinner. Tired as I am, have *that* to do" (June 11, 1927). Dunbar-Nelson's not so matter-of-fact consciousness about the sexual politics of domestic life likewise surfaces, as in this May 25, 1929 entry, written after attending the National Negro Music Festival, an event that she planned, arranged, carried out, and worked on day and night just before its occurrence:

> Nearly cracked when I got home a wreck, and Bobbo asked me if there was anything to eat in the ice-box. It was too cruel. But when I got off my shoes, into nightie and bathrobe, and went down into the kitchen to eat the sandwiches he had cooked (fried egg) and a high ball, did not feel so near to tears. I might have bawled him out a plenty.

Like Frances E. W. Harper, a nineteenth-century Black woman writer, Dunbar-Nelson was engaged throughout her life in multifaceted social activism—showing, yet again, that aware Black women felt that they could not forego such involvement. During the time of the diary, most of this work was with the state and national organizations of the National Federation of Colored Women's Clubs. Seen against the general backdrop of the women's club movement, it helps to round out the picture of American feminism and also adds details to the record of Black activism for the period. For instance, in September 1928, Dunbar-Nelson writes about a conference sponsored by women of the Inter-Racial Council of the Federal Council of Churches where, in her words,

> It was the colored women . . . who kept the discussions on a frank and open plane; who struggled hardest to prevent the conference from degenerating into a sentimental mutual admiration society, and who insisted that all is not right and perfect in this country of ours, and that there is a deal to be done by the right thinking church women of both races.

Dunbar-Nelson's work with the Inter-Racial Peace Committee tied in, too, with her racial and political views. Following the pattern of many Americans, she supported World War I but was strongly pacifist when sabers again began rattling in the late 1920s. At a 1929 peace conference, she notes the incongruity of their agenda being taken up with talk of tonnage, cruisers, battleships, etc., summing it up by writing: "Seems to me everyone is preparing for war and temporizing with the thought of it" (October 24, 1929). But her radical stance did not go so far as to encompass socialism-communism.

About race, Dunbar-Nelson's diary reveals a not-uncommon dual set of values. Looking at the Black race *sui generis* from within it, she often made critical and disparaging remarks. These even include some class-related aspersions against dark-complexioned Blacks and some comments that suggest personal alienation on her part. However, when she was mindful of the larger, social contexts, she was militantly pro-Black. One of the journal's longest narratives is the story of Theodore Russ, a young Black Delaware man who was tried, convicted, and hung on a trumped-up charge of raping a white woman. Dunbar-Nelson helped to mobilize for his defense and worked hard to try to save him. Once, after a piece of unusually dirty trickery, she wrote, "All day I hated white people"; and on the day he was killed she felt depressed and wished that "all those who sent him to his fate could swing alongside him" (August 19 and 22, 1930).

In addition to her work and civic activities, Dunbar-Nelson maintained a considerable social life. Much of it took place in New York City, Washington, D.C., and Philadelphia, but even in her hometown Wilmington, where old factional feuds and antipathies affected her popularity, there were many visits, parties, and other get-togethers. This added up to an existence that was full and hectic. Her days started early (some years with exercises and prayers) and usually ended at one or two in the morning, often with as many as four or five meetings (not to mention anything else) sandwiched in between. Dunbar-Nelson's energy was astounding, but even she sometimes flagged and, as she once wrote, "fairly fell in bed."

Her stamina becomes even more incredible when one thinks about her health—which was far from perfect. Here is a chronological list of the ailments and medical conditions that beset her during the years of the diary: "overheated, apoplectic spell"; high blood pressure and kidney albumen; "neuritis in knee and sciatica"; "suffer[ing] from what tries to be a stroke"; "lightness and vertigo"; "getting fat and dumpy"; "fatigue, blues and leucorrhea"; "a bad attack of heart and insomnia and nerves last night and indigestion this a.m."; "stomach, liver, intestines—misbehaving"; decayed teeth; "hay fever, bronchitis and prickly heat all at one and the same time"; "viciously bilious . . . recalcitrant stomach, gall bladder, and liver"; "hyper-acidity due to liver . . . jaundice threatened"; "another severe gas attack. Thoroughly frightened at pressure on heart. Thought I'd croak once."

The treatment was worse. Dunbar-Nelson took "hormotones" [*sic*], pituitrin, and calomel, and douched with permanganate of potash. Beginning in 1929, she regularly subjected herself to a horrific process of "draining" designed to clean out her "congested" liver (see September 25, 1929). And her doctor communicated that he knew nothing about her menopausal symptoms. However, the operation of patriarchal medicine is best illustrated by the examination that she went through when she tried to secure a Washington, D.C. public school teaching job in 1927. When the health department doctor failed her for a fluctuating blood pressure and an amount of albumen in her urine that another doctor thought was normal for women her age, Dunbar-Nelson, because she desperately wanted the position, tried to persuade him to reconsider. She ate spinach and hot water attempting to change her test results, took hot lysol douches, worried herself sick, and ran around to offices getting school officials and congressmen to aid her—all the while, of course, having to discuss the intimate particulars of her case. The control of her life and Black female body by the male / white medical establishment and white / male decision-makers is clearly revealed in her pithy understatement: "Never had my piddy-widdy so discussed before in my life, and by all kinds of gentlemen, from Senators and school superintendents down" (February 3, 1927).

Too much of the time, Dunbar-Nelson's mental health was also, as she put it, "profoundly in the D's—discouraged, depressed, disheartened, disgusted" (August 2, 1930). From the beginning of the diary, she occasionally falls prey to normal attacks of "the blues." During the last two years, her mental state was extraordinarily turbulent. She was worried about being "unestablished middle-aged" (March 9, 1931), bored to distraction, and besieged with fears about her worth and continued usefulness.

Undoubtedly, qualities that enabled her to survive were her strength of mind, spirituality, and psychic power, resources that have always served Black women well. Even though she sometimes went to church and so forth, Dunbar-Nelson was not solely a conventionally religious person. She had a freethinking and occult mind. One summer she wrote in the diary:

Lay on the roof in the moonlight and evolved a new cosmogony—each
planet with its own particular God. Too huge a task for one God to look
after both the spiral nebula in Orion and the plant lice that infested my
poor little ivy plant that I brought home. (June 17, 1929)

She used Unity and the Master Key (unorthodox spiritual systems that
focus on the individual's mind), had a lifelong interest in psychology,
believed in "bad-mouthing" (speaking curses on deserving people),
read her fortune in cards, heeded dreams, and relied heavily on her
subconscious mind. Interestingly enough, it appears that despite all
this—or because of it—she was not a very good judge of people when
she approached them in an analytical, rational manner.

The final area of discussion here is what the diary reveals about
Dunbar-Nelson as a Black woman writer and public figure. Fortunately for her posthumous reputation, she flourished throughout the
Harlem Renaissance, that important period from roughly 1915 to 1930
when Black American artistic and literary creativity reached a new
collective zenith. During the height of the Renaissance, her poetry
(some of which had been written earlier) was consistently published—
even though Dunbar-Nelson, strictly speaking, did not belong to the
group of bold, young, experimental poets and did not achieve new
popularity or refurbish her basically traditional style. As an older, cre-
dentialed contemporary, she enjoyed the respect of the younger writers and was sent copies of their books and asked to judge contests.
However, like many of the women writers of the period, her position
as author was adversely affected by her themes and style and certainly
by her sex, which automatically excluded her from male avenues and
circles of prestige and power.

Journalism took most of Dunbar-Nelson's time; but none of her
attempts at film scenarios, short stories, and a novel was successful.
For example, the screenplays—which she appeared to write too fast
and too opportunistically—did not suit the film companies, and the
novel, a satirical one entitled *Uplift*, was damned by herself as "inane,
sophomoric, amateurish puerility" (June 16, 1930). In addition, the
realities of her status and the literary marketplace are graphically illustrated by the career of "Harlem John Henry Views the Airmada," an
intellectually demanding, blank verse poem that she wrote in June
1931, which featured a Black protagonist who questions war against
an ironic counterpoint of Black spirituals and folk songs. She mailed
it out to white magazines, which speedily and repeatedly rejected it,
until it was finally spotlighted in the January 1932 issue of *Crisis*, the

multipurpose official organ of the NAACP, which served as a major outlet for Black writers.

Dunbar-Nelson strove to keep up her reputation and visibility. She plotted to get invited to Fisk University, valued her 1921 Iowa trip for its prestige even though it cost her money, and continued to do her *Eagle* columns solely for the publicity. Even so, this did not pay off when she needed it most—that is, when her Friends Committee work ended and she sought other employment. One cannot help but believe that, given Dunbar-Nelson's qualifications, had it not been for sexual bias, she would certainly have found something to do, say, with *Crisis* or NAACP, or the Black newspapers and press service, places where she applied. Generally, her glum November 4, 1928 prognostication unfortunately contained a measure of truth: "It shall always be my luck, it seems, to miss the Big occasions and be starred at the tiny, bum, back yard affairs."

One of the principal means that she used to keep her name before the public was platform speaking and lecturing. Interestingly, for a woman of her ability and usual confidence, she was unnerved by speaking after male celebrities like James Weldon Johnson and R. Russa Moton, president of Tuskegee Institute, or to predominantly male audiences like the one that she characterized thus: "Too many self-satisfied males—get my goat" (July 25, 1928). She also wanted to be more of a "fire and brimstone" orator. One very striking paragraph in the diary is taken up with her attempted analysis of her inability to arouse frenzied audience emotion:

> Now why can't I do that? Because I can't feel? But I do. Because I am cold? But I am not. I sympathize with the least of them. Too intellectual? Too cynical? Too scornful of bunk-hokum? Must be that. Now there's Nannie Burroughs, for instance, and Mrs. Bethune. But I've got more brains than either—or have I? Probably not—if I had, I'd be where they are instead of wondering at 55 where in God's name I'm going to turn next? (March 1, 1931)

Eventually, she developed a new anecdotal style that pleased both herself and her listeners.

The background against which Dunbar-Nelson stands revealed as a Black woman writer and public figure is also illuminated by the diary in a special and fascinating way—private glimpses of public figures and inside reports of major events, all of which provide even more information for Black Studies students and scholars. There is a 1927 view of Dunbar-Nelson and the great scholar W. E. B. DuBois cooking breakfast for themselves and poet Georgia Douglas Johnson, and one of DuBois and Dr. Virginia Alexander—a pioneering Black female Philadelphia physician—being "horribly obvious" at the Bryn Mawr (Pennsylvania college) Liberal Club Conference in the spring of 1931. And when Dunbar-Nelson tells about the famous Langston Hughes being the only *litterateur* that Bobbo ever took a liking to, Hughes's image as a "man and poet of the people" is further burnished.

The diary gives a nuts-and-bolts view of numerous national Black conventions, such as the research conference held in Durham, North Carolina, in December 1927 and the annual gatherings of the NAACP. From its pages, we also learn that, at one point, Dunbar-Nelson and Carter G. Woodson, founder of the Association for the Study of Negro Life and History, were collaborating on researching and writing a book. These are only a few of the many such facts found in the journal.

Seen in relation to her other literary work, Dunbar-Nelson's diary may be the most significant and enduring piece of writing that she produced. Unquestionably, it is a unique one that only she and she alone could have added to the body of literature. However, until such noncanonical forms as the diary are reappraised and appropriately valued, her status (and that of the many other women who write in them) will not be appreciably changed. It is also unfortunate that journalism, another form that claimed a great deal of her attention, is rendered inaccessible and ephemeral to posterity by its predominantly topical nature.

Dunbar-Nelson's diary is not like the self-consciously and / or laboriously written documents of Virginia Woolf and Anaïs Nin. Kept in the ordinary way, it has the expected virtues and limitations of the prototypical—not to say classic—diary form. Dunbar-Nelson never regarded the journal as a vehicle for creative, literary expression. Yet its style has both interest and merit. Formal British diction and latinate syntax stand side by side with Black folksay and the latest street-corner slang. There is also a great deal of tonal variety—humor, hyperbole, wit, parody, and sarcasm ("Addie Hunton comes in looking more like Death eating a cracker than ever"), brief character portraiture, high-blown purple passages, and imagistic writing:

> For my affairs are in a most parlous state. I have come to the center of a stagnant pool where I drift aimlessly around a slow oozy backwash of putrid nothingness. And Bobbo's appointment is the only thing that can wash me out of the slimy mess. (June 26, 1931)

Another noticeable feature of the diary's style is how it betrays Dunbar-Nelson's ego and her bent toward self-centering and aggrandizement. She awkwardly twists sentences to interpolate phrases like "as did by me," "as I knew," "with me." These constructions show her—a proud woman—giving to herself, in her private chronicle, the credit that may not have been accorded to her in the outside world. And, of course, there is Dunbar-Nelson's more direct self-disclosure: playing with dolls, differentiating between herself and other women who act silly, and thinking to buy a handkerchief *before* she goes into a public bathroom to cry. This kind of thing is only matched by the indelibility of a few cameos that are scattered throughout the work— for example, her bounding out of a car to break off Christmas tree branches, and her clinging to the side of a train that had unexpectedly started up.

Enough has already been said about the diary's background and content to indicate how important a document it is. Its revelations about Black culture and about women's existence are priceless. It should force a radical reassessment of the generalities we were almost becoming accustomed to accepting as truth about Black women's / writers' lives during the period. Ultimately, this diary is a singular work that has the power both of *lived* life and moving literature. As a Black woman, reading it from the beginning through to the hopefully muted end, I feel as if I have washed my face in an icy spring and my spirit in a lava bed. Every reader's response may not be this profound. However, I daresay that many will experience something of the strange mixture of depression and exaltation that always overtakes me whenever I finally come to put it down.

GLORIA T. HULL

*September 1984*

# Editorial Preface

WHEN ALICE DUNBAR-NELSON died in 1935, she left this diary among her voluminous papers and unpublished writings.* It has been perused by her niece Pauline A. Young and cursorily glanced at by a few researchers, but had never been thoroughly read or studied. The original, long in the possession of Ms. Young, has been acquired by the University of Delaware; a microfilmed copy is a part of the Paul Laurence Dunbar Collection at the Ohio Historical Society. In its manuscript entirety, the diary consists of almost two thousand (counting front and back) pages of different sizes, many of which are hard to decipher.

At the beginning of her 1921 journal keeping, Dunbar-Nelson wrote, "Bought this book for a diary." "This book" was an 8¼"-×-7", bound, unlined volume with a brown cell-patterned cover. It was predominantly handwritten on both sides in dark ink (now faded). Sometimes Dunbar-Nelson typed on the book pages; sometimes she wrote or typed on other blank sheets and pasted these to the book pages. This volume also functioned as a scrapbook. In it Dunbar-Nelson glued flyers, programs, cards, announcements, invitations, and clippings. As a result, this 1921 book is interestingly overstuffed and its pages are no longer bound to the spine.

In 1926 and 1927, Dunbar-Nelson kept her diary on 6"-×-3½", almost tissue-thin, loose, blank sheets prepunched with three holes at the top. She wrote, mostly in ink, though there are a few pencil entries, and some days are typed, occasionally on larger pages. Her handwriting is both small and cramped and is consequently even harder to read because of the size and thinness of the paper. Except for three or four weeks in 1928, Dunbar-Nelson used these same 6"-×-3½" sheets for 1928 and 1929, only they are now mostly lined. She continued to write in small script using ink, but sometimes turned the pages around

---

*For an account of how I discovered the diary, see my essay "Researching Alice Dunbar-Nelson: A Personal and Literary Perspective," in *All the Women Are White, All the Blacks Are Men, But Some Of Us Are Brave: Black Women's Studies*, eds. Hull, Scott, and Smith (Old Westbury, N.Y.: The Feminist Press, 1982), pp. 189–95.

and typed all the way across their vertical length. The interpolated additions begin to reveal her daily activities, with, for example, the appearance of American Inter-Racial Peace Committee Press Service and International Council of Women of the Darker Races letterheads.

The 1930 diary was kept in ink in a purple (now faded) 5¾"-×-4" "Wanamaker's [a Philadelphia department store] Date Book 1930." Dunbar-Nelson allowed one page side per day and confined her entry to that page even when it had to be squeezed in by disregarding the more spaciously ruled lines and writing between them. She also continued her practice of occasionally (mostly in December) typing on very thin paper and pasting this (folded) on the page for that day. Finally, a slightly under 7⅝"-×-5⅛", faded purple, water-stained book, "The Standard Daily Reminder," served as Dunbar-Nelson's diary for 1931. Its dimensions gave her a bit more space than the 1930 book, but some days are still very crowded. Her disregard of the ruled lines and use of thin, typed, inserted sheets are the same as for the previous year.

I began my editing of this material by, first, photocopying all of it on 8½"-×-11" paper. I read through the entire work, often having to compare the copy with the original. As I did so, I noted obvious cuts and bracketed tentative inclusions, working toward the goal of a four hundred-page typed diary manuscript. After the draft was typed, I did some further editing. Throughout, I strove to preserve the essence of the original, total work—its "dailiness," recurring characters, introspective modes, serial stories, dramatic episodes, and its conscious and unconscious revelations about Dunbar-Nelson and the world around her—in a more compact and readable form. My omissions from the text are indicated by ellipsis points. I have silently corrected hasty misspellings and clarified punctuation, but have not otherwise altered the idiosyncracies and flavor of Dunbar-Nelson's style.

Because Dunbar-Nelson lived such an outgoing public and private life, the diary is full of the names of friends, colleagues, neighbors, and rivals, as well as many of the important and leading members of the Black American community. Famous people in the public domain have, of course, been identified. Pauline Young provided information about family and outstanding associates, especially in Wilmington. And Dunbar-Nelson herself left behind various supplementary records that placed other individuals with whom she came in contact. Still, a host of names remains (despite some pointed editing). Yet even without precise identification, these persons function clearly in context, and, often, simply knowing whether a passing character is male or female, for example, is adequate and useful information. People are identified at their first significant appearance in the text and tagged with later reminders—although these become less frequent as the key figures reappear throughout the work. Anyone perusing the diary page-by-page will have little trouble following the persons and events; however, I have tried to provide sufficient signposts to orient the more casual reader.

# Acknowledgments

GIVING THANKS and praise, I wish to acknowledge:

First of all, Ms. Pauline A. Young, Alice Dunbar-Nelson's niece, who gave me access to the valuable materials in her home and, most important, helped me to know the people and events in the diary. Thanks are also due her for most of the photographs and illustrations.

Kathleen M. Anderson, my editor, especially for the vision which enabled her to look at my manuscript and see this book.

Betty Sherman, whose interest in this difficult project went beyond the characters that she typed.

Penny Franklin, who initiated and helped shape this venture in its earliest stages.

Barbara Smith and Geraldine McIntosh, for being props at my hopeless moments and keeping Black sisterhood real.

Margo Culley and Carol Hoffecker, who critically commented upon portions of the manuscript.

My son, Adrian Prentice Hull, for his fresh faith in me and the written word.

The special ones: my mother, Mrs. Jimmie Thompson; my husband, Anthony Delroy Wellington; and my girl friend, Terry Zingo (who also made manageable some of the final tedious tasks).

# 1921

(July 29–December 31)

*Forty-six years old and nowhere yet*

WRITING IN HER DIARY on September 18, 1921, Dunbar-Nelson decided that she was "just not a winner at anything," and then continued:

> I lay in bed this morning thinking, "forty-six years old and nowhere yet." It is a pretty sure guess if you haven't gotten anywhere by the time you're forty-six you're not going to get very far. Humiliating, of course, but we may as well look facts in the face.

Although she enjoyed brighter moods, this feeling of failure dogged Dunbar-Nelson much of these first five months of diary keeping. True, the facts that she was forced to face were generally rather harsh.

At the outset, she had to struggle continuously to adjust to the misfortunes of the previous year. Chief among these was the loss of her position as teacher and head of the English department at Howard High School. This resulted from her having traveled to Marion, Ohio, on October 1, 1920 for Social Justice Day—despite the nonsupport of the school administration. When she returned to her classes the following Monday morning, Principal Ray Wooten had locked her out of her room for "political activity" and "incompatibility." Conwell Banton, a member of the Board of Education, said that the board would sustain Wooten's action, a stance tantamount to firing her. Dunbar-Nelson, countering, stated that, regardless of the board's position, she would not return to the classroom because her usefulness as a teacher had been impaired. Wooten, a young man, had only been principal for nine days, and it seems that he felt threatened by Dunbar-Nelson's presence and importance. Although he said he was acting on his own, he may not have been, or at least he knew that his lockout of Dunbar-Nelson would be welcomed by those unfriendly to her and would find favor for him. Aside from whatever damage this may have caused her pride, the real injury was losing her salary, without which her financial problems became increasingly acute.

The other major misfortune that Dunbar-Nelson recurrently mentions is the death of her favorite niece, Leila Ruth, called Leila Jr. The oldest of her mother's four children, Leila was educated and groomed by her aunt, Dunbar-Nelson, who sent her to Sargent's School of Physical Education in Boston and provided her with music lessons. Unfortunately, because she had had typhoid fever as a child, she was never very strong. After receiving an appointment to teach physical education at the Colored High School (later the Douglass) in the Baltimore public school system in March 1918, she was able to do so for only two years, after which she returned home to Wilmington, where she died on January 17, 1921. The freshness of her death is reflected in Dunbar-Nelson's emotional memories and her accounts of the family's frequent trips to visit Leila's grave.

Because of the seemingly special nature of her relationship with Leila Jr., neither of Dunbar-Nelson's remaining two nieces, Pauline and Ethel, nor her stepdaughter Elizabeth could take her place. However, Dunbar-Nelson did attend to Elizabeth, who is a character in the diary for only this year. Born in Harrisburg, Pennsylvania, September 9, 1903, Harriet Elizabeth Nelson died in Wilmington on February 15, 1924. Described as pretty, bouncy, and sweet, she was eager to do everything but never had sufficient strength—although she was enrolled at the Interstate Commercial College in Reading, Pennsylvania, for a time, beginning in October 1921. Gradually, she wasted away, probably from incipient or actual tuberculosis. Her brief presence in the diary is definite, but slight.

The other members of the household were Dunbar-Nelson's mother, Patricia Moore (1853–1931), the quiet but strict family "matriarch"; her older sister, Mary Leila Moore Young, called Leila (1870–1942), who taught English at the Howard High School; Leila's middle daughter, Ethel Corinne Young (1899–1930), who did not work because of poor health and spent a good deal of her time visiting away from home; Leila's youngest daughter, Pauline Alice Young, called Polly (1900– ), who was beginning her teaching career; Leila's only son, Laurence Theodore Young (1901– ), who went away to college and then to law school; and Dunbar-Nelson's husband, Robert J. Nelson, called Bobbo ("Bob-O") (1873–1949).

When Dunbar-Nelson begins writing her journal at the end of July, she plunges *in medias res* into the story of her and Robert's fight to continue the Wilmington *Advocate*, a liberal Black newspaper that they had been publishing for the past two years. Because it was substantially financed by Republican party interests, it was subject to the vagaries of partisan politics (at a time when the character of the two major parties was undergoing fundamental changes), as well as to the negative effects of racism and powerlessness. The *Advocate's* problems seem to have been further exacerbated by some unlucky personnel and financial decisions. A young man named White, whom they hired to handle job printing and the mechanical aspects of the paper, proved to be incompetent, and they also sank a disproportionate amount of borrowed capital into old equipment. In many ways during this period, the *Advocate* is Dunbar-Nelson's principal preoccupation—writing editorials and compiling news items for it, raising money to keep it afloat, cooking for and otherwise participating in the all-night sessions necessary to get it on the street by Friday afternoon, even folding and addressing the out-of-town mailings. The saga ends (offstage) when the newspaper finally collapses in 1922.

The demise of the *Advocate* was also related to what Dunbar-Nelson perceived as her general loss of standing and political clout in Delaware. In 1920, she had been named a member of the Republican State Committee (the first Black woman to serve in that capacity), and, as chairman of the League of Colored Republican Women, had directed the 1920 campaign among Black women in the state. In 1921, she was chairman of the publicity committee of the National League of Colored Republican Women. However, by the end of that year, she was no longer very active or important on the political scene— though she continued to chronicle its machinations with interest, especially because of Robert's office-holding ambitions.

Participating in the activities of the Federation of Colored Women's Clubs was the second busiest area of Dunbar-Nelson's public life. She held office in the Delaware chapter and also appeared at other states' chapter functions. In fact, the diary begins with her speaking at an afternoon session of the New Jersey State Federation on July 29. Dunbar-Nelson also lectured more widely, filling a substantial number of journal pages with details of travel, hostesses who accommodated her, towns and churches, and so forth. One of her biggest triumphs (which yielded one of the diary's more interesting passages) was being a member of the delegation of prominent Black citizens who presented racial concerns to President Harding at the White House in September.

During these months, Dunbar-Nelson was assiduously working to improve herself as a person and as a writer. Being a movie addict who devoured all types of pictures, she attempted to market filmscripts—

scenarios of her stories and melodramas—to the Realart Pictures Corporation. She sought personal enhancement through the spiritual discipline of Unity and the Master Key. An early entry reports her
introduction to Unity and references recur throughout. It was a system
of meditation, mind control, practical positive thinking, and collective support. The Master Key was similar, only with a less conventionally religious orientation. These were only two of the many ways
Dunbar-Nelson tried, throughout her life, to achieve inner peace and
outward, practical discipline. (At some point, she wrote an unpublished novelette entitled *Confessions of a Lazy Woman* and frequently
referred to herself as such.)

Looking back over 1921, Dunbar-Nelson called it, in short, "one
of the unhappiest years I ever spent." She chronicled this misery in
full, copious, long-sentenced entries, often writing many pages on one
day, at one sitting, and sometimes catching up with a week or more
at a time. The fact that she recorded so much probably reflects her
initial diary-keeping enthusiasm. Though she essentially reduces the
diary to a memory device in the prefatory paragraph she wrote six days
after beginning it, it is clear that the work, from the very outset, was a
varied, multipurpose, many-layered document. This first year introduces many of the themes, large and small, that run throughout sub-
sequent years—her money worries and debt, and her love of good
food, new experiences, and pinochle—while maintaining a high level
of narrative interest. On December 31, the reader is as eager as the
hopeful Dunbar-Nelson to see what the new year will bring.

---

*In this preface, written six days after she had begun keeping the
diary, Dunbar-Nelson (D-N) remembers the summer of 1918 when
she was one of the field agents of the Woman's Committee of the
Council of National Defense. She spent several months traveling
through Louisiana, Georgia, Florida, Kentucky, Tennessee, Alabama, and Mississippi organizing Black women for the conservation
of food. In Mississippi, she had to be reminded of the committee's
policy of not endorsing other groups when she became involved in a
movement by domestic workers to form a labor union. She did not
take the rebuke kindly. Such adventures as this probably constitute the
"things" that she wished her journal to preserve. D-N also wrote an
article during this time which drew on her 1918 activities, "Negro
Women in War Work," Scott's Official History of the American Negro
in the World War, by Emmett J. Scott (n.p., 1919), pp. 347–97.*

## Preface

### Morristown, N.J.
### August 3

Had I had sense enough to keep a diary all these years that I have been traveling around, particularly that memorable summer of 1918, when I "did my bit" traveling through the south for the Council of Defence—well, there would be less confusion in my mind about lots of things. Now I begin this day to keep the record that should have been kept long since.

*Beginning her diary away from home, D-N is here attending the Sixth Annual Session of the New Jersey State Federation of Colored Women's Clubs held Thursday and Friday, July 28–29, at the Fountain Baptist Church, Summit, New Jersey. She gave "Greetings" from the State Federation of Delaware. In this entry, she mentions three other prominent women.* Nannie H. Burroughs *(1883–1961) is the dynamic educator, organizer, and churchwoman who founded the National Training School for Women in Washington, D.C., 1909.* Jessie R. Fauset *(1882–1961) is a poet and writer whose four novels— among which are* There Is Confusion *(1924) and* Comedy: American Style *(1933)—treat Black middle-class life. Her position as literary editor of* Crisis *also gave her considerable influence. D-N and* Violet Johnson, *an active New Jersey clubwoman, often called on or stayed with each other when they visited their respective cities.*

### Summit, New Jersey
### Friday, July 29

State Federation Colored Women's Clubs. Left Wilmington 6:45 . . . arrived Summit 11:13. Spoke in afternoon. Tired to exhaustion. . . . Evening session Nannie Burroughs spoke and Jessie Fauset on the Pan-African [Congress]. (Did not put it over). . . . Jessie peeved because she wanted a collection to go to the P.A. Congress. Cut me dead. I wonder why? . . . Geneva Stanly very lively all day and sang that night in a sweet, uncultured voice. From New Orleans. We had a room together at "Miss Violets"— . . . and it turns out that Geneva knows everyone "down home." She teaches at McDonough 6. A pro-

In this August 3, 1921 preface to her diary, D-N vows to begin—although belatedly—a record of her busy life.

**MES. DUNBAR WILL APPEAR IN RECITAL HERE MONDAY.**

To the lovers of literature and music, Mrs. Alice Dunbar-Nelson, wife of the late poet, Paul Laurence Dunbar, will be presented in a recital at Webb Memorial Chapel on Monday evening, August 1, at 8:15 o'clock, by the Ladies' Aid Society of Bethel A. M. E. Church. Mrs. Dunbar-Nelson is widely known and her art has won general approbation. Her interpretation of the plaintive verses of the poet goes straight to the heart. It imparts the spirit of devotion, of aspiration, of simple trust which characterized a race which, in its deepest hours, looked for relief and comfort to God. Then there are verses of lighter vein that

Alice Dunbar-Nelson.

reveal the humorous side of the Negro.

Madison, New Jersey, newspaper announcement of D-N's August 1 interpretative reading. She presented "The Serious Side of Paul Laurence Dunbar," choosing to deemphasize his humorous, dialect work.

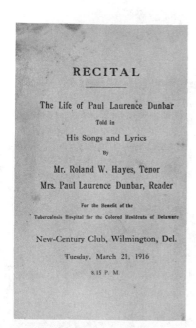

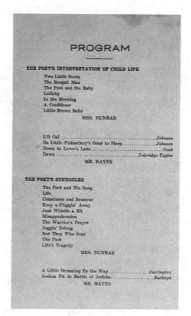

**RECITAL**

The Life of Paul Laurence Dunbar

Told in

His Songs and Lyrics

By

Mr. Roland W. Hayes, Tenor

Mrs. Paul Laurence Dunbar, Reader

For the Benefit of the

Tuberculosis Hospital for the Colored Residents of Delaware

New-Century Club, Wilmington, Del.

Tuesday, March 21, 1916

8.15 P. M.

**PROGRAM**

THE POET'S INTERPRETATION OF CHILD LIFE

Two Little Boots
The Boogah Man
The Poet and the Baby
Lullaby
In the Morning
A Confidence
Little Brown Baby

MRS. DUNBAR

L'il Gal .................................................. *Johnson*
De Little Pickaninny's Gone to Sleep ............. *Johnson*
Down in Lover's Lane .................................. *Cook*
Dawn ................................................ *Coleridge-Taylor*

MR. HAYES

THE POET'S STRUGGLES

The Poet and His Song
Life
Conscience and Remorse
Keep a-Pluggin' Away
Just Whistle a Bit
Misapprehension
The Warrior's Prayer
Joggin' Erlong
Not They Who Soar
The Poet
Life's Tragedy

MRS. DUNBAR

A Little Dreaming By the Way .................. *Carrington*
Joshua Fit de Battle of Jericho ................. *Burleigh*

MR. HAYES

Of the many recitals which D-N performed after Dunbar's 1906 death, this earlier, joint program with the famous tenor Roland Hayes was one of the most elaborate. It also recalls the fact that Dunbar himself had died of tuberculosis.

*Committee That Waited on President Harding Last Wednesday to Urge Clemency for the 24th Infantry Convicted of Being Implicated in the Houston, Tex., Riots About 5 Years Ago*

Dressed in her plumed hat, tricolette blouse, and broadcloth skirt, D-N practically dominates this photograph of seventeen of the thirty-member delegation to President Harding, September 28, 1921. Comments were made about her being "alone in a bunch of men" rather than with the other two women pictured (left to right), Mrs. Mary B. Talbert and Mrs. Carrie W. Clifford. James Weldon Johnson, who led the committee, is standing at Mrs. Talbert's right.

# Delegation of Prominent Colored Men and Women Visit President Harding

## Ask Executive Clemency for Houston Soldiers.— K. K. K. Mentioned. President Says Not Aimed at Negro

(Special to The Advocate.)

Washington, D. C., Sept. 28.—A delegation of thirty leading colored men and women, headed by James Weldon Johnson of New York, secretary of the National Association for the Advancement of Colored People, came to Washington last night bearing a petition signed by 50,000 names to President Harding asking him to pardon 61 members of the 24th U. S. Infantry (colored) now serving longtime sentences in Leavenworth Prison, convicted of rioting at Houston, Texas, in August 1917. President Harding granted the delegation an audience on Wednesday morning, September 28, at 10.20.

Upon his arrival in Washington, Mr. Johnson issued the following statement:

"Although nineteen colored soldiers were hanged and 61 sentenced to life and long term imprisonment after the Houston riot of August, 1917, colored people in the United States felt little disposed to appeal for pardon and clemency for they realized such an appeal would be fruitless.

"Now, however, under a changed administration, fifty thousand signatures have been appended to such a petition circulated by the National Association for the Advancement of Colored People, and colored Americans are looking to President Harding to redress what they feel and have felt to be undue severity exercised against a regiment with such a record of soldierly bearing, courage and devotion as the 24th U. S. Infantry.

"The personnel of this delegation is sufficient guaranty of the widespread and general desire for a pardon among colored people throughout the country."

In the delegation with Mr. Johnson, are: Emmett J. Scott, special assistant to the Secretary of War during the World War; Professor Kelly Miller of Howard University; Archibald H. Grimke, president of the Washington Branch, National Association for the Advancement of Colored People; Mrs.

(Continued on Page Three.)

D-N's "special" to her Wilmington *Advocate* newspaper, October 1, 1921 issue. The remainder of this long article listed some delegation members, reprinted the body of the petition, and summarized President Harding's response.

tegee of Nannie Burroughs. Just up from Hampton Summer School.
Violet gave me $9.00 for my fare. . . .

### Pinehurst Inn
### Saturday, July 30

Miss Violet, Nannie Burroughs, Geneva and I drove over to Newark in the morning—maybe it was noon, left N.B. at the station, thence
through all this beautiful Jersey scenery to Montclair. It seems incredible—all this loveliness. My tired and tortured spirit is soothed by the
coolness and green beauty of the hills and trees.

Pinehurst Inn, our destination, a typical Victorian house, essentially Jersey, set in a wide lawn. Inviting rooms, porches, sun-parlor,
halls. Geneva back to Summit, Violet and I to rest in a big room with
couch for V. and bed for me. . . . Slept. Ate. Went to movies.

### Sunday, July 31

. . . Quiet. Maurer, Hankins and Violet introduced me . . . to
Unity, telling me all it has done for them. . . . I shall know now of
Unity. Went for an unsatisfactory drive after dinner. Bum car, bad
driver, stupid all around. Wanted mountain scenery—got hot streets.
Wanted Montclair and Eagle Rock, got the worst end of Orange.
Everyone dissatisfied. . . .

*Here, D-N drives to Madison, New Jersey, to present an interpre-
tative reading of Paul Laurence Dunbar's work, sponsored by the Ladies
Aid Society of the Bethel A.M.E. Church.*

### Madison, N.J.
### Monday, August 1

After several false starts, got away to hunt up the person whom
Maurer says would tell me of Unity. Violet, having recovered from
the calomel and citrate I had dosed her with, quite cheery. Found a
human chauffeur and a real car. . . . Drove to Maurer's employment
office to find directions to go to Miss Dix, the Unity person. Lovely
house, artistic in a modestly beautiful way. But the faded, cheerful,
cold-eyed lady has progressed beyond Unity. I bought her literature

and paid her $2.00 as did Violet. . . . It was cheap to purchase peace at $4.35. Got a copy of Unity at Maurer's, and wrote for the paper and a letter at once. . . .

We three drove over here to Madison for the recital in the "regular" car. Passed Grover Cleveland's birthplace, a quaint little frame house near Caldwell. I always thought he was born in New York. . . .

Recital at Webb Memorial Chapel (white) loaned for the occasion. Mrs. Hines, Ladies Aid president, presiding. Fine affair. Ulysses Young, a Lincoln man and Y secretary sang. I like that setting of Henley's "Captain of my Soul." And an impossible girl got out an aimless oration about the Spirit of the Age. Geneva was good, fairly so. But the Mrs. Armistead [apparently a local songstress] who squawked was impossible. My "Serious Side of P.L.D." took well. Audience half white. Also Helen Hagan Williams [concert pianist] played— marvelous.

Violet and I shivered together that night. After the atrocious heat it was good to shiver. Midgette paid me $25.00. [The Midgette family is hosting her visit.]

## Tuesday, August 2

Pouring rain. Good breakfast. The Midgettes, Father, Mother and [daughter] Gladys, delightful. Armistead a bore. Midgette Rev. wants to ask impertinent questions concerning the intimate life of P.L.D. which are annoying and have to be skilfully evaded. . . . Then Dr. Williams, Helen Hagan's husband came for me. Lo! He is John T. Williams, the Kid Freshman of Howard. Days when Frank Steward, Pony Marshall [companions of the youthful days when she first moved north from New Orleans] et al. were together and I in West Medford [Mass.] in 1896–97. We are both 30 pounds (or more) heavier, and 24 years older. More lovely Jersey scenery—wet grass alluring. Then to his [Dr. Williams and wife Helen's] home. It is the kind of a home I ought to have, artistic, handsome, comfortable, beautiful. The living room a joy—the bed-rooms artistic comforts. Luxurious divans. Persian rugs, teak-wood chairs, open fireplace. Ah, will I ever have a home! . . .

## Wednesday, August 3

We've been in the house all day. Wet, cold, dreary. Would have had a fire in the fireplace but a bird was in the chimney. We could hear it fluttering all day. Storm blew it down. Finally it got out in the room, and Helen caught it, after I had searched for it with the flashlight. We put it out in the garden.

She practised two hours this morning. I lounged luxuriously on the couch and read Shaw's *Heartbreak House*. It was heavenly—her playing.

I hope there won't be many people out tonight. Ugh! It's cold!

## At Night

I felt stuffy after dinner and after reading on that luxurious divan awhile, listening to Helen practise, I put on boots, coat and hat and sallied forth. Meandered about the pretty town. Bought Helen a bottle of stick candy and an *Atlantic Monthly* and this book for a diary.

Violet [Johnson] drove over for the affair with some other Summit folks. At 8:30 the church was almost empty—the Union Baptist Church. Fair crowd filtered in. A hopeless affair. I had to "speak," and I yapped forty minutes on something. . . .

I've copied the diary from the scraps I scribbled on. And now to bed. . . .


*After a four-day lapse (and self-recriminations), D-N is herewith catching up on her diary. This blanket entry mentions a number of notable persons and situations. "Violets," her most-famous poem, which was also printed as "Sonnet," had appeared in* The Delmarvia Star, *the Wilmington Sunday paper. Its white editor, Martin, was something of a liberal and often reported news of D-N and the Black community in addition to supporting the* Advocate.

*The August 4 meeting is a conclave of the Executive Committee of the Delaware State Federation of Colored Women's Clubs held in conjunction with their Sixth Annual Convention. D-N gave a report as head of the Education "Department" on the afternoon of August 5, and at the evening session, rendered "Introductory Remarks." A major goal of the federation was to prevent the Ku Klux Klan from gaining a foothold in the state. Hallie Q. Brown founded the first national organization for Black women, the Colored Women's League of Washington in 1893, which eventually evolved into the National Association of Colored Women (Mary Church Terrell, first president). From Wilberforce, Ohio, she was the author of* Homespun Heroines and Other Women of Distinction *(1926).*

*The two white men whom D-N mentions in connection with edu-cational affairs are* Dr. R. W. Cooper, *Superintendent of Wilmington Schools, and* Dr. Joseph H. Odell, *Director of the Board of Managers of the Service Citizens of Delaware, a group handsomely funded by* P. S. du Pont *between 1918 and 1927 to improve social conditions in the state.*

*"Madam Lizzie," or "Big Liz" as D-N also sarcastically referred to her, is* Lizzie Banton, *a substitute night-school teacher in the public school system. Clearly considered by D-N to be an archenemy (espe-cially apparent in later entries), she was married to* Conwell Banton *(who often appears in the diary by his initials "C.B."). He was a pioneer Black Wilmington physician who was influential in local civic affairs and also owned a drugstore with John Hopkins. D-N had had an inti-mate relationship with him, which helped to foster the mutual antip-athy between her and his wife.* Fannie Hamilton, *a dressmaker, was considered to be something of a busybody.*

Edna Chippey *is an obviously dark-skinned friend of Ethel, D-N's niece. D-N's allusion to skin color reveals the kind of attention paid to that subject by Black people at the time.*

## Wilmington, At Home
## Sunday, August 7

I have been waiting to get a chance to record the days, but it seems always at home that there is no time for quiet moments. On Thursday morning last, Dr. W[illiams] drove . . . [his wife] Helen and me to Newark. We went the twenty-two miles in about forty minutes. I did not enjoy it; the beautiful landscape was a green streak, and life resolved itself into a problem of keeping the hat on the head. They left me at the station, and I checked my bag, and troddled out to shop. Net results, a pair of pink pearl earrings for [niece] Ethel; a dozen hair nets for [sister] Leila; a box of cigars (I fear they are bad) for Bob O; a jar of stick candy for Mama; a toddle top for [nephew] Laurence [seemingly a puzzling gift for a twenty-year-old]; four giant pretzels for [step-daughter] Elizabeth, one of which I ate on the train. Then home, to Wilmington, feeling refreshed by 4:30, to hear all the news. Much excitement about my poem "Violets" having appeared in the *Star* on June 26th and copied from the [*Literary*] *Digest* of June 4, coming all the way from Bombay, India, via the *Southern Workman* in Kerlin's article. The family had discovered it, through Mr. Martin's telling Bob O, and Leila went through the *Digests* until it was found. Not much news. I felt better mentally than I had for months. . . .

Executive Board meeting that night at the church. Scramble to meet Hallie Q. Mazie Mossell [Philadephia clubwoman] had horned in, and came too. Had telegraphed Mrs. Jackson [a state federation officer] who showed me the telegram, and arrangements had been made by the committee . . . for Her Hugeness.

Mazie howling for us to go into the Northeastern Federation. I did not oppose it. Eleven-thirty when we broke up. . . .

Friday, August 5 a busy day. Federation meetings all day. I was chairman of the constitution committee, as we needed a new one. Chairman of the committee on resolutions. Dr. Odell had been calling me all day Thursday. . . . He wanted to talk to me about the situation of the Negroes in Delaware. We fenced about time and place, and I said I'd come to his house, if he wanted me to. Called me Friday morning and suggested his office, to which I went about ten o'clock. Showed me the statistics of school attendance in the state. Horrible. Colored children do not go to school any better with the well-equipped buildings and well-paid teachers than before du Pont spent his millions. Dr. R. W. Cooper came in and we went into session over those formidable reports. The remedy was not apparent. I think Odell wanted me to suggest a panacea for the evil which he could take to the State Board that afternoon, but that is an evil that will have to be corrected from within. However, we parted good friends; I guess I shall hear more from him, even though I bawled him out about wanting us colored folk to "get together." I made a speech in the afternoon on the subject in my report on education.

Hallie [Q. Brown] in fine fettle that night. Good crowd . . . everything lovely. Officers elected, twelve in 20 minutes; no hitch. . . . Madam Lizzie out at night, whispering behind her hand to Fannie Hamilton, as usual, but it failed to annoy me. I can look down upon her from heights of indifference, thank God. . . .

Funny time Saturday morning. Much excitement getting . . . Hallie Q. to the station, and leaving Mazie . . . and seeing her hop a truck and get to the station before us and putting old lady Hallie on the moving train, pitching suitcase, umbrella and bag after her. I took off my hat, fanned myself, and leaned breathlessly against the wall when the train had gone.

Then I ironed, cleaned my room, picked up things, unpacked bags, mine and Bob's, broke the news to Elizabeth that she is to go to Pleasantville Monday, much to her dismay, as it leaves no time for her to sew, mess, make new things, or shop. Moreover, Ethel got up a boat ride in honor of herself and her delayed birthday festivities. . . . Leila decided to act as chaperone. Edna did not go. I don't blame her. In that aggregation of blondes and high browns, she would have looked like a fly in a flour barrel. . . . I must try to keep this diary going daily. I forget things. How silly I was not to keep one during the war; and on that wonderful trip out west [probably to the Social Justice Conference]. I've forgotten lots of things that have happened; I've even forgotten places where I have spoken before and since those days. I'm a shiftless colored woman.

Wrote Mrs. Milles about the disarmament thing she wanted in our resolutions; we put it in, and wrote Dr. Odell about the educational situation. I hope he can "use me" to the tune of a good fat salary. But I guess the budget is made for the year. Dr. Cooper says I know too much for the Wilmington City Board of Education.

White, *a young man from Baltimore who came into the* Advocate *newspaper and printing business, makes his first appearance below. Apparently, he looked promising when the partnership began in the fall of 1921, but later was let go. D-N, especially, did not "get on" very well with him.*

## Sunday, August 7

Lazy day. Bob O gone to Baltimore on the excursion to look up record of young White, who proposes to go into the printing business with *The Advocate*. The proposition looks good. If we can put it across and save a few thousand a year, we should do it; but my heart always goes down when I see Bob get out a pencil and paper and go to figuring. It's always wrong, after that.

I've read sixty pages in the Easter Key to-day; same stuff as Unity and the rest, only I've had it right here in this room, and neither read it, nor put in practice what I have read. I'm a dumb driven cattle and deserve all I get. Elizabeth just in in her [new] bathing suit, very delighted, for the second time, and very naked looking. Wants to know if it is a sin to wash clothes on Sunday, as she needs to wash out a few pieces for to-morrow's flitting. I said no. Bob O would be horrified, for he is perfectly sure it is a sin to wash necessary clothes on Sunday but not a sin to type-write, write newspaper articles, go on excursions, cook huge dinners, commit adultery, or plan political coups which will result in another man's downfall.

Mama and Leila have gone out to the cemetery with arms filled with golden glow for Leila Jr.'s grave. They miss the car, so do I. But the walk up the hill after the trolley ride will do them no harm. So shall our hearts and memories carry the glow of eternal love. But I want no grave to be cared for after I am gone.

And to think that even while the *Digest* was copying this poem ["Sonnet"] as worthwhile, I was fretting over the nasty ward politics in this town, making the weary round of office and headquarters, worrying over money to pay ward workers, anguished in spirit over the coming school election, one of the cherished ambitions of my life— to be quoted in the *Literary Digest*—had come to pass. And I knew it not, nor did my friends and enemies. So do our dreams come true— and are as naught. But never again will my soul be tortured thus. I am content.

Stormy gust, rain, wind. I wondered about Mama and Leila in the cemetery. But they came home, dry, whole and happy because the rose bush is blooming over the child's grave.

## Monday, August 8

It's two a.m. Tues. and I cannot sleep. I crept out of bed and began to write. Bobo and I had a discussion about this before he went to sleep. But he had to admit it's punishment to be compelled to do what one doesn't wish.

It was a busy day—busy with little things. Like going downstairs in cellar and getting scraps of silk and lace and pressing them to pack up to send Gladys Midgette [of the Midgette family she stayed with the previous week] for her dollies. And buying the elastic for Violet's garters. And getting samples for Helen. And seeing Elizabeth all ready. . . . Last night I went over to the Halls to spend a while before it was time to go to the train to meet Bobo. Elvira was out but when she came in, her delight was unbounded to see me. Nothing but ice-cream and cake to celebrate the unwonted call. I asked for peach ice-cream. With the first spoonful I felt a delicious thrill. *At last*, the peach ice-cream I had sought since child-hood. Then after the third or fourth, the subtle flavor had gone. So is life, too much, or enough or use deadens the exquisite flavor of an experience. . . .

Two pages is too much to write for one uneventful day. Pauline [Alice's niece] home when we arrived. She and Lovett [owner of the Hilltop House, where she had gone to work as a clerk] disagreed and he fired her. At two o'clock he thought she should say "Yes ma'am" and "No ma'am" to the guests instead of "Yes, Mrs. Jones." At three she was *entrain* for Wilmington. . . . Leila's immediate reaction was funny. "There's no money here," she said. Bobo was indignant when I told him on his return and said he gloried in Pauline's independence. But she should not have refused Lovett's check for $50 [which he eventually mailed to her]. I see Lovett's side. He is in the South and he has built up his hotel in Harper's Ferry [Va.] and there he must live. If a notion should take some of his cracker guests to say that a "Northern nigger" was clerking there who couldn't say "Yes ma'am!" his hotel might be burned down for the third time. Pauline should be home. She's thin, and her hands are too white. She's tired too. She's better off resting. The girl has worked hard enough. What good will her degree do her if she goes to lie by Leila's side? I'm going to read some in The Master Key. It may make me sleepy.

*The Monday Club referred to here was an all-Black, all-male, rather genteel and orderly group. Monday was the traditional day off for waiters, busboys, etc., but the club also included most of the professionals in the city. The exact nature of the situation that D-N refers to in this passage is unclear. It is included because of what it reveals about her attitudes and perceptions. Charles (Charlie) Colburn was a Black Republican who worked to deliver the black vote for the party.*

### Wednesday, August 10. a.m.

. . . Bobo rushes in teasing because I'm not at the office. Men do like to keep women's personalities swallowed! It is half past one in the morning now, and I am just getting back to write. Yesterday Mama had a wail about Ed Carroll because he and his Monday Club associates refused to believe [Charles] Colburn elected Grand Master. It was a blow between the eyes, I guess. Lots of things he said concerning the school election. Two stick. He was working "under cover" against [Conwell] Banton, and "It's a bad thing to be in a town with everyone against you," meaning me, because the *Advocate* fought Banton. To these I replied to Mama—I wouldn't give a snap of my fingers for a man who works "under cover." Second, the people who are against me in this city aren't worth the dust under my feet. And they are painfully anxious to have it said that they know me when they meet strangers. But I refuse to quarrel about politics anymore. . . .

Stuffy board meeting of Federation. In session until nearly twelve. Jackson is so dumb. Or is she purposely so? Cannot seem to differentiate between Executive Board and whole Federation. Wants to be in the chair and do everything all the time and has to be coached every step of the way. She's sore on that chairmanship of the Executive Board. Feels that it lessens her authority. It does—if I assert myself, which I probably won't do. . . .

Acquired Gus yesterday. He is a puppy, supposed to be six weeks old. Indeterminate breed. He might be a hound, collie, shepherd, pointer, setter, or just plain dog. Will probably be very large. Very lovable, but sick to-day from wrong diet, I suppose. I think he will be a delightful addition to the family. When Mama took him up in her lap last evening and rocked him because he was homesick, I knew his success was assured. He's howling or whining now from the cellar steps. . . .

*All of the individuals mentioned midway through this entry are political figures, whose support and influence also helped to buttress the* Advocate. *Judge Daniel O. Hastings, a white Wilmington lawyer, was the only one in the state who would allow Delaware's first Black lawyer to read in his office, then a prerequisite for practicing law in the state. He served as U.S. senator from Delaware from 1928 to 1937. Charles Warner was chairman of the Delaware Republican State Committee and head of the General Service Board of the Service Citizens of Delaware Committee. Jeanette Eckman, a white Wilmingtonian who was extensively involved in city politics, served as assistant secretary to the Delaware Republican State Committee. She was especially interested in citizen support for public education and was secretary of the General Service Board, the group of citizens headed by Warner, which explored and publicized civic and social conditions in the state.*

### Friday, August 12

There's one thing certain: Master Key, Unity, nothing will do me any good until I learn to control this body of mine. I read and meditate—every day over the Universality of things, over the control I can exercise on the Infinite Mind. How am I going to control the Infinite Universal when I am wedded to the same slip-shod habits? I dawdle and waste time day after day. I seem in a stagnant pool of inactivity. It took me all day to do what I should have accomplished in three hours. And I slip back mentally whenever I dawdle. After Monday, Tuesday, Wednesday and Thursday mornings work on the paper, I slip on Thursday afternoon, Friday and Saturday. I shall begin to discipline myself severely; it's the only way. I shall castigate myself until I can work without dawdling and can do this little bit of room-cleaning, washing, ironing etc. in double-quick time and leave time for writing and real work. . . .

Poor Bobo hasn't come in. He said he was going over to Colburn's tonight to talk over the press. Poor fellow, he's working so hard to put it across. The weary round he goes from Judge Hastings' office to Warner's, to the Bank, back to me makes me think of the weary round I tramped from Grantland to Warner to Jeannette Eckman before election, trying to get that $200 to pay my workers. I wish I could help him more than I do, yet I doubt if any man has a wife who helps him more. No flattery to myself either.

He said today he likes me at the office—evenings when he's there alone, but not in the daytime. Likes to run in the house and find me here—it's now comfy and homey. Poor fellow, he wants a home as much as I do. But we can't even pay board here, it seems.

I guess I'll give up my car for some time yet. I haven't told Bobo that I signed the contract for him Tuesday. When he's straining every nerve to get a press, it's a bad time for me to be howling new car.

Times are hard. Money tight. Debts staggering. I computed our losses Thursday. We are running behind about $360 a month or $12 per day on business alone, and since that does not include any money for Bob or me for our living expenses, it amounts to about $500. We are running on nerve, courage and gall now. It's a damn shame that Republican committee is so churchy. But Bobo and I are both fat.

I'll think constructive thoughts and attract wealth, and meanwhile indulge in some self-discipline.

*Monday, August 15*
*8 p.m.*

Here I sit on a pile of cushions on my roof, and all the lovely panorama of the eastern side of the city is spread before me. There lies that [Delaware] river, with the boats upon it, and the twinkling lights on the Jersey shore across and the masts of the schooners in the nearer creek. That river which has inspired so many worthwhile thoughts in the eighteen years I have watched it from third-story windows. It's much better to be out here on the roof with the white moon hanging in the opalescent twilight sky than down-stairs on the crowded front porch, with noisy cars going by, and noisy people, and a chattering family and Gus, whose name Leila has changed to Duke, diverting conversation. It is clear and peaceful and true up here. Mama calls, and I invite her out. She could no more clamber thru that window than fly.

Saturday night was insufferably hot, and I suggested to Bobo that we sleep out here. So with pillows and steamer rug, spread and bath-robes, I made a bed, and we stretched out. Even he sighed and said, "It *is* pleasant out here." By two o'clock, as usual, the heavy dews had wet our coverings and our hair and forced us in, but the refreshingness of the out-of-doors lasted us the rest of the night. . . .

I am learning to "go into the Silence," but I need lots of practise. My mind races about on trivialities. It's almost too dark to write more. I said just now when I was trying to conceive the Universal Good, "Even Death is not evil," and the ghastly horror of Leila's death, which is as fresh now as it was January 17 and of Bobbie's [her stepson] three years ago, arise in my mind, stark, hideous. And I must fight and square the grim hideousness of those lovely children's awful deaths with the Universal Good. Can I do it? It will be the supreme test. I have squared all the ten months nightmare of my own—the fighting and persecutions which I suffered. I alone am to blame. I will concede that. I think I am beginning to see—not as thru a glass darkly—but Face to Face.

I wrote the first line of my sonnet to Mme. Curie in the darkness.


*This passage introduces the* Advocate *staff. Edna Chippey worked in the office. Elijah Stricklin, Jr., an enterprising waiter who also sold used cars, served as business manager and generally assisted in the production of the paper. Leila's boyfriend, Franklin Robinson, also a waiter, helped out around the office for a very small—almost token— salary whenever the Nelsons could pay it. Rein was the white man who printed the* Advocate; *D-N was always at odds with him. What she calls "country stuff" was the church and social news from the small, provincial towns in downstate Delaware.*

*Wednesday, August 17*

Pauline is twenty-one today. I suppose because it is her birthday that Leila is in my mind so much. We beat her and then kissed her for her morning celebration. She is at the office doing the work of Edna and Laurence [Pauline's younger brother]. . . . Pauline likes the office these three days. The novelty of it hasn't palled yet. She even enjoys that dreaded "country stuff." My new idea for having headlines for every town works me pretty hard, going through every one and trying to find some suitable phrase, but I think, as does Strick, that it will be worth while in the general appearance of the paper. Rein, the pessimist, couldn't think of anything mean to say when he got my note, ordering the change, so he snorted and said we wouldn't keep it up.

I stayed home after dinner and made Pauline a cake and Ethel, who has been in bed two or three days, but got up for dinner, made fudge icing for it. Franklin came in tonight and we played whist. Bobo had gone to Chester, came in, grouched a bit, then finally settled down to look on, until sleep overcame him. I came up-stairs to put him to bed, having first rubbed his stiff neck. Poor fellow, he's very tired.

He and Colburn went for a loan to the Farmer's Bank for $900, and while old man Ezekiel Cooper was thinking it over, Colburn calmly went after . . . Delaware Trust. He got his $900 there and then the Farmer's loan went thru. So there he and Bobo had both loans. They took both—one to cover the other. I am joint signer on the Farmer's bank loan. But it gives a margin on that printing outfit. . . .

I think I am getting some control of myself. I can work more consecutively; I can awake at seven now, and I believe the bowels will learn to behave. I still study the Master Key every day. . . .

*Saturday, August 20*

It seems hard to realize that I have not written since Wednesday. It is 12:00 p.m. I lie in bed awaiting Bobo, a pillow on my knee, my book on the pillow. . . . Thursday Bobo went again to Chester and Media to get the political bargain with the campaign manager of the Judge who is standing for re-election in Delaware County. So I had to go to the plant. It was hot, of course, but Rein was most lamb-like and not belly-aching as usual. The printers and he commended the change I had made in the paper by using head-lines for the "country stuff." Rein couldn't think of anything cross to say, so he jawed, "I been tellin' 'em to do it right along. Wouldn't listen to *me.*"

I was sewing on Pauline's red gingham dress when Bobo came in—but I put it up to hear about his plans. Of course, it meant work for me.

## Friday, August 21

Two important things happened. I heard from Unity and the printing press arrived from New York. Between the two events was a long day filled with tedious work. There was a list of supposedly 1000 names of persons to whom the paper must be sent for 5 weeks. They are all folks in Delaware County—Media, Bryn Mawr, etc. I took charge, typing, cutting slips of each name, pasting direct on the paper, for mailing out of town. It took me all day, practically, and Bobo fussed and fumed and fretted and harassed me most annoyingly. Last night he confided to me that he hated to see me doing that kind of work. I'm too valuable. I agree with him that it is poor economy, but everyone was head over heels getting the regular edition out. Just as I had to work to get the original mailing list ready, I'll set these wheels in motion.

The Unity letter came in the morning mail, but I didn't get to read it carefully for sometime later. The principle is the same as the Master Key, though immensely simplified, and there is, of course, co-operation with others, which makes for strength. I shall try to memorize the leaflet—and practise the rules, which do not conflict with the Master Key, which I read every day. I finished it, and answered the last of the questions Thursday night. . . .

My head was stuffy after staying in the office until eight o'clock, so I went for a walk after coming home. Out 11th Street, quiet and broody under the trees, with pleasant homes; across 10th Street Park and up the stairs to the reservoir. It was heavenly up there—lovely water, soft grass, the clover leaves shut tight and shedding the dew; the moon big and red gold, hanging over the trees and matching the electric lights around the banks. Boys and girls enjoying themselves after the fashion of kids. I hungered, dreaming over the loveliness of it all. And I tried to think through this conception of Infinite, Omnipotent Good, within me, around me, ME. I went downstairs and sat on a bench in the park near a weeping willow tree, bending over the skating pond. It was as still as if it had been painted. And I tried to understand inspiration by the law of attraction.

Yes, Unity surely simplifies the Master Key by using the terms

God and Christ. But then it says call it God, Christ, Spirit, what you will.

When I returned home I found that the prodigals had showed up with a 4 ton truck carrying 4 tons of machinery, and three drivers. They were the dirtiest, tiredest lot imaginable, as they had been on the road since Thursday at three o'clock. Also hungry, and one man quite sick, exhaust gas and insufficient food. It was a big feat to tear down and bring that huge press here and White was justly proud. We accommodated the men in the basement. . . .

*The Thursday, August 25, affair referred to below was held at the Odd Fellows Hall, Smyrna, Delaware, where D-N, Bobbo, Charlie Colburn, and Rev. J. D. Bonds spoke. The handbill for the occasion read: "These Men and Women are from WILMINGTON and represent the JEWELS of our RACE in the State of Delaware." D-N was called "one of the greatest Educators of the 'Race.' " Henry Arnett, a Black Wilmington minister, was pastor of the Bethel A.M.E. Church.*

.

## Saturday, August 27

I grow worse and worse, but the days are short, and there is much to do. Since Edna has been away, and Laurence was out of the city, and the country stuff requires lots of time, and Bobo running around, it seems I cannot get time to do anything but work on the paper. I took to-day off—I always take Saturdays off, and usually Fridays too, but to-day there was so much to do with room cleaning, and settling the elderberry wine and making jelly, and washing Duke and two weeks ironing to do—that I was fagged out and very cross when I had finished. . . .

Sunday we went to Delaware City in Doraldina [the car], but Strick said yesterday that her name should be Dorothy, so Dorothy it is. It was a good trip, and worth while. We took Duke, who enjoyed his visit into the great world, and acted quite disgracefully when he saw the wharfs and the bay. He was fairly terrified. Laurence was in his glory, running the car, and ran her to death. . . .

In the afternoon I finished the sonnet on Mme. Curie and sent it to the [Philadelphia] *Public Ledger* for the [Women in History] contest [which asked contestants to write about their "favorite woman of the ages"]. . . .

Wednesday afternoon, August 24, I went after Dorothy where she was at the shop, Fifth and Orange streets, to bring her home. I swore that was the only way to get used to driving her—to drive. It was a circus and picnic in one; I locked gears, and did everything, including picking up Wallace Johns, who clambered into the car at one of my stopping places and earnestly requested himself to accompany me. By the combined efforts of the various men on the street who came out and rocked the car and unlocked my gears at frequent intervals, I was enabled to make [it] home without committing murder or suicide. . . . Bobo, Laurence, Leila, Pauline and I went up to Marcus Hook to . . . a district Sunday school convention. . . . Looked like a reunion of some of my pet enemies, but I contemplated them unmoved. . . . [Henry] Arnett had to speak, one of those response things, and he tore the tail feathers out of the eagle. It was a good speech of the ranting, spread eagle kind that he can do well, and I had to smile at him commendingly as he sat down, whereupon he deliberately winked at me. This in face of the stiffening of necks of him and Robert [Bobo] was funny. . . . When we got tired of the stupid thing—where they stood us up and "introduced" us to the audience, we went outside, and no car, no Laurence. We hung around, ate ice-cream, shivered, walked, waited and I privately confided to Pauline that there was only four gallons of gas in the car when we left, and as Dorothy is drawing a lot of gas, I feared disaster. He showed up, mad, of course, because he was in the wrong, and we started out, all cross, I eating Uneeda biscuit violently. Two miles this side of Penny Hill—silence, no gas. Laurence got out to go get some and bring back, Pauline got out to go with him. That is always the way. A man gets into trouble by his own hardheadedness, and some fool woman is always ready to help him out. Agonies for Leila, her two candy lambs were in the dark road alone, [to] bring up gallons of gasoline. I ate crackers, and surmised that they would come riding on a truck or a motorcycle, and so they did, on a truck with the two gallon can of gas, and the truck man stood around until our troubles were over, helping us make a funnel out of newspaper to get the gas in the car.

Thursday, August 25. I started out in the morning to write up the stock-takers. I made my silent prayer to Unity and read the Master Key, then I dolled up in my yellow percale and white shoes and stockings and big black hat—took my brief case and sallied forth. . . .

At two o'clock I went back to [Wilmington businessman] Patterson's office. He knew me, but I don't remember ever seeing him before. Handsome, genial, splendid man. Bought twenty shares, gave me his

check for $100, adjured me not to tell on him. Told me to go see
Irenee du Pont, president of "our company," but not to say he sent
me. . . .

I felt delighted at my success, and rushed home to show my tro-
phies to Bobo. . . . The line of talk I gave Patterson would make a
professional book agent look like a deaf mute. He had to laugh at me,
and advised me to "try it on Charlie Warner." . . .

Thursday night was the grand night for the fool thing in Smyrna.
. . . The affair was nothing. . . . It was pitiful to hear that good jazz
band going to waste. The folks sat around and looked hopeless as country
folks do, and finally I made Polly [Pauline] get up and dance with a
Philadelphia girl, who came up and spoke to us. That broke the ice,
and soon others were on the floor. We were fascinated by a dark girl
with eyes like a sleepy snake, the very incarnation of evil, she looked,
and yet you could not turn your eyes from her. She had the village
dandy in tow and asserted her authority over him. Nice looking boy,
too good looking for her with a nasty curl to his lips, as if he was
sneering at his own futility. . . .

I discovered Friday morning that I had lost my rhine-stone hair-
pin whether in the car or on the road I don't know. Somehow, beautiful as it was, I could not grieve. Just another link gone between C.B.
[Conwell Banton] and me—broken. I loved the pin for what it had
meant, but I cannot ever feel vaguely sorry for its loss. And how frantically I rushed back and forth on Broad Street the night . . . went up
to hear Jim Europe's band and the pin slipped from my hair outside
the Academy of Music, and how I almost sobbed with joy when I saw
it glittering on the sidewalk! Mutatis mutandis!


*Big Quarterly was an annual gathering and celebration of Blacks
from the Eastern Shore of Maryland and Virginia, Delaware, and
southeastern Pennsylvania. Held on the last Sunday in August, it originated as an after-harvest holiday allowed the Black slaves by their
masters. The festivities were centered on French Street near the D-N
home. D-N wrote a perceptive and entertaining article called "Big
Quarterly in Wilmington, Delaware," which appeared in the Wilmington* Every Evening, *August 27, 1932.*

*The friends with whom she is enjoying the festivities are, first,
Alice Gertrude Baldwin, "Baldikins" or "Baldy," head and sole teacher
of the Howard Normal School for teachers. The only regular Black
attendant of the Wilmington Unitarian fellowship, she was one of the*

*female teachers who lived with* Edwina Kruse. Maria, *her sister, was*
*a school principal in Massachusetts.* Marian Shadd, *a newspaper-*
*woman and interracial activist from Washington, D.C., frequently*
*visited Kruse.*

## Sunday, August 28

Today is Big Quarterly, and I am up early. I was at the office last
night waiting for the boys to come in—somebody anyhow, while waiting I tried to catch up by typing in this record book. This morning I
cut, pasted and arranged. I must keep this record up to date. . . .

It is hard to write. I was stopped last night at the office. I arose
early this morning, then Bobo got up and it was time to dress for
breakfast and all the excitement of Big Quarterly and the children
getting out to sell, etc. etc. Now I'm upstairs alone and I'm hoping to
get caught up before I am called. . . .

And the noise grows greater outside. Polly, Ethel and Strick are
holding down the stand. I must go see how they are managing. . . .

Yesterday, Saturday, August 27, my check came from Dodd &
Mead—$114. It had been mis-sent to Dayton and my ex-mother-in-
law had endorsed it by mistake. Very welcome.

## Sunday—later

. . . Maria Baldwin, Marian Shadd and Baldikins came around to
sit on the porch and see the sights. I made them go walking with me,
into the "furor" and through the next block in the thick of things.
Maria B. was positively frightened. She had never seen such a thick
press of her people—all eating, eating, eating. She said pathetically—
"How much like animals we look when we're in the raw." She was
moved to tears—pity, I guess. . . .

I see the Sunday *Star* copied my editorial on the break between
the Delaware School Auxiliary and the State Board of Education. They
changed the title to "Blocking Progress" from "The State Board and
the Delaware School Auxiliary." It is a good editorial, if I do say it
myself. Hope Dr. Odell likes it.

*Below, D-N is carousing with a mixed group of friends. Ce is*
Cecilia Dorrell, *who was married to* Victor Dorrell, *Monday Club*
*factotum and subcontractor. The* Sterretts *were relatives of theirs from*

*Harrisburg, Pennsylvania.* Minnie Stevens, *the wife of* H. Clay Stevens, *one of the first Black physicians in Delaware, played the piano and gave lessons.*

*This entry gives the first mention of* Edwina B. Kruse, *who was very significant in D-N's life. A famous Black Delaware educator and longtime principal of Howard High School, "Krusie" was very dear to D-N, who wrote a huge unpublished novel based on her life,* This Lofty Oak. *It is unclear what "sins" against the family D-N is referring to. However, Kruse was reputed to be mean and dictatorial and may have committed some act that mother Patricia considered mistreatment and that fostered her alienation from Kruse. Apparently, there has also been some diminution of affection on D-N's part from the time in the early 1900s when she and Kruse were very ardent in their friendship. Yet after Kruse retired in 1920, D-N continued to maintain their relationship with dutiful visits.*

### Tuesday, August 30

. . . Settling myself at the office when Ce came with Sterrett in his big car he had driven from Harrisburg. Wanted me to go riding with them. . . .

Ce, Sterrett and I went after Minnie [Stevens], then back to the club for Vic [Dorrell], who was "ripe" and out the State Road. Smoked some Fatimas. Back to Minnie's. A Bronx, some Pall Malls, and "Put and Take." I lost 45¢ and the game growing stale, we tried African Golf [dice]. At one time I was 97¢ to the good, but lost it all. Had some delicious toddy and they . . . drove me home 12:50 a.m. I knew Bobo would be sore when he came home after 12 and did not find me dutifully reading in bed. When he found I had been out with Sterrett, he was inarticulate with rage—and smoked! Zowie! He's been raving all day. . . .

Letter from Mrs. Hooper [Wilmington spiritualist and fortune teller] in reply to mine asking her to explain the message she gave Laurence to give me. She said that Leila, Jr. is watching our business and told her to tell Aunt Alice that a great and pleasant surprise is coming sometime in October.

The paper today (Tuesday, August 30) in the account of the meeting of the Board of Education had this ant paragraph:

The Board decided that the superintendent should interview Miss Kruse, principal emeritus of the Howard High School, and ask her to accept a pension. Miss Kruse is now helping Principal Wooten [her successor] with clerical work.

Horrible! Like turning an old horse out to graze. . . . We talked of little else today. It will probably kill her—this latest blow. I can't gloat over her humiliation, as Mama does, remembering her sins against us. I remember her good deeds and that I once loved her. . . .

Had another letter from Unity yesterday. I am not getting on very fast—too many interruptions—not enough opportunity for solitude.

I'm squaring lots of things I've read—and thought I understood—with this work I begin to see things I'd never seen before. . . .

### Thursday, September 1

. . . Today (still atrociously hot) Bobo and White started to N.Y. to bring back a motor. I to the plant as usual. Heat, Rein cross, I came back fagged out, and cried at the futility of it all.

Have not been able to concentrate—nor adjust myself, nor go into the silence for two days. Even when I lay on the roof this evening my mind raced around on trivialities. . . .

*The Pocomoke, Maryland, Colored Fair Association had invited D-N to give an "Address" and "Round Table Talk" during the fair's Woman's Day, and urged: "Those interested in the womanhood of race, come." While there, D-N stayed with a Professor Long (who was later murdered by two whites) and his family.*

### Pocomoke, Maryland
### Sunday, September 2

. . . Colburn took me to train. . . . At King's Creek car resolved itself into Jim Crow by simple expedient of white passengers moving forward. Fresh white youth wanted me to move out, to the hysterical delight of the colored passengers, who knew me. . . .

The fair was "colored." The white fairgrounds, of course. Races under racing commission of state, therefore ok., but not enough. Stands, exhibits, etc. insufficient and amateurish. Not enough games, etc. Fair crowd on grandstand. "I spoke fine." Enjoyed races. The directors or whatever they are, state officers, were pleased to be complimentary.

The Longs' littlest adopted child, Jessie, a pretty child of 10 or thereabouts, has had an ideal of me for some years—since she heard me speak at the Teachers Institute in Salisbury. Her one talk, they say, is to be a "second Mrs. D-N" and to me she said quaintly, "I want to be a second you." Lord! what a responsibility to look up to.

Little theatrical troupe gave a show in the hot, dusty, canvas and weather-boarded shack doing duty for a theatre. The five girls were shabby, dirty, in flimsy green and red, precarious chemises, but they *could* dance, and the three men were witty. I found myself enjoying them. There was a "Silver Star" band on the band stand that was good, too. Sweet.

The Long house is pretty, airy, commodious, but wretchedly kept. Colored. Bath-room could be beautiful but is unspeakable. Ellett [another female boarder] has had this room two nights, so I suppose I shall have to content myself with stale sheets. Well, she's fat but clean. And ye gods! what a bore! . . .

Ellett has piled in. Almost wish I had followed my own mind and gone home on that midnight train. Would have had to sit up all night tho. . . .

*During this visit to Atlantic City, D-N and family are staying with Dr. and Josie Terry of Pleasantville, New Jersey. Originally from Reading, Pennsylvania, he was a good friend of Robert's. The couple had six sons.*

*Pleasantville, N.J.*
*Monday, September 5*

. . . We were all set to go to see "The Four Horsemen of the Apocalypse" at Atlantic City. Ethel began puffing and wheezing in the morning however. We dolled up. Bobo in the white flannel trousers and blue coat, Elizabeth all in white organdie and Ethel in the white organdie skirt she had made and the wonderful sweater with the vest and cuffs. But alas, poor child. Brave as she was, she had to give up; her laboring for breath was painful to see, and when she finally broke down and cried from sheer disappointment and misery, I almost cried with her, and Elizabeth wept shamelessly. She's a dear child, that Elizabeth. She took off her clothes to stay home with Ethel, and Bobo and I moved off. . . .

## Wilmington[, Delaware]
## Tuesday, September 6

Here I sit in the office, pounding on the machine and very sleepy, for we had a wonderful time getting home, Bobo, Ethel, Elizabeth and I.

We got off yesterday, at last, to Atlantic City, Ethel, Elizabeth and I. Ethel was wheezing faintly, and not at all well, but only her will power, my invoking Silent Unity, and Medicated Throat Disks kept her up. She was drowsy, wheezy at times, and very dull, but so was the weather, cold and foggy and drizzly. But even in spite of Elizabeth's misgivings, we stuck it out. We took a wheeled chair on the board walk, and wheeled for an hour, although a drizzle came up just as we reached Wall's. Too many colored people, bad looking ones. It was almost time for matinee then, and by the time we had freshened up, we went in the Globe theatre. I had bought orchestra seats. . . . I was conscious of misgivings, and a pounding in my throat when we approached the ticket taker. Suppose he should not let us take our seats? Suppose the ticket seller had sold the seats to me thinking I was white, and seeing Elizabeth and Ethel should make a scene. I choked with apprehension, realized that I was invoking trouble and must not think destructive things, and went on in. Nothing happened. How splendid it must be never to have any apprehension about one's treatment any where?

Josie came in before the overture. The picture is magnificent. Each big picture that I see I claim it is the best I have seen. And I do believe that "The Four Horsemen of the Apocalypse" is the best of all. And the orchestration is splendid, and the singing superb! One soloist, and she a splendid one.

The man who rides the horse as Conquest is Noble Johnson, the half breed Indian-Negro and the first troops to arrive in France to help her are the colored troops, led by what seems to be Jim Europe's band. It is a fine thing throughout. I found myself getting all tense and excited, and crying unrestrainedly at the end of the play. Perhaps the woman next me, who broke down and sobbed at the scene where Julio's family kiss his grave, affected me. It seemed to me that the woman murmured something about "My boy." It may have been fancy, but it seemed so. Perhaps she has a boy lying on Flanders Field.

Josie and Ethel had never been to the Inlet, so we went there for luncheon, after the play. Fried oysters, lobster salad, and trimmings

put us all in a good humour, and we went thence homeward. Bobo
was lying in the porch hammock in the fog and mist and all the boys
were rubbing their stomachs to signify their hunger. Josie had to fly
around to get dinner, which was on the table by eight o'clock. Ethel
took off her shoes and played jacks with the little boys on the floor;
Elizabeth developed one of her headaches and lay in the hammock
until she felt better. Bobo and Edward, Thompson [family / friends of
the Terrys] and I played whist, and we beat the others. Tom has a
clear, logical mind, and an excellent memory. He's a better whist
player than I am, for he never tires of remembering. It was late when
we got to bed.

Up early this morning. Left on the 7:55 from Pleasantville, having
taken car over. Ethel hated to go, and hinted broadly about spending
two or three weeks there. Poor child, she does not know what a care
she is, with her wheezing, vomiting and general weakness. I hardly
care to be tried with her again. Not like she was when I used to trot
around with her to Dover, and places. She was quite droopy coming
home. It was something of a relief to me to leave Josie's house, with
all her splendid boys—if I had Lee for a son, I would be plumb crazy
over him, so handsome and strong and manly and dependable, and
Louis so much like a society he-flapper, etc. But the lack of neatness
in the house, the soiled clothes, the dubious bathroom, the sticky
things around—the—well—I love Josie, but I think two days is about
as much as I can stand. And perhaps it is mean to say that when I
realize that she made every sacrifice to make us comfortable. Lee,
tired from his night work, crumpling all his great length on the little
sofa in the dining room; Louis, all fagged out from the dance, and
having to go to work early in the morning, on a pallet on the floor—
not many people would have taken us in at such a sacrifice.

We lost Bobo in the crowd at the Camden ferry. He stopped to
light the inevitable cigar, and I moved on with the children, thinking
he was behind me. We waited for several ferries on the other side, and
finally to Broad street station, where he was as cross as he could be.
We were home by 10:40 standard. . . .

## Sunday, September 11

Sunday, and nothing written since Tuesday. Lots happened, too,
but I've forgotten. . . .

I was crossing Tenth and King Streets, coming from seeing Bobo
on the W. Chester bus, when I saw Mildred Simpson [a white woman]

in her car. She paused, and I went to the car side and chatted. . . .
Miss Simpson said that Warner, Patterson, Mrs. Ashbrook and Mrs.
Jones, of Milford, were to have a conference soon, and determine the
policies of the [Republican] party. I wonder whether I come in on the
new deals? . . .

Elizabeth suddenly decided that she wanted to go to Columbia,
and begged hard, even after she had agreed with her father and me
that she is in no physical condition this year to undertake the strenuous life of New York, and was agreed, according to Bobo's idea, to
go to Reading and to the business school there. Her sudden wild desire
to go to Columbia anyhow, I know comes only from the fact that
Elizabeth Stubbs is going to Dean to-morrow, and she wants to be in
the crowd, as usual.

I had intended to go to Reading to look up this school of Bobo's,
but he confessed to me yesterday that money was slow and tight, and
we'd have to cut corners and that a trip to Reading was an unnecessary
expense. So I wrote the H. Y. Stoner Commercial College. I hope it's
all right. I think I see the plumpness of Elizabeth's face disappearing
already, and she looked so well with her additional six pounds. Wilmington does not agree with her any more than it did with Leila.

Pauline received an urgent call from the high school in Newport
News, and departed, after much telegraphing and more or less excitement in getting ready, on Thursday. I gave her all the advice I could
on the subject of going down in a "Jim Crow" country, and had her
telegraph Palmer, the principal, to meet her at Old Point Comfort,
and write Dr. Scott's wife to take her. Had a telegram Friday morning
that everything was all right, and a special this morning with particulars of her trip, and the fact that she is to be with the Scotts permanently. That is good. I do amount to something in the kids' lives. That
trip to Newport News last April cinched her the school, and the place
to live. Leila was almost frantic over the loss of her "baby daughter,"
and only the whist games that she and Franklin, Elizabeth and Laurence play together, saved her.

Friday, September 9, was Elizabeth's birthday, she was eighteen.
Poor kid, I fear she had a rather dull day. I had to talk seriously to her
at the breakfast table on the subject of [her] not wanting to work at the
office, and it made her cry, and the rest of the day went pretty badly
for her. I did not give her a present, neither did her father, and we
had nothing special for dinner; Ethel made her a box of fudge, and
mama treated her to watermelon for the card game that night. I bot-
tled my elderberry wine, twelve quarts, and started straining off another

batch. Then I had an overheated spell, which was quite uncomfortable. Apoplectic, almost.

The car still in the shop, waiting for the clutch cup to come from the factory. The former one burned out completely. I talked business with White about taking over the car, with the result that we managed a deal. . . . That relieves me of those danged monthly notes.

Old Man Dixon was down in his Elgin, and I offered to buy it from him. I always did like that Elgin. We all rode about in it, and he said he'd be back Saturday morning to talk about my offer of $350. He did not come back however. His wife has run off with another man, and he threatens to kill her on sight. Maybe he saw her and did the deed. I can't much blame a good-looking woman, as she appears to be from her picture, for running away from a toothless old freak like Dixon.

Laurence got off for Wilberforce, via Baltimore, yesterday. Bought his new suit, and went out to the B. and O. [railroad] in a taxi, while Leila and Elizabeth meekly troddled out in a street car. Rebecca [Murphy of the Baltimore *Afro-American* newspaper family, whom he eventually married] was to give him a party last night in Baltimore. Bobo and he were at outs before he left, but Laurence collected his salary, nevertheless. Poor Leila was a pitiful figure, with both her candy lambs gone. . . .

My sonnet on Mme. Curie was in to-day's *Ledger*. That means that I have a chance at the prize. Of course, it seems best of all the published ones, to me. . . .


The *"Bowse,"* Arleon Bowser, *mentioned here appears frequently in the diary. A scion of the only Black family in Cohasset, Massachusetts (a fashionable Boston resort), and a graduate of Radcliffe College, she taught modern foreign languages at Howard High School. She never married after her family refused to accept the dark-complexioned Presbyterian minister who loved her. She was D-N's close friend and constant card partner.*

*This Recorder of Deeds situation forms a brief episode for the year. Since* Frederick Douglass *held the title, the position had traditionally been awarded to a Black man.* Lincoln Johnson, *a Washington, D.C. lawyer, politician, and the husband of poet* Georgia Douglas Johnson, *had previously occupied the post.* Robert H. Terrell, *the husband of* Mary Church Terrell, *was also a Washington, D.C. lawyer.* T. Coleman du Pont, *an important and busy member of the Delaware du Pont family, served as U.S. senator, 1921–22, 1925–28.*

## Monday, September 12

Bobo confessed yesterday that he was worried. No; it was Saturday—that he is up against it. "It isn't often I cry," he said, "but I'm
crying now." I'm sorry for him. I believe he's let White talk him into
overstocking on machinery. All that $1800 is gone, plus the hundred
I got from Patterson. I haven't seen poor Bobo so worried since we
struck a snag on the *Masterpieces [of Negro Eloquence*, ed. Alice Moore
Dunbar. Harrisburg, PA: The Douglass Publishing Co., 1914]. I went
out this morning to try to sell some stock. Couldn't get past Irenee du
Pont's secretary, and sold Grantland *two* shares to be paid Oct. 5. Not
much nourishment in that.

Bowse came in this morning before eight o'clock. She looks good.
School started off. Leila as usual, out by 8:15. Excited and nervous as
she has been for nineteen years going forth. I almost wished I were
going.

It seems incredible that I cannot get ten minutes to myself. I arose
at seven, exercised [but] before I was through—I had hoped to have
five minutes for Silent Meditation—Bobo awoke. I went down to get
my cold shower. I hoped to have a few minutes when I had finished
in the bath-room—but Bowse came in calling me, and I hurried to
dry myself and get into a bath-robe. Dressed, breakfast. Up-stairs—
hoped for a few minutes. Elizabeth came up for something. Arose,
counted clothes, made bed. Bobo came in. Sat down after he went to
bath-room. Telephone. Tried it again. He came up-stairs. Tried it
again, after he went out. Elizabeth—who just walked up, turned around
and walked out. I gave it up, and came to the office.

Bobo says he had a letter . . . this morning saying that the Senate
Committee would report unfavorably on Link Johnson's appointment.
Poor fellow! coming on top of his paralytic stroke, I fear. . . . Terrell's
letter implied that Bobo should go after the job of Recorder of Deeds.
He would have written T. C. [T. Coleman du Pont] this morning,
but I stopped him. I hate to take advantage of a sick man. But I guess
no such scruples would stop anyone else. . . .

*This entry shows D-N trying to break into movie scripting. Oscar
Micheaux is a novelist and pioneer Black filmmaker. The first of her
attempts she mentions is the title selection from her 1899 collection
The Goodness of St. Rocque, the story of a romantic triangle set in
New Orleans. "9-19-1909" was a Gothic melodrama she wrote. The
plot concerned a heroine's struggles to keep her inherited property by*

*fulfilling the conditions of an impossible will and thwarting an avaricious villain.*

*The Chester, Pennsylvania affair was a Colored Citizens meeting at the Armory on Wednesday, September 14. It was a Republican rally at which D-N, Pennsylvania state representative John C. Ashbury and other Black candidates and public figures spoke in preparation for the September 20 election. D-N alludes to 1915, when she, a committed suffragette, was field organizer in the Middle Atlantic States, which were working for state constitutional amendments.*

## Friday, September 16

And here I am again, days and days behind my schedule, and so much happening all the time that I wonder how I can remember it all.

I received the catalogue from the Inter-State Commercial College to which Bobo wants Elizabeth to go. It has a fine course, and I think E. will need it, unless she gets married pretty soon. I wrote Carrie [and Howard Nelson, Robert's sister-in-law and brother] at once to see if she will take Elizabeth this winter. It will be fine for her to be in Reading, and associated with those Pennsylvania folks, and away from the devastating effects of this town. . . .

Tuesday came disquieting word to the effect that Prof. Long, of Pocomoke, where I stayed [September 2], had been shot, as the letter said, "by two white ruffians," . . . Shocking. Nothing will probably be done about it. No matter how respected and innocent Long was, he was a Negro, and the men who stabbed him were white. That in itself is sufficient. Makes your blood boil, but what else is there to do? Riot? No use. Only more innocent ones murdered.

Went Tuesday night to the National to see Micheaux's "Gunsaulus Mystery" which was advertised. Caught glimpses of Micheaux and his man Friday, Wade, and saw them talking to White. The picture shown was a new one "Deceit," which was altogether too slow for comfort. I slept in spots. Poor action, bad English, and too many close-ups. Best thing was the acting of the child. Evelyn Preer is getting too fat, and so is Cleo Desmond. Colored actresses are not particular enough to details, anyhow. . . .

Micheaux and Wade came into the office on Wednesday afternoon, were introduced, and settled themselves to talk. . . . I gently

hinted to Micheaux that I'd like to collaborate with him, showed him "The Goodness of St. Rocque." He did not bite so readily, however.
. . .

I asked White to drive me to Chester in Dorothy, and he agreed to be at the house at 7:30 Wednesday night. After leaving Micheaux, it gave me little time to eat and dress. At the appointed time, he came. I had asked Leila to go, and she was hatted and coated for the drive. White had three women in the car, thus leaving me just one seat. I refused to go, and leave Leila, who was willing (she said) to stay. Said I'd just take the trolley. I'm afraid I was acrimonious, but there is no use in beginning what I don't intend to keep up—associating with Mrs. White's friends in Taylor street. Leila kept saying I could go with White, and being in quite a temper by that time, I told her to shut up. We went up to Ninth street, missed the car there, walked up to Market street just in time to see the Chester trolley go by. Nothing but a taxi then, as the next car a half hour later would get me to the Armory too late. Went into Barsky's, telephoned for an I.X.L. [taxi], who wanted six dollars, jewed them down to five, and in a few minutes a sedan came up the street, and who was driving it but old Friend Ralph Mustard! Looked like old times. We made the trip in thirty-five minutes. And passed Dorothy on the road. . . .

Big house, fine crowd, and plenty of speakers. I was to be first, as I had to go to Preston. Henry Arnett presiding. You can't kill him, nohow. He came clean, introduced me with a fine flourish, and we had quite a little chat before I came on. He is into the political pot, of course, by allowing the women, as usual, to use his church for meetings.

Bobo came in before I began to speak. I think I did myself proud, though Bobo was not so pleased with my speech, as he thought I did not use enough of the campaign material which he had prepared in the various issues of the paper. Did not say enough about Judge [Lincoln] Johnson, he thought. But then, Mrs. Bacon did not ask me to come to speak about Johnson, but about the whole ticket. All our old time 1915 suffrage friends on deck—Mrs. Ward, whose husband is on the ticket; Mrs. Bedford, who is growing becomingly stout; Mrs. Cheyney, who is herself on the ticket; Mr. Ward, Mrs. Bacon—like a gathering of the clans. . . .

White apologized yesterday morning for having such a car load. He did not understand that there would be two, he said, and his wife and her friends wanted to hear me speak. I accepted graciously. We had a two hour conference last night about movies. He has done some work in producing and distributing. Micheaux says his trouble is in the distribution. White seems to have it down to a science. I went over the despised serial, "9-19-1909," and we decided to film it. But we shall have to wait until next April. In the meanwhile, we will try out a five reeler. He showed me a bit of the new picture he is working on. His English is as execrable as Micheaux'. But he can't be told, of course. I shall go to work on a picture.

### Eleven p.m.

Interrupted here, and just getting back. I'm having a spell of the "losies." . . . It usually spells nervous trouble when I start losing things, but I'll have to watch out and try to forestall any such trouble.

Mrs. S. Joe Brown [chairwoman of the Negro Citizens' Committee] wants me in Des Moines, also Mrs. Francis [another racial activist] in St. Paul. I'll try to arrange for a western trip, beginning at Harrisburg, through Pittsburgh, etc. . . .

### At Home
### Sunday, September 18

I forgot to note that I went back the next day, which was Tuesday, to try to see Irenee du Pont. The gimlet eyed secretary handed me back the share blank that I had left with him, with a cold, "I have taken this matter up with Mr. du Pont, and he is not interested." His eyes looked more like black pin points in an opaque field than ever. I bowed out, hot with rage and mortification. I had one desire—to drop him out of that ninth story window. Had to run the gauntlet of stenographers, who heard the cold dismissal. I told Bobo I'd scrub or tend fires at the office, but I'd sell no more stock. Then he reminded me that out of the five people I had approached, I had written up three. . . .

That secretary's name is Davis—Irenee du Pont's, I mean. His eyes haunt me—they are so strange, so unusual. Whity gray, with those black pin points in the center.

Elizabeth's wardrobe has been under discussion. She has made herself a clever frock out of that plum colored velour coat of three years ago, and is about to remodel my light blue jersey for herself. She is certainly clever with her needle.

Bobo bought a Sunday *Ledger* on the train last night and we looked for the prize winners in the [Women in History] contest. I had given up hope on Tuesday, as no one had come for my picture or the interview which usually accompanies the announcement of the winners. I may be prejudiced, but I did not think much of any of them—even the hundred dollar one, much less of the smaller ones, down to five dollars. Slush, most of them, I thought, and Bobo agreed with me. Just as Micheaux says, if you want to get anything across, it must be pure "bunk," absolute "bunk," which the public will swallow, "hook, bait, sinker, line AND rod," and then come up gasping for more. I don't think any of the prize winners are as good as mine, and surely I might have made it on a five dollar prize. I guess I'm just not a winner at anything, that's all. Discouraging.

I lay in bed this morning thinking, "forty-six years old and nowhere yet." It is a pretty sure guess if you haven't gotten anywhere by the time you're forty-six you're not going to get very far. Humiliating, of course, but we may as well look facts in the face.

Facts. If there is anything in the theory of enemies' evil thoughts winning; if Mama is right in her sacred belief in the efficacy of evil workings of the voudooist, then those enemies of mine, of which Lizzie [Banton] is the chiefest, if they knew, could rejoice. All the things she wished against me have come true. I lost my position in school. Lost my place in the whist club. Lost my position with the State Committee. Lost my cars—both of them. I have no money, and things are far from going well with us. I lost Leila, whom I loved dearest of all. Lost Con's [Conwell Banton] friendship. To all intents and purposes I prosper, so far as the world can see, yet I cannot but think that Lizzie has triumphed mightily. Only she does not know it, and please God, she never shall.

Bobo and I had a fearsome quarrel yesterday morning, about the car, of course, and I burst out that I am tired of being the man. Bitter words passed. When I went down to the office, he was all right, and signified his rightness by giving me a package of Rexall's Orderlies!

Alexander paid him two hundred dollars Tuesday, which was something. Printing orders come in nicely, though.

### Monday, September 19

. . . Talking over the political cloud on the horizon with Jim Sewell [Black Wilmington politician who also served as circulation manager of the *Advocate*] this afternoon. He's coarse and all that but usually has the reaction of the man in the street. . . . My only dread is the launching of a Negro newspaper to offset the *Advocate*. I'll try not to think of it, lest I put the idea in motion. . . .

Funny—I menstruated today. It's so infrequent now, it always amuses me. Guess all the exercising I've been doing, plus the washing and ironing today did the business. Though these little few collars and things I wash shouldn't be hard.

Wrote out a plot for a five reeler, based on "By the Bayou St. John" [one of her short stories] last night. Showed it to White, who said he can film it. Shall cast it in scenario form.

## Thursday, September 22

Of all flivvers! Here I expected to be disporting myself in Clarksburg, West Virginia to-day, speaking at the emancipation celebration, and showing off all my glad rags, and here I am in this burg, wondering when the jinx is going to lay off me for awhile.

Had managed to extract enough money from Bobo to get ticket and reservation to Clarksburg, $19.73, had worked Schimel [the tailor] up to getting the broadcloth coat to my suit finished, and it looked most elegant, and had squeezed enough out to get myself a knee length tricolette black blouse, with fringe a foot long, and when I decked mineself up for exhibition purposes, I looked like a certified check. Was beginning to pack, when telephone call came from the Western Union, "Do not come, weather fierce. Will write." . . . All dressed up and nowhere to go. Hats, dresses, etc. all ready, shoes cleaned, all O.K. Some jinx! . . .

Tuesday night meeting of executive board of Federation. I turned out in the gray frock, which I had twinked from flesh pink accordion crepe de chine into plain gray crepe de chine, embroidered. It was very successful, and looks good with the saucy black velvet turban Laurence picked for the Atlantic City trip, and the gray bag I bought from Bowse. Meeting quite a success. Jackson stupid as ever, or pretending to be stupid about the functions of an executive board. I felt my tongue slipping several times, but kept it taut. . . .

The Wright child [a young Black woman associated with a rival political faction] was in to-day, telling about the success she has had in establishing her community work. . . . I pretended to be interested in her affair, promised to speak to Colburn about it, and interest him. Oh, I shall speak, and interest him too—to keep away. Bobo thought I ought to tell Warner. I shall think it over. I hate to be running to

white people with tattles on our folks, "White folks nigger." But even
if I decide not to make a special trip, I shall certainly tell him the first
chance I get. The danger, as I pointed out to Bobo is that if he feels
that here is a powerful machine ready to hand, he may decide to use
it as it stands, making the proper concessions to it, in order to swing
the vote when it is needed. Warner has no reason to hate all our
enemies, and in the coming warm fight, he will need all the help he
can get. He might find it convenient to get this crowd by dickering
with it. The whole thing has made me blue, actually physically
ill. . . .

### Sunday, September 25

Live and learn, so goes the world. And now it is White again. I
don't know whether I have chronicled before that I do not like him,
that I fear he is of the camel type, first nose in out of the cold, then
head, then whole body, and finally poor master has to go out and
freeze. I predicted to Bobo that we'd all be taking orders from him,
and he'd be paying us our wages. To-day I wanted the car. Sent Franklin, a very unwilling messenger boy, to his house requesting the keys
to the garage and car. Strick was to drive. Franklin came back. White
would come over. He did not come. Telephoned. Sunday was his
only day, his day of rest, he liked to spend it with his wife, give her
his company. He had planned to entertain her in the car. If I wanted
it to go to the cemetery I would have to give him more notice, etc. I
said "Yes" cooly to all his talk. Too cooly, I suppose, for he called
Bobo, and tried to do some explaining, but as I had not taken Bobo
into my confidence about the matter, he was truthful in saying that it
was a matter between White and me. Of course, it eventuated into
the inevitable quarrel between Bobo and me, the "I told you so," "I
told you not to buy that bunch of tin, etc., etc.," "Why did you let
White have that car?" and so forth. I have to explain twenty times
every time we quarrel that I turned it loose to avoid meeting the notes,
one of which was due on Sept. 9, and to avoid the payment of garage
rent, repairs, oil and all. Economy. But White hasn't put up but forty
dollars, and then won't let me light in the boat. Was ugly about Strick's
taking it to New Castle yesterday. Strick hanging around, and telephoning, to-day. Nothing doing. I have felt all day as if I had been
slapped, or spit in the face, and Leila has rubbed it in. Poor mama
has been quite pitiful. She did so want to go to the cemetery, and
asked quite humbly if she could go to-morrow. With Ethel. Just for a

few minutes to put fresh flowers about the child's grave. I would not
ask White if it was for a funeral. I'll try to get someone else.

Wrote to the Real people to-day, and tried to make a deal with
them for picture plots. I'll sell them that serial, if they will take it.
Bobo asked would I take a thousand dollars? Would I? I'd take a thousand cents for it right now. . . .

*In this entry, D-N begins her long-running narrative of the his-
toric Black delegation to the White House.* James Weldon Johnson
*headed this group of prominent Black citizens, which consisted of
such representative persons as* Robert R. Moton, *president of Tuskegee Institute, Alabama;* Robert S. Abbott, *founder, publisher, and editor of the Chicago* Defender *newspaper;* Nannie H. Burroughs, *founder
of the National Trade and Professional School for Women and Girls
in Washington, D.C.;* Mary Church Terrell, *outstanding civic and
social leader active in racial and women's causes;* Mary B. Talbert,
*former president of the National Association of Colored Women's Clubs;*
Rev. R. H. Singleton *of Atlanta, Georgia;* John Hope, *Morehouse
College and later (1929) Atlanta University president;* Dr. Charles E.
Bentley *of Chicago;* Kelly Miller, *Howard University professor, speaker,
newspaper columnist; and* Dr. W. W. Wolfe *of Newark. Also present
was* Emmett J. Scott, Jr., *formerly Booker T. Washington's Secretary
at Tuskegee Institute, who became secretary of Howard University.
During World War I, when he served as special assistant for Black
affairs to the Secretary of War, he and D-N came into contact with
each other and apparently had a romance. D-N talks aoout writing a
cycle of poems based on this relationship, called "A Dream Book,"
from which her "Violets" (or "Sonnet") was taken.*

*They had come to present President Harding with a petition signed
by fifty thousand citizens requesting executive clemency for the sixty-
one soldiers serving lengthy sentences for participation in the Houston
"race riot" of August 1917. After the Black 24th U.S. Infantry had
been repeatedly harrassed and attacked by the racist white citizens of
Houston, who did not approve of Black soldiers, fighting broke out.
No whites were ever prosecuted, but nineteen Black soldiers were hanged
(thirteen without trial) and sixty-one sentenced to lifetime prison terms.
At the time of this delegation, a federal investigation of the Ku Klux
Klan was also being conducted. What Johnson said during the con-
versational exchange with President Harding was that he could not let
this occasion slip by without mentioning the KKK and conveying that
Black people were watching the investigation with interest.*

*While in Washington, D-N stayed with Edith Fleetwood, a schoolteacher who also visited D-N in Wilmington as a helpful family friend. Because her deceased father had been in the army and had been nicknamed "Major," D-N sometimes called Edith "Cap'n." She lived with a companion, Lauralita.*

## Monday, September 26

. . . Friday was an off day for me. It was the 23rd, and Friday too, bad combination. Mama told me in the morning that Laurence had had trouble getting into his classes, as he had not paid his tuition, and Robert had failed him, for he was to write and send him the check. It mortified me and humiliated me so, and right on top of that Elizabeth got to acting up about a little housework, and I got to thinking that we were literally bumming along, and so went to feeling sorry for myself, and cried all day, off and on. Bobo went somewhere, Chester or some place, and that night I bawled it all out to him at the office, when we were alone. I was hurt all through. Man-like, his reaction was all wrong, and he at once became the martyr, put upon and abused, and we had bitter words. It resulted in his buying me a bottle of Azurea when he came home, and settling the matter with Leila in the morning. I said quite a few words, as I remember, and [?] by feeling grieved at his unrequited efforts at building up a business. Every now and then I get tired of just starting life and "building up" at middle age, when we should be settled. However, I must not feel that way. . . .

Friday also came a letter from James Weldon Johnson saying that the committee to meet the President on the Brownsville case [she means the 1917 Houston riots] will have an audience on Wednesday, Sept. 28, at 10:20. He wants all those who are going to be in Washington Tuesday night, and meet him at the "Y." Dress rehearsal, I suppose. I did not like to ask Bobo for my railroad fare, so did not say much about going. Then he went up in the air yesterday, because I did not ask him, and said I always get all the money I want, which is perfectly true. So I wrote Edith I'd be down to-morrow evening. Guess I'll go about two. . . .

## Friday, September 30

So very many very important things have happened, and lazily, or carelessly, which is it? I have forborne to chronicle. I always intended to, day after day, but there seemed no time. In the evenings it has been so insufferably hot that one could only gasp for breath. It was Monday, the last time I wrote. Monday the 26.

It was Tuesday that I got away for Washington. I did not say any-thing to Arleon [Bowse] on Monday night, and said nothing to Leila or Mama until in the morning, when Leila was making her usual rush to school. As usual, she was surprised, and wanted to know why I had not mentioned it before. I said because when I do talk about going away, I am apt to be disappointed. So I caught the two o'clock train for Washington. . . .

It was hot, but I dolled up in the broadcloth suit. When I reached Washington at 4:35 . . . went at once to Kann's and bought a face veil and a clean watch ribbon. I read the first installment of [T. S.] Stribling's novel "Birthright" in the magazine. I was sure, before I began to read, that Stribling is a nom de plume of James Weldon Johnson's, but saw his biography in the forepart of the *Century*, and Johnson told me that night that he was told by the *Century* people that Stribling is a Norwegian by heritage. . . . I started for the Y building on 12th street.

Not many present when I got there. Kelly Miller, Mrs. [Carrie] Clifford, Johnson, F. B. Ransom, of Indianapolis, Dr. W. W. Wolfe, of Newark, N.J., R. W. Stewart, also of Newark. Emmett Scott came in a bit later, and seemed surprised to see me. He always amuses me; falls all over himself, after the first few minutes of wondering how I got to places, and then acts scared. John W. Parks came in shortly after, Dr. Sinclair, and a Rev. Singleton, from Atlanta. We were well in the swing of things, Johnson read the memorial he had prepared, and as the evening papers had published—at least the papers that were carrying the Ku Klux Klan exposures—that we were going to the president to protest the K.K.K., we discussed the advisability of touching on the matter at all. Arguments pro and con flew to and fro. If we did not touch it, it would seem that we were insensible to the dangers of the situation. If we did, it might give the president a loophole to escape from the responsibility of the Houston affair. If we seemed grateful for that sop, it might be enough. In the midst of the discussion, Mrs. Talbert came in. She seemed vexed at seeing me, and I fancied the hand she gave me was quite limp. But she braced herself, doubtless remembering that I am really quite harmless, though she does do me the compliment of feeling that I am a possible rival to her greatness. Johnson finally phrased an expression which was delicately expressive of just the right shade of feeling on the matter. Mrs. Talbert, Mrs. Clifford and I decided that we would drive to the executive offices together, so as to ensure our being in time, and all together. We broke up amicably something after ten. Parks said he saw Bobo in Philadelphia as he was hurrying to catch the 5:19, and I was mystified at the ease and haste with which that husband of mine beat it out of Wilmington as soon as I had gone. It came in for some chaffing on the part of Emmett and J. W. Both seemed a trifle nervous lest I should think I wanted either to go home with me, and I hurried out lest there be any misunderstanding on their part.

Usual hushed manner of getting to bed that Edith always insists upon in order that "Baby Lita"—weighing about 250 and thirty-five if she's a day—may not be disturbed. Edith irritates me the way she spoils that accepting Laura.

I was up with them next day—Wednesday, the 28th, September. Ever memorable day. Almost a year to a day since I had made that equally memorable trip to Marion and seen Warren Gamaliel Harding for the first time. I dressed with meticulous care, unhurried and patient in the matter of complexion. It was very hot, and even the tricolette blouse and broadcloth coat skirt were oppressive. A coat was unthinkable. Reached the Y.W. and found Mrs. Talbert hatted, gloved, talking to Stewart, of Newark, who is already preparing for the N.A.A.C.P. meeting there next year. He talked pageant, Mrs. Talbert told him I'd write one for him, and I promised to let him see the one I had written for the Douglass centenary. Mrs. Clifford came in. Mrs. McAdoo chatted with us. She makes a charming secretary, as she naturally would. We skidded lightly over the fact that she was with Mrs. [Ella] Elbert [a Wellesley College graduate married to a Wilmington physician] on the boardwalk at Atlantic City, and was in this town as Mrs. E.'s guest, and did not see me. Mrs. Talbert said she had ordered Nannie Burroughs' car for us at five minutes to ten. When ten o'clock came and no car, we were all frankly uneasy, though each one told the other that it would not be late. It came at three minutes past, after Mrs. McAdoo had telephoned to Miss B., though it was on the way.

Found all the delegation, except [Emmett] Scott already at the executive offices, and he soon came in. Our engagement was at 10:20. At 10:10 all of us were in the ante-room; except the small weasel, who stood by me at the photographing. He came sliding into the executive office when we were all in there. I don't know who he is, and don't want to know. At 10:15, five minutes before our scheduled time, the president's secretary, Mr. Christian, called us. I suppose Harding thought he might as well get the disagreeable task over and be done with it.

We troddled in single file, Johnson introducing us each in turn to the president who repeated our names, giving us a quick practised handshake, and bending towards each one, with that charmingly intimate manner he has, which is disarming, though you know it is a gracious pose.

We ranged ourselves in a semi-circle around the room, and Johnson began his reading. He was plainly nervous, and had trouble keeping his glasses on. The ribbon he wears on them is very distinguished looking—I have discarded mine, but it gave Johnson trouble, and he had to hold his glasses to his eyes. The president remained standing, partly facing Johnson, three quarters away from us. I watched his face closely. It was heavily impassive, as you would expect it to be. He is a trifle thinner than this time last year. I suppose playing golf has been better for his health than sitting on the porch at Marion receiving delegations. His complexion is changed (when I told Lauralita this she said he must be using Black and White). It is no longer swarthily sallow, but swarthily ruddy, which makes him appear fairer. He still affects the short coat, which is rather surprising in such a big man, and I was really astonished at the size of his feet, for I did not get a chance to see them last year. His eyes, excessively little, are surrounded by firmer flesh than last year, but they still have that look of brilliant intelligence found in the eye of an elephant, with something of the same stubborn implacability. Remarkably small eyes.

When Johnson began to read his memorial, the president's lips were slightly parted. Gradually they began to draw together, so slowly that it was almost imperceptible. The rest of his face remained immobile. When Johnson came to that sentence, "The eyes of the colored people will be focussed upon whatever action you may choose to take," he winced perceptibly, and his lips closed in a firm line. Pleasure was the last emotion that was in his breast at that time.

Shelby Davidson [a member of the delegation], who had been very busy in the corridors before we went in, and who now stood with the bulky petition, almost as large as himself, though neatly bound, now stepped forward, when Johnson had finished, and presented his package, which the president took in his hands, and placed on the edge of the desk. "A formidable document," he said, and even this attempt at lightness and jocularity did not lighten his face or manner, which continued heavy, cold and depressing.

I thought at the minute of what Johnson had said on the evening before, when he had once had audience with President Wilson, how after their allotted time was out, Wilson sat chatting pleasantly with them, about his "old black mammy" in the south. Someone snorted and said, "Well, Harding won't brag about his mammy, that's sure."

The president began to speak; he did not think the executive (delightful impersonality) had final word in the matter. He was in the south at the time of the trial, and had naturally heard a great deal about it (southern viewpoint, of course). There would have to be investigations. We had presented the petition, but that was not all. As if we were mere sentimentalists; he was the practical one. He would look into the matter as soon as possible. We understood, of course, that other things might have to take precedence, but he would assure us it would be looked into. Bang! went the door of hope. We had indeed shot an arrow into the air, but it had fallen into slippery waters, and not to the earth.

Johnson continued, he could not refrain at this time, etc. . . . Emmett Scott said the president went up in the air. There was indeed a trace of animation in his manner at once, but whether the animation of impatience or of interest, it is difficult for me to say. "Oh, I do not think," he began slowly, "I believe," more quickly, then he turned towards the semi-circle patiently standing on the thick carpet, "No, I won't say that," with a swift shake of his head, "I won't say that, but I do not believe the Ku Klux Klan is aimed at your people." More he continued to the effect that the older organization was so constituted, but again he said, "I may be mistaken, but I do not believe it is aimed at your people."

I have been wondering what it was that the president would not say, and it has just come to me that perhaps the sentence that almost slipped out was that "if you people would cease agitating the attack upon the Ku Klux Klan, it would be more speedily wiped out of existence." I wonder if some such thought was not in his mind?

He terminated the interview, and we filed out slowly. I looked around the huge, gloomy room. I do not fancy it is conducive to pleasant thoughts; I should find it oppressive. Too many heavy portieres at the windows, too much thick carpet, desk too huge, and quite filled. Lovely roses on it, too. Outlook too restricted—the room being on the ground floor makes the view too low for my taste. Windows, circling, and taking up the west wall, only on that side. Two entrances, both on the north, one going out into the corridor, the other evidently into a communicating office, Christian's likely. He was not in the room while the interview was going on, but appeared from the adjoining office, as if summoned by magic when the president inclined his head, and murmured pleasure at having been favored with a visit from us. One slight dark man hovered in the little communicating passageway. Evidently a secret service man. Mrs. Talbert said they did not even think enough of us to have plenty of secret service men to protect the president. They know "niggers wouldn't have sense enough to attempt to assassinate the president."

I was anxious to get the press copy of Johnson's address, etc., and he told me Seligman would give it to me. We loitered a bit in the corridors, and finally Seligman darted into what seemed to be the press correspondent room, the right of the entrance to the building, and I was in possession of the mimeographed or multigraphed sheets of the N.A.A.C.P. Press service. I saw two camera men talking together in the entrance. One said, "Say, we've got competition out here," and when I went out, I saw that the "competition" was Scurlock [a popular Black Washington, D.C. photographer] preparing to take our pictures. He was a long while posing us, and we therefore were on the side of the building to the right of the entrance instead of at the entrance itself. The motion picture men disappeared, evidently deciding that they did not need black face news stuff. I don't know how I got between the two little men, Shelby Davidson, and the unpressed person. I noted Scott darting to one side, to be sure and not be by the ladies, and Mrs. Talbert getting herself near Johnson. I have heard a dozen comments to the effect that I am alone in a bunch of men, and not in the vicinity of the other two women. . . .

*Several key people are mentioned below.* Georgia Douglas Johnson *is an important Harlem Renaissance figure. She published three volumes of poetry between 1918 and 1928 (the last entitled* An Autumn Love Cycle*). Her home in Washington, D.C. was a gathering place for young writers and artists.*

Alain L. Locke *(1886–1954) was a philosopher; literary, art, and music critic; anthropologist; and black cultural catalyst and historian. His most significant literary contribution is the Harlem Renaissance anthology* The New Negro *(1925), which he edited.* William Stanley Braithwaite *(1878–1962), poet and literary critic, was best known for his acclaimed yearly anthologies of magazine verse, which he issued from 1913 to 1929.*

Martha Arnold *is one of D-N's Washington, D.C. friends.*

## Saturday, October 1

Just one year ago to-day since I made that memorable trip to Marion, Ohio, on Social Justice Day. A trip that started consequences in Wilmington, that, as Cap'n [Edith] says, will take years to obliterate, and changed the whole course of my life.

To continue the narrative. We three women drove back to the Y.M.C.A. Before we went, I saw Mrs. T.[errell] in close and earnest confab with J. W. J. [James Weldon Johnson]. She said when she got in the car that there was a discussion about a change in the office force, and that she was against any change at this time. Being a member of the Board of Directors, she had the right to voice her sentiments. E. J. S. [Emmett J. Scott] gave me a peculiar invitation to Howard. I laughed and sarcastically thanked him for his pressing invitation. He grew in earnest, and insisted that I come out during the day some time, and held out hints of Apollos. I promised, though something inside of me told me not to.

From the Y, I went to Lincoln Johnson's house. Georgia seemed glad to see me, and plunged instantly into a stream of poetic talk, mixed with hats, finding mine immensely becoming. She called Link, and he came in. Looks well, and says he's feeling all right, in spite of his stroke, save for a stiffness in the muscles of his throat. His speech has the occasional earmarks of the recovered paralytic, carefulness of pronunciation, with an occasional slurring over words with a preponderance of vowels. We were chatting when John Hope came in, and Georgia fled to change her blouse and her complexion. We all had the same reaction as to Harding's pronunciamento on the K.K.K. "That lying nigger in the White House," Link characterized him.

Funny how the general disgust at the president among our folks in Washington has resulted in calling him nigger openly. As Bobo says, some day one of these colored newspapers is going to lose patience and revive that old scandal and openly call him darky. "The nigger in the White House" is his general cognomen.

Georgia wanted to know how to put on hats, and I began to teach her. She really did not know how, and I made her practise and practise again and again. Link seemed so glad that I was teaching his wife an essential thing that he suggested luncheon, "Irish potato salad, and some of my tomatoes from the garden, Georgia, so Miss Alice can see how fine my garden is." "Well fix it," said Georgia, and he did. Two dainty plates of salad, little fine slices of bread, tea, and all. Of course, he had to push away papers, manuscript, junk from the dining room table to make a place for his tray, for Georgia has her machine, and all her literary stuff in the dining room, but we ate his salad and sliced pineapple, and everything, while Georgia showed me the manuscript of her new book, which Braithwaite is offering to the publishers. She does exquisite verses, and these are wonderfully fine—a story, running like a fine golden thread through them all. "An Autumn Idyll," it is called, the love story of a woman in the autumn of life. It makes you blush at times, the baring of the inmost secrets of a soul, as it does. I wonder what Link thinks of it? You might call it poetic inspiration, if you will, but it looks suspiciously to me as if Georgia had had an affair, and it had been a source of inspiration to her. Something like my "Dream Book," though I would never give it to the public, only the fragments which I did give—the sonnet "Violets," and the one or two others, for which E. J. S. has never forgiven me.

Speaking of him—I was much amused on Tuesday night to see him slip the Army seal ring around on his finger so that only a band showed—afraid doubtless that I had on the counterpart, and that it would be noticeable. When I saw him doing this surreptitiously, I made a point of showing both my hands, in many unnecessary gestures, so that he could see that I no longer wear his ring.

Georgia has done the big thing in letting [Alain] Locke, [W. E. B.] DuBois, and Braithwaite weed out her verses until only the perfect ones remain. What she has left are little gems, characterized by a finish of workmanship that is seldom seen in our people.

From their house I drifted over to Martha Arnold's. She raved over me, as usual, my looks, dress, etc., etc. Martha is a good antidote to the knocks and buffets I get here in this town, and the lack of appreciation. Her "Why, Alice, you treat those people in Wilmington just as if they are your equals, don't you? Take them right on terms of equality" in horror-stricken tones is as good as a month's vacation. And her wholesome advice for me to emulate Ella Elbert was good to listen to. When she started in on the Bantons, their visit last Thanksgiving being her topic, and their pretentiousness, Alice's [the Banton's daughter] uncouthness, and the horror of the little Alice [the] Christmas that she was her guest—it was almost worth the whole trip to hear.

From Martha's I went to Howard University. Something told me not to go, but I disregarded that inner voice. Every time I do, whether in a game of cards, or in more weighty affairs, I am stung It was a hot and wearisome ride, and when I got there, in all the bustle and excitement, I found E. J. S. gone over to the president's office. I left a little note on his desk, telling him that I had kept my engagement, and as I was leaving at seven p.m. could not see him again.

Then to Scurlock's to see if the group picture was ready, as I had made up my mind that it would be in this week's *Advocate*. It was not ready, and I decided to have some of myself taken. Scurlock gave me an hour, and took twelve poses. Some of them should be good, and take the taste out of those fearsome things [photographer] Cummings took last year.

It was time to go back to "The Retreat" then and tell Lita and Cap'n [Edith Fleetwood] the news. It would have rushed things so to catch the seven o'clock train, so decided to remain over for the 9:40, and Cap'n and I went to the New Republic. It is certainly a lovely theatre. I made up my mind to see Walter Pinchback and ask him what he knows about White, whom I suspected of four-flushing when he talked so familiarly of "Walter," and how the New Republic is going to run his pictures. After seeing how the theatre is run, I knew that White would never have a look-in. If Walter objected to Micheaux' English, I knew he'd kick on White's. Of course Walter had never heard of White. Did not dismiss him with scant attention, but thought and reflected, and said "never heard of him" when he had given consideration of the name. It was enough. I now know White is a liar, whereas I had only suspected it before. . . .

The nine forty proved to be a flivver . . . and reached Wilmington at 1:35. Bobo mad, of course, because I did not show up at two o'clock in the afternoon.

Thursday succeeded in getting the cut made from the picture. Letter from the Real people saying they'd take my stuff. I must get it off. I notified White that the three weeks would be up on Friday, when he would be expected to make a payment on the car. He asked me how little I could take. I told him ALL I could get. . . . Friday, Sept. 30. Had it out with White on the subject of the car. He thought I ought to accept a check from him for twenty dollars on Monday—on the $400 due me, and $40 a month thereafter. Nothing doing. We had quite a quiet scene, but I was as hard as nails. All I had to do was to remember the quiver of Mama's lip last Sunday when she couldn't go to the cemetery, and then I could make any demand on him. He said his wife is "peculiar," and I said that I am, too. He said she wanted a car, and I agreed that she ought to have one, but I didn't see why I ought to pay for it. . . .

Green came around this morning, and I told him my troubles

about the Dort. While we were talking, Bobo came in and off-hand-
edly said he'd buy the Davis car, if it could be done. I went out with
Green, drove the Davis, and found it delightful. Came home, telephoned for White to send the keys to me. He thinks I'm vindictive
about last Sunday. I am. Leila said she would have been more so.
Edna brought the keys. I went with Green to get the car, and he took
it away. . . . Green came back with the order blank for the Davis car.
Carrying that note, and the other one will make the monthly notes
$137 dollars. I don't know how we are going to do it, when we can't
pay our board, but I'd have gone to any lengths to keep White's wife
from riding in that car tomorrow. That is not according to the teach-
ings of Unity. . . .

*Broad Street Station*
*[Philadelphia, enroute to*
*Wilmington from*
*Reading, Pa.]*
*6:15 p.m.*
*Monday, October 3*

Just a year ago today, having returned from that trip to Marion, I
went down to Baltimore to speak for the Y.W. at Bethel and went to
see poor little Leila. Never will I forget the big, dreary house, the chill
that came over me when Constance Murphy [Rebecca's (Laurence's
girlfriend's) sister] met me at the train; Leila's gaunt, ill face, the dreary
halls, the flash-light she carried—all bespeaking a bleak homelessness,
that not even Auntie's cheeriness (affected) when she came in, could
obviate, nor the landlady's garrulity overcome. And the dread sinking
when Mason Hawkins [Leila's principal at the Colored High School,
where she taught], driving me to the church, told me of Leila's failing
health, patent to everyone, embarrassing to him. How often I have
wished that instead of pleading with her to come home that night, I
had picked her up and brought her. But it was perhaps better for her
to be away from the house when the storm broke over me—which it
did that next day, when little Ray [Wooten, the principal] sent me
home for A.W.O.L. It was the worst speech I ever made in Balto.,
and it shall be my last. Yesterday–Sunday, Oct. 2. Elizabeth got away
from Wilmington—and glad to go, I fancy. She seemed so listless and
uninterested towards the last. I have never known her to be oblivious

of her clothes before, and indifferent as to her garb. I packed her things for her in my big telescope, and she looked on, assenting listlessly to my suggestions. She was exhausted, when I had finished, "from watching you work, Mother." It sent a chill through me, for so Leila used to complain that it made her weary to watch her mother pack. She begged me to stay in Reading long enough to unpack her things. Mama seemed blue at her going, yet I don't know why, for she was constantly complaining of the child. It leaves a tiny household now—Mama, Leila, Bobbo, Ethel and I and Duke and Tiger [the cat]. It will be very lonely, I fancy. . . .

Howard and Carrie [Nelson, Robert's brother and sister-in-law] had been looking for us all day. . . . We had sandwiches and tea and Eliz. and I to bed together in Carrie's lovely, immaculate, bay-windowed guest chamber.

Howard has installed a shower in his tub that is quite the most refreshing thing ever. After breakfast today we three set out to hunt for "Stoners" as the Interstate Commercial College is known in Reading. Carrie and I are so big and prosperous and white-looking; she a rosy plumpness of 165–½, I a made-up face, tall, broad-shouldered Juno of 167, and poor little tiny, thin, brown Elizabeth between us, like an eerie little brown fairy—that we must have looked queer. Conference with Miss Stoner, daughter of the principal, followed up by conference with Mr. Stoner, as to E.'s career, finally settled by agreeing that she is to have the Business Course for three months, followed by shorthand and typing for six. And we went away, leaving E. in charge of her tutor, a thin young person with a wide smile and an unpronounceable name.

I hope the child will be happy, as happy as she can be with the memory of the unfortunate termination of her romance with Douglass [Stubbs]. She will be very much beloved and spoiled by her aunts and uncles and cousins and that's more than she would get in Wilmington. And she won't have mama to nag at and criticize her. . . .

I unpacked E.'s things and arranged them in her drawers. She came home to luncheon, quite pleased at what she had studied, and bubbling over with mirth at her schoolmates. She was still uninterested in her attire and seemed oblivious of the fact that she had on the same waist and suit she had travelled in.

I left at 2:55. Bade good-bye to all Carrie's menagerie—Bill Jones, the rabbit-cat, six-toed, bob-tailed, who hops on his haunches; fox-terrier Girlie, fourteen years old, with a huge tumor on her breast, who whimpers when she is not talked to; Jodie, the non-swearing parrot; and Lottie, the Maltese terrier, who when he likes you, stands on his head to show his affection. . . .

### Monday, October 10

I fear I am slipping back. I am cross, pessimistic, bitter, things are going wrong with me generally; I am nervous and tired and irritable; I cannot seem to make any headway, and above all that, rheumatism! It is maddening! Both knees as bad as ever they were when I used to suffer so terribly years gone by. The only consolation I have in the matter is that it is not a sign of age, since I have had it practically all my life, thirty years anyhow. Or more. But it is fearfully inconvenient and devastating. I want to invoke the aid of Silent Unity, but do not seem to be able to make the connection. I MUST GET MYSELF TOGETHER.

On Wednesday last, October 5 a big box came from Pauline. She had a pay-day and celebrated it by sending the whole family presents. A pussy willow white taffeta waist, embossed leather handbag, with five dollars in it, a Philippine envelope chemise, and likewise nightie for her mother, an Angora wool white and black Tuxedo sweater for her grandmother, a vanity case with a dollar in it for Ethel, a tie for Robert and a lovely ecru and navy georgette and satin waist for me. A regular Christmas box, but very extravagant, as I wrote her. I suppose the Kid felt grateful for everyone, though I guess we have all done less for her than for any child in the house, and she feels that we have done a lot.

Thursday afternoon went to the National to see Priscilla Dean in "Reputation." Good picture. . . .

Rev. King laid a circular on my desk and asked me to go to the concert which it advertised. It was at a white Methodist church, Union, Fifth and Washington. I yawned at the idea, but when I saw Freita Shaw's name, I sat up and took notice, and decided to go. . . . The concert, entertainment, whatever they call themselves doing, was rotten. . . . I went back of the scenes and asked Freita why she did not sing a solo, as only she can sing—one of those exquisite little things that she thrilled me through with out in Portland. She said there was no adequate accompanist—true, for the young man who played, as well as sang, was fearful, and she had gotten out of the habit of singing solos. Doing a lot of cheap truck, plantation stuff and the like. Funicule Funicula being about the heaviest, then a swift change into gingham aprons and headhandkerchiefs, and Suwanee River, Old Black Joe stuff. Sickening. Tiresome. But that white audience seemed to like it; it tickled their vanity. And they are working for a lyceum bureau, and have been abroad!

Minnie [Stevens, wife of H. Clay Stevens] said she was entertaining the Wright child and Fannie Hamilton [the busybody dressmaker] that evening. Funny. Dr. Stevens is working hard—for him—to make his ward come up in the community thing. His interest is in the girl. As I told him Friday afternoon, if she were some black, bow-legged person, he would not feel so keenly the need for a portable community house for the forthcoming generation. . . .

Had a letter from Brascher [of the Associated Negro Press] complimenting me on my editorial, "The Negro as a Modern Literary Subject," and enclosing copy of a letter, which he was sending the editor of the *Saturday Evening Post*, enclosing the editorial to him. The *Star* yesterday copied my editorial on "Dangerous Dallying," and very decently supplied the line, which was missing out of the editorial as it appeared in the *Advocate*. . . .

## Sunday, October 9

. . . Called on Krusie. She is very deaf and difficult to talk to. We discussed the new art teacher to come. Wooten is filling the school with men, no doubt of that.

I had to say to myself Friday night, "Mightily have mine enemies triumphed." Wooten's picture is in this month's *Crisis*. Bobbo brought it home. His biography rather fulsomely told, is there in "Men of the Month." At last has he succeeded in getting before the public the fact that he was born in the north, and not in the south. Well, I suppose he is happy, and all his friends and adherents are chortling. Joy be with them all. . . .

Bobbo saw Link Johnson yesterday, and came back from Washington very hungry, and quite full of political dope. Emmett Scott has been traitorous, and played into the hands of Link's enemies. Had a letter from Georgia sending me that poem, "A Parody," that I asked her for. I don't care for it now. It struck a mood when I first saw it.

The Autumn Fair wants me on the 24th. Mazie [Mossell, a Pa. clubwoman] writes me to "save the womanhood of Delaware," which means run around and work up exhibits for her. Nothing doing. . . . I'm not bothered about the womanhood of Delaware. It will have to go unsaved.

Emma Beckett [staunch member of the Women's Auxiliary of St. Matthews Episcopal Church] was by way of stirring up things with a stick this afternoon. . . . Every time things go wrong with that little cat she starts up a row with someone. I announced that I positively refuse to be in any fusses this winter. Absolutely, I will not quarrel with anyone, or be harrowed with gossip and tales. In order to make my point clear . . . I had to do some tall cussing. . . .

I must go to bed, but before I go, I must try to get in touch with the Infinite again. I've lost my grip, precarious enough as it was. . . .

*The three women whom D-N joins in the street here are* Anna Brodnax, *Howard High School Latin teacher who came from Plainfield, New Jersey, and graduated Phi Beta Kappa from Oberlin College;* Marguerite Hamilton, *a young, working-class Wilmington woman; and* Jo Hopkins, *a member of the* Fisher *clan that D-N sometimes mentions, a family that included her sister* Pauline *and brothers* Leon *and* Razzle.

## Thursday, October 13

I forgot to chronicle that Elizabeth sent me a special on Sunday morning. Pauline sends her mother a special every Sunday morning, and Elizabeth does not wish her mother to be slighted. It was very delightful to be so remembered. I have had no Sunday specials since Bobbo [who used to send her specials] came to Wilmington to live.

Tuesday night, the 11th, another special came from the child. She says her eyes have gone back on her; dull headaches, etc., and she was compelled to be out of school. She wanted to know if it was all right for Carrie to take her to the oculist's. . . .

Yesterday's papers announced that the husbands of Harriet Taylor Upton and Christine Bradley South have been rewarded by nice plums. "Husbands rewarded for Wives' Services." The *Age* is telling the world that I'm slated for something fat. Strick was quite impressed with the item. "You'll be riding on the moon yet," he said. But I laughed. "I write political stuff myself," I said. "I know just how much credence to put in such conjectures." . . .

The thought came to me like a flash from a clear sky that I ought to study law. Intended to get a catalogue from Temple, and see about entering in February, evening classes. Put it off, as usual. Speaking to Bobbo this morning about the death of Senator Knox chronicled in to-day's papers, I said jokingly, "Well, since one big lawyer in the country is dead, it is necessary for some one to take his place; I guess I'll study law." I expected a snort of disgust from Bobbo, and to my surprise he said gravely, "That's what you should have done long ago. You'd make a crack-a-jack lawyer. You should have been doing it all the time you were wasting on educational stuff."

"Do you think it's too late?" I asked.

He did not, and advised me to look into the matter. "It would be funny if you should be admitted to the bar here in this state," he said, "the first colored person to be admitted." But I reminded him that constitutional barriers prohibited women from practising in this state. Come to think of it, though, I believe the embargo on women prac- tising law in this state has been removed.

Bobbo has just come in to get the last of the news. The proofs came from Scurlock this week. They are so awful that I have not had the heart to send them back, or to decide which one I want. Gee whillikins! They are either hopelessly middle-aged, or passe pretty- pretty. . . .

Yesterday being Columbus Day, I had to go back in mind twenty- nine years! To the 400th anniversary of the discovery of America. How delightfully young and adolescent I was, and how old I felt! Julia [Brooks, one of her high school friends] and I walking the streets of New Orleans, all clad in new frocks, mine a dark blue chambray, which Mama had made, fondly believing it a Russian blouse, until Mamie Dessauer punctured our pride by saying it was not a Russian blouse. And Jimmie Vance and Jimmie Lewis [her beaux] adoring me, and all the happiness of the newly graduated filling my soul! Halcyon days.

Later: Will I ever get myself together? All day doing nothing. Yes- terday I bought grapes, and last night Arleon ["Bowse"] and I started my wine. To-day I put up a few glasses of jelly. Went to see "East Lynne" at the three o'clock performance at the National. Said I would not go, but saw Anna [Brodnax], Marguerite [Hamilton], and Jo [Hop- kins] going, and was out and in the street before I knew it. Played three games of pinochle with Bowse, and lost all three, after dinner. And nothing done, and now it is eight o'clock! I have been all day pasting or trying to fix up this chronicle. Everyone out now but Ethel and I, and we are up here in my room. I shall try to fix this book up. Franklin may come in. If he does to get that other piece of pumpkin pie and Leila is not here—she and Mama gone to see "East Lynne"— she will have a fit. She is real foolish over Franklin these days. I am afraid Leila is getting erotic, a development from her neuroticism. Bobbo is beginning to talk strangely about her to me. Just nerves, I guess, but it might develop into something pathetically pathological.

## Friday, October 14

Bobbo down at Salisbury and I sitting up in bed fresh from my bath. Had to work like mad today, helping to get the papers out. I don't like to wrap [the newspapers] but with Laurence and Elizabeth away and Ethel hors du combat, someone must help Edna. . . .

Bobbo went to some fool speaking trip to Salisbury. I was advertised to speak yesterday and he and I had bitter words because I did not go. It seems the man called him long distance, and he promised the man—Stewart—I should come. But Stewart failed to write; no terms were made, no hour set, no subject suggested. And Bobbo thought I should run off to Salisbury on no further data than a long distance telephone call. I raved at him! . . .

## Monday, October 17

. . . Bobbo went over to see Colburn, and came back with some political stuff. . . . I see that I am out of the game, and while it leaves me poorer in pocket, I am easier in mind. Not to be in the employ of the State Committee, nor to be required to hold meetings or get a situation straight is like heaven. I could never do it again. It may sting a bit to be left completely out, crucified on the altar of political expediency, but it is mighty comfortable on the cross. . . .

We are going to run off our own paper this week, and I guess it will be pretty much of a mess. The linotyping is being done in Philadelphia, even as White said it would be done. It galls me to the very quick that he has had his way about that. Of course, as Bobbo said, if the *Star* people did not want it, and no other people in town would bid on it, we had to go out of town, but I just hate White to have his way about that linotyping. I suppose there will be all kinds of trouble about the stuff, for I had to hurry with all A.N.P. [Associated Negro Press] stuff and news for him to take up on the 12:20. That will not be possible every week, and there will be a lot of stale news go[ing] in and a lot of stuff left out I fear. Still, it is best for us to be doing our own printing.

## Thursday, October 20

These be strenuous days. . . . White and Franklin are now in Phila. waiting for the stuff to bring down the last. . . . It is a quarter to eleven. We are at the office. Strick, Bobbo and I. When they come, I shall run home and cook some doggies and make coffee and bring it down to them. This is what it means to stick by an infant enterprise. . . .

Everyone seems anxious to see me have a job. Bowse said to-day she heard I was to teach at Dover, and she was asked about it. Makes me sore. They think my husband can't support me; he can't, as a matter of fact, but that's no one's business. Since my pay has been cut off, we are in straits most of the time, especially since every cent he can rake and scrape goes into the business. But he will be able to some day, and handsomely, too.

I can have patience and wait, I hope. I can have patience.

I dreamed of stormy waters, and huge waves in which I was swimming the other night. Now I wonder what disaster is to befall me. . . .

The Real [art Pictures Corp.] sent home the play, of course, not distinctively colored enough. They are anxious about the serial. It has the same disqualification. I shall try to get time to write another.

## Sunday, October 22

Well! The story of the past two days makes a moving tale. What Strick would characterize as "pitiful." But it is best told on the machine. [Here she switches from longhand to the typewriter.]

They [White and Franklin] came home that Thursday night; it was a quarter to one; they were cold, miserable, and cross. . . . Bobbo gave them whiskey, and I set about looking over the galley proofs. There were no headlines on some articles; and headlines scattered in a galley by itself for others. I straightened them out, as best I could, then ran home, cooked a breakfast of hot dogs, coffee, and took a basket of food, pie, bread, butter, mustard, sliced onions, and a huge pot of coffee, and with Edna's desk as a table, and the oil stove as a cookstove, made a feast. We four ate. Franklin and White said they'd work all night. We came home, Bobbo and I, and at a quarter to three I was washing up the last dish.

Friday morning; make-up not completed, and ten hours necessary to run off the paper. All day Friday lagged. Boys came to sell, people

came in, the dreary drag down stairs, the unfinished work, the linotyping still unfinished, Franklin up in Philadelphia still bringing home
bits of galleys. Mr. Martin [liberal editor of *The Delmarvia Star*] came
in to get me to sign another one of those ridiculous notes which I sign
jointly with T. Coleman [du Pont] and [Judge] Hastings [white liberal
Wilmington lawyer]. I'm in fast company he tells me jocosely, and I
laugh. It seems funny to be endorsing a note with Coleman du Pont,
one of the richest men in the world, and when I signed a check for
nearly three thousand dollars, it was ridiculous! [This Republican party-
based note-signing may be related to the *Advocate's* financing.]

Martin predicted that we would have rough sailing, but I don't
think even he knew how rough it was to be. All day Friday dragged;
White picked up and put down, Franklin set up headlines, and I o.k.'d
and suggested. Friday night came, nothing ready. Strick called up one
of the *Star* men . . . and he came to help in the making up. We came
home to dinner; I cancelled an engagement Bobbo had with Brascher,
and we went back to the office. The place seemed alive with questions. The *Advocate* late! Not out yet! What's the trouble! I burned
with mortification, and still the eight forms seemed as incomplete, all
eight of them, as on Thursday night.

No headway being made; Strick said it was a crime for Franklin
and White to work longer. Bobbo sent them home to rest, for three or
four hours anyway. . . . Bobbo and I went to bed, and were up early
Saturday morning. Strick called up. Seven o'clock, and still no headway, and then poor Bobbo's temper broke. He had been wonderfully
patient. Strick succeeded in getting Eliason to come and finish the
making up; got a truck . . . at my suggestion—and the eight forms
were loaded on and taken to the *Star*, where castings were made—as
usual—and the paper run off, as usual. It came up about two o'clock,
or thereabouts. It was time. We had been harassed by the newsboys,
the people, the questions and the implied jeers of those who were only
too glad to see us go to pieces. Bobbo was able to make the three thirty
to Philadelphia. The paper got out twenty-four hours late. One salient
fact stood out. WHITE HAD LIED, HE KNOWS NO MORE
ABOUT MAKING UP A PAPER THAN EDNA.

But Bobbo had put dependence in him, and because of his faith
in White, and White's four-flushing, we had been let into several
hundreds of dollars more than ordinarily. The paper was a day late,
and several orders were cancelled, and money had to be paid out to
get people in Chester [Pa.], etc. served. The boys had only one day to

sell, instead of two, and our receipts were thus cut in half. We left out several ads, and that's money gone!

And the paper! A screamer, and no article to go with it. Articles without headlines. Articles with wrong headlines. A poem in the editorial column—in fact, everything that I had told White NOT to do, he had done. Articles unbroken on page one and when broken, the rest not to be found. It is the worst mess I ever saw in all my life! A child starting out would have such a looking sheet. And after our twenty months gruelling work to build up a reputation, gone in one week because of a conceited fool. For if White had not been a conceited Jackass, he would have admitted to himself, if not to us, that he did not know how to make up, and would have gone down to the plant on Thursdays and watched Rein, and learned in the time he has been here. Not to mention two printing jobs that were promised on Saturday and did not get out on time. I have been mean enough to say "I told you so" to Bobbo. . . .

## Tuesday, October 25

Last night, the 24th, I spoke at the Autumn Fair as per agreement . . . to be on the program for "Dunbar Night." . . . The program was a *mess*. The Women's Auxiliary marshalled by Mazie and Mrs. Gale, mouse-colored under her make-up, took the stage. The platform faced a space of the monster place, enclosed (partly) by cambric curtains. About 600 people sat or stood in front of the stage. Beyond the curtains a carousel was in full blast, and the barkers, crowds, music and noise went on ceaselessly. People came and went, chairs scraped. Shoes resounded and beat back upon your ear drums. My throat split and went raw, my voice choked down into my ears. I babbled for fifteen minutes and gave it up. No one even on the platform heard me, nor th other speakers. . . . However, Gale honored my bill for $28.18 by cash. Emma [Beckett] went wild and insisted that I spend some of it on her. So I treated her to a fortune by the Indian Rajah.

Bobbo and I quarreled after we got home, because I told him of conditions at the office—White getting nowhere. . . .

*D-N's first speech on this "western" trip was entitled "The Serious Side of Paul Laurence Dunbar." In Des Moines, her visit was sponsored by the Negro Citizens' Committee, Mrs. S. Joe Brown, chair-*

*woman. A Davenport, Iowa, Daily Times article (October 29, 1921)*
*stated: "Mrs. Nelson is delivering a series of lectures throughout the*
*country in the endeavor to awaken a literary consciousness in her race*
*by showing them the serious side of the literature of her late husband."*

## Thursday, October 27

On Pennsylvania Railroad nearing Pittsburgh, Pa., 8:10. And the
porter making down beds. So I suppose I shall have to go to bed soon.
Car full of women—that means congestion in the dressing room.

Was in a quandary as to how I could raise the money to get out to
Davenport and Des Moines. Thought once I'd just have to telegraph
Mrs. Brown and Mrs. Rickey [her sponsoring hostesses] I couldn't
make it. . . .

## Davenport, Iowa
## Friday, October 28

. . . Reached Davenport 2:26. Met by Mrs. Rickey, charming
brown. . . . Mrs. Rickey lives with a Mr. and Mrs. Carroll. All were
out and we had the house alone and Mrs. R. had to go back to the
"Y." I was cold. Formed an unfavorable opinion of Mrs. C. because,
while every other room in the house was open, her bedroom door was
locked. Upon meeting her, did not revise my opinion. Washed up;
mended dress, went to bed—cold, and slept. Mrs. R. called me at
twenty minutes to seven. Dinner seemed to have been forgotten. I was
hungry. Breakfast and luncheon very light, and a long way back. Just
before we left, Mrs. R. gave me tea, cake, jelly, bread and butter.
Slim fare.

The Bethel A.M.E. church typical small town Negro church. About
1200 colored people in Davenport, but the "In-citys" include Moline
and Rock Island also. Good crowd out, despite the storm. I felt depressed
and did not get it across. Atmosphere heavy and I was cold, hungry
and blue. . . .

Usual agony of "reception" after and refreshments. I hoped for
coffee—alas, only pie and ice cream. Hole in coffee pot, hole in ket-
tle, girl so explained. Poured down rain, torrents—thunder, lightning.
Came home and Mrs. Carroll walked in on me in my bloomers. I am
still cold and hungry.

This is a lovely little home. I like it, and I have a pleasant room.

There was not enough covers on my bed, but I'm glad to see an extra comfort.

I turned up my nose at a woman who sat opposite me at luncheon in the dining car—and she didn't want to sit there. She had a "platter luncheon." It seemed humble to me then—all thick, greasy food. But I could swallow it whole now.

Colored audiences look the same no matter where you go. Types alike, north, east, west, south.

Was interested in a Capt. Clayton, U.S.A., 10th Cavalry stationed at the arsenal here. Very delightful to meet. So too, his wife. But of course he had something to tell from '98 to '17.

## Sunday, October 30

Had a most eventful day yesterday, delightful to the last degree. After breakfast, and if I starved Friday, I feasted Saturday. For I *ate*. Mrs. Carroll redeemed herself by a breakfast fit for the gods. It was after eleven when we got down town to the "Center" as the colored Y.W.C.A. is called. A promising looking work. Mrs. R.[ickey] fixed me up with an ancient and asthmatic Underwood, some paper and carbon, which we had collected at the white "Y" and after a brief note to Bobbo and a paragraph about my lecture for the *Advocate*, I plunged into the heat of my scenario—"The Coward." I was working at white heat and against time, as there was luncheon to eat before a two o'clock engagement. But I finished in two hours, 9 pages (carbon copy), about 3000 words. It's a sizzling drama, and I have hopes. I had intended using the plot for a colored story for the Real people—but if it fails in the *News* contest, I can still do it. . . .

## Des Moines, Iowa
## Tuesday, November 1

Mrs. S. Joe Brown is a typical club woman of affairs, and she's on my nerves. Nervous, hurried, talking always in a low incessant monotone. Kind to a fault, but indefatigable and when she has a lion [a celebrity] twists its tail until its roars fade into hoarse squeals. I am flattened out. Bury the lion.

To return to Davenport. Mrs. Rickey is the opposite—she leaves you tactfully alone. Mrs. Brown saps your every minute. I've had to sneak time just to write a line to Bobbo, to send Laurence a hasty word for his birthday and a M.O. for $3.00, and as for writing in this chronicle—unthinkable, until she had gone to bed, and she is protesting. Yet I like her lots. I miss the social side of my visit here—she evidently is not society—too much A.M.E.—Eastern Star—Club Federation. I should like to frivol. I am tired of being dragged to newspaper offices and schools. I yearn for flesh pots.

To return again to Davenport. That Saturday we had a lovely ride through the grounds of the Rock Island Arsenal. The largest in the county, they say. Rock Island is an island in the Mississippi River, between the main-lands of Davenport, Iowa, and Moline, Illinois. The ride was memorable—a whole flock of blue-birds, whirrying upward from crimson leaves, a blue jay (the first I've ever seen) chattering in a sapling, the flash of a Chinese pheasant among the autumn foliage. Then to a Girl Reserve Center in Rock Island—Mrs. Clayton's hobby—and a few bashful girls and women whom we all spoke *at*.

That night a whist party to which Captain and Mrs. C.[layton] drive us at a Mrs. Shepherd's. Funny looking aggregation of folks—worse than the Cat Fest at home, but I don't have to live among them, so enjoyed myself. And won the prize, which, as the hostess had forgotten to provide one, had to be something already on hand. A plate she had painted—lovely thing, pine cones, came to me. . . .

Mrs. Rickey sat up with me as I packed Sunday night. I am curious about her—she is so young and pretty and starry eyed—yet where is Mr. Rickey? I gathered from her that she was born in Memphis, family moved to Chicago in her infancy, and there she went to school. College education at Fisk. Had taught in Chicago. Once she said bitterly that Mr. Rickey was a "Y" secretary, had served in India and came home a broken down old man at 25. Then her voice broke and I asked no question. Perhaps I should have.

On Monday, the 31st, was up at five; the taxi came. I bade the sleepy Rickey child good-bye, and to the station. She and Mrs. Walker [another sponsor] paid me $38.60 and she gave me $1.00 for taxi fare. The train was late leaving Davenport. It was an accommodation. I was on the sunny side. Buxom youths and maidens commuted to Iowa City, where is Iowa State University. (I learned Sunday that there are 50 colored boys and 10 colored girls attending there.) Some of the buxom maidens sat with me and gave out heat. The train was roasting hot. My head swam, and I tried to sleep, after finishing [F. Scott] Fitzgerald's "This Side of Paradise." He's as good as [John] Barrie ever was in Sentimental Journey, and has [writer] Booth Tarkington's Victorian middle-classness middle westernness skinned a mile. . . .

When I arrived in Des Moines I was one heap of perspiring, dusty, hungry wretchedness. My breakfast had consisted of an apple and an orange, which a benevolent-looking old German pirate of a train butcher had sold me for a quarter, and a box of cheese biscuit, which cost the same. I had annoyed the ticket agent exceedingly by wanting a Pullman and a dining car on that cattle train.

I had visions of a bath, luncheon, a nap, but Mrs. S. Joe Brown willed otherwise. With Mr. S. Joe—a very youthful looking person, and her brother—Wilson—and a battered Maxwell, she took me in charge, and began monotoning at me. I was to be allowed to eat and wash my face—then I must roar at two schools that afternoon. The first one at two! Hers is a modest, comfortable little cottage. Took off the top layer of dirt, ate the chicken dinner, and the Maxwell took us to the Cooper school (think that's the name). Two or three grades, 3rd, 4th, and 5th, I think, piled into one room to hear me. Principal and teachers delighted, little colored children proud. Then to the next (forgotten name, but clipping tells) a Junior high. Nervous woman principal with two buildings. Efficient teacher aide. Kids standing on each other and I preached. No poems to recite. Teachers pleased. Kids vociferous. Home and coveted bath—after Mrs. S. Joe had run around a bit. . . .

The St. Paul and Chicago engagements fell down, even as did Pittsburgh and Harrisburg. So my trip will be a financial failure. The town was billed to death with those awful cuts of me. . . .

The affair last night was quite brilliant. The programs very swell. The "50 female voices" fine and the audience of about 600 responsive, eager. They drew out my best. Usual tiresome reception afterwards. . . .

I wanted to go in the Capitol to see the mural paintings. . . . But Mrs. S. Joe wanted us to go in the historical building opposite to see the [Henry O.] Tanner [celebrated Black romantic painter] portrait of B. T. W. [Booker T. Washington] which the Iowa State Federation of Colored Women's Clubs presented the state. That section in which the portraits are was locked because of repairs going on, but she teased and buzzed at the elevator, always with that insistent, unending low monotone, until the elevator man, an Ancient Mariner person, said irritably to some woman employee she had invoked, "If they'd only be still and not be so nervous, I'll manage it." I whooped. Mrs. S. Joe was on my nerves too. We went in to see the State Librarian—a Thackerayan looking old personage named (Lord knows) who took a violent fancy to me—and I to him. Lovely old book-worm.

The Tanner portrait of B. T. W. is *ghastly*. Heavy splashes of gray green for the face, merging into the background. Figure placed to right of canvas. Just bust, and so looks eccentrically one sided. Left shoulder disproportioned—very displeasing portrait, with no soul, no personality. Just chilling greenness. The [Frederick] Douglass portrait by a local artist, while not so artistic—and very conventional—is better.

No time to go in Capitol. Lunched with S. Joe. Stuffy colored restaurant. Interurban car at one for Mitchellville where we had an engagement at the Girls Industrial School. . . .

The Colored Cottage had gone into Hallowe'en heavily the evening before and Mrs. S. had seen that all decorations stayed up; the girls were excused from school. . . . The living room of the cottage was *wonderful*. The decorations, lighting, bunnies (live ones in costume) witches etc. were really marvelous. One stepped into witchland in an eerie light—with the devil, pitchfork, snake and fire all striking the eye at once. A real live owl added tone. He looked as if he were cousin to that one who kept me awake in Davenport. The girls—who were not bunnies or the gypsy fortune teller—brave in white dresses and red ribbons held the corner of the room. They performed. And I did, and we had sandwiches and coffee and cakes and Mrs. Sickels and other officers beamed. . . .

Mrs. S. Joe's feeding is a Des Moines joke. No joke to me. These sketchy breakfasts are all right, but the vile restaurant dinners are nauseating. I eat many apples which she uses for decorating the table.

Rushed me around introducing me at every chance. I always roar politely, until tonight at the concert I balked flat and refused to help out on the program.

## *Chicago Rock Island and Pennsylvania Railroad Thursday, November 3*

Just about to leave Des Moines. Tired, and begged to come to my berth, though Mrs. S. Joe would have run indefinitely. She has taken me to an infinity of places—but not *one home*. Introduced me to scores of people—but few home-looking women. She and her husband live a *strictly public life*. Strange. Not a person called on me, not a courtesy extended by a colored person, and this is a city of 8000 Negroes. I can see why the S. Joes would be very unpopular. Too pushy.

Laurence's birthday. Hope he got his M.O. No *Advocate*. Not a line nor a word from home. I fear the worst.

Think I shall stop in at the Associated Negro Press office in Chicago tomorrow and see what I can see.

There, we're off, Oh, but it was good to get to the berth, undress and stretch out! . . .

To-night addressed the Iowa State Teachers' Assn. There are 6000 teachers in attendance, but not more than half of that number was at the huge Coliseum, which seats 10,000. Some more of the lady's insistence. I hated the pushiness of it all, but she had a point to gain, and I was the instrument by which it could be gained—as Stricklin said—to be the means of shining in my sun. Well, if it made her happy I am pleased. For after all, I can boast of having sat on the platform with and being on the same program with the Governor of Iowa. Gov. Randall. Fine man, regular western type, a real bush leaguer. Handsome, self-made, etc. But with a splendid command of English (he boasts he knows but one language and he knows that well). One white hot phrase I swore I would remember. It is gone, of course. But I will write down right now Percy Mackaye's good line which struck me, "We begin to live when we have learned to contemplate."

The governor is a genuis at taking absolute commonplaceness, utter banalities, the bromidic obvious, and clothing them in choicely careful phraseology uttered with a fine and convincing earnestness until you are almost deluded into the belief that he has said something. Typically American. Not being regularly on the program I had ten minutes at the opening, after the invocation. I used six. Then Mrs. B[rown] ran me around until I howled for help, wherefore I was able to be in my berth and undressed before we pulled out at 10:55.

She paid me off.

|                     |         |       |          |      |       |
|---------------------|---------|-------|----------|------|-------|
| Yesterday           | $12     |       |          |      |       |
| Today               | 15      | cash  |          |      |       |
| Check               | 25      |       |          |      |       |
|                     | $82     |       |          |      |       |

which with Mrs. Rickey's 38.60
makes $120.60
which is a little over railroad and Pullman. These were—

|              |        |            |         |
|--------------|--------|------------|---------|
| Coming out   | 60.78  |            | $120.60 |
| Going home   | 58.67  |            | 119.45  |
|              | $119.45 | Bal. $    | 1.15    |

Of course eating on the train, tips, etc. not to mention what I've spent is going to stick me heavily, but I've had a good trip and added prestige etc. I'm only worried about the paper—horribly worried. If anything happened because I was away I'll never forgive myself.

*Pennsylvania Railroad*
*Friday, November 4*

End of a perfect day. Tempered by wonder about the paper. . . .
[In Chicago] Took trolley up to 3423 Indiana Av. to A.N.P. [Associated Negro Press] offices. Seemed to be repairing building so on to the *Defender* building a few doors away . Sent card to [Robert S.] Abbot [*Defender* editor], who came out and seemed glad to show me around. Black, smooth-faced man, diamond in the rough. A *business* man plus. That building is splendid—two stories and basement only now, but additions being made. Each editor has private office, six or seven. Front entrance like bank, grill and all. Six linotype machines. Huge rotary press, etc. etc.—like the *Star*. All that is needed to get out a 16 page paper. Splendid. Invited me to drive about city. . . . We drove in his Marmon through the parks, Lake Shore, etc. Saw the Boulevard where the Negro homes are bombed. . . . He took me to see the Vincennes Hotel, but did not invite me to luncheon. In Jackson Park I recognized the pier jutting out in the lake where Will Murphy [Paul Laurence Dunbar's half-brother], Paul and I fished all that long, hot day in August, 1899—or was it September?

Back at the office, after an hour's drive, I bade Abbot farewell and thanked him for his courtesy. He had done all that was to be expected for a total stranger. I had hunted for adventure and it had eluded me.

Took trolley down—found an inexpensive lunch-room and fed sumptuously on filet of sole, tartar sauce, baked macaroni, mashed potato, bread and butter and coffee for 40¢. Had decided to see Pola Negri in "One Arabian Night" and in hurry for the Ziegfield Theatre discovered Michigan Avenue! Not to have known Michigan Avenue before is a crime. It is lovelier than Fifth Avenue—far lovelier. Broad, sweeping, free, clear. Wonderful shops. Lake Michigan in the distance. Hotels and hotels. The familiar auditorium among them. I could love Chicago for Michigan Avenue alone.

"One Arabian Night" was all I had expected and more. Pola Negri is a delectable hussy. Ernst Lubetsch (guess that's the way to spell it) does a fine bit of acting as the hunchback. There is no question of the superiority of the foreign pictures over the American. And yet *Life* says it has been riddled for daring to say so. One dare: not write a review of this play. Foreign actors are not afraid to be natural; there are no artificial repressions. They do not fear to be brown or yellow or black—if the story calls for it. Nor are they squeamish about Negro faces in the story. The Bagdad dances before the program being pasty faced chorus girls were out of tune with the picture in spite of their Oriental dress and attempts at Oriental dancing. When I came out I revelled in the street. Tried one or two of the elegant shops. Too much service to be comfortable.

Then the Chicago Art Museum burst upon me and I hastened to pay my quarter admission and to regret that I had almost seen Pola twice over and cut off my time. A dream of beauty. Dante MS. and old Wedgewood. George Gray Barnard's "I Feel Two Natures" and [?] Man on Horseback. Michelangelo and Leonardo. Loredo Taft (and I had seen that wonderful "Time" of his in Jackson Park. Abbot drove me by. Time stands sad—the pageant of the world flows by like a wave—Enormous).

Rooms and rooms and rooms of the annual exhibition. Cecelia Beaux taking gold medal as usual. Interesting to note that scarecrow art is not there. Sweet convention and good drawing, low tones and harmony prevail. Had to hurry through for time pressed. Then to the standard collection. George Romney, Gainsborough, Corot and Breton. A whole room full of Inness[?] and Rembrandt, Van Dyck and [?]. I cannot remember the artist of the huge medieval thing in the entrance, familiar too. It was late, yet I always felt just one more glimpse, just one more room. I salivated my starved soul in the loveliness that I could easily get in Philadelphia if I were not too lazy.

Then with one farewell glance at Michigan Avenue, plunged with the traffic-defying crowd across to State Street, caught a trolley and so to my train. . . .

Well, it's been a pleasant trip after all, though I am money out on it. Hate to go home—almost—for I fear humiliation and sorrow await me. Still one must not fear. . . .

Berths all made down. Me for bed. I'm delightfully tired.

### Pennsylvania Railroad
### Between Altoona and Harrisburg
### Saturday, November 5

. . . The 6:35 that we were due in Pittsburgh proved to be 6:35 eastern—5:35 central. So it was a gold gray dawn and an early arising. But I had made my usual raid on the wash-room, cleaned up and back to bed about four o'clock.

The ticket agent gave me back $2.67 of my $5.18. I wanted it all back but he claimed the 8 o'clock out was also extra fare. Information bureau differed but $2.67 was all I got. A seat on the chair car cost $2.45. Bought one, then got *mad*. I'm always getting soaked. Took it back and asked for my money. Ticket seller mad, but I got it. Then loaded up after breakfast on baked apple, corn muffins and coffee, with a box of fruit biscuit and chocolate. Here am I then, burning it on an all day trip in a day coach, and lunching out of a paper bag—for I bought a sandwich. Very comfortable, too, by the way. Tired of being mulcted by the railroads and tipping porters.

Glad to get the *Ledger* at Altoona. "The Bat" still at the Adelphia. Believe I'll go see it tonight. Why should I hurry home? Tried the coins in my purse. Five out of eight said heads—"The Bat." A few hours longer out of bad news can't hurt. . . .

Horseshoe Curve as wonderful as ever, with usual quota of freight cars obliterating scenery at most interesting points. . . . Mountains stark and bare, shrouded in heavy gloomy clouds. Snow flurries from Kittanny Point to Altoona. We are farther down now, the mountains are clothed in crisp brown or dead red foliage, with patches of the vivid green of winter wheat. Sunshine in the valleys, sombre purple clouds over the tops. And just ten days ago, autumn rioted—even up to Kittanny Point in reds and yellows, sumacs and golden rods. The trees in Iowa were stark when I left. Though beautiful when I went.

Made a careful recapitulation of my expenses and profits. Not so bad.

*Wilmington[, Delaware]*
*Wednesday, November 9*

Back here doing exactly the same thing that I was doing three weeks ago this night—sitting down waiting for that paper to get in shape. Though this night, White is actually locking up the forms, and there will be a page proof of four of the pages before we stop for the night. All this is due to my lovely Christian cussing of the little conceited puppy, and the putting some of the fear of God in his bosom. Not enough yet, however, not enough yet. . . . Saturday night . . . to see "The Bat." Good play. No wonder there are six companies playing it now, and it has run nearly a year in New York, and Mary Roberts Rinehardt and Avery Hopwood are pulling down $6000 weekly on this one play alone. Um, yum! Couldn't I enjoy that!

Of course, it's spooky and lots of action in the dark and all that, but I couldn't get hysterical over it, as did so many of the women, and be afraid to go to bed alone, and all that. It's well worked out, and the interest is keen to the end. . . .

Twelve fifteen when I let myself in, and Bobbo in bed. He had come down on the 5:35!

We had a lovely row, because I refused to believe that the paper had come out or that it had been sent. He had Edna's word that she had sent papers to me, to Mrs. Brown, to the Iowa *Bystander*, and to the Chicago offices. Eventually I saw the two editions, and they are whangs! The less said about them the better. Bobbo is extremely tired, and has a cold. Next morning, Sunday, he took the 8:39 to Washington to try to collect a bill. . . . Came home with empty purse and full promises. Sunday, I took to unpack, and to putter around. The tale of the hectic week in getting out the paper, or the two hectic times, the long days, and the nights when no one took off their clothes came out. Poor Bobbo, he certainly picked a lemon when he got White. . . .

Last night, Tuesday, Bobbo and I went out to spend what was left of the evening after nine o'clock with Victor and Cecelia [Dorrell], and afterwards they drove us home. It was a change and a recreation for Bobbo, though after drinking some stuff that Victor called man's stuff, poor Bobbo grew very sleepy and heavy, and has had a headache all day. He is what one might call a "tin-horn sport," for which I am devoutly grateful. . . .

Elizabeth sent her report for October. She was out nine and a half days on account of her eyes, and so her marks do not run over 87 or 88, but they are pretty good.

Bowse and I went back to our pinochle with zest. She has just discovered that there is such a thing as the "project method," and is trying to find out about it. I lent her some literature on the subject.

*D-N's November 11 engagement was the third annual meeting of the Delaware State Colored Teachers Association, Whatcoat M.E. Church, Dover. She delivered an afternoon address entitled "English in the Elementary Schools." Professor I. W. Howard was president of the association. Cecie is her friend, a pharmacist, who was married to W. W. M. Henry, an M.D.*

## Wednesday, November 16

A whole week gone by and not a line added to this chronicle, and many and much has happened. Let me chronicle it as I remember under each separate heading. . . .

Friday, November 11, Armistice Day. At one o'clock this day Franklin came up to the house for a bit to eat, and I cooked some doggies and gave him a midnight luncheon. Bobbo, tired from the whist game, sat up in the kitchen and smoked while Franklin ate. All three of us reminisced over the first Armistice Day. Franklin was in France, and told us how every American soldier was a hero. Bobbo was in Harrisburg, and told how he with the rest of the populace, sat up all night to hear the bells ring in the news. And I remembered the wild scenes of this town, and that poor fellow, who dressed in his clown suit from Hallowe'en, rode from twelve o'clock midnight until six next evening on the top of a truck, yodeling and cheering, and dropped dead at the end of the day. But the picture that will remain with me until I die was the one I named "Pipes of Pan, pipes of peace," the aged Sicilian on the top of the truck, with the shepherd's pipes, blowing his weird tune, straight from Theocritus into the midst of the wild jazz and fierce blares of the twentieth century American noise.

I was due to speak at the State Teachers' Association. Left on the 10:46 for Dover, reaching there at twelve. I had my minute of silent prayer alone in the train, just before it pulled in. Hope everyone else remembered it. Went to the Henrys house, found Cecie out, so to Whatcoat Church, to get the fag end of the morning session. Luncheon later at the Henrys, dancing to the victrola while the meal was in preparation. Dorine Jolly there, a cute little brown-skin vamp from Newark school. Every time I see her, she looks cuter. . . .

Whatcoat church crowded for afternoon session. Every student and teacher from State College present, and all the teachers, preachers and townsfolks. Good speech on Elementary English. Dr. Henry delighted but surreptitiously watching clock, in hopes I'd talk past train time. But gave myself twenty minutes to make the 4:54. Collected fourteen dollars from Howard; had an ovation. Literally had to fight my way through the crowd. Mobbed with embraces, kisses and pleas to "speak at my school." I love to go down state; the people seem to love me genuinely and whole-heartedly. And they do appreciate me, there's no gainsaying that. Feeds my vanity, and soothes my wounded pride. . . .

Saturday, November 12. Nothing much that I remember; except continued admiration for the wonderful speech of President Harding's. It will go down in history with the Gettysburg speech, as I said in my editorial this week. The paper was the usual mess. It's discouraging to attempt to write for it now.

Sunday, November 13. Spoke down at St. George's. An "Educational Rally." Typical country church affair. Leila and I went on trol-

ley to Delaware City, there met by a car, and drove over to St. George's.
. . . Miss Pierce in introducing me, said I had travelled from the dashing waves of the Atlantic to the calm blue of the Pacific, and had stood in learned halls debating with the great minds of the age. Leila almost exploded, and I dared not look at either her or "Brer" Marshall. After the speaking, a huge dinner in the school-house, everything possible to eat, and oodles of it. . . .

Tuesday, November 15. Bobbo and I fought mostly all day about White, off and on. . . . Was never so depressed in my life. I wanted to hunt for a job, but where? If I could have run away from it all and left the whole thing, and started life anew, I almost believe I would have. I believe down in his heart Bobbo was afraid I would do something desperate; I was so wrought up over the hopelessness of the whole situation. . . .

### Monday, November 21

. . . I made my last entry Thursday, November 17, and said all was going well. We stayed up all night. White taking all that time to make up those last four pages. At half past four we crawled into bed. I started to scold about it coming home, but I thought Bobbo would cry from sheer weariness and worry, so I said no more. Press acted up Friday—very slow—got enough papers to supply boys and get down state and Eastern Shore mail out for the 3:46. But the folder had broken down and the folding and cutting had to be done by hand until evening; then we alternated with the machine. Slow work, eight to ten a minute off the press. Office a cyclone of paper—heaps of them spoiled, hundreds, literally. Everyone pressed into service. . . . At 11:30 we stopped for the night, not quite completed. I fed Franklin and Robert at home. We collapsed into bed after midnight. Silly White likes that sort of excitement so we must all dance while he pipes. It's only a question of time now when the breaking point will be reached.

No money. Scratching and grubbing to get enough to pay off the people. Bobbo resorting to humiliating subterfuges. I am sorry for him, desperately sorry. If I could only get some kind of work to tide over this wretched, wretched period. I wrote Unity today that it wasn't helping any of us. Even poor Strick pinned his faith to it and says it's failed him. Maybe none of us know the right thing to do. Bobbo looks haggard and I fear I am beginning to look so too. Can it be that the [?] will take everything from me? Is there to be naught but ill luck and down-grade for me? I won't believe it.

Yesterday, Sunday, the 20th, Bobbo, Leila and I went to the cem-

etery. Bleak and raw day, after a week of unexampled heat—75 and
76 degrees each day. We saw Cecelia [Dorrell] when we were getting
off the car—she was coming across the bridge, looking very jaunty—
in a little knitted cap and sweater. When we were coming out of the
cemetery and I led the way to crawl out of the corner, under the fence,
she met us with a ginger-ale bottle and tiny glass. The "ale" was something very sweet and good and *strong*, but *not* ginger ale. We walked
home with her, and while I was playing the victrola—in a hideous
house blouse—Vic came in with a Mr. Valentine Seymour and a
Miss Leitch. The former tall, angular, hook-nosed Ichabod Craneish,
the latter delicious and squab-like, black-haired, charming. Both white.
Traveling to demonstrate something or other. . . . After several glasses
of various things all around, the girl and I danced—at least she wanted
to dance with me always. Her perfume remained on my blouse and
in my nostrils all night. I hung the garment out side to air. We danced
well together and were all very merry. . . .

Don't seem to get time to read, sew or anything any more. Did get
a few chapters read in Wells' *Outline of History* and finished Maeter-
linck's "Miracle of St. Anthony." But it's just papers—papers.

Head bad. Tried my pulse with the stop watch—63 to 65 a minute. Bad.

Thursday night—the 17th, while setting up wrote out an improved
sketch of "9-19-1909," renaming it, "2-2-22" and sent it to the Real
people with a two reel comedy, "Frances Party Dress" based on the
little incident of the girls' party frock at the Industrial School at Mitchellville [Iowa]. . . .

*D-N's reference to the meeting site here alludes to the fact that
Pierre S. du Pont donated an enormous sum of money to Delaware
to build and finance public schools for the children of the state, both
Black and white. The Moors were a distinct community of people
localized in the Cheswold, Delaware area who were of mixed white,
African, and Nanticoke Indian origin. They did not identify particularly with either Blacks or whites and maintained their separateness by
inbreeding and insularity.*

## Wednesday, November 23

Same old thing, sitting up in the office, while the machine is
pounding down stairs. It will probably break down. First run should

have been off last night. Same old dumb mistakes. Same old temper on the part of Bobbo and me. Same old everything, tomorrow is Thanksgiving.

I am in a very bad humour. My head aches. Some bad stuff Bobbo got. . . . Worked hard yesterday trying to keep linotype man fed up so we could make up and get off to-morrow night, so everyone can have a holiday to-morrow. But no good. Can't get these niggers—or rather, White, to do his work in time. Promised jobs don't get out while he runs wildly up and down from Philadelphia. He likes excitement, running around, being busy and staying up all night. Never mind how many others suffer.

Last night went down to Cheswold. . . . The meeting was at the new Fork Branch school—one of the du Pont affairs. Fine one room model school house. Crowded with a congregation of Moors, and a class of beautiful children, beautiful as only those children are. Teacher in charge a Mrs. Heiskell, Virginian, massive, contralto voice, pleasant, good to look at. Only a good looking teacher would be permitted to remain in a Moor community. Usual program of singing. Parent-Teachers' meeting, with a slew of Carneys and Durhams, etc. [family names—an allusion to their inbreeding] in charge. (Shall I ever forget my first introduction to a congregation of Moors?) My speech, usual ice-cream, etc. Talk was difficult for me for I was conscious of the "inescapable differences" between them and me, for all my brave use of "we" and "our people." . . .

We drove back to Cheswold, the same group, to [her sponsoring host] Rev. Thompson's house, which was cold, as the fire in the chunk stove had gone out, but it was soon o.k. and we were warm by the time he came in, lantern in hand, having walked the whole way home. Ate an apple, and up-stairs to a cold, bare little room, and soon in bed, usual country kind, lots of heavy cover and hard bed. Slept but little. Arose at 6:20, dressed in cold room, washed indifferently, shivered, ate a cold apple, and some cold water, caught the 7:09, after a cold half mile walk with the young minister, and came on up, knitting vigorously on the lavender scarf. . . .

*Below, D-N says that Leila is traveling "au fait," that is, passing as white by allowing people to assume that she is. D-N herself sometimes did the same (as did many fair-skinned Blacks at the time) because of the wretched Jim Crow laws and accommodations. Compare "ofay," a Black, in-group term (sometimes derogatory) for white people.*

## Monday, November 28

Leila Junior used to say that I had a Pollyanna type of mind, and I suspect that ofttimes it bored her, for I had a way of seeing good in every situation and would always say that nothing was so bad that it could not be bettered. I remember her glee—and she was a bit of a kid, just past twelve, when on that dreary, bitter cold, rainy, stormy awful 25th of March, 1909 when we moved into this house, this fated 916 French Street, and everything seemed about as dreary and bad and uncomfortable as could be, she said with a roguish triumph, "Now, Aunt Alice, what good are you going to find out of this day?" and I came back promptly with, "Suppose Miss Kruse hadn't kept you kids all day, in school and at her home? And suppose she hadn't invited us all . . . to her nice, warm, comfortable house for a decent delicious dinner afterwards? And suppose I hadn't succeeded in getting the plumber to connect the kitchen stove so we could have fire in the range and hot water? And suppose I hadn't been able to get coal in the cellar and a furnace fire made? Why we have LOTS to be happy about?" And she threw up her hands in disgust at my glibness.

I was just thinking as I came up from the cellar just now, and saw with a sinking heart that the furnace fire is likely to go out, and that there is not enough coal to last another day, and realize that the reason why the coal company did not send the coal they so glibly promised is because we had not paid for the last ton, and that there will hardly be enough money to pay by to-morrow and things grow worse every day—well, there is this much for me to be grateful for—it isn't last year when the child lay ill. Then I had money of my own, and Bobbo had money, and we were able to give her every comfort and luxury and delight she wanted. I could spend lavishly on her delicacies. There was no pinch then. And all this sadness and worry that we are going through did not have to touch her, so she could go to the last happy and comfortable. Of course, Leila Senior is in comfort now, and able to help Bobbo and me, but she is able to do so only because the child left her life insurance. Enough of that.

On last Wednesday night, the 23rd, Leila got off all right, with her (my) bag all packed 'n' everything, on her little sleeping car. Pauline wrote us a card, which arrived Saturday to the effect that her "mama" had arrived safely, traveling au fait, and that she (Pauline) gave her away by running up the gang plank kissing her in full view of the horrified passengers, who probably thought the brown skin young woman very impertinent to be kissing the white lady. . . .

*As in this account of Thanksgiving merrymaking, D-N frequently referred to drinking as "anti-Volsteading," an allusion to Representative Andrew Volstead's congressional act, which became law in October 1919, enforcing the Eighteenth, the Prohibition, Amendment.*

## Tuesday, November 29

When I had gone that far [in the diary last evening], Bobbo came in, very wet and tired and heart-sick, after a hard and apparently fruitless day in Philadelphia. Helped him to get into bed, the room warm and comfortable, and when he had stretched out, to make him forget the haunting worries of the day, read to him from "The Mirror of Washington." He laughed over the portrait of Harding, enjoying Penrose, chuckled over [Senator] Knox and went to sleep over Borah. Then I took my bath and slipped into bed beside him. He is like a tired child clinging to its mother.

To return to the Thanksgiving Day. . . .

Wonderful game. Snappy from start to finish. Lincoln [University]'s first touchdown, the first time Howard [University] had been scored on this season. Men like gaunt figures carved in mud. Field so wet that ankles were covered with mud. Gray faces, dripping fingers. Heavy, soggy ball. Steam from the bodies, when in a mass play that covered the field, like a fog. Yet nothing slow about the game, every minute filled with excitement and enthusiasm, until the final score of 13–7, upset all calculations. . . .

At the field, [Howard High School principal] Wooten told me that Cornell was 27 to Penn's 0 at the end of the first half, and later found the final score 41–0, much to the disgust of the state of Pennsylvania. I suppose Wooten was surprised at my speaking to him about the game. Had a funny fuss with a man who insisted on standing on Cecelia's seat. I worried him by waving my umbrella in his face, and telling him to shut up when he tried to explain why he stood where he did. Jean Jamison [her dentist Juice's wife] and Wooten's wife in stitches behind us.

Bobbo got off at Broad street station to telephone the score down so White and Franklin could run a screamer across the page. We went on to the Dale. Mass of people in the lobby, surging, pressing, thronging, trying to get to the dining-room. I slipped a dollar bill into the steward's hands, and by the time Bobbo got to us, we were being paged to come for our table, much to the mystification of others, who had been trying to get seats for some time. Our table in the center of the room, so that we saw nearly everyone who came in and held little receptions all the while. Sarah Lee Fleming at the table in front of us, with her husband and two children. She was effusively glad that I called her to me. Jimmy Cobb explaining Link's rejection by the Senate, secretly rejoicing at it, I've no doubt. Jack Johnson [the boxing champion] passed, and was the cynosure of all eyes; went into the back room where the orchestra was. Cecelia was impressed with him. Leon Fisher came to say his party was in the next room, and for us to join them. Jo Hopkins' guest, whom she had invited me to call upon, stopped to speak, and turned out to be the identical Mrs. Winston with whom Inez Richardson and her crowd were running with on the night of the inaugural ball, and who started out cabareting with us, and whose extremely decollete gown was held in place by a single string of pearls. Why she kissed me, I don't know, except perhaps she had begun anti-Volsteading early.

When we had finished our dinner, went into the back room to see Leon's party. Orchestra, several small tables, one long one with Leon's party, all the Fishers, Leon, Razzle, Jo, Pauline, Roland, "Betts" Winston, and Jack Johnson, and his extremely pretty wife. All dancing, Roland blind. Razzle in doubt about the location of his mouth. Jo, very red under her rouge, and flirting horribly with Roland. Pauline dancing uncomfortably with Jack Johnson.

## Wednesday, November 30

Last night was interrupted again by Bobbo's entrance from Philadelphia. He looked haggard and hungry, and I suspected him of again economizing on his meals, which is just what he had done. Two days, with nothing more to eat for his dinner than a ham sandwich. I took him down stairs and heated him some of the delicious soup we had for dinner—bean soup, as only Mama can make it, puree. Mama had called to him as he came in telling him to have some hot soup. He was genuinely touched, said the kindness of the household made his heart warm from gratitude.

Yesterday was a Heluva day. I thought I'd simply give up. A succession of irate creditors, bad checks, collapses, oh, everything. Life became a nightmare for the business of the *Advocate*, and White was the cause of it all. . . . Trouble with a capital T, and no money in sight. Telephone disconnected. Trouble and more trouble. Linotype man irate because of bad check, everything wrong. No prospects of paper getting out. Bills, Bills, and more bills, and not a cent in sight, or not enough to do much good. I felt that I must get myself some work to do, so I went to see [Dr. Joseph H.] Odell, ostensibly to get the ad of the employment bureau for this week. Not much comfort there, and Odell distinctly cool. I'm afraid he saw the tears in my eyes. I hate to be a suppliant.

Bobbo said last night that if he didn't think things would break better in a short while he'd lose his mind. He talked over a new man he has in mind who is at present working for Gale in Philadelphia. To-day the man came down. He impressed me favorably. Brown, slight, modest, not cocky. [Charles] Colburn also liked him. The latter gentleman is sure of one thing—no matter what happens, White must go. Already we have had complaints all day about jobs not getting out on time, and he has nothing to do but job work and Franklin to help him. Colburn went to see his "Studio," which he has set up in the store opposite Smitty's in the theatre building. He reports it likewise a mess. Strick is afraid if he knows he is to be fired, he will damage the machinery, and has warned us both. He wrote a letter insisting upon more pay and less cussing. He'll get neither from me.

Fisher came in to-day to collect on Bobbo's ring. I told him frankly I could not keep it, and will give it back to him, and let the ten dollars stand to my account, or let him have it to pay him for the shoe leather he has wasted running after me. He appreciated my frankness, and did me the courtesy to say he wished his wife was like me—thinking how to save, instead of how to spend. I'd like to spend, too, if I could. And I'm not at all sure that Bobbo would think just as much of me if I were a doll woman like Jo Hopkins, for instance, who does nothing but demand, demand, demand, and gets what she wants, even though poor John [Hopkins, her husband] has to sweat blood for it. Bobbo says I'm his "tower of strength," and he does not know what he'd do without me in this awful crisis. I wonder. He is not by nature grateful; it is not a Nelson characteristic. They soon forget those who have stood by them in time of stress. . . . He is always scolding me because I do not forget favors. He has a creed, "stand by your friends, right or wrong, stick to them, etc." but he does not live up to that creed . . .

To return to Thanksgiving Day. Elizabeth started in to be "difficult," so I found myself saying, "Oh, those difficult Nelsons." She's like Kitty, a spoil sport. Always has a head ache, or sick stomach when she's out, or doesn't want to go some place, or looks as if she's going to cry, or wants to go in a corner and look temperamental when everyone else is doing something. Just like Bobbo. Just as soon as he is sure I'm enjoying myself in my own way, he goes off and looks either

superior or hurt, or gets sleepy, and yawns audibly. So Elizabeth went
into the sitting room and sat down alone, when we all went into the
cabaret room at the Dale. But I routed her out willy nilly, and took
her along with me. When Mrs. Jack Johnson invited us all up to her
room to freshen up, E. suddenly thought she ought to "stay with Papa."
I laughed at her, "Child, your father will be happier with a bunch of
men than having you tagging at his elbow." She went up with us. . . .
Typical actress' bedroom, and that nasty Mexican hairless dog curled
up on a cushion, looking like an overgrown, overfed rat. Ugh! Bowse
was horribly shocked when she heard that I had hob-nobbed with the
Jack Johnsons, and "couldn't understand it." But I told her frank curi-
osity was my motive, and as neither had heard my name distinctly
pronounced, they would never know me again, and I should never
claim acquaintance with them.

When we came out of her room, and down the corridor of the
hotel, after all the women had painted themselves silly, and we had
all refused cigarettes, Elizabeth with a pained grimace, Bobbo met us
and took us into an upstairs room which had been turned into a dining
room, with the Abeles and their party. "Your crowd," said Bowse,
when I told her. It was, and I felt much happier there.

We decided to go to the . . . theater and saw a mighty good picture, "The Burden of Race," a Real production. I see now what kind
of stuff the Real people want, and I realize that I can hardly hope to
come up to their standard as long as I have the kind of thing in hand
that I have. However, I have sent them stuff and will await their ver-
dict. . . .

It was a good day after all. I had made several persons happy. . . .
The only ones who were not really happy were Bobbo and I. Yet he
enjoyed the people, and seeing so many friends, though he would
have preferred dinner at home, and I—I forgot whether I was enjoying
myself or not. I don't really know to this minute whether I did.

*In regard to the Recorder of Deeds affair, D-N mentions below
two additional persons: Melvin J. Chisum, an active newspaperman
and Elk, was the Washington, D.C. correspondent for the* Advocate;
*L. Heisler Ball—U.S. senator from Delaware, 1919–25.*

*The returned scenario spoken of later was probably her "The Bayou
St. John," which the Realart Pictures Corporation of New York rejected
with a November 29 letter explaining that they were not producing
any original manuscripts, only successful plays and popular books.*

## Saturday, December 3

. . . Monday, the 28. Bobbo haunted and hounded by bills, col-
lectors, the linotype man, Stiftel. I was over there at eight with copy,
but there was trouble over a bad check, and it was blue and troublous
times. I seem to be living in a hideous nightmare. I find myself saying,
"I'll soon wake up and laugh at this." My nightly game of pinochle
with Bowse, almost my only connection with the social side of Wilmington, keeps me from being too blue. Leila arrived at 4:40 Tuesday
morning. . . . She talked lots, and evidently had a splendid time.
Pauline saw to it, as I knew she would, that she had social contact.
. . . But she finds Pauline thin and wasted looking, and says she has
no appetite. Food does not suit her. She cried and seemed to think
that life had used her hard that her children had to work so hard to
get through school that they lie down and die as soon as they are of
age. It is hard. Better for them all if they stayed in Boston, where
things might have been different. If Pauline's health breaks, I shall
feel like giving up myself. She is by way of being a useful citizen—as
was Leila. I wish, with all my heart do I wish, that she would meet
some of those splendid professional young men, who would marry
her, and give her a good home, and remove from her the necessity of
working so hard.

The refusal of the Senate to confirm Link Johnson [as Recorder of
Deeds], of course, is the most talked of thing now in the colored newspapers and elsewhere. Some of Bobbo's friends, notably Melvin Chisum,
seem to think that he should go after the Recorder-ship, now that
Johnson is elminated. . . . Colburn seems to think Bobbo should get
the "endorsement" of his voting place, and "line up" Senator Ball.
. . . I felt that Bobbo's chances were slim as a shoestring if he had to
go about it in that way. I had hoped du Pont's desire would be enough,
but he's turned out to be a pretty weak sister in the Senate. Hardly
ever there—conspicuously absent on great occasions—I fear that he is
thinking of the Senate as a delightful, exclusive private club, in which
he will enjoy himself, when there is no yachting or hunting to be
done. Ball, in the meanwhile, is assiduous in the performance of his
duties in Washington and at home. He is busily building up his fences
here, and making a hit in Washington by his very admirable conduct
of the affairs of the District. He is too poor to be indifferent, and looks
to another term. Du Pont on the other hand, seems lazy. Some think
that he does not want reelection. Perhaps he feels that he can loaf
around until nearly election time, then turn loose a couple of hundred

thousand, and turn the trick. He can if Alfred I. [du Pont] remains quiescent.

As I thought, another nigger appeared in the woodpile. Jefferson Coage, who has always felt that he should have something "big," because he votes in Delaware, and in the Second Ward, and made some speeches in the campaign, and is close to the Three Musketeers of the Second War, announces himself as candidate for the place, and goes to Ball. . . .

The ridiculousness of so small a man for so big a post, an under-educated clerk in a department, with a little ward following, posing for a national job, for Frederick Douglass' place, does not strike any of them as funny. Except Colburn. Since he has been so close to Bobbo and me, he sees things in a different perspective. He has learned to value education and looks as essential qualifications for high prefer-ment. Bobbo was irritated, and wanted to pooh-pooh the thing on account of Coage's patent inferiority. But it is not always wise to underestimate one's opponent. I realize that every time I look at [Prin-cipal Ray] Wooten. However, after many conferences and much walkings to and fro, Bobbo told me this afternoon (Saturday) that they all HAD to endorse Coage, but since he is so patently inferior and unlikely to get the place, after his application was rejected, then they would say, "Here's Nelson!" All of which I swallow with a very wry face. . . .

Melvin Chisum has gone to Washington as a sort of watch dog, to jazz up things for Bobbo's chances in something. I don't know Chis-um's influence. I always used to laugh at him, but I'm apt to be mis-taken in the people I laugh at. . . .

Bowse blew in Wednesday night and puffed me all up with vanity and pride telling me that the *Century* quotes my editorial on Stri-bling's novel. She brought me her December number, and there in The Centurion, with comments, is mine own words. I bought the December number later for myself. Tried to show off my pride at the office, but hardly anyone knew the standing of the *Century*, so it was wasted. But Whitenack and Martin knew, when Bobbo told them, and Martin said it was so rarely that a metropolitan paper or magazine quotes a Wilmington paper that he thought all the papers here should feel proud, and Whitenack borrowed my copy to write about it in Sunday's *Star*.

My cold developed into a horrible hoarseness and general smash up. I doctored myself Wednesday night, and Thursday night. Yester-day, went to Dr. Stevens. Was in worse shape Thursday than I told anyone. Temperature. Would not stay in bed, despite Bobbo's admonitions. Hate to worry the folks, and I hate the bed. Used Unity thought, as well as doctor's pills and cough syrup. Voice still awful. Hope it will get better by next Thursday, so I can go to Lewes.

Sent off some scenarios to some film companies. One back already. Entered the *Nation*'s poetry contest. Now that's what I call real nerve. With all the POETS in this country, for me to tackle a proposition like that. I went through the envelope with the typed copies of the "Dream-Book," and making a selection, called it a "Dream-Sequence," and sent the Curie sonnet, and the Dithyramb. Nerve! Received acknowledgment. Of course nothing will happen, but anyhow, I've tried. . . .

## Sunday, December 4

. . . Forgot to mention going to the Century Club to hear Madame Inouye, the little Japanese woman, teacher of Domestic Science in the University of Tokyo, who is here interesting the American women in disarmament. . . . It was a stupid affair, crowded, etc. Mme. Inouye spoke in Japanese, which was translated, very badly, by a little Japanese interpreter, herself speaking very broken English. Then Mme. Inouye read a long paper on disarmament in English. With a throbbing head, fever and aching limbs, I was not much intrigued by the long paper. She wanted to have the women ask her questions. I was much amused. The American public does not want to be uplifted, ennobled—it wants to be amused. The women wanted to know of her school life! It made me think of myself, and some of the burning messages I bring to audiences, and then they want me to recite a dialect poem! She told about the school, but I sympathized with her.

*The "Pop Jason" here is W. C. Jason, longtime president of State College, Dover (Delaware's Black college, later Delaware State College). During earlier summers, D-N had taught courses for in-service teachers there.*

## Monday, December 5

. . . Feeling that the day [yesterday, Sunday] had bored me enough, I slipped over the balcony to her [Bowse's] room and we played three games of pinochle. Bobbo would have been shocked and horrified.

He is awfully strong on that fourth commandment. I wonder if he has always been as strong on the seventh? I have noticed that the men who make the biggest fuss over a little pleasure on the Sabbath are the ones who enjoy the biggest Sunday dinners. Pop Jason and I did battle over that question for nine years.

Young Wright, the new printer, called up to say he was coming. . . . Bobbo came in, cleaned off all the seven inches of snow from the sidewalks, like a good husband, and looked all feeble afterwards. He thought Franklin, having dined with us, might have done it, but Franklin thought otherwise. Mama, of course, crept out of bed and down stairs to close the blinds, so the house would be nice and dismal looking. She gets nervous and wants the blinds closed about dark. Leila, of course, in bed, as usual.

Wright turned up about 10:45, and Bobbo directed him to Mrs. Patton's [where he is to live]. Bowse was interested when I told her he is single, and asked me to see if he is at all possible for her to play around with. She is man lonely, poor girl, I don't wonder. I don't think he is possible. And as she said, if he gets in with the Patton crowd, he will be Impossible. . . .

### Thursday, December 8

Well, here sitting in the little bare dressing room of Robinson's famed Coliseum [Lewes, Del., where she went to speak] while outside a jazz band consisting of five slim black youths are discoursing about the snappiest rendition of "Don't We Have Fun." One shimmies automatically. Even in my big coat, huddled with the proper Mrs. Miller, mine hostess, and the no less proper Mrs. Robinson, I let go, hoarse voice and all; and shake a shoulder and croak a line or two to help on the jazz noise. . . .

*"Walkerized hair" here is a tribute of sorts to Madam C. J. Walker who pioneered in hair care, cosmetics, and beauty aids for Black women, becoming a rich and successful business woman (America's first Black female millionaire).*

*The Richard Trapnell devastation that D-N muses about later in this passage remains a mystery. However, he was the white pastor of the St. Andrews Protestant Episcopal Church. When the D-N nieces and nephew were children, he ordered them upstairs (to the "colored balcony") to worship after they had attended services at his church for three or four Sundays. They rose and left.*

## Friday, December 9

It has been indeed an eventful and hectic time; it *is* an eventful and hectic time, and somehow I do not seem to be able to chronicle things as fast as they happen. If I only could, things would not fade from my memory. I stopped writing last night, when it was my turn to go on the stage and speak. The little school teacher presented me. . . . I spoke about twenty-five minutes. It was a useless effort. The few people who had braved the cold and snow to come out were for the most part young girls and boys who wanted to dance, and not be lectured to. Little brown huzzies, with Walkerized hair elaborately coiffed, bare-headed, with severely tailored effects in dress. Just the type that frequents the dances at the National, and dance lizards for escorts. What was the use of talking thrift to them or land buying, or support of colored businesses, which is what Robinson wanted me to do to boost his land project and his Coliseum? Also, I was very hoarse. But I talked somehow, and the bare pine walls of the unfinished hall echoed back my throaty grunts. It was cold, in spite of the two huge stoves with roaring fires, and the smaller one in the "dressing room." I collected my $12.50 plus eight dollars for rail road fare, from Robinson, who cheerfully made up the deficit, danced one dance with the little teacher, and left at eleven o'clock in the tow of Mrs. Miller. We had some very good home-made wine with her odd looking, cute little husband, and up-stairs to the inevitable cold bed-room. . . . Slept badly, fearing that I would miss my train. Mrs. Miller had me up betimes; was eating a delicious breakfast, when the bus came along, and had to hurry out.

Such a road! An hour and a half to go thirty-eight miles, and that on a Pennsylvania system! The snow had lightly powdered the trees and dried grasses in the fields, so that it was like a scene from a delicate fairyland, or a dainty bit of brush work from the Japanese. The pines were ever so lightly powdered, as if they were daintily powdering their noses. All up the road to Dover, the scene was exquisite, with the faint glow of a red winter dawn flushing the sky. Can't say I fancy getting up so early that one travels by star-light and sees the sun rising.

It was ten fifteen when I got home, and then the fun began. And now I must go back to Wednesday.

Bobbo had a hunch Tuesday that I had better see [Charles] Warner [chairman of Delaware Republican State Committee] in his behalf,
even as I had seen Miss [Jeanette] Eckman [a white Wilmingtonian
extremely active in city politics]. . . .

Mr. Warner was delightfully cordial. I told him about Bobbo's
candidacy for the Recordership, and he, as he usually does, forestalled
all I had to say by telling me about Coage. . . . However, Warner said
he was going to Washington on Thursday, and would see the Senator
T. C. [du Pont] and go over the matter with him, and urge Bobbo.
And I added shyly, "If the Republican party owes me anything, or
thinks it wants to pay off its debt, this is the price I am setting." Warner had the grace to blush, and tell me what they all thought of me
and Bobbo, which is very nice, but pays no board bills. . . .

Yesterday, Thursday, the 8th, dawned with varying fortunes. Shortly
after he went to the office, Bobbo came back to show me a letter he
had from T. C. There were, he said, several candidates, of which
Bobbo seemed to rank about fourth, after Coage, by reason of the
endorsement, support, signers, etc., and other factors in the situation.
"Other factors" I took to mean [Senator] Ball. If Bobbo could only
show undivided support from Delaware, he would push the candidacy.

Took poor hunted-looking Bobbo to my room, and had him dictate a letter to the senator, which I typed for him. Then I wrote one
on my own account, on my League of Republican Women letterhead, and reminded him of my "sacrifices" for the party. We put them
in the same envelope, and Bobbo took them to the post-office, with a
special. The situation took on a peculiar turn. Lord, I'll never be a
politician, for to have to depend upon a smile and a dicker with such
men as [John] Thompson and [Jim] Winchester [Black Wilmington
ward politicians],—ugh! If only Thompson could be made to turn
loose his support from Coage. . . . But Thompson, like Winchester,
is thick-headed. "If I had only known Bob was a candidate!" and a lot
of hot air and tobacco juice and noise. Likes me too, but oh, oh, oh.
I fuss because they are all so dumb, and Bobbo reminds me that he
has no claim on Delaware. He has only voted here once, and Coage
was born here. I feaze [appear unfazed] that a national position should
be given him as a national character, not as a Delawarean, and he
turns about and tells me that politics demands that a man's state, ward,
precinct support him, even if he is a national aspirant. Ward politics.
You can't get away from them. Well, I'll never get anywhere, for my
ward would never support me for a lord's mite. . . .

I started for the office sick at heart. Poor Bobbo ought to go to Washington, yet I knew he had no money. I had a little, but my telephone had been cut off, and we need a telephone. Then I thought of Pop [William E.] Grinnage [next-door neighbor, a mortician], and in a trice I had vamped twenty dollars out of him, making him promise not to tell Bobbo as it was for something for him—a surprise, and I'd pay him next week. The Lord knows how. I had another scenario come home to-day.

So when I went to the office, poor Bobbo was drooping over the machine, looking too forlorn for anything, and when I sidled up to him, and said, "This is serious," and poured out my story, he drooped still more. "And you must go to Washington, to-night," I whispered, and slipped him two ten dollar bills. "My Christmas present to you." Years seemed to drop from his shoulders at once.

So I went on to market, and to pay the telephone bill, and give Duke an outing, and home to change out of that velvet dress, and iron Bobbo some pajamas while he broke the story. . . .

Dropped into the theatre out of sheer fatigue to see a few feet of the Jack Johnson film, but was too tired to enjoy it, so back to the office, and sent Edna away. Leila dropped in, went off. [Charlie] Colburn came back, all enthusiastic over Marcus Garvey, and Aaron [Edmonds] came in full of zeal, enthusiasm and fire over the same Marcus, who is one of Aaron's idols, by the way, so that I thought he and Strick would come to blows. Edna and Ethel went on down to the biscuit social, and that brings me back to the Woman's Auxiliary, which is giving this same biscuit social at the Settlement.

My quiet, unspoken defection of the Auxiliary caused by the desire of the members not to meet at 916 [French Street, her address] was cool, quiet, but none the less determined. Emma Hall talked at me, above my head, at me, and everything. I will not go to church. I will not attend Auxiliary meetings. I send my book. Emma came and quoted a sermon which some divine from New York had preached at our service, about not having good luck if you do not work in the church. I said never a word. Many things will be forgiven by me in this world, but the circumstances which destroyed my faith in Richard Trapnell and turned me from the Episcopalian church will never be effaced from my mind. And the man who was responsible for that has a heavy weight to carry. For I believed in Richard Trapnell. I preferred to believe in him. If he had smallness, if he were hasty and too partisan, if he was too easily led by the tales he heard, I did not know it, and I did not want to know it, and I would rather never have known it. I looked up to him, and revered him. He was a refuge, a rock of strength. And when he fell, or when that other one revealed him to me, something of the faith in—something high, noble and wonderful was crushed, stained, defiled, and I shall never be the same. But perhaps, it was as well. I was setting up a man where no man had a right to be—in the place of a God. It is better to have the illimitable vision, uncircumscribed by the form of a human being. . . .

It is two o'clock. Gradually everyone has gone home, and now there are only Franklin alone down stairs, running the press, and I up here running the type-writer. I am going to stay now until Franklin can see me home.

## Saturday, December 10

Talk about a crime! This *Advocate* is worse than that. I am in despair. I wonder what is going to come of it?

Forgot to chronicle the Labor problem. Tuesday or Wednesday, the 6th or 7th, I forget which, Helen Foreman Loatman rushed in to my desk, with tears in her eyes and a hard luck story on her lips. Her brother has been out of work since August. If he gets jobs they last only a week or so. He had a wife, who left him, pawned his clothes, then had him arrested for non-support, and the court ordered him to pay three dollars a week for her support. The aged mother had been keeping him, until she was worn out, sick and worried. Helen had pinched what she could off of the pittance she gets from her husband, until she decided to come to me, "Because Mrs. Dunbar is a good woman with a kind heart."

And all the while she was talking I was thinking of [Helen's husband] Elmer's performances last spring during that Board of Education campaign, but Helen was a nice child when I taught her, and she is not responsible for her husband's vagaries, and what can one woman do when another comes to her with tears? So I wrote a note to Miss Smith at the Employment Bureau, and gave it to her. Pretty soon Jim Sewell blew in with news that there was a hurry call for fifteen laborers to go to work next morning. I spoke up for the Foreman boy. He was glum about it, but went out without saying anything. Pretty soon he called up from the Bureau, telling Bobbo that it was all right, and Helen's brother was employed. After a bit Helen ran in starry-eyed with excitement. She had rushed around to find the brother, located him, dragged him to the Bureau, and he was placed, and she is eternally grateful. Until such time as it pleases the gang to crucify me again. Mr. Colburn grunted and pshawed and growled about it. Why didn't I send her to the God, [Conwell] Banton? He had been their shrine in the spring, why did[n't] he come to their aid now. I laughed and said it was true, but why should I punish Helen and her mother for Elmer Loatman's dumbness? . . .

I did someone else a favor this week, someone who was an enemy of mine, but I've forgotten what it is.

The morning mail brought a letter from Bobbo containing further instructions. The letter was written on the train. Some of the instructions I had already carried out. He said as a post-script, "You are a good little wife." Am I?

I slept late until nearly nine, and only got out then to answer the telephone. When I got to the office found that the devil was to pay. . . .

Pretty poor vehicle is the whole paper for two of the best editorials I ever wrote—"We Need More Ghosts," and "The Advocate's Doll Babies." Even Bobbo said the first one was a classy piece of writing. It is. I put my heart's blood in it, and it can hardly be read. Yet what are we to do? All day without stopping have the press and folder run, and yet we are still about 1000 papers short. Hundreds and hundreds of people will get the paper late, hundreds will not be able to read it when they get it. All day the girls, Ethel and Edna, have sat and waited, folding and wrapping a few at a time as they came up. The boys have hung around, waiting to sell. Strick has wasted time waiting to send out, when he should have been out collecting bills. . . .

## Monday, December 12

First time in my life that I have been seventeen days to Christmas, and not one thing done—not even a list made out. Well, I have ordered the cards, and today I went and got them in fear and quaking, lest I could not have them charged, but the prayer I sent up as I entered Hardcastle's was answered, for the clerk never even questioned the propriety of the charge. I have certainly leaned heavily on the Lord lately—and my prayers have been answered.

Yesterday—Sunday, the 11th—I touched rock bottom. It seemed I could go no lower. Saturday evening, no money to pay the boys—Wright, Franklin, all looking hungrily at me. The "Indian" camped on my trail, tormenting me. I came home and went to bed. Franklin telephoned for money—none. He came bringing his pittance of cents, instead of dollars, the result of bad papers coming out late. I went to bed—and prayed—and coughed.

Sunday morning. A miserable night—and an un-glad awakening. . . .

Bowse, Leila and I went to the cemetery. We took the great armful of laurel I had bought Wednesday and holly (without berries, of course). We fixed the grave beautifully, laurel, great branches stuck up all over, like little trees all over.

Home—and misery. I ran up to my room and sat, hatted and coated at the telephone, calling Colburn. Then I plumbed misery. My spirit broke and I cried—a bit. But came back. . . .

Wrote Bobbo also, telling him all. Then had to tramp all over Market street with Duke hunting for enough stamps in Cigar and Drug stores to send both letters special.

And lost my glasses! Again I plumbed bottom. My face has grown so thin that when I had my big rubber-trimmed nose glasses with the ribbon on—there was no face. Took off the ribbon to relieve the congestion, having the glasses on a gold hook at my waist—and I suppose the heavy coat rubbed them off.

When I came home—no glasses. I was too miserable to cry. Went down cellar and found an ancient pair—too weak. Tried little Leila's—too weak. Mama's—too strong—Leila's, likewise. I went next door to Bowse's and was beaten three games of pinochle—played in silence behind closed doors. And she had beaten me likewise Saturday night. Came home, read papers with aid of big reading glass, which hurt my eyes. After all had gone to bed, went up-stairs and finished the *Mirror of Washington* with the reading glass. Then I got *mad. Mad.* I rose in my rage and I swore I *wouldn't* be beaten. The nasty bitter niggers have tried to ruin me. But I won't be downed. I rose and damned them all to hell and back again. I would live in this town and make the *Advocate* a success, and put Bob in a big position and make them all cringe and fawn to me yet. And I bathed furiously cussing all the time, and so prayed myself to bed. Slept badly. Coughed. Tossed restlessly. And faced the day. Not heavy-hearted, as feeling Bobbo defeated, the enemy triumphant, no money in bank, none in the morning mail, bills, overdrawn account, hungry creditors, irate Stiftel [the linotype man], puzzled Colburn, etc. etc. Cheerfully grinned . . . through it all. Cold office, smoky stove. I was Pollyanna. Enough money to fix up overdrawn account. Baynard's lent me a canopy frame to put in a pair of discarded lenses. Felt comfy—no charge.

Letters from Senator du Pont to me and Bobbo. Encouraging. He'd land something for Bobbo. Letter from Bobbo. Likewise. He won't get Recordership, but neither will Coage [who finally did serve as Recorder of Deeds from 1931 to 1934]. . . .

## Wednesday, December 14

Dear Me! I've plumbed bottom so often lately that I'm used to being in the depths. Yesterday was the 13th, in fact and in reality. The way I had to scratch for money, hustle about and get the paper under way will always remain a bitter memory. Went to Martin, and could not see him until nearly 12:30 and asked him to get out the paper. He did not want to do it. Too much money tied up in us already. . . .

When I came out of his office, my head was going round and round and black spots ran up and down the universe with fiendish regularity. . . . Back to [Judge Daniel O.] Hastings. Waited a half hour to see him, and found him distinctly peevish. . . . When I told him I had come to see about the paper, he went up in the air. He had too much money in that paper, and he wasn't going to put another cent in it. . . . He called his stenographer, dictated a telegram to Bobbo to get T. C. [du Pont] to finance the paper this week, and went into his next room all in a dudgeon. Gee, but I burned with rage. I am so damn tired of running to the Republican party with my hat in my hand begging for a pittance that I don't know what to do. I'd like to be able to tell the whole bunch to go to Hell and stay there. Even as Martin says, we've praised too much, and Bobbo would be lauding T. C. to the skies if I did not hold him down. My motto is to make 'em pay, even for the slightest. And I shall do it in the future, if there is any future. . . .

## [Friday,] December 23

Much water has run under the bridge since last I chronicled my daily doings, and many and various the events in my seemingly uneventful life. Two days before Christmas. I shall go back to a week or more ago since I last reduced to writing the happenings in my daily life. ·

Here's the little note-book, in which I once wrote the "Dream-Book." It has new paper in it now, and looks innocuous.

December 14, Wednesday. . . . At ten o'clock that night Bobbo came in, looking weary and quiet enough. I said nothing about his fruitless mission to Washington until I had laid all the paper situation before him. When we did touch on the subject he was as cheerful as he always is when he is licked. He had had a pleasant chat with Miss Eckman that morning, and she commented on the fact that I am a good sport, a cheerful loser. I ought to be, I've been losing all my life. . . .

## Christmas Day, 1921

Well, Christmas after all, and quite in the old way, though I swore it would not be again. I have to look back on these past few weeks and smile at myself. There would be no Christmas for me; I could not bear to think of making merry, and I would never, never, never trim another Christmas tree. Also I had no money to make presents, and would not expect any, for I had no friends. And being so horribly in debt to Leila and everyone, I could not think of Christmas. I went back in mind to last Christmas, and the two trees I trimmed, one down stairs, as usual, and the little one for Leila on her table in front of her sick bed. And how, when the day was over, she stretched out in her pillow and said it was the happiest Christmas she had ever spent—brave little soul cheering us, when she knew she was so soon to pass away. So I had no heart for Christmas this year.

Then I had to get Christmas cards. So I had them engraved at Hardcastle's. And there was not enough, so I had to buy more. Then this person and that had to be remembered, and I had no money. How I have laughed in the last weeks at my funny subterfuges to get some little gifts for the few who had to be remembered. Let's see. There was the little water color that I bought at Tuskegee, beautifully framed for Krusie. The set of book plates Laura gave me two years ago, which I put away, for Anna [Brodnax]. The yoke I bought at the Republican Rummage and Christmas sale for Leila. A lovely yoke it was, and only yesterday I scraped together enough to buy the batiste for the gown, and with a funny birthday card, and a promise to make the gown. The lavender wool scarf which I found in the rummage box which Mrs. Rhoads [possibly Mrs. J. Edgar Rhoads, of a prominent local Quaker family] sent, with the wool to finish it, which I knitted, finishing it, with the fringe, while I was in Summit, and washing it carefully and drying it in my room—which delighted Mama this morning. Three months' subscription to *Life* for Edith. Some of the booklets which I bought last summer in Montclair went to Sallie Brown, and Julia Brooks and Miss Mary Murray in New Orleans. Pauline got a Negro Historical calendar, which is a lovely thing, but she already had one. By borrowing from her, and breaking into penny banks, I managed to get money enough to pay postage on my things, and to buy the little things I needed to make Christmas cheer. Ethel got a dollar, to buy herself a coveted hand bag. Laurence got a promissory note for two dollars. Bobbo a funny card, and two chocolate bars. (His trip to Washington was his Christmas present.) I gave Elizabeth a lovely silk scarf, which cost only $1.98, and she was wild with joy; it is beautiful, apricot colored, and just what she wanted. I sent Violet [Johnson] the beautiful blue bird laundry bag which Blanche [Stubbs] embroidered for me some years ago. I had always promised it to Elizabeth, but she does not need it. Bowse got one of Elizabeth's pretty camisoles—I hardly think she cared for it, however; maybe she recognized it. It was the prettiest one, which I had put away from her stock of graduation gifts, and Edna got another. Strick got three pencils in a leather case, with his name on the case, and on the pencils. Laura got four of those silly georgette handkerchiefs, which Elizabeth and I have been collecting for some time, and Baldy [Gertrude Baldwin, head of Howard Normal School for Teachers], Emma Cottman and Mrs. Hooper [the spiritualist] got each a year's subscription to Unity, which was easy, as I have started another prosperity bank, or will, as soon as I hear from them. I finished up that buffet scarf, which I started last year as a mate to the one I had already made for Carrie [Nelson]. It was very handsome, with deep fringe, and quite keen looking; this went with a Dunbar reader from Bobbo to Howard [Nelson]. Altogether, cards, wreaths, holly, presents, everything, exclusive of Bobbo's trip to Washington, did not cost twenty dollars, and I guess everyone was satisfied. Up to date Bobbo and I have received over 70 cards.

The other evening, about a week ago, Duke and I were walking out to the doctor's, and I saw the Christmas trees around the Square. I said, "Oh, Duke, Christmas trees!" and ran to break off a branch or two, quite in the old way. It was the first time that the Christmas fever had really gotten in my blood. I brought home the branches, and put them around, first over Leila's big picture over the mantle, and the little one over the book-shelves, and then I knew that I was going to celebrate Christmas. Even Ethel's plea for a Christmas tree ceased to fall on deaf ears, and I found myself buying her little trimmings, and "Christmas tree foliage," in quite the old way, and last night, when Bobbo, Duke and I went down to the Reading station to meet Elizabeth, we walked up French Street, bought the tree, and Elizabeth and I brought it home, quite in the old way, while Bobbo lugged the heavy

suit case, which contained a quart of good whiskey sent Bobbo by
Harry, and a box of cigars from Howard [Nelson, Bobbo's brother in
Harrisburg]. Who would of thought of that innocent looking child
boot-legging! And so we brought the tree home, and put it up in the
coal, to steady it, as usual, and trimmed it late, as usual. The only
thing we did not do was to put the gifts around it—reserving them for
the breakfast table. Bobbo gave Mama the Indian moccasins he had
bought at the Autumn Fair, which delighted her soul. And Leila a
pair of silk lined gloves and Elizabeth woolen stockings, I had bought,
and Ethel one of the fat Negro dolls out of our window, which she
had wanted, and Elizabeth one also, and Ethel got her Phyllis [doll],
that she wanted. I got a big jar of cold cream, some Quelques Fleurs
talcum and Mary Garden face powder. And we had Krusie's chicken
croquettes, as usual, for breakfast. Though there was no egg-nogg.
Bobbo and I ordered the turkey from Thornton's, with the grape fruit,
celery and other things, and Bobbo brought in clear toys and nuts and
fruit cake, and I gave Mama the things to bake a big pound cake, and
altogether, the Christmas that was to have been a failure, is as bright,
if not brighter than usual, for we had expected so little. . . . And now
that all the family is here, there is noise and merriment, rejoicing,
and happiness all around. We danced last night, and trimmed the
tree, and ate candy and nuts, and Bobbo went to bed saying he was
happy.

It had looked so dark in the morning. No money in sight. . . . But
during the day somehow, money came in, Bobbo staved off the most
persistent of his creditors. I persuaded him not to go to Philadelphia,
for I was sure it would be a wasted trip. Nobody pays bills on Christmas Eve. He stayed, and held down the situation, so that he was able
to give Strick all he needed to go away, and dear little Edna refused
more than five dollars for her pay, saying she did not need it. Bobbo
and Strick gave her a Phyllis doll, and Strick took one for himself.
Bobbo gave him a pair of cuff links. And Bobbo was able to give
Franklin what he owed him, and almost pay off Wright. At least, he
was able to do something for his employees. It was a relief for Bobbo,
and for me. It is hard to have your dependents looking you in the face
for their Christmas cheer, and none forthcoming. It is a tense situation stretched over with some degree of ease.

And the merriment goes on. . . .

And now I shall take up where I left off on Friday, [when] I was
trying to catch up with the doings of the preceding week. . . .

Monday, December 19. Worry all day with Bobbo and me as to how the paper was to be gotten out this week. . . . Things looked bad.

Tuesday, December 20. Bobbo in the morning had an idea that I might negotiate a loan with the Morris Plan. I went up immediately after breakfast, and asked Miss Johnson how about a loan of five hundred. She advised asking for three fifty. . . . Now if that loan doesn't go through, we're just as Bobbo expresses it, "burnt up." I trust it will. . . .

Thursday, December 22. Awakened a few minutes after six by Duke's frantic barking. Mama shortly rushed up stairs, saying we would soon be burned alive. Looked out the back window to see a mass of seething flames and smoke, apparently coming from the direction of Tenth and Walnut streets. We thought Krusie's house seemed in danger. Dressed hurriedly, taking only twelve minutes but it seemed as many hours. It was about six or seven above zero. Went around. The Mercantile building, a seething mass of flames, and ice making fire fighting a tough proposition. Went into Krusie's and found her and all frightened, but safe, as the flames were blowing in the opposite direction. Bowse joined us. Went around to [neighbor] Mrs. Corbins, and found her safe enough, though her house was the first endangered. Very spectacular fire, and quite interesting. Glad to get home after a bit and get hot coffee, and warm up. Firemen in coats covered with ice, and icicles forming under the very flames made a wonderful spectacle. . . .

## Monday, December 26

. . . Had my hair washed this morning. Martha Clark [the beautician] said I must undoubtedly have had high fever for some time as my scalp showed every evidence of being burned out by fever, scaly and hot and tight, and hair coming out in great handfuls. . . . Shall use Glover's dog mange [hair preparation] to get scalp healthy again.

*Below,* Sadie Alexander *is one of the founders of the University of Pennsylvania chapter of Delta Sigma Theta Sorority, the third chapter established in the United States.* Virginia Alexander, *her sister-in-law, is a progressive Black Philadelphia medical doctor who was D-N's physician and friend. Herself an honorary member of the sorority, D-N wrote the lyrics for its official hymn.* Hattie Feger *is one of D-*

*N's New Orleans acquaintances. This reference reveals the rivalry that has historically existed between the two leading Black sororities, Delta Sigma Theta and Alpha Kappa Alpha.*

## Tuesday, December 27

Had to get up early and rush for train to be in Philadelphia by ten o'clock for opening session of the Delta Sigma Theta [Sorority Convention]. . . . Goodly numbers of delegates and visitors in attendance. Dr. Cole much in evidence, and irritating Sadie by her insistence on the beginning of the program. Virginia, airy as usual; lots of nice girls . . . and some girls from Cincinnati, who know Hattie Feger, who is a member of the Kappa Alpha Kappa [Alpha Kappa Alpha]. I told them to tell Hattie that she has no class.

After her opening speech, Sadie introduced me. My voice was horrible, but I did my best. Made the same speech, practically, as in Montclair, on the development of the club idea among our women, and the big job of the young women of the sorority in inculcating race pride. Some men drifted in. . . . Seemed to have put it over, the girls quite enthusiastic. Promised to be back for the reception that night. . . .

Called up Miss Johnson about the [Morris Plan] loan. Nothing doing; rejected. No reason given. I felt all sick inside. . . .

I did not feel much like dressing for the reception, and when Bobbo came in from Philadelphia looking hunted, I felt less. But put on the velvet dress, and took my satin slippers. I had quite enough of the high heeled shoes. They are too thin, and [I] felt myself taking cold from the thin soles. Second time. Also chilblains developing. Bobbo had intended giving me money to get a pair of dress shoes at Wanamaker's—the $5.65 sale, but nothing doing. I was cold, hence the velvet dress. Bobbo, after he had eaten his saved dinner, got into his wedding clothes, Elizabeth had pressed the trousers nicely. He is thin enough to wear the coat again without disaster. He had not been able to wear it for two years. Looked quite good.

Mama and Leila had gone to the night funeral of Mrs. Robinson, Laura Anderson's aunt. Bobbo had contributed a dollar toward the flowers. How things have changed. Once it was always I who paid the excess on everything, now it is Leila. . . .

We took the 9:20, and got to the party a bit after ten. The hall, pretty as usual, the girls very charming, particularly a Miss Hughes of Washington, handsome girl in a red dress, which must have taken almost a yard of cloth to make, golden slippers and stockings, showing all of a beautifully shaped leg to the knee. . . .

I felt old and tired, though I danced a few times. We left to catch the 11:40, the last train before the 3:27. Neither of us felt very festive. The failure of the loan of the Morris Plan to come through was depressing. Yet—so incurably optimistic am I, I cannot but help feeling that it was best. Only a temporary remedial agency, and it meant that we would have to come across with seven dollars a week for a year, while next week the same problem of financing the paper for a week would come up. . . .

## Wednesday, December 28

We [D-N and Bobbo] had talked over Mrs. Hooper's letter, in which she advised that I see old man Holmes, and strike him for a loan. I told Bobbo to go to him, as I believed he can do more with him than I can. He went cheerily and hopefully enough. . . .

I could tell from Bobbo's face when he came in that he had failed. . . . As soon as we were alone he told me of his failure. Holmes has invested all his money in a Virginia farm, where he is cutting off railroad ties.

I have been lost in a puzzle garden, where every turn brings you to an impasse, and I have felt just like this at that time, except that I knew I could call for help from the guide, if I wanted to get out in a hurry.

## Thursday, December 29

. . . Bobbo suggested last night that maybe Carrie [Nelson]'s uncle, Dewitt, of Bridgewater, the retired florist, might be willing to advance a loan, as an investment on the collateral of his policies, and told me to sleep over it. I did, and this morning told him to go, trying could do no harm, and though it seems a forlorn hope to me, one must do everything to try to avert the crash. Bad checks a plenty come back to us. My electric light bill was paid with a check that came back, so was the post-office account, so was the insurance bill of Bobbo's big insurance. I have gotten so that the ringing of my telephone sets my nerves jangling and my heart cold. I know it is a demand for money.

Strick went on to the *Star* with copy and more copy; I worked hard getting stuff together; ads came in. . . . Then Martin called up, and his voice was edgy. Mr. Nelson had not been to see him; he could not go on with the paper until he had some understanding. . . . Rein was delighted Martin had given orders to stop work on the paper. He saw Martin, and the order was corroborated. No money, no *Advocate*. SO!

I went home to dinner with a blind feeling. . . .

Elizabeth went off to her party—the first one during the holidays, and the Lord knows I hope she will enjoy herself. Enough that her father and I should grow old and worried over finances.

Back to the office after dinner. I've been talking with Strick and Wright about a weekly magazine, like the *Nation* or *Harvey's Weekly*. It can be done, if Bobbo will agree to turn over that junky press in the cellar.

## Saturday, December 31

Vale 1921, ave 1922. Elizabeth and I are holding watch meeting to ourselves in my room. Leila and Pauline are in bed, and so is Ethel, and Mama has gone to watch meeting at Ezion [M.E. Church]. Bobbo went up to Marcus Hook [Pa.] to-day to see the man who wishes to print our paper for us, and from there, probably to Philadelphia. Cecelia Dorrell wants us to come out and watch in the year with her and Victor, but Bobbo did not come, so there you are. I suppose he'll get in by midnight. Seems funny for him not to be here with me on this last night of the year.

I waited in anxiety for him [this past] Thursday. . . . He came in about half past eight, and the first glance at his face, I knew he had succeeded in his mission. So different from the tired, pitiful face with which he had greeted me when he failed with Holmes. . . . He pulled out a check for eight hundred dollars and showed it to me. Old man Dewitt had come across handsomely. The details were insignificant. Mr. Dewitt saw that Bobbo's security was good, and advanced him the limit of his resources (Bobbo had asked for a thousand). It will tide us over the bad places now, but only for a very brief interval. We are spending at the rate of three hundred a week, and taking in nothing just now. I told Bobbo that work had been stopped on the paper. He called Martin at once, found him at the club, and told him all was well. Martin said work would begin at once on the paper. I told Bobbo [that] Strick was sick over the situation, so he called him at the office and told him all was well. It cheered and heartened him immensely.

We were, of course, three or four hours late coming out, which made the country mail late, but we came out all right and in good shape. . . .

Quarter to twelve. Farewell 1921, one of the unhappiest years I ever spent. 1920 was bad enough, but 1921 was the limit. I lost and lost and lost, even started losing my hair, and my voice. But I face 1922 with a smile, even as I whistled and smiled Thursday night coming down the bleak and cold Delaware Avenue, when I went out to get post cards, before Bobbo came home. "I'm broke, jobless, no prospects of anything, losing my business, thousands of dollars in debt, but I'm whistling just the same, and not whistling to keep up my courage either," I sang and I almost skipped across the street.

And so, though 1921 took my heart's darling, Leila, from me—and how eagerly she lay in bed a year ago to-night, waiting to hear the Grace Church chimes ring—and took my friends from me, and showed me the hollowness and deceit of much that I had trusted, and swept away my prestige and power, money and all, crushed my faith in mankind and in religion, hurt me to the soul, and dragged me in the dust—in other words, completed the foul work of 1920—yet, I'm smiling through. 1922 MUST mean the dawn of a better to-morrow.

So for five months I've kept my chronicle in this book. To-morrow I shall begin a new one. . . .

Here comes the whistles. Elizabeth and I are going to open the doors and let in the New Year. I wish Bobbo would be the first one to step across the threshold. . . .

*If Dunbar-Nelson did begin a new diary (and there is no reason to think that she would not have done so), it has disappeared. The next extant portion of her journal resumes with November 1926.*

# 1926–27

(November 8, 1926–December 31, 1927)

*Deliverance from this House of Bondage*

WHEN DUNBAR-NELSON'S DIARY resumes on November 8, 1926 no internal evidence gives the slightest clue about the unexplainable, almost five-year lapse in the extant manuscript. In fact, the content, tone, and style all suggest that she has kept a journal throughout this period—or, at least, certainly for 1926—and it has simply been lost from among her surviving papers. Nonetheless, external data proves that, in the interim, she has maintained her usual, busy life.

One of her most important involvements was heading the Delaware Anti-Lynching Crusaders. As part of a national effort, the group agitated for congressional passage of the 1922 Dyer Anti-Lynching Bill, legislation that was aimed at curtailing the killing of atrociously large numbers of Blacks by lawless whites, especially in the south. (The bill was defeated.) Her political activity further reveals that by 1924, she had completely changed her affiliation from the Republican to the Democratic party—as had other Black people in the country— for from headquarters in New York City she directed the 1924 Democratic political campaign among Black women. Her article "Politics in Delaware," which appeared in the November 1924 *Opportunity* magazine, shows that this defection from the Republicans had much to do with events in her home state. In 1922, the Black voters of Delaware—who held the balance of electoral power—had subverted tradition and helped to place Democratic candidates in office primarily because the incumbent Republican congressmen had not supported the Dyer bill. One of these in particular, T. Coleman du Pont, a former ally often mentioned in the first year of the diary, was a special target. These political upheavals were closely tied to the 1922 closing of the Nelsons' Wilmington *Advocate* newspaper.

Earlier, in 1920, Dunbar-Nelson had joined with other women of the State Federation of Colored Women to found the Industrial School for Colored Girls in Marshalltown, Delaware, a facility for delinquent and homeless female juveniles. In her "Politics in Delaware" essay, Dunbar-Nelson notes with satisfaction that "when appropriations to State institutions were being cut and slashed in the interests of economy, one institution escaped, the Industrial School for Colored Girls, which received an appropriation of $53,000, more money than was ever given to any colored institution at one time in the history of Delaware." This enterprise yielded her employment, for in 1924, she took charge of its public school department, where she would remain until 1928. As a writer, Dunbar-Nelson continued to produce and to see her work appear in print. Between 1922 and 1926, she published poems in *Opportunity* magazine, a piece called "Negro Literature for Negro Pupils" in *The Southern Workman*, and an important two-part article on Delaware for *The Messenger*'s "These 'Colored' United States" series (August and September 1924). Her literary standing was also enhanced by her inclusion in Robert Kerlin's critical anthology *Negro Poets and Their Poems* (Washington, D.C.: The Associated Publishers, 1923).

By 1926, the family has changed residences. On June 30, 1923, they moved four blocks up French Street (where they always resided) from 916 to 1310, into the house they were to occupy for their remaining six years in Wilmington. In an effort to systematize their "haphazard" household economy, Dunbar-Nelson and her sister Leila establish more businesslike arrangements, which leave Dunbar-Nelson with the major responsibility for money management and cooking. Dunbar-Nelson's youngest niece, Pauline Alice (born in 1900 and named for Paul Dunbar and her aunt), has returned and become an integral member of the family. She had taught high school for one year in Newport News, Virginia, then worked for two years on the press staff of Tuskegee Institute, Alabama, before finally assuming a position at Howard High School as history and Latin teacher, and later librarian (a post she held until she retired). The diary for this period shows "Polly" helpfully driving her aunt about while otherwise pursuing her own full life, and until the journal ends, she will remain a character in it.

Dunbar-Nelson's work at the Industrial School (which she described in ironic understatement as "no sick woman's job") consisted of diverse tasks—teaching mixed-grade classes, attending court parole sessions, directing musical and dramatic presentations, and so on. In addition to this day work, she also taught Girl Reserves classes at night. And, from January 2 to September 18, 1926, she contributed a weekly column to the Pittsburgh *Courier* newspaper entitled "From the Woman's Point of View" (changed in February to "Une Femme Dit").

Despite the centrality of these activities, the contours of Dunbar-Nelson's life were also largely determined by her and Robert's association with the Improved Benevolent and Protective Order of Elks (the Black Elks). In 1925, Robert had become managing editor of the Washington *Eagle*, a newspaper that functioned as both their official, fraternal organ and a wider-circulating Black weekly. This job kept him in Washington most of the time, where his wife frequently visited him. While in the city, he lived with J. Finley Wilson, the Elk Grand Exalted Ruler, and his wife in a small room in their house. For her part, Dunbar-Nelson wrote a column for the paper, "As In a Looking Glass," ghostwrote speeches for Wilson, became an Elk Daughter, attended conventions, and the like.

Yet at this point, Dunbar-Nelson is utterly dissatisfied with what she is doing, and restlessly casting about for more stimulating and lucrative work. One of the most moving sagas of the year details her desperate attempt to secure a teaching position in the Washington, D.C. public school system, beginning with her collecting of credentials in early December 1926 and climaxing in a round of disappointment and doctors the following March. Furthermore, she spent the second half of 1927 angling for the secretaryship of the Society of Friends' American Inter-Racial Peace Committee, a subsidiary of the Friends' Service Committee aimed at promoting inter-racial and international peace. From her first mentioning of the possibility in early June, Dunbar-Nelson envisioned the position as "deliverance from my House of Bondage." At the very end of the year, she is offered a profitless part-time arrangement that, at least, gets her "foot in the door"—and she accepts it. Her pressing need for money added even more urgency to these job efforts. At various critical points, she and Robert contemplate questionable business schemes and she herself plays the illegal numbers game hoping for a "hit."

Stylistically, the 1926–27 diary entries contrast markedly with those of 1921. Dunbar-Nelson seems to have had fewer satisfactory opportunities for writing. Notably, her only New Year's resolution at the end of both 1926 and 1927 is to keep her journal up-to-date. She does not, lapsing in 1927 for periods ranging from a few days to two months. These derelictions—which resulted in hurried, catch-up entries reconstructed from memory—help to explain the abbreviated, even perfunctory nature of her inclusions. This is not to say, however, that what she writes lacks interest or a pithy kind of depth, for even in brief, Dunbar-Nelson's thoughts can be quite arresting.

The biggest disclosed secret is a second marriage that she made on January 19, 1910 to Henry Arthur Callis in Old Swedes Church, Wilmington, Delaware. Her first cryptic allusion to that event occurs this year, 1927; then, on January 19, 1931, she unequivocally states that they were married. It was a well-kept secret and is not mentioned in any other of D-N's papers or in any of the published research about her or Paul L. Dunbar. However, Charles H. Wesley's *Henry Arthur Callis: Life and Legacy* (Chicago: The Foundation Publishers, 1977) contains one sentence mentioning their "friendship and marriage" (p. 44). Callis was born in Rochester, New York, on January 14, 1887, attended Cornell University, where he helped to found the Alpha Phi Alpha fraternity (the first one for Black men), and went on to receive his M.D. degree in 1921 from Rush Medical College, University of Chicago.

He and Dunbar-Nelson met when Callis, just out of Cornell, taught from 1909 to 1911 in Howard High School's English department (which Dunbar-Nelson headed). She was 34, he 22. Why they united and/or why they parted remains a mystery—except for intriguing comments that Dunbar-Nelson records about not marrying for spite and about destroying their relationship to save him. Later, Callis married a woman named Pauline, and had two daughters, born in Chicago in 1916 and 1917. He made another, actually a third, marriage with Myra Hill Colson on September 2, 1927. In 1930, he came to Washington, D.C., where he taught at the Howard University Medical School and maintained a private practice. Dunbar-Nelson speaks of him in succeeding years with increasing frankness. (See below, especially September 19, 1930 and June 4–5, 1931.) Though Dunbar-Nelson always marked important anniversaries such as this wedding in her diary, the immediate concerns of her trying existence are what kept the ink in her pen flowing.

---

*The State Teachers' Association below was a statewide organization of Black schoolteachers and administrators who, because of segregation, could not belong to the same association as their white counterparts. Mrs. Aiken was a well-to-do woman who owned a farm with her husband near Dover; Isaac Howard taught elementary school in the lower part of the state; and Blackburn was a downstate principal. Grossley succeeded Jason as president of Delaware State College.*

## Thursday, November 11

. . . Sunday on the 8:19 for Dover. Cold and raw and I shiver in my new red satin dress and the fall coat.

State Teachers' Assn. Questions interesting morning session. Election of officers in p.m. Talk of me for president. . . . Nominating committee brings in my name among candidates for president. Mrs. Aiken and Prettyman ask me to stay on. Jason and Grossley excited. The idea is to save Howard by deflecting votes from Blackburn. So I run—much to the disgust of Dr. Henry [downstate M.D., husband of her friend Cecie]. The vote is: Howard–39; Blackburn–32; Nelson–23. Not so bad since it was a hurried affair and I did no campaigning. Quite a buzz. I was the lamb led to the slaughter to save Howard. He seems to realize it. He would never have been elected had I not allowed myself to be run. . . .

*Eva Hall, with whom D-N attends the sesquicentennial celebration of the U.S. independence in Philadelphia, taught English at Cheyney Normal School (later Cheyney State College), Pennsylvania and was the sister-in-law of artist Laura Wheeler Waring who painted D-N's portrait. D-N's totaling of her expenses here is incorrect (the sum should be $7.24), and suggests a mathematical carelessness which may help explain her frequent difficulty with her personal finances.*

## Saturday, November 13

Eva Hall and I go to the Sesqui together. I met her in the station. . . . We finally get off, and have a lovely day. She is charming to go around with. See lots of old things, and things new. Eat in China, Russia and Mount Vernon. In the evening to see Cyrano de Bergerac at the Forrest. A beautiful picturization of the lovely story. Foreign. Either Italian or French. The women's names seem Italian, but the leading actor is named Louis Magnier. In color. Preceded by a pretty story of Mona Lisa.

Except that the dumb orchestra played "Nearer My God to Thee" when Cyrano died, it was perfect.

| Home by midnight. | Fare | $1.92 |
| | Luncheon | .75 |
| | Tea | .72 |
| | Dinner | .60 |

# SONNET TO APRIL

I had not thought of violets of late,
 The wild, shy kind that spring beneath your feet
In wistful April days, when lovers mate
 And wander through the fields in raptures sweet.
The thoughts of violets meant florists' shops,
 And bows and pins, and perfumed papers fine;
And garish lights, and mincing little fops,
 And cabarets and songs, and deadening wine.
So far from sweet real things my thoughts had strayed,
 I had forgot wide fields and clear brown streams;
The perfect loveliness that God has made—
 Wild violets shy and Heaven-mounting dreams.
And now—unwittingly, you've made me dream
Of violets, and my soul's forgotten gleam.

**Alice Dunbar-Nelson**

D-N's most well-known poem, also called "Violets" and, simply, "Sonnet."
Its appearance in this form on the April 1968 cover of the *Negro History
Bulletin* attests to its and D-N's enduring popularity.

# From A Woman's Point Of View

## By
## ALICE DUNBAR NELSON

"The women of a race should be its pride," sang the poet Dunbar some years ago, and this race of ours has much for which to pride itself in the long array of fine women, doing unselfish deeds all over the land. For instance Jane Porter Barrett. Quiet, unassuming, unobtrusive, yet putting over one of the biggest jobs in the State of Virginia. When her husband, who was in the business office at Hampton Institute, died about 16 or 17 years ago, she did not nurse her grief, and sit down and bewail the hard fortune which had taken her mate from her when they were both young and avid of life. No. She gathered up the mantle of her grief, and went out to see what she could do for others, less fortunate than she, even in the bitterness of her bereavement. And she found out, as so many colored women have found, that the girls of the race need all that can be done for them. Outcast. Homeless, forlorn. Misunderstood. Imprisoned, when they need guidance. Whipped and reviled, when they need a friendly word, and a chance to make a decent living. So she gathered together a few outcast girls, and at Peake's Turnout brought them together in a log cabin, resolved to give some few a chance to make good, and not have the initial mis-step be the beginning of the descent into Avernus. That was the beginning of a group of buildings, school, administrative building, domestic science, farm and dormitories. The little group grew; the one woman in charge had to bring in other workers. The little pittances coming in from a few philanthropists grew, there came a state appropriation. And Peake's Turnout is famous because of its Girls' Industrial School. And all Virginia is proud of Mrs. Barrett, and respects the school.

Of course, she is a club woman. Chairman of the Executive Board of the National Federation of Colored Women's Clubs—so elected at the last Biennial at Chicago. But her being a club.woman is, in her life, of secondary importance to the fact that she has set many stumbling young feet in the straight path, and guided them aright until they ceased to falter and stumble, but could walk proudly erect.

And she will not tell you a thing about it all unless you pump and quiz her about her life work.

The beginning of D-N's January 23, 1926 Pittsburgh *Courier* column. She wrote it (title later changed to "Une Femme Dit") from January 2 to September 18, 1926.

# NOTICE!!

## Mrs. Paul Laurence Dunbar COMING!

### Mrs. ALICE DUNBAR-NELSON
of Wilmington, Del., formerly the widow of the Greatest Negro Poet, Paul Laurence Dunbar

-Will Lecture At~

## THIRD BAPT. CHURCH

## FRIDAY, OCT. 7
### 7:30 P. M.

As a great Lecturer and journalist, Mrs. Dunbar-Nelson is one of the outstanding characters of the day. She is certainly well known in the Literary World throughout the length and breadth of this country. Her name was among the few that was broadcasted over the Radio Sept. 12, when Mrs Ruth Dennis stepped before a broadcasting station and made a speech on "SOME NOTABLE COLORED WOMEN." She is attractive in Features and in appearance.

This is Mrs. Dunbar's first visit to Portsmouth and she says: "I can give you an 'Evening with Dunbar."

The lecture will be illustrated with Readings from the poet. The program will be interspersed with Music by the Choir.

All are invited to attend.

### Admission, 25 cents
#### DR. B. W. DANCE, PASTOR

Somerville Printery, 812 Columbia Street.

This incompletely dated flyer is particularly interesting for its unabashedly dramatic style highlighting D-N's qualifications and attractions.

| Bell | .15 |
|---|---|
| Beads | 1.00 |
| Basket | .20 |
| Papers, carfare | .40 |
| | 4.82 |
| Theatre | .50 |
| | 5.32 |
| Supper | 1.00 |
| | 6.32 |

## Sunday, November 14

Sleep late. Clean furnace. Plant hedge. In front of kitchen. Have conference with Mrs. Tatnall [Quaker woman who served on the board of trustees of the Girls' Industrial School]. She was elected chairman as well as treasurer yesterday. . . . And I was made chairman of the parole board. Stop by Minnie [Stevens]'s and spend the evening. Buy a box of fried oysters and some gingerale, and we have a party. Polly home from her Baltimore weekend, tired but happy. . . .

*A part of D-N's Industrial School job was to attend and witness court cases involving girls from the school. The following case concerns a young woman, August, who—after delays and maneuvering— is finally paroled under Pauline's care.*

## Tuesday, November 16

Hideous rain and wind. Storm rages all day to the detriment of the kitchen roof and the back yard fence. In all the welter of wind and rain, get out to court by 10. Another *whole* day wasted. Try to get Hagner to drop case. August has a bad municipal court record. Can't get the case up. Go home at 12:15 and wait until 2:30. Back again and hang around again. No action. Case finally called at 4:10. August recommended for parole after Polly had agreed. We collect out $4.00 each and flee home, very tired and cross.

I give Bowse [Arleon Bowser] at her home, one of the new Hering Revision Binet tests. Girl Reserve Class and still more big old women out. . . .

Pauline has a new Baltimore fish [a boyfriend named] Brooks— who misses his train and we help him catch his trolley. . . .

## Thursday, November 18

Weather continues warm and close. Rain at night. Have one of my queer collapses. Bowse in. Polly has a bad cold. Quite distressing. Night school too much, I guess. Too tired I am to write Bobbo. Too much furnace and the rest of it. Bowse says Bootsie [Bowse's pet dog] has a "tired heart"—Guess I have too. . . .

## Wednesday, November 24

Miss Mason [perhaps a patron] comes to school and spends the a.m. with me. The "little children" have their monkey little plays and everyone happy. I close school at noon and get in town for my slippers. . . .

Leslie Pinckney Hill, *who appears below for the first time this year, is to become an important character in the diary. A poet of some renown, he was principal (president) of Cheyney Normal School, Pennsylvania. In 1920, he had written an introduction for D-N's* The Dunbar Speaker and Entertainer. *Now he is chairing the American Inter-Racial Peace Committee and, thus, figures prominently in her life during this period.*

## Tuesday, November 30

Cut school. Tummy bad. Heaps of desk work to do. "Clerical work." And going to make the 1:20 anyhow. Which I do. The Conference on Peace a notable affair. In addition to the listed speakers, many others—Dr. Hubert Harrison, a polysyllabic monkey chaser [derogatory term for a West Indian Black]. An I.W.W. [International Workers of the World] also black and foreign[was present, too]. . . . Leslie [P. Hill] presiding. White predominantly. [Howard University President] Mordecai Johnson acting like a nigger—not appearing and sending no word.

I, too, disappoint my hostess by coming home on the 6:18. In bed early. . . .

## Wednesday, December 1

Go to Dover on the 8:19. With committee . . . harangue State Board of Education. Over at 11:30. Grilling interview. Afraid we stressed salaries too much and high schools and supervisors not enough. . . .

*The officials from and for whom D-N is here gathering credentials
are* David A. Ward, *white, superintendent of Wilmington schools,
and* Herman Long, *Black, assistant superintendent of schools, Washington, D.C.*

## Thursday, December 2

Try teaching for a change. Hard to get down to it. Then Polly
comes for me early and I go to see Boiled Fish Ward about giving me
a signed statement of my years of service in the Wilmington schools.
He promises it. Spend the evening gathering up and arranging my
oodles of credentials. There is a considerable bundle. Fill in application blank and mail it with photo and letter to Long telling him I'll
bring the precious bundle for him to see. Quite cold.

## Friday, December 3

Mrs. Lockridge [superintendent of the Industrial School] suddenly
decided to go to Stockley [a facility for the mentally retarded overseen
by the Ennises] today instead of tomorrow. It is cold, down to 20
degrees and threatens snow, but we bundle up—I borrow a woolen
dress. . . . When we get down in Sussex County [Del.], the gorgeousness of the "holly and the pine" get into my blood. Leonard [the school
driver] stops the car and I climb out, and searching for a still brighter
bunch of berries, plunge deeper and deeper into the forest. Dwarf
pines I pull up by the root and Norway spruces for Mrs. L's urns, and
armsful of holly branches rich with berries. I am absolutely happy.
Christmas holly—that—I am plucking myself. I fill the front seat of
the car with my holly and spruce.

Stockley turns out to be quite a place—800 acres, quite a few
buildings, barns, furnace rooms, laundry, dynamos, turkeys, 1,000
pound hogs, etc. Mrs. Ennis—tight lipped, taciturn, but tremendously courteous and anxious to please. We see the new $27,000
building for the colored feeble-minded. And only one colored little
girl in it now, with seven white ones. Such pathos! Men and women,
boys and girls, and so pathetically hopeless and helpless! It is a place
of magnificent distances, for the segregation of males and females is
absolute. A wonderful place is the "Colony," and a marvelous man is
Ennis. Ex-Service Man, Rehabilitation, Vineland [New Jersey, where
a similar institution was located]—all the earmarks.

It is four o'clock when we leave and we stop and pull some little
Christmas trees, and so on home, eating our sandwiches—what is left,

and stopping for hot coffee. Home by 7:30, to find Mama all peeved about my not telephoning Pauline not to come for me, and so making dinner late.

I am thinking about bed, when Leila and Polly come in from the barber's and their conversation reminds me that I promised to read for Anna [Brodnax] at her church entertainment. So I dress, cajole Polly to take me over on du Pont street, read two selections, "Cano"—trying it on the dog, and the [Dunbar poem] "Christmas basket." So home and to bed by 10:30. Mama has an attack of indigestion, and I am up with her until two o'clock. . . .

## Saturday, December 4

Bitter cold, but not so cold as yesterday. Still threatening snow. Letter from [superintendent] Ward, giving me the requisite data. Am waiting now to hear from the Baltimore child about speaking at Morgan College, so I can go right on down to Washington and present credentials and see questions. Struggle with the furnace, my dirty room, and planting the little pine trees in the frozen window boxes all day. Mama still in bed. Go to bed early. . . .

## Sunday, December 5

Bitter cold—twelve or fifteen degrees, and a heavy snow storm. I spend the better part of the day firing the furnace, staying in the cellar to read the papers. Then in the afternoon, shovel snow. Go down to Krusie's [Edwina B. Kiuse] to get her signature on a statement of my grading while she was principal. That, added to my other certificates, will be valuable.

Copy some poems for the *Opportunity* Contest. Am sending out four this time, "Cano," "I Translate," "Snow in October" and "Pan Pipes of Peace." Going to fix fires and go to bed.

Funny, no *Eagles* came this week. Wonder if Bobbo did not use my article and did not send me a copy therefore?

## Tuesday, December 7

At night go to N.A.A.C.P. meeting at [the Thomas Garrett] Settlement [House]. Not so cold, but still plenty of snow and ice. Jack [the family dog] picks me up on Walnut street, and goes to the meeting with me. Social hour, and he has a wonderful time eating butter thins. Get the Branch to promise ten dollars to . . . Negro History. . . .

*For the remainder of the diary, George A. Johnson, mentioned below, is principal of Howard High School, having succeeded Ray Wooten in 1923.*

## Thursday, December 9

. . . Girl Reserve class at night, postponed from Tuesday. The fat sisters seem to have dropped out. Lizzie [Banton, her old enemy] gets peeved because I seem friendly and chatty in the office with [Principal George A.] Johnson, and calls him out. Her funny triumphs amuse me.

*The "Other Wise Man" by Henry Van Dyke tells the story of a fourth wise man who did not arrive at the Nativity because he repeatedly stopped along the way to help people in distress.*

## Friday, December 10

To Howard School by nine to speak for "Freshman Day." Tell the story of Van Dyke's "Other Wise Man," which I have been practising on my poor kids all the week. It goes over nicely.

Find things at school in a turmoil, and I am made errand girl. [Leonard] Fenimore [the school driver] in the Franklin brings me in town, and I shop and market. Warmer weather, and fur coat and galoshes a nuisance. . . . Mrs. Swift [from the school] brings me back to change the things I got wrong, and Polly picks me up and returns me to the school. . . . Went over the road five times. Struggle with Sunny Boy the Furnace, and give Jack a much needed bath, and now feel as if I'm going to develop grip[pe]. That won't do. Too much at stake next week.

## Saturday, December 11

Trustee meeting and luncheon at school very harmonious. Luncheon very pretty. . . .

Bowse in at night, also Minnie [Stevens, who is beginning to go insane]. She's doing perfectly atrocious things now—such as taking money from anyone, and selling *everything*. . . .

### Sunday, December 12

Spend most of the morning struggling with Sunnyboy. Mrs. [Julia] Robinson [a well-off Black neighbor] calls with Alice Kent's things [Alice Kent is a young woman from the Industrial school] and gets the rest of the time. Then we go to the cold, dreary wet and soggy cemetery and plant little pine and holly trees. And come home to a cold and cheerless kitchen. Polly very cross. But what's the use. Mama is old. . . .

### Wednesday, December 15

. . . Reach Washington by 2:15. Straight to Franklin Building to present credentials to [Herman] Long [for the D.C. public school teaching job she is seeking]. Said credentials fill Polly's brief case. Such a time as I had collecting and collating them! Long's office messed up with important looking people. He takes me into a private room and we go over the age situation. Since I am eleven years past the statute of limitations, I am to agree to abide by decision of Board of Education on appointment, even if I pass. I leave the precious pack of papers with Long. . . . Copy exam questions. . . . Snow and bitter cold. I had to put on my invisibles in the station as I came in from Baltimore and buy a pair of rubbers.

Something happened to the train and we don't get home—at least I don't reach Wilmington until twelve o'clock. Fagged out. . . .

### Thursday, December 16

A frightfully busy day. Make the children work extra hard to get their Christmas things under way. Mrs. Lockridge tells me of the children having to sing at Mrs. W[arfield]'s funeral, [a Wilmington Black woman who earned her living as a domestic], so I have to prepare a quartette and rehearse them, in addition to the Christmas music.

Go to library in afternoon and get Barr on Feeble-Mindedness. . . . Spend hours at night hunting for my "psych" notes. . . . Upset cellar, library, everyplace—finally locate them in the cellar. Breathe again. . . .

## Friday, December 17

Decide not to go to the church funeral with Mrs. Lockridge and the girls. They can sing well enough without me, and Mrs. L. likes the credit of taking them. Just as well, for that funeral will take hours. Mrs. Warfield was a "Jiner" [joiner, as in clubs] plus.

Have dinner, dress for the evening and get away in the 4:55, with a huge hat box filled mostly with note books and tomes. Robert late meeting me, but we connect finally, and go to the church. . . . Fair crowd, for a dollar admission. I "speak fine" on the "Value of Political Organization," and collect ten dollars for expenses. . . . All I was interested in was getting my rail road fare. . . .

## Saturday, December 18

No letter from Long telling me whether or not I can take the exam. So I call him up. He asked me to come right on down to his office. This upset me so, I did not want the breakfast Mrs. Finley [wife of J. Finley Wilson, Bobbo's boss] had left for me, but drank two cups of sugarless tea, and went on down to his office.

He had prepared two or three copies of an agreement to be signed by me whereby I agree in case I pass, and the Board of Education *may* not see fit to appoint me, I will not sue or try to coerce them. I hesitated, but finally signed. Nothing else to do, or no exam on Monday. It was such a relief to find that it was nothing more serious, that I could have sung when I came out. Went down to Steve Lewis' for the dental work, but found he had gone up to the Penna. sanitarium. . . . So to do a bit of shopping and to the office to get Bobbo, get some lunch and home to study.

Stuck close all afternoon, boning and grinding like a good fellow. Bitter cold out and the house quite cold, which I had to myself. But there was sunshine part of the time, and being alone helped. I boned hard. We all had dinner together in the kitchen about eight o'clock, and I went back to boning until bed time.

## Sunday, December 19

Oh, such cold! I felt congealed all day. Finley off early to White Plains. Bobbo and I breakfast together. Mrs. F. lay down to rest a bit before filing a monstrous pile of letters, and I shivered and studied and studied, and Bobbo TRIED to keep quiet, with indifferent success.

We went to dinner with Edith [Fleetwood] at 3:30 at her home. Nice dinner with the near-bald Mrs. Watson [a friend of Edith], but we shivered before the open grate in the living room, until Edith finally suggested we go to their room, and we four, Laura [Edith's housemate] and all basked before the oil stove, electric stove and radiator in their room and thawed out—I for the first time in three days.

Back home to find Mrs. Finley just getting up; she had slept all day, exhausted. We bought her some ice cream, bitter tho the weather. Froze and studied and went to bed by nine o'clock.

## Monday, December 20

The day of days! Did not get up after all as early as I wanted, for was awake so early that dropped off. But up anyhow, and rush out. Ran into Martha [Arnold]'s and asked for breakfast and get service, from all hands. At the Franklin Building in Long's office I cheerfully asked for the "torture chamber." It caused merriment. These Washington teachers take themselves too seriously. Glad it did. Upstairs in the assembly hall was the place. About 30 being examined in various things. . . .

It was an "inclusive" exam. Nothing left out. I wrote three ink-fulls, and called it a day. . . .

Tired out by twelve o'clock. We had until 12:40, but I was through. Scheduled for oral exam at three. Walked to the library, and thought I'd rest there, but hated the sight of a book. After all, fled back to Bobbo at the office. We had a bite together, and I rested with him, and back for my three o'clock. . . .

The oral exam was amusing, tho Long, after letting the others play with me, took charge and put me through my paces. Fast and furious we bandied technicalities. . . . Felt I had scored well. . . .

Down to Steve Lewis', and found him awaiting me. Had some temporary work done, and came away with certificate to hand to dentist on to-morrow's physical exam.

Edith took me to a movie, after Bobbo and I had dined. . . . An innocuous picture, but a relaxation. Dropped in to see Martha, and picked up Bobbo there, and so back home and eventually to bed.

## Tuesday, December 21

Breakfast with the Wilsons and then off to Miner Normal [School] for the physical. The "Class of '26" as I dubbed the examinees all on the anxious seat, and many important looking doctors, dentist (Clif. Frye), two nurse attendants, and a haughty Duchess to test the eyes. Clif. passed my teeth, altho they were not up to par, there being no occluding molars. The eyes with the glasses were normal. The weight nine pounds too much. And the long waits. It seemed every woman was finished before me, and then my turn came at the blood pressure. *178!* Passed to another doctor, and another machine! Old Dr. Freeman. So particular and precise. Tested. *178!* "I cannot pass you on that."

Something went all sick inside of me. Failed in my physical test. High blood pressure. I went to the office and told Bobbo and we mourned together.

Mrs. Finley took me to the station, and I caught the 1:05. Get home by 3:13, stop down town and buy a few Christmas doo-dads, and home in time to start dinner, Mama still being too feeble to do any cooking.

After dinner I gently break the news of my high blood pressure to Pauline and Leila, and using that as an opening wedge, tell of the story of the exam. Call up Mr. Evans and have him bring my engraved cards around, and sit up late that night addressing Christmas cards.

Bowse coming in to play cards, and Minnie coming in just for plain foolishness delay me somewhat.

## Wednesday, December 22

Three days before Christmas, and I am just about beginning my preparations. I feel suffocated in the rush. Christmas work to be finished by the children at school. Cards to be sent out. Purchases to be finished up. Packages to be wrapped and mailed. However, I find time to go to [Dr.] Harvey Murray's and have him take my blood pressure. He makes it 164, and is not alarmed. Diet, rest, freedom from worry will bring it down. Lord bless us! Three weeks from now he will examine me again, and in the meanwhile, I'll leave off the hormotones [hormones]. The pituitrin is not so good for high blood pressure. When I start on them again, leave it out. . . .

## Thursday, December 23

Last day of school, and I have the children finish up, and I pack and collect all their things, the 66 wreaths, 70 yards tree trimming, 18 gold lanterns, 40 calendars, 25 big candy boxes, 40 candy baskets, 20 little boxes, paper feathers and doo-dads, not to mention the books of Christmas carols. . . . Started to make the properties for the play, but Polly came early as she had a train to make to get to Phila. to a Delta meeting. Very much of a scurry and a rush and a shopping in haste all around.

Mama is unspeakably depressed and dejected and thinks she's horrifically ill. She does not seem to want to fall in with our plan of having Christmas in Philadelphia.

The furnace still wearing me out body and soul.

### Friday, December 24

Up early, for there is much to do on Christmas Eve day. Washing windows, and tending the furnace—Sunny Boy is getting to be more like Moloch [the furnace] of 916 [French St.] than ever. Of course, if he has no shaker, and his insides get clogged with ashes, he is inevitably cross. Late in the afternoon, after things begin to shape up—we three, Leila, Polly and I, fliv out to the cemetery and fix wreaths and holly and things. . . .

I had trimmed the tree, MY tree, that I cut myself down at Stockley, and the little trees and [the family dog] Jack's two little artifical trees on the buffet, and the new red wreaths, which I fixed with holly myself, and all the holly around. Pretty. Bobbo was tickled pink with his bath robe—handirobe—and slippers to match.

*The "Jean" of this entry is* Jeanette Stubbs Jamison, *with whom D-N and Pauline frequently socialized. The daughter of a Wilmington physician, she married Francis T. Jamison ("Juice"), who was D-N's dentist.*

### Christmas Day!

Polly awakes us with a special to me from Ethel [her niece]. Leila off to St. Matthews' Church early. I get breakfast—Krusie's croquettes. Mama up early, "trying her legs." I have some pretty things. A blue rayon bed spread from Edith; two monogrammed pillow cases from Krusie; a bureau scarf from Anna [Brodnax]; the corduroy bath robe and Chinese slippers from Bobbo; a perfectly gorgeous envelope pocket-book from Polly, big and flat and lizard-y. Leila had given me my stockings before I went to Washington for Thanksgiving. Violet

[Johnson, her New Jersey friend] sent me a lovely Italian silk Undie.

We get off finally about one or a bit later, all five of us, and reach Philadelphia without disaster. Lovely day, not too cold. See a good show at the Stanley, John Gilbert in Sabatini's "Bardelys the Magnificient," with a good program of music and dancing. Mama bears up wonderfully, for a lady who had determined to die. Then to the Marion Tea-room for our dinner. It was a turkey dinner, and I have eaten better ones, but anything's better than cooking and worrying in the kitchen for two whole days. . . .

Reached home about nine o'clock. Jack on guard, and perhaps wondering if this is Christmas he [has] had enough of it.

Jean had a party, and Polly took a nap before going. Malcolm [Polly's boyfriend, possibly], Bobbo and I played poker. We cleaned Malcolm of 40 cents, and afterwards I won it all from Bobbo.

And so endeth Christmas 1926. The glory of it has passed away. It's just another day now. I told St. Anthony perhaps I did not feel it in my heart because I had not made anyone else happy. I miss children.

## Sunday, December 26

Breakfast to cook, and help with dinner, and get together the costumes and properties for the [Industrial School] children's play. Polly and I start out to the school at 2:30, and when we get there the dinner not yet over, so we come in for some dessert and speechifying. . . . The [Starlight] Club gave me a box of correspondence cards, and expected me to make a speech about it! Everybody speaks on every and all provocation.

The children did their play, "Christmas Everywhere," very acceptably. At least that was over. Costuming them alone was a job. Then we departed for home, Polly and I. Mrs. L.[ockridge] gave me the bridge set I coveted, and sent Mama a tray cloth. And that's over. Bobbo very busy "seeing a man."

## Monday, December 27

. . . Went over to Minnie's for her punk party. The Shills or whatever their name is, the guests of honor. Ordinary young white couple. Elizabeth Stubbs. We talked psychiatry. Polly blew in and took Elizabeth home, as she had to make the 10:05. I stayed after the Shills left. Walked home alone. Very cold. Punk evening.

## Tuesday, December 28

Such bum holidaying. All morning at the furnace, trying to get some action and heat. The coke came, and the last state of it is worse than the first. . . . Mama lapsed into invalidism again, only more so. Leila complaining. Polly [behaving] like she had good sense, going to parties all night, and sleeping all day.

## Wednesday, December 29

Bathe Jack today, and that's a job! Play some 500 with the two "Shieks" and Polly. Party at H.H.S. [Howard High School] at night, and about 2:30, a mob of about thirty invaded the house. Three carloads of "Debs" from Phila. with their own hamper. I had gone to bed, and did not get up. . . .

*Here D-N refers to Agatha Lawson, who taught art at Howard High School and had a home and husband in Philadelphia. Ethel, D-N's niece, liked and visited her (as well as Mrs. Julia Robinson)— but Mrs. Lawson and D-N had quarrelled in the past.*

## Friday, December 31

The last day of the old year. Polly to go to New York, driving herself to Phila. then to pick up her party, and a man to drive to N.Y. Her idea to take Leila and me to Phila. for a day of it. Mine to take Mama too. Mama balked. Don't blame her. We would have to come back on the train. Then Leila wanted to see Ethel at the Lawsons and I had no stomach for that. Pretended that I had business to attend to, and backed out. Not much on leaving Mama alone anyhow, even if she is devilish. . . .

And now I've been ever since dark trying to get this diary written up, since December 15. If I make any resolutions for the New Year, the main one will be to keep this diary up to date. Mama went to watch meeting. I walked down with her. Bobbo called up from Washington. He is coming on the 1:50. Leila came in from Phila. complaining how "TERRIBLE" Phila. is. Snow and rain outside. The men from the coal yard cleared the coke from the coal, and by having a mixture, am able to get a decent fire. House warm, so is the weather. Going to clear this library of unread papers, and dust the desk. Have cleared it some. Bought a new blotter.

Well, 1926 farewell! You've been a cruel year in some respects, and yet you could have been infinitely worse. What will 1927 bring? Prosperity and good fortune and happiness, I think. I am sure it will. Farewell!

### [Saturday, January 1]

Happy New Year!    $1927 = 19 = 10 = 1$

According to numerology this is to be a wonderful year; its guiding number 1—let us hope.

### [Sunday,] January 2

Running true to form did not make entry yesterday. . . . Arose early. Worked all day cleaning. . . . Helped with dinner. Leila grumpy and wanting "more business like arrangements." Decide, after thinking it over, to do as she suggests. Bobbo warns against it. . . .

Today, arose in the dark to see after the furnace. Bitter cold all over house. Get things warmed up. Leila still upset. . . . Anderson [probably Leon] comes bringing man [to do household chores]—named Bartley. We strike bargain. $2.50 per week. Well, that takes Sunnyboy [the furnace] off my back. Then Leila and I talk "business." She had thought $10 per week per piece [person] good pay and I began figuring on $80 per month—coal, chore man, gas, electric, telephone and food, and getting it out. Then right off she wasn't sure whether Pauline could pay all that—well that's her funeral. I can't manage on less. However, we agreed to try it for a month. Maybe by that time I'll have a charge to go to Washington.

We begin new arrangement tomorrow. Our living has been haphazard and expensive. I'll keep strict accounts. And to begin, I'll cash that $53 check on my Metropolitan loan to use it to finance me until the 20th. I guess Polly will always be behind in her accounts. . . .

### Monday, January 3

Up at six o'clock to begin the new schedule. Since I am going to keep boarders, I'll keep them *right*. So I get breakfast, though Leila is still buzzing around. Bartley comes and finds out that Sunnyboy's shaker wasn't broken, merely locked with a clinker and that he was fearfully dirty, his upper draft not having been cleaned. He also agrees to put the broken lining in the kitchen range. So it looks as if we would have some comfort.

At school—things as usual. Room clean and warm.

Decide to go home at noon to get money and start this marketing off. . . . Market and stock up *right*. Get dinner, so there's a decent meal for once. And yet Leila comes ambling in with some perfectly inadequate chops and lettuce. We'll get shaken down eventually! . . .

## Wednesday, January 5

On the way out to school Polly suggests that she should have a party. The Christmas party she had been talking about. In honor of Tribbet. And Twelfth Night too. Nothing for me to do but plan a menu for said function. Go to Juvenile Court to relieve a strain on the school. . . . Ex-Chancellor Curtis at work. I like him. No beaming optimism, but apparent sincerity. No girls [who might find their way to the Industrial School], so I slip out, phone Polly and she and Tribbet come for me.

We do a mess of marketing. Rush home. I cook dinner—then go right into making shrimp salad, custards etc. for the party. It is ten o'clock and the guests are arriving before I finish, but I lie down for a nap before I arise at eleven and dress. Same little old "crowd." The party a success and a "pleasant time was had by all.". . .

## Monday, January 10

Depressed. "Frustrated hopes. Frustrated life" keeps running in my mind. Maybe Zona Gale's "Preface to a Life" has depressed me and made me morbid. Bitter cold and windy. . . . My cold is bad and helps to make me miserable. Anyway, the "Professor," as Polly calls Bartley, keeps the house warm and comfortable. Leila doesn't like him, of course. Does not trust him and resents him. But he means a world to me. Especially as I am doing the cooking. And the latter I do easily. *And*—I'm wondering how I'm going to squeeze through until the 20th. Money quite low. . . .

## Wednesday, January 12

Still bitter cold. Leila slips me a twenty spot and life is roseate again. Sorry I wrote Bobbo for money. . . .

## Thursday, January 13

Bobbo writes cheerily. Incidentally sends me excerpt from Eugene Gordon's estimate of me in January *Opportunity*. He feels that I was a distinct loss to the [Pittsburgh] *Courier* when I left it and hails me as a *big* columnist. [Superintendent of D.C. colored schools] Garnet Wilkinson's letter also reporting blood pressure and suggesting a re-exam. . . .

## Monday, January 17

Leila [Jr.] died six years ago today.

Still bitter cold. Bobbo has a tooth pulled and when I returned from school find him in bed; taking calomel and groaning with his face. So what with my usual cooking and waiting on him, my hands are full.

Go to [Dr. Harvey] Murray's to test his new blood pressure machine. Thorough test. Pressure gone up to 180! Whew! Thought something was wrong from the pounding in my throat and temples. Lost a pound and three-quarters. Put me on nitroglycerine three times a day. Epsom salts every other day and no meat. I don't feel very happy. . . .

## Wednesday, January 19

January 19, 1910–1927. This is the date, is it not [that she and Arthur Callis secretly married]? Laurence [her nephew, who is attending school in Chicago] writes that Arthur and his wife are getting a divorce and that the former said to him, "Laurence, never marry to spite anyone." Well, who told him to marry Pauline? Seventeen years we *would have* been together—fourteen he has struggled with her and nearly eleven with Bobbo and I. . . .

## Sunday, January 30

To the doctor's early. Blood pressure down to 142, weight 155–¾. He says I am ready to go to Washington [to retake the medical exam for a teaching position]. . . .

## [Washington, D.C.]
## Tuesday, February 1

The beginning of a hectic time. All primed for the successful passing of the exam. I go to the District Building, 14th and Pennsylvania

Avenue, and present myself to Dr. Murphy, of the Health department. Takes blood pressure. Varies from 162 to 178! Horrors! Examines heart. Irregular, but no valvular trouble. Insists upon his own urinalysis, saying the one from the health department of Delaware not authentic. I leave sample. He tells me he will not pass me. Stumbling in tears, I flee back to the office. Things all black before me, so I run to Bobbo as a child to its mother. Having eaten nothing but a drink of orange juice, I am hungry.

Moon around awhile, and then decide to go see Wilkinson. Wait an interminable time, and then have but a sketchy interview. He decides to wait and see result of this latest urinalysis. Decide not to go home tonight, but wait for developments. Eat dinner with the Wilsons, listen to the radio, and so to bed. When I was waiting for Wilkinson, ambled into [Herman] Long's office, and see all my examiners, who hailed me as a long lost child. Long told me I passed. Wilkinson also—and inferred that said passing was brilliant.

It's all over town about me and my "brilliant" exam.

Do my column today.

*Tessa below is* Theresa Lee Connelly, *a socially active and prominent Washingtonian, who was a favorite "running buddy" of D-N.*

## Wednesday, February 2

Groundhog Day. And he surely sees his shadow, for a more lovely spring-like day it would be hard to find. I have a brain-storm. Maybe that specimen of urine I submitted to Murphy was affected by the orange juice I had drunken. I take a specimen at home, and trot down to his office with it. He tells me the report was adverse. There was albumen in the specimen. That, coupled with the high blood pressure he found, points to a serious complication of kidney trouble. I might teach a few months, and then be a pensioner on the bounty of the District for years, because of a stroke. He had already written me to that effect, but I had not received the letter. I protested. Almost wept. He could not do otherwise. I ought to be glad of the experience, which would give me an opportunity to "live right." Back up to Bobbo's office. He was out, but I figured that he was down at the New Liberty Hotel with [Melvin] Chisum, with whom I had talked over the phone yesterday. He was. I took a taxi, and soon was with the two. They conferred. Chisum would put Madden, from Illinois, Chairman of the Appropriations Committee on the job. . . . But I thought that I ought to see Robert Houston, of Delaware, my own Congressman, after the District Health office, for he is on the District committee. Bobbo and Chisum think this a good idea. We take a taxi to the House offices. Soon Bobbo and I are in Houston's office, and I tell my story, also telling him of the urinalysis by our State Board of Health.

He immediately calls the Health Department and gets the head, Dr. Fowler. Fowler, he explained, is not only the head, but he is the last word and immediately amenable to Houston. Fowler's talk was wordy, but in the end he asked if I would come over right away. Bid Bobbo farewell . . . and rush off to the District building. Stop at Murphy's desk, and ask him about the new specimen. Albumen, and unfavorable. So into Fowler's office. A lank individual, with low blood pressure and pyorrhea. He talks a lot of slow speech about conserving the government's money. A narrow-minded bureaucrat of the lowest order.

He called in Murphy, and I am damned as an individual who would be refused by any life insurance company. The bacteriologist called in said there was an infinitesimal quantity of albumen in this new specimen submitted. He, Fowler, asked Murphy to take my blood pressure. I said it would be unfair. Had not eaten anything since morning when I had an egg and tea at Martha's [Martha Arnold]. Head ached from worry and fretting, and rushing around. But Murphy insisted. It was 182, of course, but ran down to 150. Fluctuating. Bad circulation said Fowler. No such thing, said I, but irritation. Kidney lesion said Fowler. No such thing. Headaches constant, said Fowler. Never have them. The State report, which I had abstracted from Murphy's desk in the morning, and showed to Houston, he (Fowler) did not think worth anything.

Would I bring another specimen in the morning, and have another blood pressure test? Of course. I suggested, I am paying a substitute. But we'll let it go at that.

Back up to Wilkinson's office in the Franklin building, and wait an interminable time for him to come in and get off the other callers. Among them Otelia Cromwell [historian John W. Cromwell's daughter, who was a writer and taught English at Miner Teachers College], who congratulated me on being in National Guy's place [as teacher in the D.C. school system]. Mollie [Mary Church] Terrell [famous D.C. clubwoman and activist who was formerly D-N's neighbor] had called up at the Wilsons' [where Bobbo lives in Washington] to congratulate me, and the District was buzzing [prematurely] with the news of my appointment.

Wilkinson and Long looked despairing. They conferred about extension of time. It seems my time expired today, or tomorrow. I judge Wilkinson was all ready to submit the appointment at the Board meeting this afternoon. But here was this adverse report from Murphy.

I paid my respects to Fowler—to him and Long. Showed my Board of Health urinalysis. Told of [Dr.] Harvey Murray's findings, and Murphy's frank puzzlement at my fluctuating blood pressure.

Wilkinson and Long looked wise. Figured on some technicalities which would give me ten days longer. Said it was now up to me either to satisfy Fowler, or to "reach" him. I went out sick with a blinding headache. Hungry, but afraid to eat.

Waited at the office for Bobbo. He was late, and I was hungry. But called Tessa. She swore over the phone over a decimal fraction of albumen in my urine holding me out of a job. But suggested I go to Elmer Terry, the "best diagnostician in the District." And while Bobbo was working on Browne, [Delaware senator] Bayard's secretary, to write Fowler just where he got off, and Chisum was invoking Madden, I got a car and went out to see Dr. Terry. And on the way out it occurred that the albumen was due to leucorrhea!

Elmer was as tense and violent as ever. Cussed all the Health Department for fools, twice damned. Showed me an eminent medical authority who said a small percentage of albumen was due in the urine of any one over forty-five, especially women. Murphy had said that women were apt to have a small percentage of albumen. Then why the fuss?

But he took me in charge, even as Tessa had suggested. Pills (nitrite sodium), no dinner, or at best, a little spinach. Hot bath. Hot lysol douche. Bed and rest. Hot lysol douche in the morning. NO FOOD. Then for exam. Back to office. Bob and I at Thurston's [restaurant], where I eat a horrible meal of spinach, carrots and hot water. Buy a douche bag, and lysol, etc. and tramp wearily home. Bobbo had to go back to Chisum. Sick all night from worry and fatigue.

### Thursday, February 3

Head going round like a top. Take Terry pills, douche, etc. in the a.m. Get another specimen. Never had my piddy-widdy so discussed before in my life, and by all kinds of gentlemen, from Senators and school superintendents down. . . . Sleep a bit more. Mrs. Wilson brings me a charming breakfast up, but I shut my eyes, take the glass of water, and dress leisurely. She drives me down, being careful not to drive too fast for fear of starting up this blood pressure.

Murphy on the job. Pressure fluctuates from 142 to 170. But Murphy thinks 142 is about what it should be. Leave the specimen. Told to return at 2:30. Murphy is sympathetic. But suggests that Fowler is fussy. Get breakfast. Read exchanges at the office. Bobbo busy with make up of paper.

Back at 2:30. Murphy is out. See Fowler. Call in bacteriologist. Fowler nasty. Evidently the pressure brought to bear on him by [Senator] Bayard and [Congressman] Houston has just made him stubborn and nasty, after the fashion of a little man with a little power, determined to show it off. Bacteriologist says a tiny trace of albumen—but "No pathological significance." Even that does not satisfy Fowler. He thinks the fact that he did not send the first unfavorable letter is a great thing in his favor. But the fluctuating blood pressure! Ah-ha!

Was leaving when Murphy ran in. I begged him to work on Fowler. They have a lengthy conference. Then Murphy came out saying he could not move Fowler, but he thought he would make up his mind soon. Nothing to do but wait now, until the ass makes up his mind. With a blood pressure hitting normal at times, and a urinalysis practically all right, what was holding him seems nothing but stubbornness.

Well, nothing to do but to eat, drop by to see Martha, go home take a nap, and go out alone to the Dunbar School to see the "Krigwa" players. Run into Recorder of Deeds Froe on the car, and we went together. The three little plays were well done, especially Narka's characterization. See lots of people, and have to accept more premature congratulations. Bobbo comes for me, dead tired.

## Friday, February 4

Nothing to do today but to wait for Fowler's letter to be sent to Wilkinson. . . .

Bobbo and I in bed when Finley [Wilson] comes home from the Mus-o-Lit Club saying that he had seen Garnet Wilkinson, who told him that he had a letter from Fowler in the p.m., and it was favorable [for her appointment].

A load off my breast. I had been so far in the dumps that I had even broken training enough to eat marshmallow cake and drink wine and "corn" with Mrs. W[ilson].

Nothing to do now but make plans anent the appointment.

### Saturday, February 5

. . . At the office Bobbo calls Houston, who says Fowler recommended a temporary appointment of a year, my health to be under supervision, and another exam at the end. Fowler is a first class fool. . . .

### Sunday, February 6

Lazy day. Breakfast with the Wilsons. Read paper. Call on Martha, on Georgia Douglas Johnson. And on Edith. Just have time to pack bag and make train dinnerless—but not hungry. Arrive home at ten. Polly up. We exchange gossip. The town ringing with my "appointment." Things just the same, otherwise. . . .

*Opportunity magazine's annual literary contests for Black writers were very important, and winning a prize in them an honor. They were inaugurated to foster Black creative expression. Note that D-N entered and won an honorable mention this year using a* nom de plume. *(See also May 7 below.)*

### Monday, February 7

. . . Read a letter from [banker] Hoch which was on my desk Sunday. Is going to foreclose mortgage Thursday if I don't pay up. Write him. Do my article. Revise "April is on the Way" for *Opportunity* Contest. Get to bed about two a.m. Things at school same. . . .

### Wednesday, February 9

Go to see Hoch again. Tell him a wild tale about his being to blame for [me] not getting my job due to reading his letter as I was going out for my physical exam. We argue, but wind up by his making suggestion of taking out another second mortgage on house, which will clear off old debts, and arrange so that I will only have to pay $7.00 per week. It relieves me so that I go home "spurning the ground."

Tell him to go ahead and fix it up. It will mean five years to pay, but what's five years, if the strain of the $20 per week is lifted?. . .

## Tuesday, February 15

A hell of a day. To Hoch's office early staying from school, to sign bonds, mortgage, notes, etc., as it had to be done during banking hours. Find an impasse. He had dug up some information about back city taxes. They have not been paid since 1922, and there is a judgment against them on the 1923 tax. This, coupled with the last payment on the Macaullay judgment, makes a total of $90.01 which must be paid before the second mortgage of $1260 can be recorded. Hoch and I have bitter words and we sit and talk, but nothing is done until we both begin to get angry. I call Bobbo in Washington and he advises me to go to Baker of the Delaware Trust and get a note discounted. This puts me in tears, and I lose what little self-control is left. Go off and cry in the bank, having first bought a handkerchief, and after waiting around for Baker to come back from lunch, approach him. [Banker] Reilly had said it was all right. He felt that way because he liked the Lincoln-Douglass article in last week's paper.

Baker was acquiescent for $100. Found [Charlie] Colburn [local Black politician friendly with the Nelsons] in the street just as he was leaving the public building. Took him in the library and got his signature. Wrong, of course. Back to the bank to be told it was wrong. Out again and luckily run into Colburn as he was going in. Get the right signature. Back to the bank. Get the money, after slight delay. Back to Ford building and pay last of account against me at Hering's office. Back to public building to pay 1923 taxes. In City Solicitor's office, and clerk out to lunch. Wait a bit. . . . Back to Hoch's office. Wait for him. He comes in finally. Get all signatures made and after waiting for Gluckman, get them straight. Over to Industrial Trust to get check, money, and little yellow book. After three and we are locked in the bank. I have been hopping around all day without anything to eat but the morning grape fruit and coffee. Splitting headache and probable blood pressure of 200.

Home at last, and get dinner. . . .

## Monday, February 21

Mrs. Rose and I spend the morning interviewing possible candidates for trustee [for the Industrial School] from rural New Castle. . . .

### Friday, February 25

Tonight and the Alpha-Delta [Alpha Phi Alpha fraternity–Delta Sigma Theta sorority] dance. I've been talking about going for a month. But when I say to Pauline in the morning that Bobbo will probably come and take me and ask for room in Henrietta [Pauline's car]—lo— she has promised to take Annie [Douglas] and Jean [Jamison] (spatting with Juice) and Blanche [Stubbs] and so there is no room for us. Hardly any for Mitchell [a pharmacist in the Hopkins-Banton drugstore], her escort.

Bobbo here when I get in from school. Bad, rainy night—so I don't feel like going on train. Tooth and whole face and neck raging pain. But I would have gone to the dance.

Cross currents surge to and fro, but the party finally departs and I rush upstairs to hide my tears of rage and disappointment.

And suffer with that abscessed tooth all night.

### Saturday, February 26

Not speaking to Pauline. Go to Juice's to see about tooth coming out. Too sore to touch. So buy myself a spiffy pair of shoes and stockings at Monaghan's. . . .

### Sunday, February 27

Have to speak for Mrs. Hughes at her husband's church—John Wesley M. E. in W[est] Philadelphia. . . .

Church luncheon and "I speak fine" though Mrs. H[ughes] only gives me five dollars. I'm always threatening to quit "speaking round" at little dinky church messes. . . .

### Tuesday, March 1

. . . And biggest job of all. Wrote up this diary from February 16 to today—12 days. Lord, but I'm shiftless!. . .

*D-N here mentions Langston Hughes' latest volume of poetry. She was one of the few commentators to give it a favorable review.*

## [Enroute to an engagement in Roanoke, Va.]
## Thursday, March 3

. . . It makes me cross—the disappointment of having to spend a night on the train—but it was the best after all. . . .

In spite of the cough it is infinitely more restful than it would have been with Bobbo coughing a duet with me. Read Langston Hughes' "Fine Clothes to the Jew."

## Friday, March 4

Arrive [in Roanoke, Va.] at dawn, after a wretched night of coughing and bad dreams. . . . Dress and find the red cap waiting to escort me to "the Professor" who turns out to be "Professor Holder" in charge of the high school. We go to Mrs. Dean's [with whom she stops]. . . . Pleasant southern home. Wherever you look in every direction, mountains, the Blue Ridge, now snow covered after the recent blizzard yet things are peeping out, forsythia, peach blooms, iris tops— amid the remnants of snow in the warm spring sunshine. . . .

It is 11:30 when I get back and I go to bed and stay there, sleeping and re-reading DuBois' "Gift of Black Folk" and making notes for the "lecture." Cough raspy and annoying and voice criminal in spite of drastic methods. . . .

## Saturday, March 5

Decide to stay over until tomorrow on a chance of getting to see Natural Bridge. Been reading about it all my life and having the chance concluded to take it. Guess Bobbo will be disappointed at my not spending Sunday with him, but he probably will be relieved at not having to buy my dinner. . . .

## Sunday, March 6

It was on a Sunday that March 6 fell in 1898, twenty-nine years ago when Paul and I were married! 29 years!

We start for the Natural Bridge at 10:45. . . . A lovely day and a lovely drive. . . . Debark, enter the little house, pay $1.10 each, register and admitted to the park. Start down to steep path and stop to put on galoshes. I must remember the high points: 1) The Cascade; 2)

The Arbor Vitae Trees 2000 years old that guard the path; 3) The bridge, incredibly high and majestic; 4) George Washington's bona fide initials carved high up; 5) Saltpetre cave; 6) Lost River; 7) Lace Falls. And the long, long lovely trail by Cedar River, the hepaticas and anemones out, shyly peeping lizards, fishing birds singing, stalactites and stalagmites falling from the rocks across our path.

And the majestic omnipresent awful bridge. . . .

*When she returns to Wilmington, D-N finds messages from Issaac W. Howard, president of the Delaware Federation of Colored Teachers, who led the fight for the equalization of teacher salaries. Writing in one of her Associated Negro Press "Little Excursions" columns, D-N said: "Wilmington teachers always had had equal pay for equal work, men, women, whites, blacks. But sad inequalities prevailed in the rural sections, despite the definite wording of the famous du Pont School code on the subject of equal salaries."*

## Monday, March 7

Awoke early passing through Manassas [Va.]. Reach Washington 7:05. I call Bobbo, but he is very gruff and uncommunicative. Leave on the 7:25, get breakfast on train and arrive Wilmington 9:58 and in school by 10:40.

Polly comes for me at usual hour and so home. Find I *have not* won prize in [Philadelphia] Sunday *Ledger*. Things the same. . . . Ike Howard sending SOS to go to Dover for vote on House Bill 109— equalization of salaries. Call up [principal of Howard High School, George] Johnson and ask him to drive with Polly and me at noon.

Then I have my old enemy, neuritis in knee and sciatica.

## Tuesday, March 8

Gray and rainy in early morning but clearing to perfect day and March winds and belling clouds. Polly and Johnson and Henrietta pass for me at 12:15 and we hie to Dover. The State House swarming and alive. . . . Bill has been reported out of committee. General air of favorableness. Howard speaks and [W. C.] Jason. Also I and Johnson as a representative of Wilmington teachers. Some debate and [?] makes a poor showing in his opposition. Vote—33 to 3. In the lobby Democrats and Republicans vying with each other to take the credit for the vote. Some congratulatory buzzing around, and we start home. Reach there by 5:30.

Knee paining like hell. Bobbo called me at 7:30 this a.m. asking me to lend him $15.00 and to telegraph it. Luckily I hadn't banked my money—so passed by Western Union before school and sent it. Poor fellow—sick and broke.

### Wednesday, March 9

I write Bobbo and tell him to come home immediately after making up the paper. There's one thing—he has a home and a warm one too. Raw and cold in school and have to teach all day in main building. . . .

### Sunday, March 13

Warm spring-like weather and I put in a strenuous day—just getting meals. It is a luxury just to lie down after a strenuous day and catch up on the papers. . . .

*This entry reveals the outcome of D-N's quest for the Washington, D.C. school position. Another woman, a former teacher, is given priority for the job.*

### Thursday, March 17

. . . Go to library and read the Washington *Post* to see what happened at School Board meeting. Rule passed giving re-instatement applicants precedent over new ones. That puts Mary Baker ahead of me. Oh, well, poor devil, she needs the job more than I do. . . .

### Monday, March 21

First day of spring. And a gray gloomy cold day it is. Decide to have my tooth out. Infecting my throat now. Go to Juice's and after some trouble (couldn't do much anesthetizing owing to infection) it finally is yanked out.

Go home, finish dinner, wash dishes, "produce literature" and go to bed.

## Tuesday, March 22

Decide to stay in. Cold. Feel shaky. Stay there until two o'clock. Get dinner and serve it. To Mrs. Rose's for [Industrial School] Parole Committee meeting. Home. Write an editorial on Kelly Miller's segregation article in Current History. Arleon [Bowser] and Anna [Brodnax] in and we play bridge. Tapioca custard and hot cocoa. . . .

## Friday, March 25

Blue. My God! I'm so blue that if I were a dog, I'd sit on my haunches and howl and howl and howl. . . .

## Saturday, March 26

. . . Blue because I don't know where to turn. Threats to turn off water if water rent not paid by the 30th. Bobbo sends me a V which keeps marketing and pays Bartley. Pauline's derelictions as to Board have pained me. . . .

Cold, rainy, bleak. I go to little Italian movie and see Colleen Moore in "Twinkletoes." Then to the library and read [James Weldon] Johnson's new poem "Go Down Death" in the April *Mercury* and home to a cold dark house, where Mama and Leila have long been in bed. . . .

## Monday, March 28

Awake early with the grim duty ahead of me—to raise money. Instead of going to school, go down to Harris' pawn shop next to Danforth's [drugstore] and there suggest to the youthful and pimply Shylock that I'd like $25 on my ear-rings—he offers $15 and sticks—nice stones, but small. The engagement ring is full of carbon and the platinum set diamond too small. But among the lot I raise $25. To the bank and deposit $15, pay for a half ton of coal, get out to school by ten o'clock and on my way home in the afternoon stop by and pay the water rent. It was to have been shut off on the 31st.

At night we drive up to the Professional Woman's Club in Philadelphia, who had asked me to address them since January. Meeting at Dr. Jaffe's, 265 South 22nd Street. A palatial place—prove to be all Jews and Arden-ites (had met some of them last summer) [Arden was a liberal, theatrical northern Delaware community] and *wives* of professional men.

Very stimulating gathering and I "speak fine" for an hour. Then much discussion. Coffee and cakes. About a hundred out. Very fine affair. Home by 12:40 to find Bobbo there on his way to Salisbury [Maryland]. We have whiskey sours. A relief from the nervous tension of the night. . . .

### Wednesday, March 30

Time for the [new Howard High cornerstone laying] exercises and a pouring rain. [Conwell] Banton in the limelight, of course, being Grand Master of the Masons, who have charge. But I am in the cornerstone, for my biography of General O. O. Howard, written during the campaign, goes in, and my idea of Dr. Stevens' [deceased pioneer Black physician, husband of Minnie] picture is carried out by Pauline. . . .

### Thursday, March 31

. . . Chill day—yet it was gorgeous to see the two blackbirds cavorting in the little trees near the school-house. . . .

### Friday, April 1

All Fools Day. Mama and Pauline catch me early and I retaliate on Miss Dade [Industrial School teacher] when I get to school. Cold, bleak, cheerless. Spits of snow, sleet, and hail.

Start some drastic reducing dieting on 1200 calories per day—trying to. . . .

*D-N's April 4 diary entry (not included here) mentions that* Estelle Miller *(one of the school's delinquent girls) had "run away from the Baby Hospital" and that she had gone with Mrs. Lockridge "to swear out a warrant for Estelle's arrest." Green is probably* Percy Green, a white Wilmington lawyer.

### Tuesday, April 5

Booker Washington's birthday. Do not go to school early, but wait to confer with Green about Estelle and sterilizing her and about Frances Huffington [another delinquent girl]. . . .

## Wednesday, April 6

. . . Decide that I am a small soul in a little place—a mite and had best stay among the little.

Organize the Girl Reserves at the school. . . .

## Saturday, April 19

Rather eventful day. I was to give a talk on projects at the Settlement [House] at the Jim Crow county meeting. Dr. Hosie [?] of Columbia spoke to the handful. Then left, as usual. I displayed my projects. Then sailed into them on the unnecessary Jim Crowing. The city teachers having one meeting—poor county teachers J. C.'d. But Stewart was not with me—he likes his brief authority as chairman. Poor Jim Crow souls! They like their inferior status. . . .

## Sunday, April 10

Palm Sunday! Grandma was buried 31 years ago today. Seems like last year. Brilliant, cloudless, cold. We all rose early—I to do my leftover Saturday cleaning. And to church. The rest to St. Matthews [P. E. Church]. I to the [St. John's P. E.] Cathedral. Found the service unspeakably tedious and uninspiring. Glad to come out and home. . . .

Diary stops here [after April 12] until Sunday, June 5—over two months. The rest must be reconstructed as best from memory. Only high spots here and there stand out. . . .

## Wednesday, April 20

Our anniversary! Fourteen years since Bobbo and I met. Eleven years since we married. . . .

## Saturday, April 30

Trustee Meeting. Election of officers. I have to preside and step on the gas of the little red steam roller. . . .

*A number of Harlem Renaissance notables are mentioned in this account of the* Opportunity *magazine literary awards dinner held in*

*New York City.* James Weldon Johnson *(1871–1938) is the famous lawyer, musician, poet, writer, anthologist, teacher, and public person. Seemingly admired by D-N, he is executive secretary of the NAACP during these diary years.* Countee Cullen, *highly praised poet, won the Harmon Gold Award for literature for his first book* Color *(1925).* Carl Van Vechten, *a white writer and photographer, gained notoriety for his 1926 novel* Nigger Heaven *and for his pictures of Black celebrities of the period.*

## Saturday, May 7

Pauline yanks me out of bed early. "Get up and come on and go to the *Opportunity* dinner." I demur—sick, no money. Leila lends me $10. And I get better.

So after buying Mama's things for Mother's Day—tomorrow—and after many false alarms and disappointments we get off to New York City. . . .

Reach Fifth Avenue restaurant 8:50. Dinner nearly over. Scared to go in. Do so finally and check bags. Had telegraphed for reservations. Find them. Welcomed effusively by Jim [James Weldon] Johnson, Countee Cullen, Carl Van Vechten.

Have table set up for us.

Moved from table to [white writer and critic] Dorothy Peterson's table. Sit near speaker's table and close to Paul Green whose play "In Abraham's Bosom" just won Pulitzer Prize.

My poem "April is on the Way" won honorable mention under name of Karen Ellison. . . .

## Sunday, May 8

Pauline and Jean [Jamison] . . . go to breakfast. I stay at the Parks' and wait for their return so we can start home.

And wait.

And wait.

Eloise home by 1:30. Said they were coming home.

I go out and walk around. No address book so can't remember where anyone lives. Go to a Spanish theatre. Teatro Apollo on 125th street. Good show. Wonderful real Spanish dancing. Home by 5. No girls.

Send Papa Parks after them. No news. In disgust pack bag and go. A ticket to Newark and $2.00 my all. Too proud to ask for money home. Too mad to wait any longer.

So to Newark. Get train for Summit [N.J.]. Find Vi's [Violet Johnson] house. Go to church and get her.

Sanctuary.

### Monday, May 9

. . . Home by 10 [p.m.]. Excitement has prevailed. I had dropped out completely and they were all panic-stricken. Leila had just called Bobbo who was able to tell her I had been in Summit.

Polly and Jean had come home on train Sunday night—afraid to drive all night unchaperoned. The boys had driven the car to Lincoln and Polly and Jean had gone to get it. Everybody mad. . . .

### Friday, May 13

Field Day! I have the bus which I chartered some time ago and we set out at 10 a.m.—36 and four adults. . . . Cold and rather bleak, but we have a very successful trip to Middletown [Delaware], a good day there and a good trip home. Mrs. Tatnall [Industrial School Trustee] and I had to put up the money—she $15, I $10. . . .

### Tuesday, May 24

We go to circus! Polly, Leila, Ethel and I. Ringling Bros. and Barnum & Bailey. Five rings and everything. A really magnificent affair and most thrillingly gorgeous. I don't ever remember enjoying myself more.

### Wednesday, May 25

Graduated from Straight [College, New Orleans] on this date in 1892—just 35 years ago today! And it's just as clear and vivid as if it were five years. . . .

### Thursday, June 2

Get my rating—A1. . . .

### Sunday, June 5

. . . I have reconstructed all the above as best from memory. Don't know why I stopped keeping the diary. Some things forgotten doubtless. . . .

One item I forgot—on Friday, June 3 . . . went to W.[est] Philadelphia Belmont Center to address a G[irl] R[eserves]. Mother-Daughter
banquet at the Bethel Baptist Church. Very monkey. But ran into
L[eslie] P[inckney] Hill in W. Philadelphia station en route to Nashville to deliver baccalaureate address at Fisk. Tried to talk to him about
putting me on as Field Secretary for the Interracial Peace thing. . . .

### Tuesday, June 7

Commencement Day at [State College] Dover. . . . I went primarily to see and talk with Leslie Pinckney. He was talking when we
got there. . . . Don't know whether he was lying or not when he
promised to do his best to put *me* across. . . .

### Friday, June 10

No check this a.m. Made me *sick*. A busy, mostly harassing day—
what with hanging charts and putting up work and the million other
things. My feet swoll horribly and Pauline "didn't know I was expecting her," so have to come home on the bus. But after eating I soak in
hot water. Soak off the real estate acquired, picking daisies and eating
surreptitious wild strawberries. Then . . . up to Morton [Pa.] to . . .
school commencement. The Phyllis Wheatley school. . . . I am the
speaker. So much program, I cut my talk to 15 minutes. All about
strawberries and daisies. . . . Home by midnight. A lovely drive. . . .

### Saturday, June 11

"God made this day" for us. Perfect weather. Clear, brilliant sunshine, lovely blue sky. Strong, cool west wind. My check comes and
I do some business at the bank before Polly takes me out [to school]
early [to prepare for commencement]. Work unceasingly—placing
chairs, decorating pillars and front, and a thousand, thousand things—
going every minute until finally dressed in "Mother Platers' " room by
two o'clock.

Everybody early—not a hitch—not a ripple to mar it all. . . . The
lovely dances of the children. The crowds. The exhibits. Everything
perfect. Even Leila says so.

Home by seven. Stop and vote at school No. 5 for school board.
. . . Get some dinner. Tired as I am, have *that* to do.

Bowse comes in later. She had to go to Philadelphia and missed
coming out. Then later, Bobbo comes. Elks conferences, of course,

had kept *him* away. I act peeved, too. Pretended I thought he had stayed in Washington to see [aviator] Lindbergh. . . .

## Tuesday, June 14

Flag Day. And a blowing, cold, wretched stormy day all day. Finish school work. Do my *Eagle* column—review of . . . "South African." Wretched day.

Had thought I *might* be able to rest this summer. So had Bobbo. But too many notes, bills, obligations. I am almost wild. Accumulations. And my extravagancies, I suppose. And Polly's not paying board. . . .

## Wednesday, June 15

Cheyney [Normal School, now State College] Commencement Day. A lovely day, but quite cold. Shivering in the morning. Somehow I put this day as the decisive point in my summer plans. I don't know why I hoped Leslie [P. Hill] would give me a definite hope for the Field Secretary job. But I did. A hopeless and futile hope. Had me shaking with nervousness.

The whole damn family gets off. We are a bit late, but get in via the fire escape and good seats. The usual commencement with Leslie P. talking too much, as usual. Harry Burleigh [composer and musician] giving an illustrated (by song) talk. Allston Burleigh [his son, who also directed choral groups] worshipping his father. [Henry O.] Tanner's new picture "Christ and Nicodemus" unveiled and commented upon. (I don't like it. Christ too cadaverous and head gear, as Mrs. Hill says, like a slicker hat.) The crowds, the supper, the gathering in Lottie's [Lottie is the head secretary at Cheyney] rooms . . . the various newly weds and Brides to Be and all. The dance afterwards by the Alumni. The good music. The midnight drive home in the wonderful moonlight. And under it all a great ache in my disappointed heart. I had hoped, hoped that Leslie would say it was all arranged. I would get the job—why I don't know. Instead—he had been too busy to think. He would "keep me in mind." The meeting would not be until the 26th etc. etc. Evasive. Could I attend the meeting? No, 'twould spoil my chances. I felt the door slam in my face.

So amid all the joy and beauty I carried a sinking heart home. I had hoped to sell the idea of Inter-racial, Inter-national Peace to great gatherings. Instead I shall have to sell little one volume encyclopedias to tired mothers. I see nothing to do but to go to Baltimore and learn how to be a book agent for the "Library Volume" folks. Ye gods! . . .

### Monday, June 20

This is the day I was to have started my book-selling training in Baltimore. But decided that there is no particular reason why I should peddle books. True I am in debt up to my eyes. But—it's not my fault and I'm not going to make myself ridiculous and unhappy about it— peddling books! Time Robert was coming to my rescue. Struggling with my finances as per usual. Even Bowse comes on me for what I owe her. Flat. . . .

### Friday, June 24

. . . Get down town and get my rings and ear-rings out of the pawn shop. Cost me $32.50! Think of paying $7.50 for $25 for 3 months! . . .

George S. Schuyler *is, at this point in his life, one of the 1920s New Negro radicals. He was best-known for his hard-hitting, irreverent "Shafts and Darts" columns, which appeared in the Pittsburgh* Courier *and the* Messenger, *the socialist magazine founded in 1917 by A. Philip Randph and Chandler Owens. D-N had contributed a number of articles to the* Messenger *this year. The "retrenchment" is probably relevant to the fact that the magazine ceased publication in 1928.*

### Monday, June 27

Feel better, have a lot to do too. Third blue Monday. Got a letter from Schuyler saying the *Messenger* has to "retrench," so my articles will not be needed. That hurt. Another instance of being terribly wonderful, but not needed. . . .

### New York[, N.Y.]
### Thursday, June 30

[In Summit, N.J.] Awakened by pattering of rain and I *cussed.* Why did it have to rain on my holiday? . . . I get away on the 3:28

standard for New York. . . . God, but New York is beautiful! It grips
you by the throat. . . . And now—to have a smoke and to bed.

*D-N refers here to Robert Browning's character in his* Pippa Passes, *obviously a poem that she liked since she knew it well enough to do an impromptu parody of it (see March 23, 1928). She is making something of a weekend holiday of this speaking engagement in New York City.*

## Friday, July 1

Edith [Fleetwood] came to my room [at the Y] early—though I
had been up and to bed again. We decided to be like Pippa and lose
no time of our day together. And out of all the big day's doings this
was the schedule.

1. Edith and I to station. Check her bag and get breakfast. I am
suffering torments with my leg all the time. 10,000 red hot devils
careering up and down my spine and around my knee.
2. To Roxy Theatre where we have to stand in line for doors to
open. Once within, the mind refuses to grasp its immensity and beauty.
A wonderful show too. . . .
3. Time now to go to station to meet Laura [Edith's house-
mate]. . . .
4. Put Laura and Edith into taxi for the boat.
5. Go to the Rialto to see . . . "The Way of All Flesh." Other
than that and some good singing, a lovely presentation of life of Chopin, with pictures, illustrated by orchestral and vocal selections from
his works.
6. Next, to the Gaiety to see "The King of Kings" which I had
bought ticket for in morning. A fine presentation by Cecil de Mille of
Christ's last year. But spoiled by having H. B. Warner (Christ) made
up as traditional blonde Nordic weakling. And Simon of Cyrene a
white man. . . .
7. Home after midnight—*dead*. Bought some collochin hoping
to apply it and get relief from that awful sciatica. One thin letter from
Bobbo. . . .

*Below,* T. Thomas Fortune, *often called the dean of Black journalism, was, during the 1920s, chief editor of Marcus Garvey's* Negro

World *and also of the New York* Interstate-Tattler.

*Here is the first mention of* Helene London, *a Chicago artist originally from the Omaha–Des Moines area, who becomes a key figure in the 1930–31 diary. Perhaps the debt was incurred during D-N's 1921 lecture trip to Iowa.*

### Sunday, July 3

. . . Luncheon. Then to the [New York] Forum [lecture series] where I am introduced by Mrs. [?] and "speak fine." Tom Fortune there looking like a scarecrow and poking holes in my speech. . . . And oodles of others. . . .

Polly brought me a batch of mail, among it a letter from Helene London enclosing check for $10—that old debt. . . .

### Wednesday, July 13

A blazing morn. Polly and Jack and I early (eight o'clock) to Ralph Mustard's and get Jack clipped. The rest of the day is spent more or less ministering to him, for he must be brushed and greased, then bathed and greased. I sweat through my galoshes. At night to Juice's. Drink punch and look at the moon on their porch. Eliz. Stubbs has thrown up that job that I'd have given my eyes to have. . . .

### Thursday, July 14

Bastille Day and as hot as Hades. The torrid wave is generally prevalent—106 in Phoenix, Arizona. Bobbo writes that the Elks will meet in Jersey City. Bates [Grand Elks Secretary] pulled that, says the *Courier*—it being his home town. Farewell Bobbo's hopes of secretaryship. . . .

Sleep in library again. I'd sleep on the roof porch if it wasn't too much trouble. . . .

### Friday, July 15

. . . So hot that I melt the rubber in my step-ins and they almost fall off. . . .

*D-N and* Perry Howard *had an interesting history. The Wilmington* Advocate *of December 16, 1922 had branded him "Traitor To*

*His Race" because Howard, a Mississippi Black appointed by Harding to a Justice Department position, had attacked the NAACP and worked against passage of the Dyer Anti-Lynching bill. During this political intrigue, Howard wrote a November 23 letter to Delaware senator T. Coleman du Pont, who had just been defeated in the 1922 elections by Democrat Thomas F. Bayard. In it, he said:*

> *The purpose of this letter is to call attention of you and other outstanding statesmen to the fact that the National Association for the Advancement of Colored People is purely a Negro Democratic organization and has always been found on the side of the Democrats in the final analysis. This organization was used by Bob Nelson and others, and you owe your defeat to no other agency.*

*This situation was probably a key factor in the* Advocate's *losing Republican-du Pont financial support and subsequently folding.*

### Saturday, July 16

. . . Up betimes and plan for leaving for Washington [on a month vacation]. . . . Bobbo on hand to meet me. Tells me we are to spend the day with Perry Howard at Highland Beach [outside Washington, D.C.] tomorrow. Mine old enemy!

### Sunday, July 17

Leave at 12:45 for the beach. . . . The place is lovely now. I could scarce recognize it—after 27 years. The Howards' house is quite lovely. Mrs. H. a charming hostess. . . . We all [the Howard, Nelson, and Wilson couples] go in the water. I had to pry Mrs. W[ilson] into Mrs. H[oward]'s bathing suit. Water lovely—though warm and quiet, remembering the Atlantic waves. We stay in two hours. Then dinner. Leave about eight o'clock. . . . We are all so sleepy when we reach home by eleven that we can barely climb into our beds. . . .

### Tuesday, July 19

My birthday! 52 years old. Ye gods! Can you believe it? I feel about 32; look 42. So that's serene. . . .

### Wednesday, July 20

. . . We three [D-N, Tessa, Estelle Mayes] then go down into N. E. Washington and the home of one of the Turner twins. The mother

does a "hot" business between there and New York. Has her apartment where Helen is. I buy a dress—voile, handmade and embroidered for $3.50. . . .

*The following is an account of D-N being a special guest at one
of* Georgia Douglas Johnson's *Saturday Nighters soirees. Mentioned
are* Willis Richardson, *a young dramatist who received the* Crisis *magazine prize for his play "The Broken Banjo: A Folk Tragedy" in 1925,
and* John P. Davis, *who headed the Fisk University Publicity* Department.

## Saturday, July 23

. . . First I went by Georgia's [Georgia Douglas Johnson] and there
Mrs. W[ilson] picked me up and I persuade her to drive with us. Hard
work too. Then get the men who were at some "Chitterling Club"
down south-east. Get lost in Arlington. Finally find [D.C. area phy-
sician] Dr. Holmes' house. Georgia looking like the Tragic Muse
thinking of the little poets she had invited to meet me and how it was
getting on to nine o'clock. Good highballs and I get in two games of
"500" with Mrs. Holmes and a weird soul. Get lost leaving there, but
finally reach Georgia's at 9:45. She and I make explanations. A near-
high [?] bunch. Willis Richardson and his wife, the most interesting
and little John Davis. Much poetry and discussion and salad and wine
and tea and Bobbo rescues me at midnight. . . .

## Friday, July 29

Incidental meals, heat, and my annual summer attack of squeamishness are wearing down my morale. Stay at the house and work on
clippings all day. About to eat dinner, when a lot of Elks and Daughters come in, looks as if dinner is to be indefinitely delayed, so go
down town, bawl Bobbo out, and get a chance meal at Thurston's.
Then I go down to the Broadway and see a cracker-jack picture—
"Slide Kelley Slide," all about baseball, and it takes my mind off my
woes. . . .

. . . Put in time at office reading papers, until Manning Jones
chases me out with his crazy declarations of love. Hide in drug store
across street.

Bobbo and I go to Broadway to see John Barrymore in "Don Juan."
Wonderfully worth while. Get back to house and see the New York

fellows, who are guests of Dr. Holmes of Arlington. One of them is a
Dr. Thompson, a well-to-do physician of Mt. Vernon, New York. He
turns out to be George Thompson, of the class of '93, at Straight. . . .
We have a great get-together. Bobbo is being groomed for secretary to
succeed Bates, and is quite anxious about it. Pleased when I know any
of the brethern. I honestly don't think he has a Chinaman's chance,
but $4000 a year is well worth making the fight for. . . .

### Tuesday, August 2

 . . . Coolidge electrifies the world and starts the biggest contro-
versy in history with ten words. "I do not choose to be a candidate in
1928.". . .

### Thursday, August 4

Chilly enough for a coat. Tessa and I go down town and I buy a
dress at Landsburgh's. At least lay it away and have it fitted. Don't
know where the money is coming from. Dig up some figures in Library
of Congress for speech. Go to N[orth] E[ast] Federation meeting and
speak. . . . Mollie Terrell catty, as usual. . . .

### Saturday, August 6

Put in a thirteen hour day. Finish the address book, then help
Mrs. F[inley Wilson] file letters. Very unsystematic and unbusiness-
like methods. Wasted energy and lost motion. . . .
Bobbo and Mrs. F. get off on the midnight excursion train for
New York. Bobbo must needs show himself among "the boys" in New
York in the interest of his Grand Secretarial candidacy. . . .

### Monday, August 8

Two new books in the mail—Cullen's "Copper Sun" and "Black
Cameos." Also some dunning letters and notice of note due in bank.
Put in day at the office, producing literature. Do a free verse poem,
"The Proletariat Speaks"—on the smells and sordidness about me—
which I send to "Mercury." And the beginnings of my articles for
A.N.P.—"Excursions" etc.
 . . . To the Lincoln to see a rotten picturization of "Soundings"
(Hamilton Gibbs). This trash played by Lois Moran was called "The
Whirlwind of Youth," and Gibbs should lynch the producer. . . .

## Tuesday, August 9

Tessa [Connelly] has some wild idea of going to see Carl Phillips, head of Bureau of Conciliation [where Georgia Douglas Johnson works], about going to Moscow. The Sacco-Vanzetti case has the air pregnant with the Third Internationale and echoes of the bombs of the proletariat girdle the globe. Carl Phillips is pleasant; he and Georgia give us the hour graciously while I look at photos and read reports and listen to advice from Phillips to let the Communists alone. Georgia and I discuss the Bethune banquet, which she had attended in New York the night before. Phillips drives Tessa and me home. Puts me on the front seat with him and takes Tessa home first. . . .

## Wednesday, August 10

Bobbo and I have a honeymoon breakfast at the house. . . .
    . . . To the [Washington *Eagle*[ office intending to finish my story for the *World*. But write 13 letters instead and suffer from acidosis. Stay late and go home with Bobbo. . . .

*In this entry, D-N and friends present themselves to be initiated into a Temple of the Daughter Elks, sister organization to the male IBPOE (Elks). Because of petty resentment and "secret society" technicalities, they are refused. The following week (August 17), D-N is admitted by a different chapter, which makes her eligible for the higher degrees conferred at the national convention.*

## Saturday, August 13

    . . . Night came, and time to go to Fairmount. "Utility white dresses" said Mrs. Trammell, so had Mrs. Wilson purchase a Hoover apron for me. So equipped, Tessa, Mrs. Jones and I . . . hie us to Fairmount, where after a seance with the doctor, Mrs. J. emerged with her certificate.
    The hall typically Negroid. The women likewise. We waited with nine other candidates down stairs, after we had waited upstairs, and surprised hostile glances at us. Poor Mrs. Trammell non grata. Some technicality of the law. The other nine taken up. We did not take our dismissal lightly. We protested. There was a "fending and proving." To no avail. Neither Mrs. Trammell's tears, nor Daughter Estelle's orations, nor the defiant speech of the little dish face cockeyed soul.

We sat below in isolation until 11:30 when Mrs. Jones' brother came. Mrs. Trammell devastated. The others indifferent. "Dicties coming out from town to tell them how to run their Temple!"

Sorry for Tessa. She had given up a job at the Country Club, and lost money thereby. Bobbo said they were right. Mrs. Wilson properly indignant.

### Sunday, August 14

Bobbo and I ready to go to Wilmington early. . . . Glad to get home. Looks good to me. The month at Washington fades into an inconsequential nightmare. . . .

### Tuesday, August 16

. . . Do a peroration for Finley's speech and send Bobbo. Minnie [Stevens, Dr. Stevens' widow, who is becoming neurotic] in at bed time, as usual, with her hard luck stories. . . .

### Wednesday, August 17

. . . At night—ten o'clock present myself at the "Elk's Home" for this initiation. Add considerably to my store of knowledge, including why an Elk's eye is red and what eleven o'clock means. I am properly initiated, at the expense of my nerves, and succeed in getting my "Degrees"—three of them, all there are, so that I can get the "Grand Lodge Degrees" next week in New York. How surprised all those catty Columbia and Fairmount Temple Daughters will be! . . .

*Emma J. Sykes, whose husband was a dentist, was an active Wilmington woman who worked with John Hopkins and usually held small political jobs. From this point on, D-N frequently placed numbers bets with her.*

### Thursday, August 18

. . . Learn . . . that Emma is a "Number" agent. So after writing a half dozen letters, all but one being about school affairs, put on my things and go over to her house. My store of knowledge is still further increased. I learn the ins and outs of the scheme, and let myself in for a dollar and a quarter, variously placed on 29 numbers. If I win, I'll win big. If I lose,—I'll be running true to form.

But I shall stick until I make a killing. . . .

*Here D-N coins a term for Black people, Senegambians, a tele-scoping perhaps of Senegal and Gambia. During this week in New York City, D-N is attending the national convention of the Elks, the fraternal organization for which Bobbo works. She also engages in a hectic round of socializing—principally for pleasure, but also with an eye for possible business and professional opportunities.*

### Saturday, August 20

Get the 9:48 (standard) and find Tessa [Connelly, her Washington, D.C. friend] on it surrounded by Senegambians in all stages of eating. So we take a parlor car in peace. Reach New York in time, taxi to the Y.W. and after a bit are settled. Then begin "bumming." . . .

### Sunday, August 21

An unsatisfactory breakfast. Then we start out looking for a "hot" Spanish shawl. With a Miss (sounded like Wilstock) we go next door and find a weird exotic apartment, all padded and quilted and tapes-tried and incensed, with teak and ebony, jade and soapstone things, and colored shades—a bit of Orient. The mistress of this place was out but a maid showed us things—none looked good to me. No shawl. Then way down 137th Street to squalid apartment house, and a crowded family and harried lady who sold hats. Didn't look as good to me as some fresh ones in the stores. So back to the exotic apartment. The mistress—a little wizened brown soul, young but haggard, in. Miss W[ilstock] chaffered. Tessa and I were cold. She talked in terms of a hundred dollars for shawls. I laughed. . . .

To St. Mark's Church for Pan-African meeting. . . . Very tire-some. A list of speakers from here to Africa. . . . We left after the man from the Bahamas had talked. . . . Home with Mrs. Miller and a high ball—then to Violet Wilson's for dinner, with Miss Irwin. A lovely dinner—good eats and liquor. We leave about eight. Tramp down 7th Avenue. See Bobbo. See everyone in the world. Tessa looking for someone to give her a large evening. Call on her [friend] "Sol John-son." Nobody home. Go to Julia Coleman to see Violet. [Arthur] Schomburg [West Indian bibliophile whose donation to the New York Public Library became the famous Schomburg Collection] there and lots of others. Some good gin. Sell two subscriptions, one to Vi, one to Schomburg. Out again tramping here and there, hither and yon, running into people—Countee Cullen among others. Finally at mid-night Tessa gave up and agreed to come in. I guess she had a disap-pointing time.

Personally I don't like to work so hard. My feet hurt from tramp-ing.

### Monday, August 22

Today is the day Sacco-Vanzetti are to die, every means of respite having failed. Well, I'll ride in no subways. If I am to be bombed, it must be in the open air. Early breakfast and down to Bloomingdale's via surface car. . . . Find a hat for myself on Broadway. $12.50, but get it for ten. It's worth it. I love to buy hats! To Billy Pierce's [popular New York dance teacher and Broadway choreographer] and see some actresses going through their paces, have a long talk with Billy and acquire a sealed quart of Bacardi rum and so up on the bus. . . . Tessa and I do some golddigging. One Milles of Richmond, staying at the Hotel Dumas has good Canadian Club in his room. We come to the "Y" for the Pan-African reception. See all the high-brows and have a lovely time. . . .

### Tuesday, August 23

. . . When I went back to "Y," to dress for Grand Temple stuff, found Mrs. Rose and Mrs. Badson and a telegram to [from?] Leila saying that Sheriff Poole had been to house and inventoried things and what should she do. Brought on an attack of high blood pressure at once, which kept me uncomfortable all evening. Go to Mt. Salem Church and sit there from 6 until eleven. Get all the mummery of the "Grand Temple" degrees off. . . . Home. Write convention arti-cle for *Eagle* and addenda to Leila's letter asking about the sheriff—go out to mail them. 1:20 a.m. find Edgar Still to buy me a bromo seltzer and lend me a stamp, and so home to suffer from what tries to be a stroke. . . .

## Wednesday, August 24

Tessa and I have an early breakfast with [Recorder of Deeds] Froe at the lovely little St. Luke Dining Room. Then I go down town to investigate the rumor of teachers needed. By the time I have batted around, found the Board of Education, interviewed various clerks and found the rumor unfounded, filed for exams etc., it is noon. Drop into *Opportunity* [magazine office], have luncheon with Noah Thompson at a H.[orn] and H.[ardart] cafeteria on 5th Avenue. . . .

## Thursday, August 25

Decide to stick around today and try to help Bobbo's candidacy [for the Elks Grand Secretaryship]. He's so confident of election. Of course Finley [Wilson, the Elks Grand Exalted Ruler and his boss] will pull him through, he thinks. Talk with John Hall, Will Purnell, Algernon Jackson [all Elk brothers]. They don't sound good to me. "Too many offices in the *Eagle*." Bobbo still confident. . . . [I] Get nervous as night progresses. Try to take nap. Tessa suggests curling our hair. In shampoo parlor and hear cheers and yells. Hurry to street and hear the whole administration has been re-elected. . . . Poor Bobbo! It makes me sick for him. Poor, poor trusting, optimistic Bobbo! I hate to face him.

We go down to midnight show. Geraldyn [Dismond, attractive New York society woman, whose husband was a medical doctor] had left passes to orchestra seats for us. I love *Africana* chiefly because of Ethel Waters. She's loveable. Geraldyn introduces us to her and she's lovely to meet. She sings *everything* on request even "Elie, Elie" in Hebrew. I would like to know her.

Taxi to Geraldyn's home, with its quaint built in beds and have a high ball, which quite spiflicates us, but doesn't seem to bother her or her aunt, Mrs. Laurence.

Drop into the chop suey place for a sobering dish, and see Froe and Harry Jones passing by. Get them in. They are cussing, popping, furious. Bobbo had been double-crossed. Sold out. I had suspected as much. Finley in conference with Perry Howard, Houston, Bates, Carter and all, had decided to let the steam roller crush Bobbo and save the administration. Poor George Benson had not been allowed even to place Bobbo in nomination. Ruled out of order. Bobbo led up to the slaughter and Finley did it.

We all cuss ourselves blue in the face. Froe certainly likes Bobbo.
I write a note to the *News* asking that my letter be killed and Harry
agrees to put it in the box. Why should *I* boost Finley's administration? Home by 5:10 a.m. Can't sleep for hurt rage!

*D-N devoted one of her A.N.P. "Little Excursions" columns
(Washington* Eagle, *September 9, 1927) to Sol Johnson, who was
formerly from Washington, D.C. and had been an Ellis Island immi-
gration official for the past twenty-four years. (One cannot help but
wonder what he could have achieved—with his personality and command of six languages—had he not been Black.) In it, she tells an
anecdote of his putting a scared Italian family at ease by joking with
them in their dialect and playing with their little boy. The piece was
reprinted in* Heebie Jeebies (?): America's News Magazine *(Chicago),
September 10, 1927.*

*Roscoe Conkling Bruce had recently been named to head a Rock-
efeller Foundation project for Blacks. Its details had not yet been completely unveiled, but a major part of it was a 541-apartment, 2,000-
person cooperative housing idea (Washington* Eagle, *September 9,
1927).*

## Friday, August 26

Can't sleep, so rise, bathe and downstairs. See Bobbo across street
and run over to him. He plainly was *not* trying to see me. I greeted
him with, "So that dirty little gutter-snipe double-crossed you?" Bobbo's head up and his arrogant, "Who do you mean?" "Finley"—"Oh,
no, it wasn't Finley, it was the other fellows." But I soon had witnesses
to prove the secret coalition. Bobbo's reaction was a cold fury, and
shortly he excused himself to go into the convention. . . .

Hurry back to "Y" to pick up Tessa, race for "L" to Battery, chase
after the 2:45 ferry for Ellis Island.

Arrived at the immigrant place . . . met by "Sol Johnson." I have
not seen him for 30 years. Very fascinating to watch him handling
cases of immigrants and their hopeful escorts; to hear his easy fluency
in a half dozen languages. Got out of his uniform at last and back on
the ferry to New York. Taxi to East 12th Street in the Italian section
to "John's" and have a *perfect* dinner. I mean perfect. . . .

Then uptown to "Mac's" place—a lovely little restaurant—another
high ball. Mac, who looks like Belasco sobering up from a two week

jag. We went to talk business [the details of which remain unclear], so up in the "Club" in a back room where we go over his business proposition—Mac, Tessa and I while Sol sleeps. Looks good to me, though Tessa was the one he wanted. Sol awakes when I suggest my terms $75 a week guaranteed for three months. We decide to meet tomorrow and go over it again.

Tessa and I home in the rain. It is eleven o'clock. Bobbo had called twice. I try to get him on the phone. Tessa and I talk over our business ideas—her dress plan, *my* ad. scheme. Tomorrow I'm going after Roscoe Bruce and see what I can do for Bobbo. I hate to think of his going back to the *Eagle* for that dirty little gutter snipe.

## Saturday, August 27

Before I can get dressed, Bobbo here to breakfast with me. I have only a cup of coffee in the cafeteria with him, while he tries to explain away Finley's treachery. Then when he goes to the convention, Tessa and I proceed by taxi, as it is raining, as usual, *always* cold and rain-ing—to Roscoe Bruce's place. A ground floor office and here we see Roscoe, fat and portly and happy with his life-time position of $12,000 a year, and little seventeen year old Burrell at a desk, and soon Carrie, his wife, still limping from her elevator accident, but wearing her Phi Beta Kappa and a smile of satisfaction over her $3600 position, and Clara, the senior in Radcliffe, at a desk too. What luck! And Carrie just refused a settlement of $50,000 for her accident! We talk over Roscoe's plant, the wonderful Rockefeller foundation, which he is to run for life! I ask for a job for Bobbo. Of course, there is none there. *Of course.* . . .

Dinner at Craigs . . . Sol comes in and we go to his house. Send a boy in a taxi for Bobbo and soon he and Emmett Scott [D-N's old boyfriend, now of Howard University] come and then over four bottles of champagne and imported gin and rye we cuss out Finley—though Bob is still loyal, bless his heart.

Home by nine thirty, sleep and arise, dress and to Mrs. Sidney's reception over her Venetian tea room. . . .

## Sunday, August 28

. . . Bobbo decides not to go at five. He and Harry Jones come in. He tells me all privately about this "Civil Liberties Commission" which is being cooked up to placate him at $2500 a year. I listen and argue—

poor boy. I hate it, but $2500 is a good addition to $1200 and if they want his good will, let them pay for it.

. . . Dinner at the Venetian. Here we [D-N, Tessa, Lena Holsey, one of their conventioning friends] are joined by Mr. Holsey. I am afraid of him. His wife beats women about him.

I have to leave them at table to meet Bobbo at nine o'clock. So we get off in the driving rain and get the 9:40 (8:40) for home. . . .

## Thursday, September 1

. . . Finished George Moore's Memoirs of Dead Life and returned it to Reilly. He offered me Boccaccio, but I said I had it. Told me to let him have "anything good," meaning literary pornography. . . .

*In this entry,* Laurence Theodore Young, *D-N's only nephew (born 1901), gets married to* Rebecca Lee Murphy, *of the Baltimore Afro-American newspaper family. Because he was away from home, he seldom appears in the diary. Directly after graduating from Howard High School, he attended Wilberforce Commercial College, Ohio, and then Ohio Univeristy, Athens, Ohio, where he received a B.A. degree in commerce in 1925. He then spent one year at Howard University, Washington, D.C., as Emmett J. Scott's secretary. After he and Rebecca married, they settled in Chicago where Laurence earned a Doctor of Jurisprudence degree in 1932 from the Chicago Law School. Their two children,* Laurence Jr. *and* Gracie, *were born between 1928 and 1932.*

## Saturday, September 3

Mama is up at three, but is coaxed by Ethel to go back to bed. But she gets us up a bit after six anyhow. . . .

Reach Baltimore finally—taxi to house—1741 Druid Hill—where all is confusion, bridesmaids dressing all over the place, Rebecca calling for us to see her . . . , Leila needing help in getting into her things, Pauline paralyzed into inaction, presents arriving, Robert and Mr. Murphy [Rebecca's father] in the library looking solemn. And finally time to go to church. . . . Laurence and Jordan enter the chancel, both very pale and very clean.

On the minute of 11:15 (standard) the organ pealed, "I Love You

Truly." On the minute of 11:58 it began the Lohengrin march. On the minute of 12 the lovely bridal party reached the altar and grouped itself like a beautiful pageant of flowers and pretty dresses and the bride's shimmering gown and veil. Quite the most beautiful wedding I ever saw. And then after the conventional "O Promise Me" and the vows and all, the Mendelssohn march and Rebecca clinging triumphantly to Laurence's arm, both tall and slender, he pale and stern, she looking as if she was saying, "I have him; now touch him if you dare!" Connie [Rebecca's sister] weeping, unrestrainedly, her maid of honor bouquet drooping; Pauline sniffling, and the two little boys, William and Houston, giving way to unrestrained grief—and the wedding was over and Baltimore drew a deep breath.

Then to the house, to stand on line for several hours, to grin and shake hands, and look at Baltimore's dowdy frumps as they filed by feeling stylish; to eat hungrily of chicken salad and ice cream, to get the bride sent off properly from the station, whither we went in a caravan of hooting cars, Laurence's traditionally tied up with signs and white ribbons and tin cans; and the station a mess of pounds and pounds of rice and noise and jollification, and finally off on the Twentieth Century Limited. And so back to the house, and Bobbo and I take the train to Wilmington, leaving Mama, Leila, Ethel and Pauline and the bags to come home in the flivver. . . . We get some dinner, the others get in about ten, and soon all are asleep and exhausted.

## Sunday, September 4

Everybody floppy. . . . Call from Philadelphia in the afternoon from Sammons, the Thermocomb Man. He begins babbling about a business proposition. . . . I cut him short by saying that if he wanted to talk business I'd see him in Philadelphia. Called Bobbo to phone. We agreed to meet him. We were in West Philadelphia station by four thirty. He met us in his run about, drove us all over parks, parkway, out Norristown way, unfolding his scheme, which is a good one. Opening shops for selling of women's suits, coats, dresses, etc.—as he has unlimited credit with Kolinsky, a wholesaler—and by advertising that ten per cent of the profit goes to charity—saving women and girls, as Sammons grandiloquently puts it,—making a big bid for business. His details were fascinating. . . .

Bobbo and I home by 11:30, full of the scheme, which is to spell deliverance for me from the school room.

## Monday, September 5

Sammons telephoned early for us to come up and see Kolinsky, the wholesale dealer. . . . Have an illuminating interview with Kolinsky, short, fat, typically Jewish, and with his assistant. We all part enthusiastic over the business we are to do—only I have my misgivings when I get a close-up of Sammons' suit, which is pitifully thread-bare and worn. . . .

*Apparently, nothing came of these meetings with Sammons and Kolinsky for, in this entry, D-N is once again beginning her fall teaching at the Industrial School.*

## Tuesday, September 6

Bobbo takes the 4:53 train, and the awaking in time for it, keeps me awake most of the night. Make him some coffee, though I do not drink any myself, as I go back to bed and to sleep. Decide, as I am so fat that I'll go out to school on the bus mornings, so as to get some exercise. I think this is pleasing to Pauline. So up, dress, get the 8:15 bus and my year's work begins.

I have 44 children in NINE grades. I look at them despairingly, arrange my books, classify, grade, and plan a program. . . .

## Thursday, September 8

. . . Get mail—a letter from Miss Hawse at the "Y" in New York [where she stayed] telling me both my checks were bad—the three dollar one on my bank, and the $25.00 one from the Washington *Eagle*. Almost made me have a stroke. I don't like to get as angry as that. Seems like no matter where I go, if I have a pleasant time, there is always a nasty afterclap of bad checks following me. . . .

I wrote Bobbo a scorching letter taking him to task for allowing the *Eagle* and Finley Wilson to make him the goat in the business. . . .

## Saturday, September 10

. . . We go down to hunt up Bobbo, meet two trains [from Washington], and he is not on them, but finally comes in about 10:30.

Gruff over my letter, but sneakingly meek and depressed. We make up, however.


### Sunday, September 11

. . . Bobbo has some kind of Past Exalted Rulers' Council of which he is Chief Antler. This followed by a dinner given by the "Daughters" at the Tent Hall. I get in in time for dessert, and everyone gives me an ovation. Afterwards, Bobbo and I walk down Market street, look at the decorations in honor of the Tri-State White Elks, and window shop generally. He leaves at 10:23 for [his job in] Washington. . . .


### Monday, September 12

. . . School all readjusted now. Program working splendidly. So am I. No sick woman's job.

Bowse comes over at night and we play bridge. Afterwards I produce literature. Leslie [P. Hill] wrote that he wanted a formal application for that [Friends American Inter-Racial Peace Committee] field secretaryship. I sent him one, with specifications. . . .


### Tuesday, September 13

These hot days and damp, chill nights give me the heebie-jeebies, or malaria, I'm not sure which. I know I am tired and languid. Lovely letter from Sol Johnson. Lovely letters last week from Roscie Bruce, and Charles H. Johnson [of the Urban League] and Jim Johnson. Lots of irons in the fire—but where is the deliverance from my House of Bondage? . . .


### Wednesday, September 14

And now all the excitement is to get Myrtle Robbins [apparently of the Girls Industrial School] off to Nannie Burroughs' school [the National Training School for Women, Washington, D.C.]—if it can be done. There are so many obstacles in the way that it looks like a Herculanean task. . . .

*Here D-N is speaking for some sort of political rally in Chester,
Pennsylvania. The entry spiritedly shows her anger at Alexander, the
organizer who engaged her, for his sexist devaluing of her participation—anger that spills onto J. Finley Wilson for a similar offense.*

## Thursday, September 15

. . . Alexander buzzing around. Fair-sized audience and a mess
of candidates. I make a cracker-jack speech. All about vice in Chester.
And that tight-wad of an Alexander pats me on the back with some
well-done Girlie stuff. When I talk money, he looks vague. Promises
a check. I insist upon cash. Ducks behind—no check book. I'm through
with Aleck. That's twice he's buncoed me. Chauffeur wants me to go
to Darby [Pennsylvania] Monday night—but I'm too mad, when I get
in the house at one o'clock to think straight.

Shortly after got in telephone rung. Finley calling up from New
York asking me to get flowers for Benson's [apparently an Elk brother]
funeral for him. To spend about $25.00. And that makes me mad,
too. The nerve of all these little men! . . .

## Friday, September 23

. . . Mrs. Samuel Bancroft [a white woman] mailed me her check
for $250—for Myrtle Robbins' expenses for the year. Shall deposit it
to-morrow. . . .

*Although the precise identity of these characters is not known, D-
N's account of them is interesting because it documents her frequently
voiced tenderness for children.*

## Sunday, October 2

King Watkins and his little [6-year-old nephew] Charlie Johnson
had been at church and Sunday School all day—so he [Watkins] goes
out after we get home, leaving Charlie in bed. Poor kid gets lonesome
and frightened, so we [she and Bobbo] take him in our bed. He clings
to my neck the rest of the night.

Finley said at breakfast that he "never double-crossed a friend." I
got it. . . .

D-N makes this trip and boat ride the subject of her "Little Excursions" column, Washington Eagle, October 21, 1927. Her focal point is the ridiculousness of the segregation that begins in Maryland. Often D-N's daily experiences were directly translated into these articles. Compare, for instance, this excerpt from the column with the diary entry:

> It was a gorgeous moonlight and sunset scene the other night, a three hours sail of breath-taking beauty across the Chesapeake, with a bit of an excursion into the Atlantic. And the forward end of the boat was the preferred place to enjoy the loveliness of sunset and moon rise. Therefore, the white passengers, many of them, came and sat among the colored passengers, and "Oh'd and Ah'd" at the scene. The captain descended from his eyrie and sat at the side of some of his dusky passengers and commented upon the beautiful evening. It was the preferred place, temporarily, and Nordic superiority did not disdain to reach out for the prize.

### Friday, October 7

This is the day to go to Portsmouth, Virginia to read for the Rev. Dr. Dance. . . . At Salisbury . . . betook my place meekly in the Jim Crow section of the boat. Such a gorgeous three hour ride on the Chesapeake and into a nice swell of the Atlantic sunset. Great black clouds. Then wonderful. Clear, lovely. The captain even grows sentimental in the lovely night and tries to be "fresh.". . .

### Sunday, October 9

Have a hectic day what with straining off my grape wine and hunting through the cellar for letters of Paul Dunbar in order to get an autograph for Carl Van Vechten. . . .

D-N had already commented favorably on James W. Johnson's novel The Autobiography of an Ex-Colored Man, mentioned below, in her September 2 "As In A Looking Glass" column.

### Monday, October 10

. . . Lockridge says no word of my absence Friday, so I know she knows I was lying when I sent word I had indigestion. . . . Do the review of Autobiography of [an] Ex-Col.[ored] Man for Opportunity and get it off. Due on the 11th.

## Tuesday, October 11

. . . Entertain the Bridgets [her Wilmington bridge club]. Give them a gorgeous supper of shrimp salad, [?] and butter sandwiches, punch with [?] in it, figs with whipped cream and saltines. Warmer and more pleasant.

*D-N, like everyone else who knew* Clarissa Scott Delaney *(b. 1901), considered her early death a tragedy. Emmett Scott's daughter, she had taught at the Dunbar High School in Washington and was a poet (published in Cullen's* Caroling Dusk*). She had quit teaching and married* Hubert Delaney *in the fall of 1926.*

## Wednesday, October 12

At school mostly getting ready for the matinee. . . . See a baby snake. When I come back to kill it—gone. We go on the bus more or less hecticly. Thurston [nationally known magician] at his usual tricks. Bore me to tears, but I like to see the children's enjoyment. . . .

Bobbo's letter fills me with sadness. *Clarissa Scott died* yesterday. It made me faint when I read it. Wrote them at once. . . .

*Here D-N is attending the Fall Conference of the secretaries and advisors of the Girl Reserves of the Middle Atlantic States at Camp Arcola, Pennsylvania. One hundred fifteen women (nine Black) gathered for "lectures, conferences, round table discussions, songs, information, psychology, methods, ways and means" ("Little Excursions," St. Louis* Argus, *October 28, 1927). All of the women mentioned are Girl Reserves conferees.*

## Friday, October 14

We lose our way at Collegeville, [Pa.] but finally after panning the brake in a farm yard and getting it unjammed by me with a stone, reach Camp Arcola. Here a clutter of people surging around Emily Brown on a huge stone porch, with a paper busily assigning people to rooms up on the second floor of the immense barn. Mrs. "T. T." [Williams] and I are in Aubride [?] No. 13 and find that we are to be with a Miss Payne and a Miss Hill, neither of whom came that night. We grab the blankets from their bed.

Supper proves a lovely meal, then up on third floor of barn to the Assembly room where there is an open fire. In spite of it, the cold is ghastly. Miss Ann Rice—too sticky sweet—lectures. Then is a song led by Annie Gilbert—barely fighting middle age. Then wash up in the washroom—across the walk—a chilly process—and to bed.

A very cold and miserable night. Dawn to bird song and activities way up above our heads under the eaves and rafters. . . .

### Sunday, October 16

. . . Joined a camp fire crowd on the Perkiomen [River] bank, and seated on an up-turned boat, read "Dusty Answer" and revel in the lovely sun-soaked landscape. Dinner. More psychology. The lecturer appears to be a kid. Tea. Lovely cakes and things on the porch at 4:30. Then start home and reach there at 6:45. A gorgeous drive. And so ends two practically perfect days. . . .

. . . *My horoscope here* [home in the mail].

### Monday, October 17

Pouring rain. Glad it held off Saturday and Sunday. Go to see Ethel Barrymore in "The Constant Wife." *Soul satisfying*—that's what. She is more like me than ever. Worth standing out in the rain to crash a seat. . . .

### Wednesday, October 19

. . . Go to Howard School and meet my group (Dramatic) of the Girl Reserves. Big crowd in spite of the rain. I plan and start a "Hiawatha" play. . . .

### Thursday, October 20

. . . Still studying my horoscope. It is worth $15.00. Evangeline P[?]ams knows her onions. Glad I got it. It has helped me to realize the futility of my bitter cravings and strugglings and foolish hopes. . . .

### Friday, October 21

. . . I come home and take up my plants, potting them, making a hanging vine basket in the library, clean the latter room and my own etc. etc. A very profitable holiday for me. . . .

*Cheyney Day was "a fair held under the auspices of the Cheyney
Community League, which represented the extension service of the
Cheyney Training School for Teachers. It was a movement for a progressive Negro citizenship in which the students of the school join
with the colored people of the neighborhood in working out community problems" (Washington* Eagle, *October 28, 1927).* James W.
Johnson, *executive secretary of the NAACP, was one of the speakers.
Also on the program this year was* Madame Lillian Evanti, *a colora-
tura soprano from Washington, D.C.*

### Saturday, October 22

Cheyney Day . . . It was a perfect day—with nothing to mar either
the beauty of the weather or the genial pleasure. [Leslie Pinkney] Hill
a bit flustered in his too evident desire to play up to Bob and me. I
guess his conscience hurts him about that Field Secretaryship. I never
so much as betrayed by the flicker of an eyelash that I cared. Jim
[Johnson] was adorable. Narka [Lee-Rayford, one of her Washington,
D.C. friends] came with Lillian Evanti. Home by midnight. It was a
lovely day.

### Sunday, October 23

. . . Bobbo and I play poker in the bed. . . .

### Monday, October 31

Mama develops a fit of temperament. I forgot to open her door
last night before going to bed—so she said she almost choked to death
and was ill—certainly wasn't going to get up and wait on "my company." . . .

### Thursday, November 3

. . . I resigned last night from the Dramatic Unit of the H.H.S.
[Howard High School] Girl Reserves. Too much work. Patsy [Mama]
still temperamental. . . .

### Thursday, November 10

Get off on the 8:19 for Milford where the State Teachers' Association is meeting. . . . Carter Woodson [historian and founder of the

Association for the Study of Negro Life and History] disappoints for the night session. With my husky voice I read one of the sermons from [J. W. Johnson's] "God's Trombones," the one about Noah. Quite a hit. And read [her own poem] "Cano" for an encore. . . .

### Saturday, November 12

Feel sort of let down today and don't get much done. Bowse in and we play two games of pinochle. Go to see Dr. Murray about this lightness and vertigo but he knows nothing about it. . . .

*It seems that D-N has written a somewhat controversial editorial relevant to the D.C. schools in the Washington* Eagle. *The manner in which she shrugs off the reactions suggests that by now she does not harbor any expectations of ever teaching in Washington.*

### Tuesday, November 15

. . . Letter from Bobbo. His interview with Wilk [Garnet Wilkinson] nothing much. Wilk was shrewd enough not to lug me in. Seems that Perry Howard thought the editorial fine—and one Hayden Johnson, of the school board, was panicky. Oh, well. I don't want to teach anyhow, so we may as well go on and have fun. . . .

### Sunday, November 20

. . . Special from Robert telling about his luncheon with Wilkinson, the shrewd, and how cleverly did Wilk manipulate matters to put Bobbo and the *Eagle* in the wrong for the editorial. Couldn't do anything for me now—would seem like coercion. Very clever Wilk. Bobbo and I are but suckling babes in his clever scheme to keep his place. I am the pawn in his clever game. . . .

### Friday, November 25

[In Washington, D.C.] Skinner drives me out to Nannie Burroughs' school in that fearsome car of his—"Crispus Attucks' News Service." See Myrtle [Robbins, from the Industrial School]—but school is in session, so can't bring her in town. Slip her a dollar. Look around and leave. . . .

### Saturday, November 26

A quiet morning [in Washington]. Then Mrs. B.[urroughs] and I go down to the National [Theater] to see Otis Skinner, Mrs. Fiske and Henrietta Crosman in "The Merry Wives of Windsor." A most notable production. Almost historical and mighty well done. Otis Skinner a rollicking Falstaff and Crosman a delightful Mistress Ford. But Mrs. Fiske inclined to rant and too obviously and pointedly kittenish—heavy. Made me think of Hallie Q. Brown [her associate and a nationally prominent clubwoman]. Age *does* tell. Yet that last lovely scene where the elves and fairies dance—and then these three, these ancient three, play a ring-a-round rosy is worth all the memories of youth. . . .

### Wednesday, November 30

. . . Wondering if the check I gave Nannie Burroughs for Myrtle will be protested. [It later was.] Horrors! I am cold and sick inside at the thought. I could not have made such a hideous mistake in subtraction. Well the horoscope warned me in October about spending too freely. . . . It's a mess. I've been just about two hundred dollars behind the game for over thirty years. And it's flicking on raw nerves now.

However—went to see "Bless You, Sister" at the Playhouse with Polly. . . .

*The kind of contemporary reading that D-N does this Saturday afternoon was used as raw material for her "As In A Looking Glass" articles. In her next (Friday, December 12) column, she mentions the following: a review of "Porgy" in* Outlook; *a story, "Rose Hill," in the* Yale Review; *an article, "Teaching Art to the Talented Student," by George Oscar Carrington, Howard art teacher, in* School Arts Magazine; *an article on Gary, Indiana, school segregation in* School and Society; *an article on Central Africa in* The Living Age; *a poorly written article on Blacks in* The Southern Workman; *an article saying Blacks are not biologically inferior by a University of North Dakota assistant professor of sociology in the* American Journal of Sociology; *and an article on African folk medicine, "The Savage as Scientist," in the November* Golden Book.

## Saturday, December 3

. . . Got home—after shopping for the school at Butler's [stationery store] and boning up on contemporary magazines at the [Wilmington public] library. . . .

## Sunday, December 4

Awake to the driving of sleet, hail and snow against windows. A blizzard rages all day. A lovely day to be at home and secure within warm walls, with good food, and comfort. We four, Mama, Leila, Pauline and I and Jack alone all day. A lovely day. Sweet, secure. And yet I think of poor Bobbo, alone and batting out in the storm for his food. Poor Bobbo!

*A young, energetic Black woman from New England,* Crystal Bird *had come to Philadelphia and eventually secrued a position with the Friends Service Committee. D-N looked back to this evening for her final "As In A Looking Glass" column for the year (December 30, 1927). She wrote:*

> And some of us dumb ones are still wondering what the "Inner Spiritual Significance of Negro Spirituals" as projected by the American Friends Interracial Peace Committee has to do with Interracial, International Peace. With all Europe an armed camp, and Asia in the throes of a conflict that threatens to spread into Europe, with militarism stalking abroad as haughtily as it did in 1912–13, the Prince of Peace knows that we need the thought of peace hammered home into the heart of the world as never before. For the next war will make the frightfulness of the last one seem like children playing with harmless sparklers. Therefore, we need no dallying with pretty words, but cold, bitter, hard facts on the waste and futility and terror of international conflicts. Dilletantism has no place on the program of 1928.

## Monday, December 5

. . . Hurry home to produce literature early—so as to be ready to go to the Unitarian church to hear Crystal Bird. . . . A good crowd out. Crystal Bird—who [Dunbar-Nelson mistakenly believes] got the job I wanted—talking on "The Inner Significance of Negro Spirituals." Talking pleasantly—by collating all the introductions of all the

books of Negro spirituals. And singing—very badly. Now what that
has to do with Inter-racial International Peace, I know not. Dope for
aged Quaker ladies. . . .

## Wednesday, December 7

. . . Charley Avery meets us [in Durham, N.C., for the "Fact-
Finding and Stock-Taking Conference" on Blacks in America], and
takes Georgia [Douglas Johnson] and me in charge. . . . We are put
together at the very palatial home of the Scarboroughs [with whom
they boarded]. Most gorgeous place. (But the meals are always cold,
we find out later.) Snow degenerates to slush. We go down town. . . .
Pleasant to see so many folks. It looks as if everyone is here. After
session, go downstairs in one of the offices and get out my A.N.P.
[Associated Negro Press] release, which Ormes [of the A.N.P.] wires
to Chicago for me. To our home, rest and have one of those cold,
funeral meals. Scarborough's wife is the second one, young and scared
in all this magnificence, with a lovely 8 month old baby which Scarborough worships. . . .

Very peppy night session. [Howard University president] Mordecai
Johnson especially good.

Georgia elects to walk home with an old flame—President Neale
of some Nashville school. I am swept up by Geraldyn Dismond [her
New York City friend] and Bess Whitted and we go to Martha Merrick
Donnell's. Here we stage a Dutch supper, plenty of liquor, and dance
by the Orthophonic. A jolly gang. . . . It is two when I get home and
have to get both Georgia and Mr. Scarborough out of bed to let me
in. . . .

*The young people mentioned below are Gwendolyn Bennett—
poet and artist, of the Barnes Foundation at Merion, Pennsylvania;
Eugene Corbie—New York law student; Allison Davis—teacher at
Hampton Institute; John P. Davis—head of the publicity department
of Fisk University. In her December 16, 1927 "As In A Looking Glass"
column, which was completely devoted to this "Fact-Finding and Stock-
Taking" conference on Blacks in America, D-N called these youth
"the delight of the conference" who "spoke early, often and late. They
tore the old folks into shreds. They turned the stop light of youthful
intolerance on all the shams and shibboleths, the evasions and com-*

*plexes, of conservatism. It was a joy to watch and listen to them, knowing that they, too, will be conservative twenty years from now, even as most of us were radical twenty years ago."*

The *"distinguished ladies"* are Mary McLeod Bethune—*founder (1872) and president of Bethune-Cookman College, Daytona Beach, Florida;* Charlotte Hawkins Brown—*head of the Palmer Memorial School, Sedalia, N.C.;* Mrs. Benjamin Brawley—*whose husband was a noted Black cultural historian and critic.*

## Friday, December 9

. . . Georgia and I settle with the scared bride—who only charges us $3.00 each. Thanks be. Miss much of morning session—educational part. [W.E.B.] DuBois and I sit back and observe youth (Gwendolyn, Corbie, Allison and John Davis) being radical, and speculate on how long it will be before they are conservative. I am all day trying to write the article Ormes wants. Mrs. Pearson has a luncheon for the distinguished ladies—Mrs. [Mary McLeod] Bethune, Charlotte Hawkins Brown, Mrs. Benjamin Brawley, Georgia and myself. "Luncheon" meaning a most elaborate turkey dinner from cocktail to demitasse! Bethune's bags papered with labels. Back to work and stick at hearing papers, discussions and reports until nearly seven. Then a rush to the station. The article finished by 7:10. A special sleeper for us. Gwendolyn, Georgia and I and eleven men. Leave at 7:55. Jolly party to see us off. . . .

## Saturday, December 10

Arrive Washington at 7:25. Found that Georgia had invited DuBois to share with me that early breakfast. So we taxi up. DuBois wisely suggests that we go marketing. We do and buy cream, butter, eggs, bacon, rolls. Back to Georgia's and after some vicissitudes as to coffee, percolator, etc. get together a breakfast fit for the gods. At least DuB. and I—the cooks—think so.

Warmed and fed and smoked, we separate—after having vainly tried to telephone over Georgia's "temporarily disconnected telephone." I walk to Bobbo's office and surprise him. He is still all full of the Elk's Civil Liberties thing, the politicians milling around because of the meeting of the National Republican Convention.

Seems that Emmett [Scott] had wanted to see me and Bobbo. The latter calls over [the] phone to say that I am in town and in a few minutes a taxi invites Bobbo and me to Howard University and Emmett's office.

Poor Emmett! Shriveled and gray. [His daughter] Clarissa's death hit him hard. But he has a great scheme for making money and Bobbo and I are to be a part of this "National Negro News Service." We discuss ways and means and depart well pleased with ourselves and each other. . . .

## Monday, December 12

Christmas hecticness begins at school. . . . Girl Reserves meeting almost put me in the grave. . . .

## Tuesday, December 20

From now on it's hop, skip and jump. But Polly and I drive to Philadelphia to see "Show Boat." If these mean negresses Leila, Bowse, and Polly, had gotten a ticket Saturday the 10th when they went, as I asked them, I wouldn't have had to pay $3.85 for a seat. . . .

But *Show Boat!* All that was claimed for it. Wonderfully satisfying. Those colored performers fine, though Julius Budson, good as his voice is, always irritates me. . . .

## Wednesday, December 21

Official beginning of winter and shortest day in the year. All too short for me, as I can't seem to get caught up with myself. . . .

## Saturday, December 24

. . . And no croquettes for Christmas from Krusie [her old principal and friend, Edwina B. Kruse]. She has abandoned her custom of the past 35 years! [The wandering] Minnie [Stevens] in and I invite her to dinner.

## Sunday, December 25

Christmas Day! Bobbo says I get a kick out of Christmas. I do. I love it. . . . The Sunday *Star* reproduced my article on Christmas (from the *Eagle*) and Bobbo's editorial on John Thompson [Black Wilmington politician]. . . .

## Wednesday, December 28

. . . Mama and I sit up alone and gossip over old New Orleans days. The Xmas tree lights don't function. My luck. *My* lights *would* go out.

*This entry marks the beginning of D-N's work with the Inter-Racial Peace Committee and spells out the initial terms of her appointment.*

## Thursday, December 29

If I make any resolutions for New Year's, it will be that I will write in my diary *every* day and let not battle, murder, nor sudden death keep me from it. For here I have been for an hour or more writing up my diary since December 16 [?]. Which is a pain. Take the twelve o'clock boat for Philadelphia with Leila. Since it is only 25¢ round trip, thought I could afford to attend Leslie Pinckney Hill's pussy-footing meeting. . . . Few present . . . They had been discussing me and the secretaryship. It seems Crystal [Bird] is not the secretary, after all, but in another branch. The $3000 it seems is problematical after June 1. Hill called me in to another room and seemed to talk money. Then he and [Wilbur K.] Thomas [executive secretary of the American Friends Service Committee] conferred—and then I was offered! Saturdays and part time work. *No pay.* But expenses. After June 1, *perhaps* pay.

I accepted without batting an eyelash. Even in the face of Dr. Thomas' saying they'd rather have a "young college person." Foolish? Perhaps. But something tells me it will pan out Big. Bigger than Emmett's scheme which has filled Bobbo's mind [but eventuated in nothing]. . . .

## Friday, December 30

. . . Funny not a soul has been to see us through the holidays. Not a soul. Night after night we Three Musketeers light up the Christmas tree (I got it fixed tonight) and sit in lonely, silent splendor. No callers. But then Leila and I never go anywhere. . . .

### Saturday, December 31

The last day of 1927. An indifferent year of pleasures and no accomplishments. And I finish my diary in the station awaiting the 9:20 from Washington and Bobbo. . . . And I am very wet. All day I traveled with rain boots and umbrella in the muggy, drizzly, foggy heat and tonight discarded them. And lo, as I stepped from the library— a seeming cloud-burst. Hurried to shelter but legs and feet sopping wet. Finally—in a brief respite—to the trolley. Now I am drying out. Coat in front of radiator—shoes under it—gloves upon it. Stockings rubbed dry on my ankles. Some amused women looking on. I should worry. . . .

And my new mattress finally came. Bobbo and I will christen it together tonight. . . .

Well, 1927 will go. I will write no more, but let the year go its way. Bobbo and I will doubtless go home, drink some one of his decoctions—and awake to 1928. Not even a party to go to—at least none to which I am invited. Ah well! Vale 1927! Ave 1928!

# 1928

(January 1–December 31)

*Battling with trains, producing literature*

DUNBAR-NELSON'S EXPECTATION of beginning a dull, sub-dued New Year at home did not come true. Instead, she danced in 1928 at a holiday party, and this unexpected festivity heralded a change-filled, eventful year that picked up the general tempo of her life.

Initially, she is still working laboriously at her Girls Industrial School duties and engaging in such volunteer civic activity as training the Elk Daughters for a spring cabaret show. When her part-time American Friends Inter-Racial Peace Committee (AIPC) job becomes full-time and paying on June 1, she jubilantly closes one chapter and begins the next with energy and enthusiasm. Almost daily she is "battling with trains," commuting to the office at 20 South Twelfth Street, Philadelphia. However, promoting the aims of the committee involved, not so much routine office tasks (although answering letters, writing reports, etc., were necessary) as calling on people, attending meetings, speaking at conferences, sponsoring programs, and similar outreach strategies. The additional traveling makes her life even more peripatetic. In certain respects, her hunch that this job would pan out "big" proved to be accurate.

Yet as early as the first few weeks, signs of trouble—which become more portentous in succeeding months—can be seen. These seem to have originated in ordinary office and organizational intrigue, racial conflict, and personality clashes. One of the principal actors to whom Dunbar-Nelson frequently refers from now on is Wilbur K. Thomas. Dubbed "Frozen Face" by her, Thomas, a white man, was executive secretary of the American Friends Service Committee, parent body of the AIPC. In that capactiy, he ran the office, raising in Dunbar-Nelson a variety of ambiguous attitudes about him. She was on firmer grounds of friendship with Helen Bryan, a white woman who also worked for the AFSC. However difficult, this job—along with Rob-ert's position as a regional director of Al Smith's Democratic presiden-

tial campaign against Herbert Hoover (for which she also spoke)—
blunted the sharpness of their financial worries. Dunbar-Nelson is
even able to refurbish and redecorate the house, an undertaking that
recalls her oft-voiced yearning for her own lovely home.

Of course, she is still kept busy during this year "producing literature," her catchphrase for writing her poems and articles, and the
obligatory newspaper columns. That the diary writing becomes a larger
part of her authorial consciousness is indicated by her dedicated striv-
ing to keep it current and her prescient remark that it is "going to be
valuable one of these days." By mid-year, the journal really perks up
and continues strong throughout the numerous coursings and calam-
ities of the next four years. Her entries become more revelatory and
unguarded, blunter and more direct.

In addition to disclosing the tension caused by her husband's jeal-
ousy, Dunbar-Nelson also says exactly what she thinks of her sister
Leila's disposition. Mary Leila Moore Young, five years older than
her younger sister, had married in New Orleans before moving in
1896 to West Medford, Massachusetts, where her four children were
born. Her husband, James Ross Young, owned a prosperous catering
service in Cambridge, but left the area about 1901 because of personal, familial, and financial difficulties. After this, Leila, the four
babies, and mother Patricia joined Dunbar-Nelson in Washington,
D.C., where she was living with Paul. Leila stayed for about a year,
looking for employment, then followed her sister to Wilmington where
she, too, began teaching English at Howard High School (and did so
until her retirement in 1931). Dunbar-Nelson, always the more ram-
bunctious of the two, often found her less social, more sedate sibling
an annoying "drag."

On the whole, 1928 was for Dunbar-Nelson a rather good year,
especially when contrasted with some of her earlier times. Yet certain
dissatisfactions still bother her. December finds her mourning her loss
of social touch and ending her annual diary on a very jaded note.

---

### [Sunday, January 1]

1928! Hail! After all there was a New Year's party. Jean [Stubbs
Jamison]'s 10th anniversary. Polly and Dallas back about nine—or
ten. Bobbo and I coming in from the station and Jean on the phone.

# MRS. A. D. NELSON IN PEACE WORK

## Becomes Executive Secretary of American Inter-racial Committee

## ALWAYS ACTIVE IN UPLIFT MOVEMENT

Headlines announcing D-N's position as Executive Secretary of the American Friends Inter-Racial Peace Committee, The Wilmington, Delaware *Evening Journal*, July 2, 1928.

## The American Negro Labor Congress FORUM

Hall, 610 S. 16th St., cor. Kater St.

Sunday, August 5th, at 2.30 P.M.
EVERETT MEVES
Subject: "The Need for Birth Control"

Sunday, Aug. 12th, at 2.30 P. M.
ALICE DUNBAR NELSON
Of the Society of Friends
Subject: "Inter-Racial Peace and its Relation to Labor"

Sunday, Aug. 19th, at 2.30 P.M.
J. St. G. WHITE
N. A. A. C. P.
Subject: Cause and Cure of Mob Violence against Negroes

Sunday, Aug. 26th, at 2.30 P.M.
HAROLD L. PILGRIM
M. A. P. E.
Subject: The Need of Unity among Workers

Admission Free    Questions and Discussion

You and your friends are cordially invited.

During her speech for this 1928 forum series in Philadelphia, D-N angered some of the radical laborites.

## AS IN A LOOKING GLASS

### Alice Dunbar-Nelson

TO talk about anything else this week but the convention of the National Federation of Colored Women now in session in Washington would be a sheer waste of time and energy so far as colored women are concerned. It is "The one great divine event, Toward which the whole creation moves." Or to paraphrase it, the one great event in the life of the club women of our race, toward which their energies are bent for the two years intervening between conventions.

*    *    *

SIDE lights and high lights are plenty. Everyone who has a program to put over, an axe to grind, a bit of publicity to be gained, a resolution to be endorsed, advertising to put forth, a friend to meet, a date to make, someone to find, old friendships to renew, old acquaintances to seek, new contacts to be made, propaganda to spread, subscriptions to take to publications, articles for which to take orders, pamphlets to hand out, cards to distribute, pictures to take, pictures to sell, gossip to disseminate, joy to spread or gloom to distribute—all such persons, and their name is legion, are to be found around the halls, in the lobbies, in the auditorium, on the platforms, in the committee rooms, in the yard of the Armstrong Technical High School, and at night buzzing up and down the stairs and in the lobby of the Metropolitan A. M. E. Church. For if you stand still long enough at either of those two buildings, you will come pretty nearly running across every colored woman in this country who is in public life, or who hopes to be in public life, or who has been in the public eye.

THE presiding of Mrs. Mary McLeod Bethune is a joy to behold. Absolutely fair and impartial, judicious, pleasant, cheerful, unruffled in the face of upheavals, giving everyone a chance, without crowding out anyone, compelling obedience without arousing antagonism, refusing to allow the Association to commit itself to anything of which it might afterwards be ashamed, maintaining an attitude of strict impartiality and neutrality in the face of all efforts to swing her to one side or the other—she is a marvel to behold. You wonder how her physical being stands the fearful strain of wielding the gavel all day from nine to five, of attending executive board sessions every morning from eight to nine or ten, of presiding over long evening sessions from eight to eleven and eleven thirty, dedicating and opening various buildings, cottages and Association activities, socializing with the friends who must have her time—and then appearing every morning on time, fresh, smiling, happy, firm, physically fit. You marvel at her every day, and wonder at nature in putting so much that is splendidly worth while in one body and mind.

One of D-N's "As In A Looking Glass" columns, the Washington *Eagle*, August 3, 1928. She contributed these weekly articles from 1926 to 1930.

So we all four drive out in the flivver. One of Jean's "twilight parties."
Liquor etc. Pleasanter to dance 1928 in than to mope it in. . . .

Awoke this a.m. about 8:45. . . . Bobbo and I out calling. Bitterly
cold and windy. Such a biting wind that froze everything and made
you shiver horribly. Such a change from the heat and mush of the
week. We made seven calls. . . . Pretty good for us. Won't do it again
for another year.

Home—and . . . Polly and I play pinochle while waiting—she for
Jean and [her dentist-husband] Juice to come on the way driving up
to Dallas' "dawn" party—and I for the ktichen fire to burn ere I banked
it and Bobbo drinking bi-carb soda after his bath. And now to bed—
having kept this first day's resolutions. . . .

*The work from which D-N copies her poem below,* Ebony and
Topaz: A Collectanea, *was one of the key publications of the Harlem
Renaissance. Edited by Charles S. Johnson and published by the Urban
League in 1927, D-N discussed it in her March 16 "Little Excursions"
column.*

### Tuesday, January 3

. . . Come home grippy in an engulfing wave of disgust. Feel too
rotten to "produce literature." Copy "April is on the Way" from *Ebony
and Topaz* for my column. Bowse in. All disgusted and [?] sick, go to
bed at nine o'clock.

### Wednesday, January 4

. . . Play bridge at Arleon [Bowse]'s. Promised the Tri-Hi girls to
read for them—but throat too bad for one and preferred to play bridge
for another. Got Polly to call . . . and make my excuses. Too cold to
take out the flivver. Come home and find Minnie [Stevens] parked on
the doorstep, wanting to come in and get warm.

Feel bum. . . .

### Saturday, January 7

Aspirin last night made me feel human again. This a.m. better.
After I had sweated a barrel wrestling with the furnace—which needed
dumping and the shaker broken—and evolved the idea that the pain
in my throat was rheumatism and wrapping the neck in warmth made
it better—decided to keep my engagement with Leslie Pinckney [Hill]
at Cheyney. Day balmy and spring-like, but I went togged in the vel-

# STOP-LOOK-LISTEN

## Where Are You Going?

# Thursday, November 1, 1928

### AT EIGHT O'CLOCK P. M.

#### ············TO THE············

# A. M. E. Zion Church, East Main St.

## UNIONTOWN, PENN'A.

### Of Course.   What's Going On?

# Mrs. Paul Lawrence Dunbar Nelson

**will speak there in behalf of the Democratic Party
on Radical Problems, also**

# Dr. Whitson of Monesson & others will appear

**The Smith for President Club will have Mr. William
Craig, of Pittsburgh, present to address the meeting.**

**There will be Special Musical Features on the Pro-
gramme.    The above will be sponsored by the Lucy
Humes Welfare League.**

**Mrs. L. D. Connors,**
President and Mistress
of Ceremonies.

**Mrs. S. S. Moore,**
Chairman Ways & Means Com.

**Mrs. Lucy Humes,**
Assistant.

An example of D-N's political campaigning for Democratic presidential candidate Al Smith. The names and addresses on the flyer probably represent
D-N's enrollment of new members for her Inter-Racial Peace Committee.

vet blouse (high about the neck), a woolen scarf and galoshes. We ran hour late, but got in considerable talk. Stayed to dinner in the dining hall. . . .

Home by five thirty (stopped for shopping). At the bank Reilly quite excited over "April is on the Way" which I used for "As In A Looking Glass" as I felt too bum to do any column this week. Leslie quite excited over it too. . . . Read papers, dozed. The damn throat hurts. Going to bed at 8:30. . . .

*Lil Gardner was a member of the numerous Anderson clan, while Josephine is obviously one of the homeless girls from the Industrial School who has gone to live with her—a kind of "farming-out" arrangement that was sometimes used for students without viable families.*

### Monday, January 9

. . . Lil Gardner came in with Josephine. She's boy-struck and otherwise fourteen years of age, and Lil and I fussed with her for an hour. Like pouring something over a smooth and polished surface. I'd hate to see her go back to the school, but if she won't do—she won't do, that's all. . . .

### Tuesday, January 10

. . . Bought some lace from a Canadian woman peddler. Probably smuggled.

### Wednesday, January 11

. . . Hill called about three o'clock to say that he couldn't get to Philadelphia, so didn't have to go up. Bought a hat instead—$1.95. Hope deferred maketh the heart sick. . . . I am breathless with anxiety. . . .

### Saturday, January 14

What strange tricks does Fate play us. Here I was a few minutes ago lying on the couch resting until time to go to the train and meet the 9:20 from Washington and Bobbo. Dreading the trolley trip—yet jubilant at the thought of him, with perhaps some good corn in his bag, home and lemons and ice, Leila uniting for a "party." The telephone rings, Leila answers. Robert in Washington. I get up to the library. He has been struck by an automobile. No bones broken but the doctor ordered him to bed. Would I come down on the excursion tomorrow?

So I come upstairs to bed and rest for the B. & O. excursion tomorrow—instead of going to the station. . . .

### Sunday, January 15

Back at home after a hectic day in Washington. . . . Found Bobbo sitting up in bed eating breakfast and [his friend] Froe watching him lovingly. [?] of Gary was at the house and Perry Howard came in twice and half of Washington, it seemed, called up. . . .

Bobbo pretty battered. A badly sprained ankle, a contusion on the head (no fracture), soreness but no internal injury. Struck by a Chevrolet and the owner (who was driving on the wrong side of the street car) . . . an oldish gentle soul, probably a government clerk and came to see him. He had been there last night. Seems scared. Offered to bring Bobbo a chicken dinner, which offer I graciously refused—as did Mrs. Wilson.

Bobbo's ankle bathed twice in Epsom salts. Dr. Fisher [M.D.] on hand. Oodles of men and the usual hectic time when Finley is home. Eight for dinner. . . . Called up Emmett [J. Scott, Jr.] who said the deal [of beginning a national Negro news service] had gone through, first a question now as to time. A telegram sent to "the West" on Wednesday last, should give him definite information by Thursday next. . . .

Came home and hunted up Bobbo's *Public Ledger* [insurance] policy and sent in notice to Philadelphia. Also wrote him a line and flivved I to the P.O. and now must rest for next week. I'm in a hell of a pain about money and Bobbo's accident prevents him from giving me the help I should have. Guess I'll be on a hot griddle. . . .

### Tuesday, January 17

. . . Burned my hair today trying to locate a clinker in Moloch [the furnace]. Head went against hot poker. I cussed a blue streak.

Anna [Brodnax] entertained the Bridgets. Again I played in rotten luck.
The cards have been against me for three weeks.

I am getting fat and dumpy. Must weigh tomorrow.

## Wednesday, January 18

Drunk! at 12:30 and glad of it. For I was about to sit on my hind
legs and howl when Jean and Juice [Jamison] came in and took Polly
and me to their house and filled us with corn liquor and chessy [?].
Whereupon I am not as indigo as I have been for the past 24 hours.
A stupid teachers meeting at H. H. S. [Howard High School] after
school, lasting until six. After a lonely dinner, wrote some letters,
among them a plea to [banker] Baker to extend my note to February
11. Then Bobbo called up. He has had an X-ray made. Fractured
tibia and plaster cast. He's in for a hell of a time. Wherefore, from
fatigue, blues and leucorrhea, I was glad of Juice's invitation.

## Thursday, January 19

. . . Tedious days—the school a nerve-wracking thing. Bobbo's
letter not so reassuring about his fractured tibia. Sent the insurance
blanks made out for the carrier to sign. Said Emmett wanted to see us
together when I come down Sunday. Wish Emmett hadn't said anything to me about it. Another case of hope deferred and actual physical illness from disappointment. God! Will I ever get out of that barn
[the Industrial School]! I feel like a trapped thing. . . .

## Saturday, January 21

Cold as the devil today. Took the 8:25 to Philadelphia. . . . Stopped
in Wanamaker's and heard the R. C. Ogden band giving a morning
concert. How lovely to go to work with music. Reached the Friends
Building by 9:30. Leslie had phoned that he was ill and couldn't come
in. Got out letters. Pamphlet material. Conference with Newton and
[Wilbur K.] Thomas. The latter put me in a train of thought. Inter-
racial peace (Negroes non-combatants) is a preservative of the white
man. Can't use that thought but it's a whopper. . . .

Went in [Wilmington] library and finished "Right Off the Map"
and saw exhibit of Japanese dolls. Very beautiful, but not homey and
cuddly like the ones *we* sent to Japan. . . .

## Saturday, January 28

. . . Have been lame and sore all evening. A lameness and soreness superinduced by shoveling five inches of snow off the kitchen roof. There are perhaps ten more. We have seldom had such a blizzard. . . . I changed the parting of my hair and cut bangs.

## Sunday, January 29

. . . I preside [at Wilmington "Peace" meeting]. Meeting pretty good—but I missed the [Cheyney singers'] music.

"Wars are made by old men, fought by young men, and suffered by women and children." Mine own epigram. Home by 10:30 or thereabouts.

Well, that's over.

I broke my resolution. Forgot to write in my diary and put this in Monday night.

## Monday, January 30

. . . I feel perfectly stultified. Also the downstairs part of the house is cold. No matter how much fire—it stays cold. Especially the dining room. Ugh! I *hate* winter. . . .

*Below, D-N is reading* Plays of Negro Life, *ed. Alain Locke (New York: Harper, 1927). She led her February 17 "As In A Looking Glass" column with favorable commentary on this collection, especially praising Locke for his "spirit of the true artist" in saying that "it is not the primary function of drama to reform us."*

## Wednesday, February 1

. . . Had to wait a half hour ankle deep in snow, mud and slush for a bus this p.m. Got home and found Sarah [Fleming] strumming on the piano; Ethel waving a paint brush—having dismantled Pauline's room—after she had arranged and cleaned it beautifully after the papering. Pauline stormy with rage. I [?] to my room, shut the door tight and with a cigarette, read Locke's edition of Negro plays— until Sarah had gone; dinner over and the atmosphere less tense. . . .

*These kind of astrology notes occur throughout D-N's diary and are included here as a brief sample of such entries.*

## Early February

Magnetic. Crave sympathy and understanding. Be discreet. Inspirational.

## February 1st to 9th

Hectic. People get on nerves. Guard against trying to accomplish the impossible or working in impractical manner.

Be skeptical of business propositions.

Slow about new ideas of radical character.

Apt to suffer from indigestion and nervous headache. Keep calm and serene. . . .

## Thursday, February 2

Groundhog Day. Had a heck of a day. Late for school—got there after plowing over hummocks and skidding over icy roads and found the schoolroom 52°. Something cracked. I saw red. Dismissed the kids and beat it up the road without going to see anyone. Another half hour wait for bus. Stopped at county office and reported school too cold and closed. Found sympathy. Got some oysters for an oyster pie and home. . . .

The state of turmoil that I am in is extraordinary. I don't ever recall being in just such a state before—for no apparent reason. I believe it is sub-conscious worry over waiting for Emmett's rescue [of the projected news service venture] and the hideous financial snarl. Awful. Rotten. . . .

## Sunday, February 5

. . . Tore up my old will tonight. It was a foolish document anyhow.

## Monday, February 6

. . . Took the 10:50 to Philadelphia and to the Land Title Building and Marston and Smalley's. Arranged for a loan on my policy. It matures in three years—what a pity. But I have to raise the money for those taxes. . . .

Pauline and I went to see "The Vagabond King" at the Playhouse. S.R.O. So we sat on the cold, hard, concrete steps. But the play was well worth it. After having sung that Vagabond chorus for two years, it was good to hear it correctly sung. . . .

## Wednesday, February 8

Nothing special. . . .

## Saturday, February 11

Lead [Inter-Racial Peace Committee] discussion group. Luncheon. Go to Longwood Gardens [Pa.]. A dream of loveliness. Tropic inside and snow without. Luncheon and organ. A perfect day. . . .

## Wednesday, February 22

Krusie's birthday—and George Washington's. I send her a Chinese bell. . . .

## Thursday, March 1

I am minded of that flash of a "blue bird's wing" I once wrote about on March 1. But all I do today is to hurry to catch the 7:35 for Wilmington [from Philadelphia] and on out to Marshallton [where the Industrial School is located] and work. . . .

## Wednesday, March 7

Go to Daughter Elks meeting and promise to train them for the minstrel show. Also interest myself in little destitute girl. . . .

## Sunday, March 11

. . . Madre [a friend of hers from Washington, D.C.] is here at Ezion Church for Woman's Day. . . . I go in the afternoon. Madre pulls a lot of slush and soft soap. She had done it in the morning. Put me on some wonderful pedestal. Embarrassing. But good to let folks here know how folks away think of me. . . .

### Wednesday, March 14

Begin work on minstrel show. Meeting at National [Theatre]. Rather discouraging outlook. Lot of fat, heavy, lazy women who want to sit on side-lines and laugh instead of working.

And I'm rehearsing daily on the Peace Pageant at school. Home to find the house a riot what with the Jamisons and Annie [Murray, their French Street neighbor] and Bowse. . . .

### Saturday, March 17

. . . And up early in the morning for exercises and prayers.

### Sunday, March 18

There! What a relief! I let this darn diary lapse from February 9. It has lain like a weight on my heart to get it up to date. I've carried it around to school and to office. And like some inhibition, I could not bring myself to write. And tonight, when I ought to be in bed, the spirit moved me to straighten it out. . . .

### Wednesday, March 21

The first day of spring and very cold and blustery, though bright and frosty. Up early. Have lots to do. In afternoon, lead County Reading Circle at school. Take 7:45 for Philadelphia. Have some trouble finding John Wesley M.E. Church in West Philadelphia [where she is to speak]. . . . Locate it finally. . . . Usual "cullud" affair. Freebies as usual. My expenses. That's all. The older I grow and the more I do, the cheaper I get. Home by midnight.

Heard a wren today—and saw and heard a curlew. . . .

### Friday, March 23

Polly drives me to school because I have so much junk for the [Peace] Pageant. Stay at school instead of coming home. Rather restful. Children acquit themselves rather well . . . and Mrs. Lockridge [school superintendent], Miss Dade [another school officer] and the girls work hard with their chicken and waffle supper. I recite a base parody on *Pippa Passes*—"The Little Blackbird" and Mildred Fields discovers it. Made it up as I went along. . . .

Frogs singing in the ponds tonight as we walked up the road towards the church. Thunder waked them yesterday. And an occasional bullfrog calling for "Mon ami." And the stars! Wonderful in their brilliance!. . .

### Tuesday, March 27

. . . Pauline entertains Bridgets [bridge club] early as I have minstrel rehearsal. Those females will *not* come out. Always a meeting or a funeral or something. Disheartening. . . .

### Thursday, March 29

Intended to go to bed early, first doing up letters and getting my scrap book brought up to date. But Juice and Jean and Blanche [Stubbs] came in to hear the Lincoln [University] quartet over the radio here. . . Messing with Easter things now at school. Lillies and things which I bring home and wax and shellac. . . .

### Saturday, March 31

. . . Bobbo meets me [in Washington D.C.]. Nothing doing all evening but dinner, buy Yolande DuBois [the famous W. E. B.'s daughter] and [poet] Countee Cullen's wedding present in Gertrude's, sit in [*Eagle*] office and hear [what] the Sanhedrin [a sarcastic reference to the Elks ruling circle] has to say. . . .

*As this entry reveals, the subject of war and peace becomes one of D-N's preoccupations during this time (partly because of her Inter-Racial Peace Committee work). She criticizes the warmongering spirit of the United States in her "As In A Looking Glass" column of March 16, and on April 20 writes: "It is heartening to note the increasingly large number of the great minds of the world, who are not only expressing themselves upon the need for world peace, and the sheer futility of the war spirit, but are bending all their energies toward making war impossible."*

### Sunday, April 1

April Fool's Day. Also Palm Sunday. Camille Nickerson [a very old friend from New Orleans] on hand. We go over her father's life and the dear old [New Orleans] days of the Student Orchestra. . . . But do not speak of his suicide.

Mrs. [Carrie] Clifford takes us for a drive. Open car and chill winds, but the "sea of golden daffodils" along the margin of the Potomac River on the Speedway amply repay[s] us for the chill.

The dinner is at three in Amazon's Flagg's "arty" dining room. Thirteen of us. . . . Very lovely affair. . . . We go from there to the "Y" and I have my first experience in a rumble seat—in Narka [Lee-Rayford]'s car. E. C. Williams presides over the "Literature Lovers" and in spite of Mrs. Clifford's injunction, I pull a Peace talk. The younger writers' lack of interest in war. Discussion waxes warm. Mollie [Terrell] tries to hog the limelight and a pleasant time is had by all. . . .

The gym of the "Y" looked interesting, so we dropped in to hear a yogi and learned the difference between a mere Swassie and a Yogi—such as this wonderful "Yogi Hari-Rama." Bobbo bored and walks out and even Narka and I give him and his flaming orange robe, his hushy voice and ascetic frame and his Nordic barkers up and leave. . . .

## Friday, April 6

Good Friday—and a holiday. But I must cook for Edith [Fleetwood]. And try to do some cleaning. And market. And get pots for the cemetery. And fix window boxes. Very pretty—if someone did not steal one of my geraniums later.

Pauline all agog to go to Atlantic City for [Conwell Banton's daughter] Alice Banton's party which was to begin at midnight. . . . But Mama is taken violently ill with severe vomiting and things look dark for a while. Polly continues to dress. Edith runs out to get peppermint at the drug store and in obedience to Mama's admonition to "put up the latch" fastens the knob latch. When the car comes for Polly at ten o'clock, we cannot unfasten the door and all our efforts are unavailing. She goes through the alley and I spend a hectic hour taking off locks and knobs and prying the door open. Order restored and Mama's vomiting quieting down with soda and peppermint and hot water, we finally get to bed.

## Saturday, April 7

. . . Am trying to blow . . . when telephone rings. Leolya Nelson [a young sorority woman] telephoning from Elbert's drug store. With five other girls had "biked" from New York. Looking for place to sleep for night. Ensued some hectic hours. House messed up with hot, tired, khaki and knickered girls and bicycles. Pauline and I succeed in getting them a place . . and peace and quiet and the Easter rabbit finally descend upon the house. . . .

## Tuesday, April 10

. . . [Daughter Elks] rehearsal Tuesday night. I have to "produce literature" first. Cold and raw these days. Back to the old fur coat. Miserable weather. Reorganize the show. Discard minstrel idea. . . .

## Thursday, April 12

We go at night up to Philadelphia to Wanamaker's Egyptian Hall to the really very wonderful program of the Urban League. Hall packed and jammed and hot. But program worth while. Crystal Bird paid me a tribute. . . .

Saw *everybody*. Home by 1:30. . . .

## Friday, April 13

Jinx day. But not for me this time. . . . We finally get off for Middletown [Del.] . . . [competitive] program finally gets under way. . . . Music . . . orations. My [Industrial School] quartette wins first place, gold pins and go to Dover [the state capitol]. . . .

Jubilantly we get home. Two o'clock.

## Saturday, April 14

Well, the German fliers were found in Labrador. At least they did not die.

Raining and raw and cold. I make the 8:25 [for Philadelphia]. Wait for [Leslie P] Hill, who said he wanted to see me. Does not come, so I to the W.I.L. [Women's International League]. He finally shows up. Heap much talk. Drives me back to 20 South 12th [the Friends office] See Crystal [Bird]. Some conferring. [Wilbur K.] Thomas pouting like a spoiled baby. Hill uneasy. I, too, have my bad hours. Looks like my future job is precarious. I have a pretty bad afternoon and evening. Worrying, worrying. I had hopes that all would be well— but I have long felt that Thomas does not like me, personally. Well, I suppose it's the barn [the Industrial School] for me for the rest of my life. I have a very unhappy time with myself.

# 228

*Give Us Each Day*

However—go to see "Chicago" with Phyllis Hower [?]. Takes my mind off myself. Go to bed early. . . .

*Louisville, Kentucky*
*Thursday, April 19*

Early up. Breakfast. . . . Reach Louisville at 11:50 central time . . . Take taxi to address sent me by Mrs. Wilson [who engaged her to speak]. Mrs. Emma Keye's . . . [with whom she is to stay]. . . . Funds so low that I watch the meter with anxiety. Mrs. Keye out, but her sister . . . whom I take for the maid—directs me to the church where the K.N.E.A. [Kentucky Negro Educational Association] are meeting. Ride down on the funny one man trolley, find Mr. Wilson, but no Mrs. Keye. Back to house, and go to bed.

In despair about my voice. Can hardly speak above a whisper. Intend to go to the doctor . . . recommended by the porter on the train—but don't. Work on throat with aspirin gargles, soda mint tablets, eau de cologne gargles.

Find I have a roommate. . . .

Get up to dress for dinner—still gloomy about my voice. Have been having ten double duck fits because Dr. Thomas Elso Jones, President of Fisk University, speaks same night I do. And now with this *voice!*

But it clears out surprisingly. And—so inspiring is that big crowd of 13 or 1500—with the mob standing and another mob surging to get in—that I "speak fine."

Dr. Jones apparently impressed. Invites me to Fisk. Which was just what I wanted. Told him I'd wire him if I could come. Got him to promise he'd write Ray Newton [of the Friends Service Committee] about speech. He said I "stepped on it."

Folks seemed much impressed. Saw all the folks I knew long since. . . .

Home at last exhausted and all the household . . . to bed including my bed mate . . . in no whit disturbed by my outrageous coughing, quieted by . . . paregoric.

Mr. Wilson paid me—$95.74. And surprisingly bleak and cold. The fur coat very comfy.

*So elated was D-N about Fisk University and this visit to it that she used a substantial portion of her April 27 "As In A Looking Glass" column to praise the school and the president, noting in particular that "Fisk flung out the challenge that all education is 'higher'—but refused to climb upon the band-wagon of manual efficiency."*

## Nashville, Tennessee
## Friday, April 20

. . . Fisk University! The longing of 40 years granted at last!

## Saturday, April 21

The great lovely room like a Wallace Nutting picture gave me a good night's rest. Bird song and lashing rains alternately lull and wake me early in the morning. When I am dressed and down stairs find two youthful Jones—David, aged nine, and Canby, aged seven, playing the victrola. Emerges Mrs. Ennis, the missionary from Portugese West Africa home on leave, and Mrs. Gilbert, a Harmon foundation specialist, on research visit. Also Dr. Jones for breakfast.

Rain ceases, cold moderates enough to permit the spring coat and sweater, instead of fur coat. Mrs. Jones takes Mrs. Ennis and me on tour of inspection. See all the buildings, etc. Am most impressed of course with Jubilee Hall, with the chapel, where the magnificent life-size painting of the original jubilee singers dominates the organ and chancel. With the chemical laboratory, presided over by Dr.—what *is* his name?

Good-bye to Mrs. Ennis. Back to the house and library to finish up some letters. Then Mrs. Jones has to drive to the other side of town to take David for a day with a playmate, and I go with her. Back just in time for luncheon at Jubilee Hall

At 2:30, . . . we start out again. Call on Mrs. Boyd—all dressed up and conscious of her beautiful home. Then to Mrs. Napier's. She was most enthusiastically welcoming. And as Mrs. Jones had both a tea and a dinner engagement—I was glad to lay off my things and give myself up to an afternoon of most delightful and unalloyed pleasure. Lovely old Southern home. The aviary with the 13 radiantly singing happy canaries. Mr. Napier, lame from his broken leg, but roguish and happy. Darby and Joan [a cartoon couple] to the nth power and joy personified. A really lovely time. We were all three sorry when Dr. and Mrs. Jones came for me.

They had to dress hurriedly to go to some banquet and bade me good-bye. Mrs. Jones had made my reservations and delegated a Professor Shaw to see me to the train. While packing, Mrs. Gilbert came in and we had a pleasant and informative chat. She is all burned up with zeal and horror over prejudice and Jim Crowism.

Finally Professor Shaw and his frau come. The "frau" is French and lovely, if withered. The reservation okeh, though I do have to change cars in Knoxville. . . .

### Bristol, Tenn., and Virginia
### Sunday, April 22

Had a narrow escape this a.m. at Knoxville [Tenn.]. Got off dining car to send telegram to Bobbo and got back on car which was to be cut. Thrilling ride of a few minutes clinging to outside of Pullman. Rescued by a brakeman. Finally get to my car—"Mt. Home" was the name and home indeed it was to me. . . .

*Usually, D-N did not note her engagements and obligations in the diary by such an extended list as the following. However, this seems to have been an especially busy period—even for her.*

### Monday, April 23

[Had stopped overnight in Washington] . . . Home. Change shoes and stockings and get rain boots. Find Mama the personification of gloom and Ethel likewise. Kitchen leaking like out of doors. Cheerful home coming. . . .

Schedule:
Thursday, April 26—Better Business, Philadelphia, 8:30
Friday, April 27—Dover—State Musical and Oratorical
	Contest
Saturday, April 29—20 South 12th to distribute literature.
	Jane Cowl—if possible
Tuesday, May 1—Meeting 20 South 12th, 4:00 p.m.
Thursday, May 3—State Federation, New York City
Saturday, May 5—20 South 12th
Thursday, May 17—Club Ritz-Carlton. National Theatre,
	Wilmington
Friday, May 18—Washington, D.C. Marie. Madre
	Marshall

Sunday, May 20—Institute, West Virginia
Sunday, May 27—Donation Day. Industrial School
Saturday, June 2—Commencement, Industrial School
Saturday, June 16—Commencement Address, B.T.W.
   School, Dover
June 5—Berean School

## Thursday, April 26

Leila still stays at home. Clear and cold. I mean cold. Hard work at school—so much trouble with the damn exam papers. They are whangs—the scoring of the language papers and the distributions.

Leila holding forth. Mama still devilish. Ethel trying to get to Dover [to stay with friends].

Leave on the 7:09 for Philadelphia. Go to the Palais Royale for the Better Business League. . . .

Sadie Alexander [Philadelphia M.D. and sorority sister] and Lena Trent Gordon [Sadie's relative] on hand. We three to the platform where Sadie presides. Lena dispenses her usual hot air and unfinished outline. I bark hoarsely about peace and we call it a night. . . .


*Famous for his daring investigations of southern lynchings,* Walter White *wrote two novels,* Fire in the Flint *(1924) and* Flight *(1926). He was assistant secretary of the NAACP from 1918 to 1931, then succeeded J. W. Johnson as executive secretary.*

*D-N's exhausting entertainment of White provides interesting documentation of exactly who was doing all of the private home, inter-city hostelrying required for Black travel because of segregation. (See also, below, May 5).*

## Saturday, April 28

. . . When I get home and call up Polly to haul me home, she tells me that someone has been waiting for me all day. . . . When she drove down, lo, it was Walter White fresh from Europe. Gathering data. More hecticness. Leila too fagged to do much marketing and Mama determined not to let anyone be more ill than she. So I have to buy chops and cook dinner for Walter and me—then market for next day—then go down to meet Bobbo—then back and drink some of Bobbo's brew. Then Walter and Polly get off to Jean's party—and I can stagger to bed. Three hours sleep in 36 not so comfy. . . .

## Thursday, May 3

Get off to New York . . . To Abyssinia Baptist Church [where she is speaking]. Have a flashlight group picture taken, which when it comes home later proves to be a scream. Talk about Delinquent Girls, and since Mrs. Mayfield seems to be high in the counsels of the City Federation and was there, shot some bull at her. Went over, too. Leave on the eleven something, and home sometime in the wee small hours. . . .

## Saturday, May 5

To the [Philadelphia Friends] office betimes . . . I tell him [Hill] not to be too wordy in his presiding—and go on to Broad Street Theatre to see [Paul Green's] "In Abraham's Bosom" [a play she defended as "universal" against militant Black critics].

. . . Home, and collect all my materials for the dandelion wine. Start it, and am working at it when Robert comes home—brought in by Pauline. I scold at the prospects of the Wilsons being on hand for breakfast in the morning, and he counters that the dandelion wine isn't a sine qua non. I might be resting.

## Sunday, May 6

Leslie's and my big day [for the Inter-Racial Peace Committee program they organized] dawns auspiciously. Finley [Wilson] and Mrs. F. arrive on a morning train [from Washington, D.C.], and I give them breakfast. Rhubarb and grapefruit and devilled kidneys and corn muffins. Then it being one o'clock, Leila, Polly and I go [to Philadelphia], since we are flivving up. Leaving Bobbo to bring them up on the train. Finley rehearsing his speech the last thing I heard.

Uneventful trip up. Broad Street Theatre packed. Art exhibit excellent. Mrs. Musserone nervous. Hill also. Finley makes a good speech, but not the one Bobbo wrote. Hill presides beautifully. DuBois whacks his Quakers. I make an appeal, which nets $155.00. Everybody pleased, even Dr. Thomas. . . .

## Tuesday, May 8

Ritz-Carlton rehearsal. I'm getting nervous over this thing [the Daughter Elks Cabaret dramatic show]. . . .

## Saturday, May 12

A most astounding state of affairs is revealed to me by Helen Bryan. Thomas not at office. Newton ready with more plans, which I copy. Helen and I leave early, as she says she wants to talk to me. Some inkling of what it's about leaks out, when she tells me that she is leaving on July 1. We go to a quaint little tea-room in an artists' center, and she makes me cognizant of a strange conflict going on, of which I am the [?] and unconscious center. Waves of dissension, double-dealing, hypocrisy, deceit, manipulating and what not are beating on me. To hire me or not hire me seems to be the question, and Thomas is my enemy, Newton my non-friend, Helen my ardent supporter, and about to lose her job for it, Hill my advocate, and Crystal Bird my staunch ally. The situation is appalling. Helen had made an engagement for me to see Hill at Cheyney tomorrow.

Helen's revelations leave me limp. . . . Arrive home about three and find Pauline's bridge party in full progress. Finish up the salad, and help serve the brilliant crowd. By six o'clock, all cleared up, we can sit down to rest. Of course, no playing for me, just maiding it in the kitchen.

A lull before the second party begins. The crowd from Philadelphia, ready to drink punch, eat sandwiches, and dance. About twenty to the bridge in the afternoon. About fifty to the night affair, including [nationally known singer-actor] Allston Burleigh who brought his guitar, and sang his little song from "Abraham's Bosom." This lasts until three or later. I fairly stagger to bed.

## Sunday, May 13

Yank Polly and Connie [Murphy, her daughter-in-law Rebecca's sister, who had come up from Baltimore for the big party] out of bed and we fliv to Cheyney. There we have dinner. And there Hill confirms all that Helen had told me, only more so. In brief, Thomas does not like me, as I always knew; does not want me, as I always knew; and will stoop to any subterfuge to avoid having me. Even to complaining about my lipstick. Sickening. . . .

## Thursday, May 17

. . . The "Club Ritz-Carlton" comes off very satisfactorily. Packed and enthusiastic house. Numbers according to specifications, songs, dances, etc. Altogether I feel repaid for my worries of the past two months. . . .

### Friday, May 18

Again I must be nagged at about my school by a set of inferior nincompoops. And it may be that there is no way out—that I may not be offered the secretaryship of the I.P.C. [Inter-Racial Peace Committee]. Whew!. . .

### Monday, May 21

. . . Sit up until two o'clock writing up this damn diary—when I've got so much else to do.

### Wednesday, May 23

All day the drums have been beating in my head. My fate is being decided. Saturday at the Inter-Racial Committee. Today at the Peace Committee. And it spells just the difference between reputation and obscurity; between life and stagnation; comfort and pinching penury. God! to be at the mercy of *one* man—Wilbur Thomas. I always did hate that name Wilbur. Somehow I feel as if I have lost out and next September—the same old barn and Lockridge with her treacheries and deceits. Why I have not screamed all day I don't know. But I haven't. I have rehearsed the children. And played bridge at Arleon's— who was feeding the Bridgets. Ye gods! . . .

*In this entry, D-N rejoices at her American Inter-Racial Peace Committee secretaryship finally becoming a paid position, thereby enabling her to quit her job teaching at the Girls Industrial School.*

### Thursday, May 24

Hooray! Freed from the barn. And again hooray.

After a more or less hectic day at school . . . Polly came for me. While hanging around the [train] station, the Hills . . . drive up . . . Hill enroute to Bridgeville. But we had ten minutes talk and I got the news of Saturday's and yesterday's meeting. And after due consideration—I was named for the Executive Secretary last Saturday at $2,000 per year. And after due consideration yesterday, the $3000 was voted by the Peace Committee.

And so—adieu to the Barn and the Morons!

So I was able to view the fall down of the pageant at Ezion Church with equanimity. Even Blanche Richardson's bad palying only momentarily annoyed me. The whole thing was a nauseating mess.

Brought Mama home. Then looked around for something to do. So Polly and I out to Juice's for a game of bridge and supper. . . .

It was a pleasant diversion and the crab Newberg and wine were good. Celebration of my Emancipation from the barn—and the Morons—and "Miss Bee" [Girl's Industrial School official].

Found 9 four-leafed clovers this morning on the roadside going to school.

## Friday, May 25

. . . Jean and Juice drop in and I introduce them to the Arabian Nights—which they enjoy. Quite a literary evening!. . .

## Saturday, May 26

. . . [Leila] and I to luncheon [in Philadelphia] then to see *Porgy*. Ah, but it is soul satisfying. Rose McClendon and Frank Wilson and Young Carter—superb. And those scenes—lovely,—no not lovely, terrifying splendid. . . .

## Monday, May 28

. . . . [President William R.] Valentine called me long distance from Bordentown [Manual Training and Industrial School] breathlessly asking me to be his Commencement. I accepted and his voice sounded relieved. His original speaker probably disappointed him and he's using me for a pinchhitter. Oh, well, the more places I speak— the better for the Executive Secretary of the American Inter-Racial Committee. . . .

## Thursday, May 31

. . . *Southern Workman* paid me $12 for that Peace article [probably "The Negro Looks at an Outworn Tradition," May 1928].

## Friday, June 1

. . . Down to State College. Oratorical contest. I am one of the judges with two pink gentlemen, one a professor from University of Delaware. Having judged and announced, we drive to Dover for a look at Cecie [Henry, her good friend] and so home by midnight. Find Bobbo and some good pre-Volstead [liquor] at home.

## Saturday, June 2

Awake to the gentle patter of rain. Groan in disgust—and turn over to sleep. By getting up time—rain over, but clouds lowering. Go out to school on bus. Soon the sun came out with heat and humidity, but by noon the wind [?] to west and the day was lovely. Clear golden sun, west winds blowing cool and dry, blue sky and great lovely fleecy clouds.

It takes hustling for me to get the decorations done. Then I dress in the school-room, peacefully. . . .

[Commencement] Exercises lovely and everything moves like clockwork. The children did well, Sadie [Alexander] spoke well. Eva [Hall] spoke nicely. Miss Mason was good. Everyone pleased. Luncheon served okeh. Home by five o'clock. Exhausted but happy—another chapter closed. . . .

## Wednesday, June 6

. . . Took a nap and went to Daughter Elks' meeting. We cleared $190 on the concert. They offered me money. I refused for myself and suggested that Edith be given a donation—but as for me I did what I did for the good of Pocahontas Temple etc. etc. Pure hokum.

## Thursday, June 7

. . . I came home and copied the speech for Cramp [Dr. Crampton, an old friend and Harrisburg, Pa., physician]. It's four years old. Hope he won't recognize it. . . .

## Sunday, June 10

[Minnie's deceased husband] Dr. Stevens' birthday. Cool and lovely. Bobbo gets off to Seaford [Del.] where he goes to "antle" [participate in an Elk activity]. I bathe and put up jam and plant my little pine tree and wash my hair and do up my cumulative record cards and arrange the school cards, records, etc. I can hardly realize that I am all through at last. . . .

## Monday, June 11

. . . Busy day. Start my dental work with Juice. Ghastly but not as bad as I thought. . . .

## Thursday, June 14

. . . Commencement [at Bordentown] begins—out of doors, of course, with a pavillion for speakers. . . . Terrific thunderstorm arises. I finish my speech hastily and the crowd—hitherto patient and courteous—crowds into the auditorium. Lights go out and much darkness; but no disorder. The glee club and the band being lost in the melee—and there being nothing else, [President] Valentine asks me to speak again. So I make *another* speech. And the Commencement goes off smoothly. Valentine is grateful. So grateful that he follows me all day thanking me. . . .

We [D-N, Pauline, Leila] start out immediately. Reach Philadelphia downtown by midnight. . . . Go to Horn and Hardart's on Market opposite 16th. Are not served. Sit and wait—no one comes to take our order. Go to the Roadside where a honky-tonky band is playing and get a sandwich and coffee for Leila and coffee for Polly and me. . . . And so home by 1:45. Mama and Jack [their dog] had had a terrible time with the devasting rain storm and the cellar is flooded.

Hoover nominated for President on first ballot. . . .

## Saturday, June 16

. . . Been expecting Edith [Fleetwood] all the week and now tonight we are all going to Dover. I pin a sign on the door for "Miss Fleetwood to ring Mrs. [Annie] Murray's bell, 1308" and leave . . . a letter for Edith and the house key.

Mama, Leila, Polly and I reach the Booker Washington school. . . . The exercises . . . are very monkey. . . . But worst of all was having *two* commencement speakers, Hyland Moore and myself. The former youth arose and talked for one hour and five minutes and there was not an ology or an ism that he did not touch. I was so irritated

*Give Us Each Day*

that I don't know what I said—and cared less. . . .

Foolish Blackburn [the principal] gave me five dollars for my wretched night.

### Sunday, June 17

. . . Do my article for the *Eagle*, and an A.N.P. Little Excursions and then pack [for her trip tomorrow] and it's after two before I get in bed, and daybreak before I fall into a fitful sleep. . . .

*The People's College, below, was a Danish-model experimental school about which D-N wrote: "And all the while I was wondering if in its ideals of perfect democracy and sex equality the school would welcome one of our race in its delightful atmosphere of freedom and beauty. But since ours is such an unequal battle in the body politic, I felt glad that we have no money to expend on educational experiments, but must needs travel the beaten paths which lead to economic independence" ("Little Excursions Week by Week," Washington* Eagle, *June 29, 1928).*

### Monday, June 18

Get off with great eclat . . . for Pocono Summit [Pa.] and get . . . here at 1:24 (2:24), the hotel bus brings us up a mile and a half. Quite a beautiful caravansery. Six stories high and all kinds of service etc. etc. I have a lovely room. Mountains all around. 2,000 feet above the sea. Addie Dickerson, Addie Hunton [both prominent clubwomen], Crystal Bird, Leslie Hill, two Lincoln boys furnish the color in the 200 or more delegates. Luncheon immediately and then a fifteen mile drive to the People's College, a very remarkable and inaccessible school with peculiar ideals. Back to the Manor (Pocono Manor) by five o'clock and a meeting in the auditorium. The lovely goldenness of Saturday and Sunday has given way to lowering mists.

I am so tired. But a good hot bath and dress for dinner make me feel better. Wilbur Thomas and Ray Newton. The former pretending, as usual, not to see me.

I slip out of the night session as soon as Norman Thomas (socialist candidate for president) has spoken and up to my room and soon in bed and asleep. I'll get *one* good night's rest, anyhow. Heavy, blanketing fog over everything.

## Tuesday, June 19

. . . Sessions and meetings and round tables and talks.

The day moves on apace. You meet people and talk and are talked at. Then after the night session Leslie and I sink in the soft chairs which are all over the great rooms and talk and talk, . . . and finally to my room to read divinely in [Warwick Deeping's] *Sorrell and Son*.

Leslie presided over the night meeting. Very well done, too. Brought in idea of *all* the darker races. . . .

## Thursday, June 21

. . . Home [from Howard High School commencement] and half of Wilmington and Philadelphia pour in. Literally. Sadie and her mother leave at midnight and the other half of Philadelphia, New York and Baltimore come. Plenty of pretty girls—but it all seemed silly and senseless to me and I felt soiled somehow. . . .

[Dr.] Cramp[ton] called up to say the speech was okeh and he was sending me a check.

## Friday, June 22

. . . Josephine [a young student-friend of hers] had left her report card for me to see—she had been doubly promoted to 7B. So bought her a little wrist watch for $3.50. A real good one, guaranteed sport model. . . .

## Saturday, June 23

I've had a clearing up time all day. Have just finished—2 a.m. getting my desk, letters, etc. straight. At the [Friends'] office today Helen and I concocted my biography for the [press] release [about her new job]. Then on my way down thought of my war work and rewrote it at home. Got in a bit after two and after dinner, had to go to Juice's with that damn tooth. Helped Mama buy diapers for the prospective great grandchild [Laurence and Rebecca's] and had to supplement her meagre cash. Collected $60 for my Hampton expenses at the office. Telephone memo saying Mr. Walls of the Industrial Trust wanted to see me at seven o'clock. I knew he wanted money, so went over at seven and paid $50 and $2.50 in fines. Then went in to see him. He was mollified and said when I had paid in $50 more he could rearrange the loan so I would only have $7.00 weekly to pay. I sweat with gratitude at that. . . .

*D-N is traveling to the Hampton, Virginia Conference of the Interdenominational Institute of the Middle Atlantic Section to pub-licize her AIPC work.*

## Monday, June 25

An anniversary of ours—Bobbo's and mine. It was on the 25th of June 1913 that we went to Cape May [N.J.].

It was hard to get up this morning at five o'clock when Mama called me for I had not slept more than an hour or two. Aching tooth, fatigue, nerves. Did not get to bed before two. . . .

Beautiful morning. Driving was lovely. It was a quarter after ten when we stopped a few miles beyond Salisbury [Md.]—which is 103 miles from Wilmington and had our second breakfast in a lovely pine grove—gorgeous with bird song. Polly stretched out and rested and I read and listened to the birds.

Soon it grew hot. When we passed Accomac, Virginia, the road was a "dirt road"—brilliant white sand that choked with dust and beat on the eyeballs with its awful whiteness. Made me think of Laurence's "Revolt in the Desert." Finally, concrete road and then Cape Charles—200 miles from Wilmington. It was just two thirty o'clock—that is one thirty standard. We found that the boat left (as I knew) at 4:30, three hours to wait. We had the car looked over (a foolish battery), parked on the sea side, ate luncheon, washed our hands in the bay, read some and finally to the boat wharf to go through all the intricacies of freight-ing the car, having it drained, buying tickets, etc. $4.73 for the car, 87¢ apiece for our own tickets, made it a dear trip. And here we changed our watches to standard time.

It was lovely on the boat J[im] C[row] notwithstanding. Lots of ministers, going to Hampton. Some found it rough—the boat did rock quite a bit, and one brother was very sick. Two hours on the lovely water cooled us off. And then landing at Old Point Comfort, more intricacies of getting the car off and getting gas in her and soon Hamp-ton and Holly Tree Inn.

The sour manageress said she had no letter from me, but let us have two rooms. No meals. We bathed, dressed, found the restaurant and ate—the administration building. . . .

Negotiated for meals. Saw Mr. Wash. as he came in. Made myself solid with him. Attended the church service and heard Dr. Hayes preach. Got in touch with Dr. Downing, head of the brethern [all officers and members of the conference] (there must be 300 of them), asked for consideration, and so back to the Inn. *Dead!* A busy day.

### Tuesday, June 26

. . . Then I began to buzz and operate. Found Clarke Hall, the conference headquarters . . . and finally got Mr. Finnegan [the executive secretary] for a five minute conference. He agreed to sandwich me in tomorrow afternoon. . . . And to have my literature [500 leaflets] placed on exhibit and for Mrs. Isham to push it. Felt it was a good day. . . .

After dinner . . . we three [D-N, Polly, Madeline Foreman Dabney, Newport News, Virginia friend of Pauline] drove to Langley Field. Saw aeroplanes take off and land, go into hangars and come out. One near where we had parked interested us very much. So Polly and I got down to investigate. It proved to be an amphibian, hence its queerness. The mechanic showed us all about it and we clambered up its sides and in the pit. It had just returned from Greenly Island. . . .

### Wednesday, June 27

I don't know why I pulled that jasmine—gardenia they call it up our way—but Cape Jasmine to me always. But I wanted it *so* badly. It was a solitary bloom on a little bush by the Teachers Dining Hall. I said some midnight I would steal it—and tonight when we brought Hattie Feger [an associate of theirs] home from Madeline's party, I pulled it. Luscious, creamy, fragrant. And now what? Before I get it home, it will be black and dead. And I cannot exhibit its beauty here. Human nature—to destroy what it loves. . . .

Made my speech at four o'clock. A big audience and it seemed to go over big. Spoke fifteen minutes. Now for some follow up work. . . .

### Thursday, June 28

. . . Smooth sailing to Richmond. Found Richmond a lovely city. To the St. Luke Bank [and Trust Company] for Mrs. [Maggie] Walker [Black woman founder and president], but she has her headquarters at the St. Luke building. Thither to find an imposing six-story structure. Up in the elevator to top floor where sat Mrs. Walker like a queen— at her desk, or perhaps a school-mistress with her forty or more clerks before her. And then I found that her throne was a wheeled chair for she was helpless from arthritis in her knees. . . .

Sailing joyously along the gorgeous road. Zoom—flat tire. Miles either way from a garage. We got out and stood looking ruefully at a rag of a tire off the rim. A passing colored woman cheerfully opined that there was a garage "not more than a mile away." Then a Fordson passed with two Virginia crackers, three children and an Airedale. "Want any help?" was joyously greeted by us. An hour's wait, while the children, the Airedale and I picked and ate blackberries and blueberries.

We hunted for the Arcadia Tea Room, a very gorgeous place kept by "Race" people. . . . But they J.C.'d Polly, so Leila and I would drink no tea there. And the repair shop had had most of their equipment stolen, and I refused to buy an inner tube there. Howbeit, the boys tinkered at the engine and at six o'clock, we set out again—sixty miles from Washington.

With no more trouble we pulled up to the [*Eagle*] office at nine or thereabouts. . . .

### Friday, June 29

. . . [In Baltimore] went to see Reverend George Braggs [relative of the Murphy's, who had written a history of the Afro-American church] who read me voluminous extracts from ancient documents and gave me the list of inter-racial folks. . . .

Mama frantic with joy to see us home safe and sound. She spends the time when we are away in a state of terror lest she be left alone. . . .

### Saturday, June 30

We moved into 1310 five years ago today. I celebrated by getting to the [Friends Service Committee] office on time. We had a grand foregathering. It was Helen [Bryan]'s last day. The releases were all ready and I had brought the mats from Washington. So Martha [the secretary] had a day's work for her to get them out and a batch of mail.

Bobbo dropped in and created a flutter among the females. . . . Hot and I was glad to get home and attend to household affairs. . . .

### Sunday, July 1

A hot lazy Sunday. I really rest. Wash my hair, read papers. Take life easy. Go to bed early.

The Sunday *Star* carries my release and picture, with a gorgeous banked headline. Did not alter so much as a comma. . . . Quite impressed by my own story, I was. Bobbo and his Irish friends still buzzing.

## Monday, July 2

. . . Went to see Dr. [John] Turner [Philadelphia physician active in education and politics] in the a.m. to get him to serve on our committee. Marvin, his wife, showed me a picture she took of Paul [Laurence Dunbar] before he died. He was seated in a chair under the grape arbor of the Dayton home. It was the last picture he ever had taken.

Produce literature at night and get to bed late.

## Tuesday, July 3

Day begins with blazing heat, worse than yesterday. We have Board of Directors meeting at office. . . . Present my report. Apparently satisfactory. Got permission to go to seven conventions. Best of all—the Elks in Chicago. Could have whooped with joy. But looked modest. And then—though it was as hot as blazes, went out and walked my luncheon hour. . . .

## Wednesday, July 4

. . . Special from Bobbo enclosing copy of part of letter from Tessa concerning New York gossip . . . about Bobbo's possibility of heading up Al Smith's campaign among Negroes. Sounded encouraging.

Like everything of Jean's, the picnic was lame starting, but finally off, five carloads, usual crowd. A place by a little muddy creek, more or less damp and hot. Some played cards, some waded—the young girls, and all ate enormously. Blanche and I gossiped gorgeously. Black clouds warned us to pack. . . . We drive and drive to get cool. The thunderstorm descended upon us in fury. Finally home. I read all afternoon and rested. . . . Listening to the radio. I pray for Bobbo's success. . . .

## Friday, July 6

Weather quite more bearable. Routine day and routine evening. Nothing of moment. . . .

## Monday, July 9

Blazing sun in a blazing sky. I don a short-sleeved red gingham frock and hie forth to Philadelphia. Leslie P. in for a conference. Wants a monthly bulletin. Good idea, but a lot of work. Gave me a lot of who struck John—this time it's my rings—putting it as usual on Wilbur Thomas. Poor Thomas would doubtless be surprised. Hill thinks he's fooling me and I let him think it. Best way to get along with him. And then his anxiety is natural. He wants me to make a good appearance for his sake, as well as my own. I had already discarded the rings. He departed, after telling me that I looked "nice" three times. So I knew I looked like a dowdy, shiny-nosed frump. . . .

## Wednesday, July 11

. . . Got my check today—$166.66 [her month's salary].

## Friday, July 13

St. Anthony's Day—one of them. After a busy morning dictating, filing, etc., go out, feed myself and hunt up E. Washington Rhodes [editor] of the *Tribune*. . . . Promised me a hundred dollars. Hope I get it. Used a slick "line" with him. Want the *Tribune* to be the first paper to give us a big contribution.

Even Frozen Face thaws when I report this at the office. . . .

*D-N's reference in this entry to Nobile and the Artic tragedy is an instance of her occasional inclusion of current events items. General Emberto Nobile and his crew had embarked on an expedition to the North Pole on May 24 in a dirigible balloon, the* Italia. *On the way back the next day, the airship crashed, killing or losing about half of the men. Nobile himself was rescued on June 24, and the remaining survivors on July 12.*

## Monday, July 16

Bobbo and I to the station together and he gets off on his usual 8:10 and I for the 8:25. Hot as blazes all day. Usual routine and I am busy all day. Heat intense. See by the papers that Europe is sweltering and scores are dying in Paris, Austria, Germany. Much excitement over the Arctic tragedy. Looks as if Nobile and the rest of his crew were a pretty yellow lot. . . .

## Tuesday, July 17

. . . When I got off the train found Polly awaiting me. It was a relief to be able to drive up [the thirteen blocks home] and not have to fight trolleys in the blazing heat. Leila had quite a lovely dinner— sirloin steak and fixings and Ethel had made a coconut layer cake. A pre-birthday dinner [D-N's own]. Also Leila and Polly gave me a lovely bath gown, shimmering green satin, far too beautiful for daily use or for traveling. I shall exchange it for a more practical one.

Leila had had three teeth extracted and was in great pain. Pyorrhea is getting worse.

Call from the Artisan's Bank and I went down. Mr. Boyer [the banker] had the new mortgage all put through. I had to sign a bond, a few other papers. Bobbo will have to also. Had to take out tornado insurance also. Altogether my bill was . . . $7.25 and that coupled with the $45.00 interest money . . . and the original $20 sent for search to the title and the $4.75 tornado insurance . . . makes it quite an expensive proposition.

Then to Juice's [her dentist] to have my tooth treated. Home, packed my bag. Played some pinochle and caught the 10:12 (11:12) Federal Express. It was hot sleeping and a very uncomfortable night—even in a lower berth.

Slipped away from the office today and went to see "Ramona" at the Market Street Theatre 330. Lovely picture and Dolores Del Rio splendid. Warner Baxter as Alessandro smiles too much.

## Wednesday, July 18

Up early and dressed. . . . Got some breakfast in the station and wait for eight o'clock train Morning papers carry glaring screamers about assassination of President Obregon of Mexcio. That with death of young Carranza the aviator makes Mexico's grief a profound affair. . . .

Reach Newport [R.I.] eventually at 10:45 daylight. Take taxi to 79 Thames Street. Find it a church and parsonage combined, as is usual with these New England colored churches. But I am agreeably disappointed in Mrs. Jeffries [her hostess]. She is young, slim, fair, pleasing, with a lovely smile. We get out soon to the church where the

[Northeastern Federation of Women's Clubs] meeting is held. A.M.E. Zion church. . . .

The day drones on. The heat intense, even in Newport, by the sea. Dinner eventually and I am very hungry. An excellent dinner. Tedious afternoon session of Ex.[ecutive] Board. Five o'clock when we get out and I don't want any supper—only a bath and sleep, which I get—to the accompaniment of the Navy band playing snappy tunes at a lively, cheering baseball game in a park back of the house. Can see the Narragansett Bay, too. And a cool breeze makes it comfy.

Arise eventually, dress, make friends with the family dog, have a glass of milk, cake and fruit and we sally forth, after an "outgoing" prayer by the Reverend. Church crowded. Song program. The Mayor speaks—Sullivan, Democrat, Harvard accent. Lizzie Carter [the presiding officer] calls on me suddenly to respond. Scares me out of a year's growth. But I pull some sort of a response. Remember that the Knights of Columbus sponsored *The Gift of Black Folk*—since Sullivan recalled Negro's part in making of country.

See lot of old friends. Eat ice cream and get home, talk, eat a peach and go to bed. Nice and cool. I have a lovely room.

## Thursday, July 19

My birthday! Fifty-three today. Feel much younger than when I was 33.

Hot, but tempered a bit. Eat breakfast at the church. And sit and listen to interminable [talk] until I itch and grow frantic. And when dinner is about ready I slipped out, caught a bus to the beach. Went in the first place I saw—it looked high class, certainly the prices were, for my bath, suit, privilege of place, etc. cost $1.75. But the ocean was lovely. It was worthwhile. Did not stay in long, and I missed having a cap and couldn't dive. Then went in a funny cafeteria where a good orchestra played and had a lobster salad and iced coffee. . . . Took the bus back to the church and blazing heat again and more talk until supper. . . . Got my supper and came home to lie down and enjoy my regular afternoon temperature.

Got a card from Bobbo and one from Mrs. Jeffries. Gave her and her husband a copy of "Toussaint L'Ouverture" [Leslie P. Hill's blank-verse drama, which D-N praised as "a notable addition to the Negro Renascence"]. Hill sent me six for sale. . . .

Speak at the evening session. "I speak fine" and much enthusiasm manifested. *Now* I must clinch it tomorrow.

Then we come home, . . . have tea and toast in a restaurant, talk a bit mostly about religion, and I finish "Bambi" which is certainly one of the most lovely books I have ever read. . . .

## Friday, July 20

Very full day. . . . My own performances were:

1.  Elected alternate from N.[orth] E.[astern] Fed.[eration] to National. Could have been elected delegate if I hadn't been so darn dumb as to say I was chairman of a minor committee.
2.  Elected 9th V.P. or Vice President from Delaware.
3.  New department put over—Inter-Racial Relations. Made head of that.
4.  Resolution written and put over endorsing A.I.P.C. [American Inter-Racial Peace Committee] and calling for the North East Federation to put over policies of A.I.P.C.
5.  Keep Mazie [Mossell] from getting through resolution endorsing John R. Hawkins.
6.  Help write resolutions censoring G.O.P. for indicting [her old enemy, then, later, associate] Perry Howard for sale of offices. . . .

Home by eight o'clock. I pack and we start out again . . . for the boat and soon I am aboard and having tea and toast in the dining room. The water is rough and the boat tossing pleasantly, as I smoke (how good this Old Gold is!) in my stateroom. A profitable convention. . . .

## Saturday, July 21

The boat docked [in New York City] before I was awake. Had intended to spend the day in New York . . . but as I was dressing occurred to me that I had better get to the office as soon as possible. So got a bit of breakfast on the boat and hurried to the Pennsylvania station. Got the . . . train for Philadelphia. Reached there promptly at ten (eleven) which meant one hour for work. Glad I did, for mail was piled up and if I am to be away, need to get things adjusted.

Worked until twelve. Went down to the Benjamin Franklin leather shop and bought or rather finished paying for my leather case. Bought a cake for the family and got the 1:18 home. Surprised the family by getting in and was glad to be on time for a good dinner.

After dinner change the lovely green kimono for a more servicea-

ble one of red and gold. Buy two new dresses. Go to Juice's and he
isn't in to ease my aching tooth. Then with Mama as a passenger—
we go to Chester. . . .

Then home. Play some pinochle, listen to the radio, bath, bed.
Hot and muggy weather. Found cards from Edith and Bowse and a
*lovely* bed doll—white haired and sophisticated. She is just adorable—
trousers, shoes and all. Laura dressed her. . . .

Annie Andersen-Murdah [a Wilmington acquaintance] in with some
gossip about Alice Banton's losing her job in Atlantic City "for conduct unbecoming a teacher." Married man. May be sheer gossip. . . .

### Wednesday, July 25

Reach Charleston [South Carolina, where she is speaking about
the AIPC at a teachers' convention] at 6:40 [a.m.]. . . .

Get to the high school ten minutes after eight [p.m.] Somehow, I
never do well with these teachers. Too many self-satisfied males—get
my goat. I am the first speaker and talk about 20 or 25 minutes. And
I feel as if I am not altogether putting it over. I feel cold towards the
audience and they seem to react coldly to me. Never get any fire in
my message. Applause perfunctory—so it seems. However, later lots
of folks say otherwise. Perhaps I should have more fire. Next time, I'll
be fiery.

Dr. Mordecai Johnson followed. Usual ballyhoo and after hammering on the iron which I had left cold, he gets them all warm and
whooping. Just what the audience wants. Hoo-roo! . . .

At last the agony over. I suffered from a sense of defeat. Folks said
nice things—very nice things. Perhaps, after all, they will remember
my simple story, after they have forgotten Johnson's perorations. I
gave them *meat*. . . .

Liddy [Elizabeth Stubbs] told me to "look over" Betty Lindford.
She is very good looking but getting plump. Sings beautifully but a bit
too dramatic, is a fast worker and cunning vamp on the ballroom
floor. Shall report. Understand she is engaged again.

### Thursday, July 26

Up early—over to the school to be carried out to Institute. . . .
Succeed in locating Eva Bowles and having a satisfactory "conference" with her. Maybe she was lying in her proposition that we coop-
erate always closely and work together—but at any rate it was good to

have her say so. Also had satisfactory interview with Monroe N. Work
[compiler of *The Negro Yearbook*]. . . .

### Friday, July 27

Reach Washington at 7:40. Bobbo meets me. . . .

I am suffering horribly with leuchorrhea and chafing. Can hardly
walk. Get the 8:15 home and taxi up. Folks surprised to see me. Lunch.
Bath. Bed. Sleep. Needed very much. . . .

### Saturday, July 28

To the office as per usual. . . . Get some work done up. Hot as
Hades today. Go down to "Jew town" to market. Fifth street from
South on down. Like a bazaar in the near East. Bit of foreign land in
America. Market and find things abnormally cheap and fairly stagger
to the 2:40 train. Have to call up Polly to get her to come after me. . . .

It is late when we [D-N and Polly] leave [a party]. . . . See helpless
colored girl apparently suffering across from Hotel Dupont. Foolishly
play good Samaritan and take her to a house in Chippey Street. Man
lying there either dead or drunk. We hurry away as a motorcycle cop
comes up and takes charge of the girl.

Home by 4:45 a.m. . . .

*D-N's August 3 "As In A Looking Glass" was related to the follow-
ing entry. She began the column thus: "To talk about anything else
this week but the convention of the National Federation of Colored
Women now in session in Washington would be a sheer waste of time
and energy so far as colored women are concerned." Their two major
successes for this biennial meeting were the opening of a national
headquarters in Washington and the dedication of the caretaker's cottage at the Douglass Home and Shrine at Anacostia.*

*The two clubwomen friends of D-N who "strike up a heavy flirta-
tion" here are Mrs. Narka Lee-Rayford of Washington, D.C. and Mrs.
Lethia C. Fleming of Cleveland, who was president of the Ohio State
Federation of Colored Women's Clubs.*

### Wednesday, August 1

Executive Committee [of the Federation] meeting. Fight over
endorsing National Colored Republican Women. Don't do it. I get

the A.I.P.C. [American Inter-Racial Peace Committee] endorsed. Long morning session. Bobbo comes and is "introduced." I finally speak. . . . "*I speak fine.*" Go to office. Produce literature. Dr. M[ossell, Mazie's physician father] drives Jeannette [probably Jamison] and me to Douglass Home. Dedication of caretakers cottage. More hot air, oratory and lime-light hounds. . . .

. . . Narka and the rest appear. . . . Narka comes to the house for "comfort." We want to "make whoopee." So we telephone Mrs. Pettis' home to see if Lethia Fleming is there. She has just come home. We go. They are eating cream—Lethia, Mrs. Glass and another little soul or two. After a bit enter Mrs. Pettis, just from her Masonic block party. She and Mr. P. laden with chitterlings, hot tamales. Life looks interesting. Enter now a tray, small glasses, Three Star Henessey brandy. Life is glorious. Good home made white grape wine. We really make whoopee. Lethia and Narka strike up a heavy flirtation. My nose sadly out of joint. Something after two Narka starts to drive home alone, just as Bobbo comes up. Such a gorgeous moonlight night. . . .

### Friday, August 3

. . . [National Federation of Colored Women] Executive Board meeting lasts until 10:30. Then the tedious day session until 2:30. Charlotte Hawkins Brown [founder and president of Palmer Memorial Institute, North Carolina] won out over Mrs. Burnett. Dirty little rat! She used unscrupulous methods. And a respite all too brief for lunch-eon—which I find in the neighborhood. Then a stormy and bitter Executive Board session from 3:30 to 7:00. Terrible. Lots of dirty linen washed. Tears. Undercurrents that I knew not of. Realized sharply that I am an "out." Rebecca Stiles Taylor canned by Mrs. [Sallie] Stewart for Executive Secretary and a bitter war precipitated thereby. Too exhausting to think of. . . .

### Saturday, August 4

. . . Going with Bobbo to get his new suit and shoes and re-read-ing the fatal telegram from Bessye Bearden [her New York friend]— "Julian Rainey selected" [instead of Bobbo, to head Al Smith's presi-dential campaign among the Black electorate].

It made me sick. But Bobbo was game. The telegram came to the house in the morning before he left and he met it with the same brave smile with which he meets all his disasters. He refused to believe it.

Something wrong. So he went about getting his suit and shoes and all to go to New York. . . .

When we got off the train at Wilmington a curtain of heat enveloped us. There had been no cooling thunder shower and Wilmington still lay gasping in its torridity. Though it was half after eleven daylight time when we drive up to the house, everything was open. Mama, Jack on the steps, Ethel in the kitchen and Leila, though in bed, wide awake.

Ensues some hectic telephoning. Mooney had called and Bobbo called back. Mooney said that Senators Gerry (R.I.), Bruce (Md.), Bayard (Del.), Harrison (Miss.) had sat in conference and he, Bobbo, had been definitely selected. That Bayard had said that he would like the pleasure of notifying Mr. Nelson, but that Gaston said he would write him. Now Gaston, it seems, is the liaison man. Gaston is from Massachusetts and Gaston and Rainey are friends. I figure that Gaston had promised to put Rainey across and failing to do so, had made up his mind to do some funny business to put him over, anyhow. . . .

### Sunday, August 5

Pitiless heat. We gasp for breath. . . .

Leila still suffering with her mouth. With all her teeth gone she is hardly recognizable. . . .

### Monday, August 6

. . . No word at home from Bobbo. Polly saw Rainey in New York at the Dark Tower [famous New York townhouse of A'Lelia Walker, daughter and heiress of Madam C. J. Walker]. He told her he had been appointed as National Director of the Democratic campaign among Negroes. That Bobbo was to be Regional Director of the South East Division with offices either in Washington, Richmond or Greensboro, North Carolina. Which latter was so ridiculous that Polly says she asked him how was his wife and received no reply. . . .

### Tuesday, August 7

Ethel told me when I came in Saturday that Emma [Sykes, with whom she places numbers bets] "had something" for me. I felt happy thinking that I had "hit" the numbers that I left with Emma before I went to Washington. But when I called her up it was just a "bolita" of $2.70. My modest little plays of 15¢ a day aren't much, but at least I don't lose much. Bobbo had a string of "sure hits" but none have come out yet. Rumor has it that Mrs. Rose has hit it for a thousand. I wonder. . . .

I weigh 165 pounds. Too little exercise. Got some hormotones [hormones] today. . . .

## Thursday, August 9

. . . Great excitement in the office. Some one of the girls discovered that Bedell's is selling out and extraordinary values in frocks, shoes, hats were being offered. Gladys [a secretary] started the ball rolling with a black satin back crepe and black satin slippers, the former $10, the latter $2.19. Hurried exits and soon clothes begin to pile up in the cloak room and everyone intensely excited. I could not get into the fray until after luncheon, for I had an engagement. . . . I go to Bedell's also and after a hot and hectic time, get a lovely evening gown in black, for $10.00 and a hat for $1.79

*In this entry, the actual outcome of Bobbo's hopes for a paid position in Al Smith's presidential campaign efforts among Blacks is clarified.*

## Friday, August 10

. . . Crystal Bird comes in—she and F. F. [Frozen Face, i.e., Wilbur Thomas] have a long conference and then she and I have a lively chat. She is leaving September 1 to spend a year resting with Birdie [her sister-in-law]. F. F. wanted her to take Helen's place, she said.

We go to the station together. She says F. F. has a sex complex, hence his grouchiness. Maybe so, maybe so.

It rains and thus gets a bit cooler. Bobbo comes in at 9:30 (10:30) and Polly and I meet him. We have cracked ice and spiritus fermenti in the kitchen. He has the regional directorship of the Middle Atlantic States at $125 per week and expenses (when on the road). Gaston is director. He is young, ambitious, rich—worth $20,000,000 and is putting up money for the division. [Julian] Rainey is secretary. Morten, Chairman Executive Committee. [Lester] Walton [journalist] head of publicity—as four years ago. They appreciated the fight Bobbo put up. He is glad to be in the picture somewhere, anyhow. So am I. I would have been broken hearted had he not been considered at all, for I think it would have so broken his spirit that the effect would have been disastrous for him.

We talk late. He is happy. So am I. . . .

## Sunday, August 12

The tropical storm which has ravaged Florida and the Carolinas has moved up the coast and begins to ravage here. . . .

Clears off finally and Leila, Polly and I drive up to the [socialist-communist] Negro Labor Congress meeting [in Philadelphia]. . . . I talk about 45 minutes. Follow questions and discussions. Heap much speeches. A Hungarian girl denouncing Hoover for stopping the Hungarian revolution. "Comrade" Patridge, white, Ohio, voluble. "Comrade" something or other, brown, old, militant. "Comrade" something else, white, bitter. Then giving the chair to another, Warren takes the floor, assails the A.I.P.C., bitterly denounces Wilbur Thomas and has a good time generally. However, I have the last word, and "clean up."

"Comrade" Warren is so peeved he doesn't even shake my hand goodbye. . . .

*While visiting New York, as here, D-N often saw Bessye Bearden, a journalist, educator, socialite, and politician, who was also the mother of Romare Bearden, who became a renowned artist. During this Business League convention, D-N combines recruiting members for her Inter-Racial Peace Committee with a great deal of socializing and party going. All of the individuals mentioned are leading members of the Black community—educators, teachers, physicians, journalists, bureaucrats, etc. Anne Dingle and Eunice Hunton Carter were a lesbian couple. (Later this year, D-N refers to one of the Friends Peace Committee members as a "male Anne Dingle" in alluding to his homosexuality.) Dingle was the first national treasurer of the Delta Sigma Theta sorority. As these entries show, D-N is beginning to speak more openly of lesbians and homosexuals in the diary.*

## Wednesday, August 15

Leila and Polly, after much family discussion, decide to go to New York with me. . . .

Hot on the road. We stop at the Linwood Grove outside of Brunswick [New Jersey] . . . rest under the trees, get a luncheon, and so on our way. It is quite an experience going through the Holland Tunnel. I wanted to go through since it was opened last December. Like a clean bath room, and perfect ventilation and lighting. . . . to Bessye [Bearden]'s. 173 West 141. Bessye lives up four flights, in a rather shabby apartment, but her own apartment is beautifully kept and furnished. Bessye is volubly glad to see me, comes down to the car, greets the Pollies [Polly and Leila] with joy and acclaim, and so we go upstairs. . . .

Bessye and I to the Venetian Tea Room, and then to the session of the Business League. . . . Packed meeting. The "Late Mayor Walker" is late, as usual, but immensely interesting when he does come. [Tuskegee President R. R.] Moton indulges in sheer drivel for his annual address. Meet lots of people after it is over, and have a good time "gassing." We go to the "Dark Tower" for a salad and a cup of coffee. Irene Alexander [Sadie's sister-in-law] is hostess, and looks too foolishly pseudo artistic for words. Anne Dingle and Eunice Hunton Carter very much together. See everybody. Spend some time there. Eventually get home, the Pollies going on their way. Not such a giddy evening, but I am very tired from the long hot trip.

## Thursday, August 16

. . . Spend profitable time picking up news, "making contacts," etc. Get Moton to join the committee, and pay his dollar. [Her niece] Pauline is put on the resolutions committee, which is good for the committee for eventually she and Lester Walton keep the committee from endorsing Hoover. But that does not come out until the next day.

Polly goes off with Moon for dinner, and although Leila sits tensely watching Seventh Avenue from Bessye's window all afternoon, she does not show up again. It is very hot. I relax, and try to get Leila to do the same, but she is always happier when she is uncomfortable. . . . Bessye and I go to the [Zion] church. Not as large a crowd as the night before. Settle myself for peace and comfort, and [Charles C.] Spaulding [president of the North Carolina Mutual Life Insurance Company] introduces me, and I have to make a speech, a whole day before I was expecting to. Don't know how good it is, but everyone said it was all right. I know it would have been better if I could have had more preparation. . . . We start out. The crowd grows, until we finally have twelve in the party. . . . We go to the "Cotton Club," the Harlem cabaret which does not welcome "us." Quite the most beautiful cabaret I have ever seen, and a gorgeous show. We stay a long while, and then on to "Mexico." By that time the others separate from us, and Bessye is left with her escort . . . and I am still with Roddy. The "Mexico" is one of those Low-downers, with plenty of local color, a bar, good beer, and good food, quite reasonable. We run into Sol Johnson . . . and promptly get dated up.

Pretty near day-break when we get home.

## Friday, August 17

. . Eventually, after many happenings, we get to the ball. I wear my new gown, and everything proceeds according to Hoyle [the card authority]. The Renaissance Casino is a very beautiful place and the crowd was just about large enough to make it a pretty party, and not one of New York's awful crushes. I dance all dances but one or two. With Eugene Kinckle [Jones, executive secretary of the National Urban League], with Imes, with Sol Johnson, who came to see us at the Venetian, and told me all his troubles about Tessa, with Dr. Ross, who is a lovely dancer, in spite of his bigness, and with others. . . . It is after three before we leave. Pauline is suspicious of Bessye and me, thinking we are going to stage another cabaret party without her, but we are both all in, and ask only to get home, and get off our slippers. And so to bed.

## Saturday, August 18

I rise early, intending to slip out and get my breakfast down town, so I can make time. But Bessye awakes, and I have to have breakfast with the gang. Haven't said anything about Howard, Bessye's husband, who is very delightful, and Romare, Bessye's overgrown adolescent boy, who is no less Harold Teenish. . . .

Leila and I have dinner at the St. Regis, stroll around a bit, looking at Broadway, but Leila always suffers so from heat, or feet, or something—in fact, she always has something the matter with her, and is so generally unhappy when she is out that it is a pain to try to be nice to her. So we take the Fifth Avenue bus and up to 125th Street, and then a taxi to her abiding place. . . . I am glad to take off my clothes, and crawl in her bed and sleep. Dead tired and hot.

Rise about eight, dress, bid Leila farewell, for she refuses to go out again. . . . Buy Bessye some flowers, and myself a new compact. . . . Home to Bessye, whom I had left purposely alone all day, so she could get her [Chicago] *Defender* [newspaper] page out. . . . (Just think, she gets $50 a week for that page!) As Pauline says, there is no use having a college education!. . . . Eventually, Bessye and I get dressed, and Sol comes for us in a taxi.

It takes quite some time to round up Dr. Ross, who had surgical cases calling him. In the meanwhile, Bessye gets her to-morrow's chickens, and parks them in Marshall's car. We get under way a bit after ten. Stop down in the Italian quarter and get a gallon of good Italian claret. And the others eat raw clams. Then a long drive, away out in the country, over toward and beyond Pelham Bay, and finally to a quaint German roadhouse, where we have a private room, a pull with the German proprietor, and a very lovely dish of soft shell crabs, with our own highballs and claret.

None of which I touch. Pretend to drink, but dispose of it. Bessye gets "high," and about one thirty we leave. Bessye insists upon driving on the way back. It is a reckless, feckless drive. But eventually, she "passes out," and then the problem is how to awake her.

However, to Jay Clifford's. He is staging a big party. Half of it seems to be on the sidewalks. The other half is in his futuristic apartment, with divans, and love seats, and funny looking walls, etc., and most of those inside, as well as those out are pie-eyed. But not more so than Bessye, who insists upon saying Good night to Central, because Jay has a French telephone, and she had never used one before.

Sol runs into his son, whom he had not seen for four days. Everyone in the world is there. Pauline seems disgusted, and was ready to go when I got there.

The salad is gone, the punch unspeakable. I do not refresh myself. See Jay. . . . It is the worst mess of an affair that I ever saw—what even hard-boiled New Yorkers . . . designate as an orgy.

Howard Bearden is there, and Marshall is scared stiff about him—fearing trouble about his having been out with Bessye. Sol is uncomfortable, and Marshall spends most of his time pushing the bag of chickens at me.

Finally, we all decide to go to Mexico. When we drove up, Binga, Floyd Snelson, and a Dr. Spanish-named something stopped our car, saying that Mexico is slated to be raided. We drive on. Pauline was in her car, but never came while we were there, and I spent some unhappy hours wondering if she went on in.

We go home, Bessye still "high," and have lamb sandwiches, and claret. . . . It is after four before Sol goes. . . .

Daylight or later, after six, to be exact, Polly comes in to get her key. . . .

### Sunday, August 19

. . . Eventually, we got off at 2:10, leaving many good-byes and much promises. . . . Finally home by 9:15, all of us more dead than alive. Mama wild with joy, and Ethel in the same sardonic and angry mood that she was when we left. . . .

Find that Bobbo had been home Saturday—and to the office in Philadelphia looking for me! I wonder if he thought I would run away from New York to have a few words with him! Makes me tired. Excited, as usual. Nobody in the campaign will work as hard, do as much, be as excited, or make as little out of it as he. . . .

### Tuesday, August 21

. . . Polly meets me at the station with the *Evening Journal* and a screamer across the top. All the "number" kings, barons, and under-lings have been arrested and dragged to jail, including John Hopkins, Buster, Maceo Smith, Roland—about 100 in all. Rozelia and Mar-jorie, it seems, just escaped. They usually counted money—but Old Man Fisher smelled a rat and warned them not to go to work today. Emma [Sykes] seems to have escaped. An awful scandal, the papers bristling, the sidewalks sizzling—no other topic: "Dicties" in a jam, a scandal. Polly says Philadelphia is a tame, dull place compared to Wilmington.

Have tooth treated. Juice and Jean over to the house afterwards. Juice says he got out of the number business weeks and weeks ago. Scared. And was wise. Great gloatings going on.

### Wednesday, August 22

. . . Reached home and while at dinner a telegram from Laurence to Leila. "Boy born this morning. Mother and son wonderful." So Laurence Theodore Young, Jr. came on Wednesday, August 22. And I am a great aunt, Leila a grandmother, Mama a great grandmother and Pauline is already calling herself "Aunt Polly." We wired family congratulations.

Listened in to Al Smith's acceptance [of the Democratic presidential nomination] speech at Albany. Terrible rain made the exercise damp there and heap much static over the radio. But it was a mighty fine speech. Clear, definite, cogent, lucid.

## Thursday, August 23

The little Quaker lady from the Swarthmore meeting came into the office and added considerably to the gayety of nations by her stringent objections to the Negro in general and Negroes in Quaker meetings in particular. Her aspersions and complaints could not have been more bitter if she had come from Georgia. "I've had colored servants etc. etc." We all had a good laugh after she had gone. If she had known I was colored she would have died. Spend the day reading reports and theses on activities of the A.F.S.C. [American Friends Service Committee]. . . .

(This is the write up of my diary after I returned home—
September 7, 1928)

*D-N's AIPC-sponsored trip to Chicago gives her the chance not only to recruit members and get her committee work endorsed at the Elk National Convention, but also to visit her nephew Laurence, his wife Rebecca, and their newly-born son Laurence Jr. At the same time, her niece Pauline is visiting and Bobbo, her husband, is also attending the convention, which included auxiliary meetings of the Elk Daughters. All of the people mentioned are Elk officers, members, friends participating in the official—and unofficial—activities of the meeting.*

## Sunday, August 26

Awoke too early, after a good night. Ate a breakfast, which I did not need, and read until train reached Chicago. . . . Took taxi in Chicago. Begin at 25 and 35 cents, and the meter clicks every two blocks. . . .

Bathe, dress, and go at once to the hospital to see [Laurence's wife] Rebecca. It is a good little walk from the house, and the sun is hot. I dress in the outfit which I wore at Beck's and Laurence's wedding. It is one o'clock when I reach there, but as I am a stranger, the usual formalities are waived, and I am allowed to go up an hour ahead of the regular visiting hour. On the way to the ward I pass through the nursery, and asked the nurse if I might see if I could pick out Laurence, Jr. among the babies. There were four of them. I looked them over, and then selected a snub-nosed one, who was Leila, Jr. to the life. I was right and great was the marvel among the nurses that I could so unerringly select a five day old infant.

In an hour in come Pauline and Laurence, delighted and surprised to see me. We had a grand time fussing. Pauline averred that Laurence had walked her to death and fed her indifferently. . . . We go to the Chicago airport, and spend a lovely time there. See the huge Ford fourteen passenger airplane, see some planes land, and some take off in the glare of the search lights; then some ice-cream cones, home, and drop Pauline. Laurence insisted that we come into his apartment. It is a very pretty one, nicely furnished, with just enough things, not too cluttered. Reception hall, living-room, with day-bed, opened up for Pauline, bed-room, dining room, kitchen, bath. All neat, new, spick, span, lovely. For this he pays only $57.50. We leave here and home to bed. . . .

## Tuesday, August 28

. . . I am wandering around Pershing Road when Colonel Marshall and Roland Johnson hove in sight. Wanted to know if I would ride in the [Elks Convention] parade with them. Delighted, and hurry home to tell the folks to go on, and not wait for me. Run into Bobbo taxi-ing over to tell me *he* is going to ride in the parade. Give him the haha, and proceed.

Will ride in no more parades. Too tedious. Glad when the five mile journey from 69th Street to the Grand Stand at 35th and Wabash is reached, and we debark. SOME grand stand. Low rickety seats under a flapping canvas, reached by stumbling through weeds. But here we are. The parade did not measure up to the New York one, although there was better weather, clear skies, and a rapidly cooling atmosphere. Only took a bit over two hours to pass, as against New York's four. . . .

In the afternoon session, or rather the evening session, like a clap of thunder out of a clear sky, came [J.] Finley [Wilson]'s nomination from the floor and he was elected [Grand Exalted Ruler] by acclamation. Nicely put over, without any excitement and he is safe for another year.

When the Lindsey party was over, we went to the huge Coliseum where was the ball of the Elks. The usual awful horde, huge, undigested mob, Bobbo sat down on the steps and went to sleep. . . .

*In the following nine entries D-N is once again catching up her diary, this time from a three-week lapse.*

(Written September 21, 1928—This diary has gone long enough now. It is almost a month since it has gotten away from me, and I am sure I don't need to forget now. So many interesting things have happened and life has been so colorful that it seems a shame for me not to have kept up. And now I have forgotten most of the delightful occasions, but not all of the uncomfortable ones. However, I'll do the best I can.)

## Wednesday, August 29

. . . We were finally sent for. It was thrilling, to see all those men. I spoke first, and I spoke fine. Really did. Much demonstration. Bishop Sampson Brooks introduced me. Isaac Nutter arose and made a motion that an endorsement come from the floor. Rising vote. Mrs. Williams made a corking good speech, but her appeal was a strictly local one— only for the health work in Arkansas. Very good. Finley said we could take up a collection, but I felt it would be better to get on the appropriation for the educational program, and waived the collection. Maybe I had better taken it. . . .

Went over to the drug store to luncheon, and heard that the Daughters expected to put on their election in the morning. Knew it would be fatal for me to attempt to speak under those circumstances. So went home, changed into white dress, and back to church, and sat in the gallery. Bombarded [Grand Daughter] Mrs. [Ella G.] Berry with cards which I sent up by the ushers, and finally at a quarter to five, she called for me. I had to stand in the gallery and speak. That irked me, but I put over the message as well as I could. She spoke very feelingly, Mrs. Berry did, I mean, saying that she is a member.

Well, then, my job so far as speaking and covering the convention was over. . . .

## Friday, August 31

. . . All the log-rolling about the opening of the new Binga bank. Said reception to be at the new Savoy ball-room. Pauline did not want to go, being tied up with some ink-spot who had a Nash car. . . . However, as the Inky Nash "stood her up," I took her along with me to the affair. It was stiff and stilted and a lot of speeches, but finally wound up in a very gorgeous dance. . . . Geraldyn [Dismond, Chicago socialite and columnist] told of a party at Mrs. Earl Dickerson's which would be after the Savoy affair. . . .

The party was a "Low Down." The basement floor is waxed for dancing, and very attractive place, like some of the Bohemian New York restaurants and cabarets. Semi-lights, blues, and a punch that made you dizzy to smell it. Fellow by the name of Williams seemed to have annexed me as his personal property. Learned during his talk that he is the son of my old flame, Captain Williams, of Boston, who stirred my girlish fancies when I was twenty-one and he was forty-odd. However, the only girls smoking were the Philadelphia girls. . . .

It was four o'clock when I got home, [Dr.] Bias [Tuskegee veterinarian] taking me there. Bobbo in bed and raised hell. Had to cuss him out good to get peace. He couldn't get over it—that I was so late coming home, that I came home with Bias, and that I cussed him to get him to shut up. However, the party bored me to distraction, and Williams' violent advances made me tired. . . .

### Sunday, September 2

Bobbo was to leave today about noon for Washington, and I was to go to Benton Harbor to meet Blanche and Jessie for the two days rest and vacation that I felt was coming to me. So in a driving rain went down to the boat at the Municipal Pier. Such a storm! And such a taxi bill! A huge boat, larger than a Fall River line, or as large, but common and cheap in comparison. . . . Lake Michigan lovely, even in the rain. Slept two hours in my stateroom. Amused myself watching the dancing down stairs. Played the roulette game, and won two boxes of candy,—good candy, too. And finally at half past two docked at Benton Harbor.

Ensued then the most humiliating adventure in my life. No signs of Jessie or Blanche. Did not know where to go. Had no idea of the name of the place where I was to stop. Was not sure whether it was Benton Harbor, or St. Joe, which is just across the bridge. Jessie and Blanche had gone the day before, but if they gave me the address I did not remember it.

Spent a hectic two hours riding around in a taxi cab with a sympathetic white driver—for the colored drivers were haughty and unsympathetic. Called up Mrs. Morris, who tried to find out by telephone where was such a place, but distinctly high-hatted me. These Chicago Grande Dames are a pain! So provincial. I can remember the people who stranded in Wilmington have called me from drug stores or stations, to receive in response to their distress signal, my hearty, "Come right up to my house, and I'll see what I can do for you!"

In place of that Mrs. Morris' airy, "I'm sorry I can't have you come to my house, but I have an unexpected guest, etc." Even if Bobbo and her husband are bitter enemies.

So, after combing every possible avenue, I gave up, and sailed back to Chicago on the four o'clock boat. Did not take a state room this time, but passed the time watching the funny dancers and playing the roulette wheel again. Won another box of good candy. Two boxes I shall take home to Leila and the girls in the office, the other I gave to Jean.

The waves were quite violent on the lake, and the boat pitched quite a bit. More rain. Though it was bright and sunny, and blazingly hot in Benton Harbor. Jean was surprised enough to see me back so soon, bag and all, after I had made such a high departure. We could not understand why Blanche or Jessie had not met me, or why it all happened, so after wasting an hour in conjecture, I went to bed. And put another black mark against Chicago. The umpteenth. . . .

### Tuesday, September 4

. . . Go over to Maudelle Bousefield's school, the Keith. She is principal—the only colored principal in the city.

She is glad to see me, and the school was all organized and running on greased wheels as early as ten thirty a.m. the first day.

Have packed my bag. . . . And so get off alone in the taxi to the B. and O. station for the noon train. Chicago has not been hospitable. Somehow I have not made the grade here. Lots of functions to which I was not invited. . . . Well, I never did like the town, but this last trip was a bit of the worst. Was glad to see it fading from my view as the train pulled away. . . .

*D-N's "rough-necky" Wilmington friends below are* Arthur Wheeler, *who taught physical education at Howard High School, and his wife* Madeline. *He was the brother of the well-known artist* Laura Wheeler Waring. *What they interrupt is a "high brow" philanthropic meeting between D-N, other officers from the State Federation of*

*Colored Women's Clubs, a visiting white clubwoman, and her hostess.*

## Friday, September 7

Mrs. Rose had called me last night, telling me that Mrs. Falconer is in town, and making a survey of our school, and of the needs of the city. So had had Gertrude Henry call a meeting of the Executive Board of the Federation at the house. Purchased a lovely Canton China chocolate pot at Snellenburg's, and some cakes and cocoa and sherryjell at Hanscom's, and proceeded to entertain. Mrs. Falconer, who was Mrs. Tatnall's guest, came with that lady, and some other folks. . . . Mrs. Falconer spoke appreciatively of the needs of a working girl's home, and we formed a committee, etc. I served the chocolate and cake, and while we were all sitting around being high brow, the Wheelers [Arthur and Madeline] came in all rough-necky. I put them in the library, and Pauline soon had them down in the kitchen to get their refreshments. . . .

The ladies finally left, and I cleaned up the dishes. Then Arthur and I sat down to beat Madeline and Polly a rubber of bridge, and I gave them dandelion wine, and they left after midnight. Madeline said she wanted to see her friends before they got in jail, speaking of the "number raid" of John, etc. . . .

## Wednesday, September 12

. . . Begin my absolute fast today.

## Thursday, September 13

Go into [Philadelphia] office and read mail, and get ten o'clock train for New York. In the Democratic headquarters by a bit after twelve. It being the second day of my fast I was a bit weak, but drank much coffee without sugar or cream. Had to be drastic. Weighing 167 pounds and poking out back and front. Stuck to my diet of water and sugarless black coffee.

Lester [Walton, publicity director] takes story, and promises to play it up big. See Gaston [the campaign director] and talk with him. Rainey out of town. Never saw such a bunch of ineffective futilities in all my life. . . .

## Friday, September 14

. . . Broke my fast today by a bit of bread and warm milk for breakfast, and soup for luncheon. Found that I lost eight pounds. Whoopee!. . .

*The conference described here was initiated by the women of the Commission on the Church and Race Relations of the Federal Council of Churches, in cooperation with the Council of Women for Home Missions, and the National Board of the YWCA. The meeting was biracial. D-N made a significant statement about it when she said: "It was the colored women, by the way, who kept the discussions on a frank and open plane; who struggled hardest to prevent the conference from degenerating into a sentimental mutual admiration society, and who insisted that all is not right and perfect in this country of ours, and that there is a deal to be done by the right thinking church women of both races" ("As In A Looking Glass," Eagle, September 28, 1928).*

## Tuesday, September 18

. . . This second biennial Inter-Racial Council of the Federal Council of Church Women [at Eaglesmeer, Pa.] began at once, as soon as we had registered. I have a pleasant little room, albeit cold, for this is a summer hotel, and equinoctial gales already begin to blow. . . . And here is Dr. [George E.] Haynes [executive secretary of the Department of Race Relations of the Council of Churches] buzzing about and his secretary, little Miss Jeter, and Mrs. [Richard] Westbrook [the chairwoman] all smug and satisfied and too smiling, and all the rest of the churchly ladies, . . . and we settle down in the big living room in easy chairs and on couches, and everything before a big open fire, and the prayers begin and the conference is on.

There is tea at five, and I buy cards, and we dress for dinner, and eat together at various tables throughout the conference, trying to break up our relations and know as many as possible as we did at [the June 18–20] Pocono [meeting].

The night session is the same only more so. A furiously large program with a tremendous amount of topics on it, and not much time for any of it, and less time for healthful discussion. I feel that I am going to get irritated, and Helen [Bryan] is frankly so. It is after ten before we break up, and nearly half after eleven before we get to bed.

## Wednesday, September 19

A good warm bath in water that is as red as brick dust, but plenty of it hot and plenty of towels, and a sparing breakfast of orange juice, rolls and coffee. Then the first session. Then a photograph out on the front with a cold wind shivering us, and a brief cessation of the rain. Then luncheon. Then more session. . . . Head aches from being indoors so much, so I slip out between sessions and take a lovely walk in the mist and wind down to and about the lake for a bit. Fifteen minutes in the fresh air is helpful.

I pack my bag, but dress in my lace blouse and blue chiffon for dinner as I am to speak tonight. Succeed in getting Mary Whitten to talk, as she was being crowded out, and I knew she had good material. Our little party at dinner complained about the lack of time to hear real contributions. By the time it is my turn to speak, I am thoroughly cross, but do not stick to my subject, and ask for clarity of thought and frankness and truth. Makes an impression in some quarters but is the only speech which Mrs. Westbrook challenges.

Lucy continues throwing monkey wrenches in the works after I get through. She had been not so strong in her own sct speech but some of the irritation at the smugness must have gotten under her skin as it did under mine and Helen's and Miss Eastlack's, for she asked some pointed questions of the Washington church women. Altogether we gave the hypocrites an uncomfortable fifteen minutes.

But Mrs. Randolph and May Belcher brought it all back to sugary sticky sweetness and love with their closing prayers. And I changed back into my ensemble suit, which Pauline made me bring, and which I had had pressed by the hotel people. And we start out in the bus a bit after nine for a wild ride down the mountain side in the rain and wind. Not so good. I felt that if there was a bit of a skid it would be all over with us, and nothing to do but to go down the side of the mountain. But the twenty-four of us reached Muncy without any accident. Got the train, in the rain. I had an upper berth. . . . But a good looking gentleman, hearing me say sadly, "Mine is an upper," exchanged with me, and I was happy, and soon asleep. . . .

*D-N wrote about the Redding-Hastings situation of this entry with quite a different tone in her July 6 "As In A Looking Glass" column. She rejoices that Delaware is finally about to have a Black lawyer after much agitation and using the cry of "no lawyer" as a political and campaign issue. She mentions that* Louis Redding *is a native son and a graduate of Brown University and the Harvard Law School and concludes by styling* Daniel Hastings *as "one of the shrewdest and most astute politicians to be found anywhere in a month of Sundays" (in the light of this diary entry, not entirely a complimentary reference).*

### Friday, September 21

Put in most of the day at the office making up my diary. Seemed an awful thing to do just to spend that time, but my diary is going to be a valuable thing one of these days. Bobbo dropped in the office to say Howdy, having come to town. He seemed perturbed. Things worried him. I met him after hours at the Citizens' Hotel, and we had dinner together. Home on the 6:15. Louis Redding dropped in to call. Pauline had gone to Washington. . . . But he seemed to want to come in anyhow, and sat nearly two hours, while Bobbo went out and came back, and was cross, of course, as he always is, when I show any interest in any male or female, either. Louis and I talked, read papers, but something seemed on his mind. It came out just as he was leaving. He has already discovered what kind of a man Hastings is, and that he must compromise with his own soul if he is to remain in Hastings' office and "get on." His father is very keen on his being the "first colored lawyer" in Delaware, but Louis is already wondering if the price he must pay in compromise, renunciation of ideals and all is worth the dubious honor. He wanted advice. I wouldn't give it. Told him that was something he would have to fight out for himself. Don't want old man Redding thinking I have interfered in his affairs. And after all, Louis is going to do as he wants anyhow. Bobbo says I should have advised him to clear out, rather than compromise with right and wrong. Hastings is the lowest form of animal life. He would corrupt Satan himself. Bobbo says the boy came to his old teacher asking for bread and I gave him a stone. Perhaps. But far better for him to make his own decision, than for me to guide him. . . .

### Wednesday, September 26

. . . The big thing in my life was the meeting of the Peace Section at four o'clock. Such a bunch of disapproving-looking, stern old Quakers. They make *me* quake. Presented my report. Vincent Nicholson presiding is a male Ann Dingle only more so. Their austere attitude toward me was in striking contrast to their reserved pleasure at the reports from the Peace Caravansers—three of whom were present. Gave me a nervous headache. . . .

## Thursday, September 27

. . . The girls in the office thought I should go to the big meeting of the A.F.S.C. [American Friends Service Committee]. No one had invited me, but Gladys [the committee secretary] said I could go with her. . . .

So we rushed over by three o'clock. And sat until six while the ancient Quakers talked. I was gorgeously snubbed by the wizened little Henry Cadbury, the new chairman. He went all around, mentioning names of about everyone who was a stranger or visitor there, including the Belgian Hare (Milton Davis)—but not a word about me. Let us be charitable and say that he put me in the class with Gladys and Blanche— adjuncts to the office. And Vincent Ann Dingle Nicholson made the statement that the most important thing the Peace Section had done was the Peace Caravansery. However I have no quarrel with the Quakerfolk. I can watch them and weigh them and feel superior to them— and *not* impressed. . . .

## Wednesday, October 3

I knew Mama couldn't stand the strain. So many men, so many things to look after; telephone men, paper hangers, roofers, delivery of packages, laundry men, etc. etc. She's a wreck this a.m. and barely able to crawl out of bed so Gardner can paper her room.

I puzzle for help until Henrietta [another Friends' office secretary] suggests that Ethel go home and help out. No sooner said than done. I phone . . . Ethel and get her promise to meet me for the five o'clock train. She ought to be home instead of staying up here [in Philadelphia] a month. I'll have to pay, of course, railroad fare and bribes. However she met me and we went home to a frightful clutter. . . .

. . . Wait for Tom Clarke on the 6:16 from Washington. He arrives, pompous, dignified. Thank goodness, he had had his dinner. Had to fix Bobbo's dinner and mine. Pauline washing. House cluttered up with folks who wanted to see Bobbo. Paper hangers still there, Leila in tears over the hopelessness of her room and Mama's. Ethel mad because Mama isn't as sick as can be; Mama collapsed. Bobbo impatient and irritable. All of us hurried.

We finally get off for Dover and arrive at 8:43. Pythian Hall packed

to the doors and outside. A fine [Democratic political] meeting. . . .
Clarke and Bobbo . . . speak convincingly. And I, too, give an Al
Smith address. Short—but pointed.

We leave at 10:40. Stop at Smyrna and get some hot dogs, home
by midnight promptly. Polly to bed. The men get some chop suey and
we have tea with it and send Clarke to Annie Mabry's [where he is to
lodge overnight] in a taxi.

Forgot to say that I slipped away from the office and went up to
the Aldine to see Al Jolson's latest Vitaphone picture "The Singing
Fool."

Bought some bitter-sweet today. . . .

## Friday, October 5

This date always fills me with amusement—October 5, 1892, and
how heartbroken I was when Bis Pinchback went away and life was all
black. And exactly a month later, November 5, began my romance
with Nelson Mitchell [both sweethearts from her younger days]. . . .

## Saturday, October 6

. . . I hurry from the office at noon, . . . arriving at 1:17 in
Wilmington. . . . I rolled up my sleeves in my smock and dust cap
and went to work to try to get some semblance of order out of chaos
in these parlors. Scrubbing paint, washing pictures and putting things
to right. About nine o'clock when things seem about straight, into the
library and the files of *Eagles*. Another two hours' work, then hot bath
and bed. . . .

## Sunday, October 7

When I awoke felt as if I had been beaten. Would have given ten
singed cats to be able to stay in bed. . . .

## Monday, October 8

. . . Lovely Indian summer weather—lovely. And I buy my
needlepoint armchair, too. Had made up my mind to have one, and
found a soiled one at Snellenburg's for $16.75. And some darling
lamps. And an enamel polly white to replace the violet covered one
Bobbo broke. That's almost the last of the violet toilet set I bought

when Paul and I first set up housekeeping. And a new clean enamel pail for my bedroom. . . .

## Tuesday, October 9

. . . Have a rotten cold. I mean *rotten*. Buy a plant—one of the new "African violets" . . . at Snellenburg's for Krusie [her old friend and former principal Edwina B. Kruse], and stop by to see her on my way home. She is in bed permanently now, better than Sunday, but childish, not right mentally. She chuckled with delight at her having killed Dr. Stevens [deceased pioneering Black physician who had been married to Minnie] because she was tired of him. . . .

## Friday, October 12

. . . To the [Philadelphia] station and napped while I waited for [her niece] Ethel's train [from Wilmington]. Meet her and to the Academy of Music with her little fat bag, which I characterized as "a bag of bricks." . . .

The Academy of Music was filled by ten o'clock—for the audience was all evening getting in, getting settled, getting the right seats—in short the worst exhibition of poor taste, bad manners and worse management that I have ever seen. Marian [Anderson, world-renowned concert singer, friendly with D-N and Ethel] looked lovely and sang divinely—after her year in Europe. Milton Davis [a white acquaintance] was particularly charmed with her German songs. Marian's dress of gold lame and tulle was more than lovely.

Stood at the stage door to see her come out. . . . Pecked at Marian's cheek. Then drove home. Glad to get a ride down. I do so hate battling with trains. . . .

## Saturday, October 13

. . . The Graf Zeppelin reported near Bermuda with a broken pin shaft. For the next 36 hours we could get news of her always around Bermuda, but unable to get away. Adverse winds forced her 1000 miles off her course. . . .

## Sunday, October 14

Cooler this a.m. More like real October weather. A day of such perfect gorgeousness that Mama and Leila yielded to my invitation to

drive over to Downingtown [Pa.] with Polly and me. And it was splendidly worthwhile. Autumn at its best and loveliest. We reach Downingtown early—walk a bit and soon the "vesper service.". . .

It was a nice little service and we get away at 3:30. Loaf through
the park of a lovely estate we found on the road. Buy some cider and
cakes and bring a jug home. We hunt for bittersweet and find only
autumn leaves. And so home by five o'clock or thereabouts. Dinner.
Cold roast, hot gravy and rice.

Annie [Murray] and Arleon [Bowse] in as we read the papers. Later
Jean, Juice, Liddy [Stubbs] and Charlie Stewart. Party gets wild. I go
to bed and Mama raves about the [Sunday] dancing.

The Graf Zeppelin still hanging around Bermuda.

### Monday, October 15

Put in noon time buying drapes, etc. Spend a lot of money. Everyone on the streets excited over the Zeppelin. Stores filled with photos
of Hindenburg, and the crew of the Graf, miniature Zeppelins, etc.,
and the *Bulletin* stated that she has passed over Wilmington at 2:15.
It was 2:30 then and the streets were packed, roofs, windows, all. I
rushed in to [her Philadelphia office to] tell the girls and all ran out.
We almost missed it due to the narrow streets, but I saw the rear end.
Just enough to say that I saw the Graf Zeppelin.

At home dig into the library to get books weeded out. Find about
a hundred more. Looking like the devil when Bobbo comes in. . . .
My dirty face, short frock, and dust cap enrages Bobbo and he generally acts like the devil. He's half sick and about to develop one of his
nasty bronchial attacks. By the time I get him fed and coddled and in
bed, he's cooled off from his rage at seeing me look "like a chimney
sweep." It is 11:30 now and I go back to the books and the tapestry
binding and hit the hay about 1:30.

### Tuesday, October 16

Leave Bobbo in bed. Have a strenuous day at office. Suffering
again from that devilish acidosis. Makes me quite unhappy. Also it is
unseasonably and unreasonably hot and humid. Bobbo drops in to see
me and we decide to go home on the 5:15 together. When we reach
Wilmington he starts his ragging again and my appetite fails. Poor
Bobbo, he's so childishly afraid of being in second place. Had to get
downright firm about his growling. . . .

## Friday, October 19

Bobbo off, growling as usual. He is frightfully difficult these days. And that is putting it very mildly. Devilish is better. But then, he has a lot to contend with. . . .

Still shopping for things. House shaping up slowly. Some sweet day maybe things will look right.

Charlie Stewart and Chita McCard in town [from Baltimore]. So of course, Polly dippy. I finish the books in the library. It won't be long now. And put up the pictures. Pauline and I have our usual little chess game about that $15 check [Pauline's household expenses]. . . .

*This situation mentioned here provides a particularly striking example of the kind of unique slurs and prejudices to which Black women are subject and to which D-N strongly reacted. Governor Bilbo of Mississippi had said that Hoover danced with a Black woman. Hoover's assistant, George Akerson, issued a denial of the "charge," calling it "unqualifiedly false" and "the most indecent and unworthy statement in the whole of a bitter campaign." D-N was properly incensed and wrote this "scathing editorial" (unsigned, Eagle, October 26, 1928) entitled "The Ultimate Insult," which began ironically: "The ultimate insult has been given to Presidential Candidate Hoover. He has been accused of calling upon and dancing with a colored woman!"*

## Sunday, October 21

. . . Do a scathing editorial on Akerson's reproof of Governor Bilbo anent Hoover's dancing with a colored woman. . . .

## Tuesday, October 23

Find when I get on train [for her commute to Philadelphia] that Pauline had forgotten to give me my ticket. Could have bitten a ten penny nail in two at having to pay a dollar and a cent fare. . . .

## Wednesday, October 24

Helen continues to rave over my going to Rancocas and the "Peace Picnic" re Vincent Nicholson. Today Ray Newton invited me to go with many apologies and stammerings etc. I declined on the plea of a previous engagment. Helen was peeved, very. But I was obdurate; Ray was visibly relieved.

The Peace Section met at four and I read my report. No comment. Lot of futile discussion. . . . I left to hurry for the 6:15 which gets in at 7:23. Made me cross and tired. Afterwards Bobbo went out and I painted the stairs coming from my third floor and when he came in we had to sit down stairs until they dried.

Bobbo ruined one of my best bath towels and a guest towel mopping up blackberry wine from his clothes.

### Thursday, October 25

The day of Bobbo's big Wilmington meeting and here I am to be sent on a wild goose chase to Buffalo. Accumulated wrath, irritation, lost sleep and suppressed desires and what not break and I rave over finding that Bobbo has forborne to use the towels provided and plunged into guest towels. My ravings are wild and raucous. . . .

Sent Bobbo a telegram in the a.m. apologizing for my blow up.

Very cold. My two coats and fur hardly keep me warm.

### Friday, October 26

. . . Reach the office by 9:30 and get down to work. Planned to leave for Atlantic City at 12:10. Find to my dismay that the 12:10 runs only on Saturdays and the next train was at 1:40. An hour and a half to get into mischief. I succeed. After a luncheon at the Sandwich Shop, ankle up to Broad Street and hearing the amplifiers outside the Smith headquarters working overtime, conclude I'd drop in to see Mrs. Bergey. She was at the desk in front; the place was packed and jammed, a big meeting was on—about four or five hundred folks. In less time than it takes to tell, I am surrounded and embraced by Mrs. Bergey and the other lady who was at the dinner, hustled up to the front, introduced to the audience, and lo! I am before a "mike" while my speech is being delivered outside on Broad Street via the amplifiers. . . .

I reach Atlantic City at 3:05 without disaster. . . .

Back to the stuffy church and the fat women. Addie Hunton comes in looking more like Death eating a cracker than ever. I discover that I can get an 8:50 from Atlantic City to Philadelphia and there make good connections for home. [Her good friend] Violet [Johnson] quite peeved, but I am obdurate. . . Home by 11:36. . . .

## Sunday, October 28

. . . Hurry to dress and get ready to go to Philadelphia. Gamma Chapter [Delta Sigma Theta sorority] meeting. Pauline [like D-N, a member] balky about going. . . . She wavers quite a while but we finally drive up—and Leila goes too, much to Mama's disgust.

We drive to [Philadelphia physician and soror] Virginia [Alexander]'s new house and office. Everyone is late but eventually the Delta members arrive, about fifteen of them. . . .

We have a three hour session—the first part devoted to me and the A.I.P.C.—valuable for me and my project. Then the fateful elections. It were best to draw a veil over the harrowing scenes—the passionate appeal of me in the chair, the fateful blackballs, Wilma the proud, the tears of Clementine—well, all five candidates were lost, Clementine's hysterics and Wilma's passion—well, we came out nearly seven o'clock, and I've seldom had such a splitting headache. . . .

## Monday, October 29

. . . At noon go to Mansen and DeMany's [store] to change the pony coat. Eventually decide on a gray caracul trimmed with gray squirrel. Very beautiful and as near squirrel as I can afford. It cost $40 more, making total cost $275—not so bad, when we consider the $50 rebate on the old seal coat. . . .

We hear Al Smith's Baltimore speech over the radio. He pays his respects to the [Ku Klux] Klan most masterfully. Said he would rather go down to ignominious defeat than owe his election to a body like the Klan.

Bobbo loves my coat.

## Tuesday, October 30

Rewrite my "Why Vote for Al Smith." . . . .

Travel continuously and then do not arrive at the Kensington [Pa. High] School until 9:10. . . . Am hurried to the platform to meet the little principal—Miss Fenimore. 1500 pairs of young girls' eyes are facing me. I stand and tell the story of the Negro's gifts at Miss Columbia's birthday party [Miss Columbia represents the United States of America]. Receive a lovely ovation, and words of beautiful commendation from the vice-principal. . . .

### Thursday, November 1
### All Saints' Day

Get the 8:48 for Uniontown [Pa., where she is to make an Al Smith campaign speech]. . . . I can hardly recognize the town since 1915. My abiding place is down an impossibly rutty street—really dangerous looking, but the house not bad. The home of Mrs. Lucy Humes, after whom the "Welfare League" is named. There is an unconscionable wait and finally dinner—quite a pretentious affair in horrible taste, is served. Mrs. Connors, the president, is present. Then off for the church. A huge and barn-like structure which was not there when I was here before. And lo, some wiry little white sisters who remembered me in the suffrage campaign of 1915 when Mrs. Umbles had me staying at the hotel, came to hear me. But it seems the brother minister of the church had other ideas. He had invited a brother pastor from Washington, Pennsylvania, to have a service and that service must be had. The church was crowded with the congregation and the brother pastor was late, of course. We could not have our meeting until his sermon was over. We had reached an impasse. The suffrage sisters spluttered and were for doing something violent. A Mr. Moore was for going somewhere else. Outside the band was blaring and parading. I counselled peace and patience and my counsel proved good for the Washington brother finally came, and before preaching his sermon, talked for Al Smith, the band lugged in an additional crowd to the church congregation, so that the large building was packed and jammed and when religion finally gave way to politics—when Mrs. Connors had gotten her speech out of her system as presiding officer and the various local talent had sung and played and I finally got up to speak, I had an enthusiastic and wholly sympathetic audience. Therefore, "I spoke fine." . . .

Mr. Humes "almost persuaded" by my speech to vote for Smith, but fearing a Catholic.

### Friday, November 2

. . . And here was I marooned for ten hours [in Pittsburgh, Pa.]. . . . Called Julia Jones at the Pittsburgh *Courier*. Her welcome was hearty and unequivocal. Took a taxi to the *Courier* office.

Julia unaffectedly glad to see me and so was [editor] Bob Vann, mysteriously in town. . . . Had a delightful chat with him in his sanctum, whereupon he decreed Julia a holiday and placed his Cadillac at our disposal and called up his wife to entertain me.

Ensued a lovely day. . . .

### Saturday, November 3

Laurence's 27th birthday. Arrive Englewood [Chicago, Illinois, where she is speaking for the Democratic Party] at 8:35 and taxi to his apartment. Gray, chilly, drizzly day, but not cold. Good hot bath and coffee. Beck and the baby fine and soon have enjoyable time when Laurence comes in. . . .

### Sunday, November 4

Laurence got a good breakfast of calves liver, waffles, etc. which we ate late to the tune of the baby. Then we took pictures on the sidewalk in front of the house for it was a lovely spring-like day, hot as blazes in the apartment. Then the three go to the park leaving me alone, as I did not want to be possibly out when Mrs. Outlaw came for me. . . .

Finally Blanche Shaw and Mrs. [E.] Franklin Frazier [wife of the noted scholar] call, and Blanche's monologue is interrupted by Mr. Outlaw's arrival. We got together, they to be dropped at the Armory where Oscar de Priest [Black Chicago politician who served in the U.S. Senate] is staging a big meet with Roscoe Simmons [New York politician and writer] as speaker. They tell me that I should have been here on the 1st when an audience of 10,000 turned out at the Savoy and Armond Scott failed to put it over. Mozelle's fault. It shall always be my luck, it seems, to miss the Big occasions and be starred at the tiny, bum, back yard affairs.

The first place we stop is a hall with a band and a handful of dopesters and thugs sitting about. . . .

So we go to a church—a St. Matthew's A.M.E.Z. Here was Earl Dickerson and some dumb brothers from Indiana and the city. And an audience so stodgy that it was sickening. Like a January prayer-meeting. North-side Chicago not convincing. Flatter myself that I waked them up. Earl Dickerson grateful. I could like him. Tall, rangy, good-looking, pathetic, too, in a way. Cut socially because of his unfortunate divorce.

From there we get to the Colonial Tea Room back up in our

district. Here the Theta Sigma graduate chapter (Delta's) were staging a pretty little dinner for me. Very delightful of the sorors . . .

Home finally by eight. Laurence and Rebecca lying across the bed worshipping Sonny Boy. Earl Dickerson had promised to come for me at 8:45. . . . Get my reservations, have an interesting chat with Dickerson and so board my train.

Laurence, Rebecca and I had an illuminating talk in the a.m. all about his legal ambitions etc. I shall try to get Dickerson to help him. Gave Rebecca $5.00 to have the baby's picture taken. Gave her also a dollar to get it some oranges. Altogether give these two young folks $12.00 for my stay there. . . .

Well, travelled from Wilmington to Chicago with no more luggage than a brief case would hold, including my book. And the one black satin dress and suede shoes do valiant duty.

## Monday, November 5

Awake in my berth repeating the old phrase, "To my friend of November 5, 1892."

. . . In the Wilmington station at 6:08. Was glad to walk up from the station. Five days of inactivity had me feeling as Al Smith says, "Tight in the waist." The house is a pandemonium. Men men and more men, tramping to and fro and up and down. Mama in a state of collapse. Bobbo a bundle of nerves, chewing cigars or cigarettes or what have you. I change my clothes, eat something, tell the story of the baby to an admiring family—get a peck at Bobbo. And still the procession of men, men, men. Later Polly and I play pinochle and Bobbo joins us in a poker game wherefore I clean up from both of them. We get to bed about eleven, after I have unpacked and gotten straight and heard Bobbo's tale of woe. Josiah Marvel crooked—sold out—Democrats putting up no money; Bayard too high-minded. G.O.P. stopping at nothing.

## Election Day, November 6

Dawns clear and bright, spring-like. Too beautiful a day for Democratic victory. . . .

House a pandemonium. Polly told a tale of excitement. Eddie Chippey and Boots Evans [two of their working-class, Wilmington

associates] arrested for bribery. Bobbo disappeared for hours. Leila and
Polly worried and phoning everywhere for him . . . and all excite-
ment. Located him finally at the [Black, male, private] Monday
Club. . . .

There is a steady stream of men. Tense atmosphere. Make my
bed. About six turn on the radio.

Returns begin to come in. Good for [Al] Smith. Men, men, men.
Leila goes to bed worn out from looking after Bobbo and Lem all
day. . . .

Radio continues. Mama freezes to the living room. She has been
particularly devilish these days—nervous strain too much for her.

Bowse in for returns. Then Louis Redding. Smith's lead in New
York good. Then comes the debacle—state after state, county after
county—Hoover leads.

Juice and Jean come. We listen—at first hopefully—then at ten
o'clock the New York *World* concedes that Smith has lost New York
state. At 10:30 both the *World* and the *Times* concede Hoover's election. We go to the kitchen and have liverwurst sandwiches and Bronx
cocktails—Louis as superior as ever, Bowse glorying in being an Aunt
Dinah and a handkerchief head. The radio goes on with its tale of
disaster. We wash up the dishes and Bobbo and I sneak upstairs and
have a good old fashioned period of strafing and cussing before we get
to bed fairly exhausted. Poor Bobbo! As he sank to sleep he said, "We're
always on the losing side, aren't we?" . . .

### Wednesday, November 7

Awake rather early. Bobbo says he must shave and go forth with
head up and filled with pride. Poor Bobbo. He really expected Smith
to succeed. Though I knew he hadn't a ghost of a chance. I did think
he'd get 114 electoral votes. But to lose Texas, Maryland, Florida,
Virginia, North Carolina, Tennessee, Kentucky—to lose the solid
South! Hoover's strength is great in the fundamentalist sections of the
South! . . .

At the office various sentiments. F. F. [Frozen Face] I think was
disappointed though he voted—not for Hoover, but *against* Smith,
and that probably accounts for the huge vote.

. . . Go to the Fox Theatre to see the Russian picture, "The End
of St. Petersburg," a marvelous production, by Russian actors, directed
and produced by Russians, a pure propaganda for Kerensky.

The rest of the program is Russian and Peace. Best of all the Tchaikovsky overture "1812." . . .

### Thursday, November 8

Things are slowly shaping down to normalcy [from the election excitement]. . . .

### Saturday, November 10

. . . After a luncheon, and walking and seeing the same old Armistice Day parade twice, go to Wanamaker's to the toy store—"Venture Village," dwarfs, snow-maidens, Mother Goose rhymes and all—and *enjoy* it. Then rest in the restroom before setting out to the "Y."

[Artist friend] Laura [Wheeler]'s exhibit is really quite fine. I like best "Boy" and the French dolls. Laura all fat and radiant in a white lace frock. And husband. And the Quaker folk. And Nellie Bright pouring tea. Enjoy mineself and leave on the 5:57. . . .

### Tuesday, November 27

. . . Eventually get to . . . Brooklyn, via subway, taxi, and the grace of God. . . . Addie [Hunton] comes up as I debark from the taxi.

She has a delightful apartment. We have a rather elaborate dinner. . . . Afterwards to Annie Hawley's home where the Circle of Peace and Foreign Relations is meeting. All the old Brooklynites— Mrs. [T. T.] Fortune [wife of the radical journalist], etc. come in. I talk and we have an interesting time. . . . Get practical promise for them to come into the A.I.P.C.

Afterwards we play bridge. . . .

Home with Addie and try on her glad rags which she is taking to Washington for the game.

### Wednesday, November 28

. . . To Laura Pollock's and dinner. . . . After a very lovely dinner, some folks in . . . and the fortune teller. This is a professional lady invited by Laura to enliven the occasion. We go to her one by one for a seance in Arleon's room. She tells me a lot of interesting stuff and when I ask her a question about Bobbo's new scheme with Gaston, makes a favorable prediction about it. . . .

*Helen below is Helen Curtis, New York friend of D-N, whose husband was a diplomatic envoy. She had four Black children, the "African farm," living with her.*

### Thursday, November 29
### Thanksgiving Day

. . . The streets are full of "Ragamuffins"—kids dressed in ridiculous Hallowe'en costumes, begging for pennies. A quaint New York custom that I did not know about—never having been in New York on Thanksgiving, even when I lived here. . . .

Meet Bobbo at 1:30. We come on up to our room—which pleases him immensely. It is full of gorgeous fripperies and comfortable withal.

We dress and to Helen [Curtis]'s. She has the Mrs. Graham—ex-attache of the Liberian embassy, and with the African farm, we have a pleasant Thanksgiving dinner. . . .

Helen, Bobbo and I down to theatre. "Blackbirds of 1928" justifies to us its long stay on Broadway and its second company on the road. Particularly do we like "Bojangles" Robinson's famous tap dance up and down the steps. . . .

### Saturday, December 1

. . . After a funny dinner and some good trimmings, we go around to [housing project administrator and friend] Roscoe [Conklin Bruce]'s. The affair develops into bridge for the women—I stay awhile, with them, but soon drift out to the poker table and the men. Bobbo passed out early, but revived. I am two dollars sadder and wiser when we break up about 2:30 and Sol [Johnson], Bobbo and I stop and get citrate of magnesia on the way home. . . .

### Tuesday, December 4

. . . Lists from the Armstrong Association Study Class at the Meeting House and I am sleepy, as usual. All these "problems of Neutrality" don't seem to me to get anywhere. . . .

## Wednesday, December 5

. . . Start the history class at the Y.W. Girl Reserve. Twelve interested and enthusiastic girls—mostly juniors and seniors—high school. Think it is going to be interesting for me. . . .

## Thursday, December 6

. . . Inter-Racial Committee meets. A.F.S.C. [American Friends Service Committee]. Very interesting—if tiny. Succeed in getting elected as one of the delegates to the Inter-Racial Conference in Washington. And Mrs. Yarnall insists that I re-write the article that Helen and Mr. Thomas had written for the Inter-Racial Committee for the *Christian Century*. Funny.

## Friday, December 7

A hectic day. . . . Make nine o'clock time at the Selzburger Junior High. . . . Delight the children—about 600—ninth graders with Dunbar readings of about 15 minutes . . .

Hill comes in during the morning, all in a hurry as usual. Has time to turn pale when I tell him that Rhodes may not speak for us but looks better when I suggest Ed. Henry [Philadelphia magistrate]. Has his usual lot of "who struck John" before he leaves. Get down to Ed Henry's court by one. He is all tied up with speeches and conferences Monday and unavailable but willing. Says, however, that he thinks "Gene" [Rhodes] will be back.

Get some hot water (called chicken soup) and tea at the Marion Tea Room. Rush back to office to meet Helen and we take bus to Camden to the Chamber of Commerce where Bruno Lasker is holding a question and answer conference on Negro labor. All Bordentown and Atlantic City there and some of Newark too. We have to leave at a high point of interest and hurry back to Philadelphia for the Philadelphia Inter-Racial Council at the Ethical Culture. Here I have to act as secretary for nearly two hours and am fairly headachey by that time. . . .

Find some of the Executive Committee of the Federation at the house and eat a scrappy and disjointed dinner ere I go in to the meeting—which is quite lengthy. I am pie-eyed now but Mrs. Rose drives me down to Bethel Church where the N.A.A.C.P. is ending its baby contest. I had been assiduous for several days and collected $13.20.

Added $1.80 to make up $15—and carried check in (and nothing in the bank to meet it). There are all of eleven persons out—exclusive of the "judges" and we speak our pieces to each other.

Laurence Jr. comes in third—and gets a prize of $1.75—five cents less than I had added to the amount. So I pocket it and call it a day. Long after eleven when I get home—exhausted after five meetings in one day. . . .

### Saturday, December 8

. . . Morning mail brings check of $112.53 from Democratic Committee being the Chicago trip. I hasten to bank and deposit. Thank goodness for that.

Dog catcher after Jack. Had complaint from police blotter. Nobody but the Murrays [their neighbors]. Mean niggers. Shan't send them any Christmas card. Of course, Jack *did* howl. But that was Mama's and Leila's fault for locking him up when he was "at stud." . . .

### Monday, December 10

. . . See [lawyer] Hastings has been named to succeed du Pont who resigned Friday because of ill health. "Senator" Hastings! Ye gods! . . .

### Tuesday, December 11

. . . Anna [Brodnax] entertains the Bridgettes, most gorgeously. Oyster croquettes, etc. Insists that I go up to speak to Krusie. Horrible. Wish she hadn't. She looks like an animal—puffy under the eyes, just alive, eating, stupid. Dear God, let me die while I am useful.

*Here begin rumblings of uncertainty about the continuation of D-N's job. Though they are premature (her work does not end), the American Friends Service Committee does enter a period of organizational upheaval and financial stringency that keeps her more or less unsettled for a while.*

### Wednesday, December 12

As soon as I got to the office . . . , Ray Newton wanted an interview. It was heart-breaking. No $2000 by June—no more job. Lots of time saying it and many words, some talk about the office etc. etc. Left me blue all day and into the night. . . .

Well, everyone has something to be blue about. I felt that my happiness was too beautiful to last. . . .

### Friday, December 14

A day of climate—fog, rain, heavy, pouring, incessant, omnipresent. . . .

### Saturday, December 15

My glasses come to pieces in my hand as I am dressing and I have a very unhappy day. . . .

*The meeting that here brings D-N to Washington is the National Inter-Racial Conference. In her December 14 "As In A Looking Glass" column, D-N declares that the idea of inter-racial cooperation, which was initially sneered at, is now growing and gives as an early example of such cooperation "the historic meeting of the white and colored women at Tuskegee in 1920, and the furore which it created."*

### Sunday, December 16

. . . Reached Washington at 2:15. Went to office on trolley. We [D-N and Bobbo] sat and talked. I changed my dress. Ate at Thurston's new place. . . . Then to H.U. [Howard University] alone. Everyone gathered together. Quite a good time with [President R. R.] Moton and DuBois. Walter White and about everyone else in meeting. Moton and I have a lovely time. Walter White and Helen [Bryan] get together. Bobbo and Leamus come in. The meeting in the library a fearful bore—Charles Johnson [of *Opportunity* magazine and later Fisk University] dreadful. However, we get out, and home eventually. Think I'm going to have a good time.

### Monday, December 17

Up betimes. Take a cup of coffee at the corner and taxi down to the Department of Interior, where . . . I put in a hectic morning ushering, which largely consists in keeping out people who want to crash in without having paid their five dollars. It is really quite pleasant. At noon we lunch in the roof garden cafeteria. Shelton Bishop, Helen and I lunch together. Afterwards, a walk around the block and discuss Crystal Bird. Bishop told us that the whole story of her breach of promise suit against Roland Hayes [famous Black concert tenor] and the settling for $30,000 was in the New York *News*. And then, Helen had known it all along!

Enjoy meeting Donald Young [sociology professor] of the University of Pennsylvania, and lots of others. All along in the back of my mind is that constant nasty nagging of my loss of social touch everywhere, save in Manhattan. People don't invite me to parties, *anywhere*. Why?

But that is not an Inter-Racial Council problem.

Helen [Bryan] and I go up to [the Elks *Eagle*] office after close of afternoon session and get Bobbo. Office never looked filthier than when I saw it through Helen's eyes. We have dinner together at Thurston's. (The place is really very beautiful—new, clean and artistic.) Then Helen and I to Finley [Wilson]'s to clean up. Mrs. F. takes Helen for colored and makes a *faux pas* which is pricelessly funny. So to Howard University Medical building where Helen has a conference with Algernon Jackson, and later the evening session (part of which I sleep through, when the room is dark and the slides illegible and the speaker (from Johns Hopkins) unintelligible). Narka has come for us, and after much gassing around with everyone and Helen getting pinker and more excited every minute, Narka, Bobbo, Spaulding and I to Harrison's [restaurant] for devilled crabs. It is pouring rain. After we get home, I hate to see Narka drive off for her ten mile lonely drive home. . . .

*In this interesting entry, D-N does not mince words over her feelings about Washington, D.C. and Bobbo's situation there. After the presidential campaign and with no other prospects materializing, he has once more settled down in Washington to edit the Elks' newspaper, the* Eagle, *and is rooming with the J. Finley Wilsons, the Elk Grand Exalter Ruler and his wife.*

## Tuesday, December 18

Decided not to go to Conference this a.m. but to office and do my column. . . .

. . . We [D-N and Edith Fleetwood] go down together to Department of Interior [where Georgia Douglas Johnson worked]. . . . Have fun reading Georgia's new book of poems—"Autumn Love Cycle." . . .

Edith, Bobbo and I walk home—the latter [Bobbo] so grouchy and cross that I have to stop speaking to him and don't begin until next morning. Bobbo pretended he was angry because I kidded Charles Hall and the "gang" on the street. Really he was generally sore over the NAACP bunch and the party being staged for them, to which we were not invited. When I left Washington five months ago in August I vowed I'd not come back soon. When I leave this time, I'll stay away five years. Washington is a changed place to me since Bobbo came to live at the Wilsons. He nor they have neither social flair nor social contacts and my old friends have fallen away from me. It is humiliating. Bobbo feels that he has adequately entertained me and given me the proper setting when he has allowed me to sit around in that filthy pig pen he calls an office, and share his barren little room. Mrs. F.[inley] when she has given me a greasy meal in her cluttered kitchen. Disgusting. And outside of Narka [Lee-Rayford]—no one invites me anywhere. So I am quite bitter when Bobbo gets snippy with me. . . .

### Thursday, December 20

. . . After twelve when I reach the office. Martha [who works in the office] proceeds to "dish the dirt"—privately, of course. W. K. T. [Wilber K. Thomas] has resigned and things are to be topsy turvy. The office is to be closed from Friday to Monday. Talk of salary reductions, lost jobs, upheavals etc. Unrest and agitation all over the place and Blanche, incidentally, collecting money for a birthday present for W. K. T. ex F. F. [Frozen Face] for tomorrow. I contribute my dollar and put in considerable time trying to get a line on the situation. Looks bad from every angle. . . .

### Friday, December 21

Shortest day in the year and official beginning of winter. And it is winter. Crisp, clear, cold, about 20°. Fine and encouraging for the death of the flu epidemic. Quite a festive air about the office, with little packages being slipped on desks and greetings exchanged. Then we give F. F. his very beautiful set of George Eliot and all wax sentimental over it. It is his 46th birthday. Later he called me to his desk. Showed me his resignation and unburdened his soul. He feels hurt, but declares a load is off his shoulders. I express sympathy, genuine—too. He *is* out of a job and nowhere, at present, to turn. He will be with us, however, until February 1.

I went up to Philadelphia laden with bundles and come back likewise on the 5:15 plus a tiny Christmas tree for Kruse.

More addressing of cards and mailing them and wrapping parcels—not many—and in and out and up and down. Trying to catch some of that joyous thrill I always feel at Christmas—but unsuccessfully. Am I growing old? It is the first time in my life that I have had no thrill, no eagerness. I am doing the usual things—but dutifully, not joyously. . . .

### Saturday, December 22

. . . Home on the 5:15 lugging another Christmas tree. . . . We have a hectic evening marketing, green grocering, ten cent store shopping, buying wreaths, coming home to hang them—and playing pinochle to wind up. And *still* I don't feel Christmassy. . . .

### Christmas Day

Flawless weather, all day and a white moon at night. Awoke late, feeling of contentment. Everyone looked after—Paul, the furnace boy, the postman, all. . . .

The usual quiet day, breakfast. Then dinner, play cards, doze and to bed. . . .

### Wednesday, December 26

The morning after look over everything and everywhere. Bobbo and I up early, he to make the 8:05 for Washington. I for my usual 8:28 for Philadelphia. . . . Peace section meeting, and it lasts from four to six. I make a verbal report. Considerable discussion over budget as of June 1929 to June 1930. Ray [Newton, also a Friends Service Committee officer] has been howling at me all day. Atmosphere tense, anyhow, with W. K. T.'s resignation. I ask [chairman] Henry Cadbury point black to ask if the work of our Committee is to be budgeted along. Seems it is. . . .

Polly is giving a party—the same bunch which was at Alice [Banton]'s. I close my door and put silence and sleep between myself and the festivities. . . .

## Thursday, December 27

All thoughts suspended today for the "big" Service Committee meeting. . . .

I had prepared a report for W. K. T. to incorporate in his report to the committee. Though the agenda was long, nothing much mattered until we came to the reading of his report—which was masterly, especially his notice of the length of service of his workers. Follows the resignation. Follows one hour and a half of talk. Discussion. Talk. More talk. All about the resignation. W. K. T. and the Ex. Committee. . . .

My head began to split and stomach turn. Talk. Talk. Until Lucy Biddle Lewis [an influential committee member] gets sob-stuffy. Finally in sheer futility the meeting breaks up at 6:25 with half the agenda unfinished. A committee on reorganization appointed and a committee to confer with the Ex. Comm. and W. K. T.'s resignation unaccepted, save tentatively.

It is pouring rain when I come . . . home and find Polly with the new car, Mlle. Francine, called Frankie for short, ready to come after me. . . .

## Friday, December 28

Nothing much. Lull at the office. Everyone dead, emotionally exhausted. W. K. T. off to New York for that job he said he had to clinch. Ray Newton bears watching. He carries water on both shoulders. His speech yesterday shows that. Dr. Mossell [Philadelphia physician] called me up today. I went down to see him and Mazie [his daughter] at headquarters. Poor fellow. I think he's in a bad way. The future of the Douglass Hospital campaign will kill him. I promised to help. He offered me $500—poor fellow, they won't take in much more. . . . Mazie's hair is whitening and she is patient with her failing father. It's rotten and I, of course, must get in on this lame duck situation. . . .

## Saturday, December 29

. . . Out to Laura [Wheeler]'s—arriving there by seven-thirty. Her affair began at four and went on indefinitely. One of those highbrow things where you drink tea and indulge in improving conversation. . . .

Arthur [Wheeler] comes in to see about Polly and finds she has driven to Philadelphia, her car being intact and only the other one battered. She is still "Model T" conscious with her feet and does things in an emergency that shouldn't be done with a gear shift model. I quail a bit at the thought of going to New York under those conditions—but must always be a sport. . . .

### Sunday, December 30

Mrs. Lockridge delayed me this morning coming to talk about Alice Kent [from the Industrial School]. She has apparently dropped out of sight having left Tuskegee on Friday night (expelled doubtless) and having arrived nowhere. I tell her that having telephoned Tuskegee, telegraphed everywhere, stayed up all night to meet trains, put Travelers' Aid to work, etc., she has exhausted her resources and should go home, take a bath, go to bed and forget Alice. . . .

. . . To the Club Harlem [in New York City] where the Whoopee Club is staging a benefit. Packed, close, etc. etc. Same stuff. Little naked girls showing how they can "hand it up" etc. etc. . . . Since I am sober, I am bored early in the evening. Home about 5:30 a.m. . . .

### Monday, December 31

Am up and alone. Bessye [Bearden] downtown being sworn in as 5-year member of Board of Education. Polly asleep. This is the last I shall write in the diary this year. We shall probably go from party to party tonight and drink the New Year in. Then home tomorrow. God bless us everyone. I wish I were home. The kick soon goes out of dissipation for me. No sentiment. A real *affair* now—but I can't even get up emotion for that. Guess I'll stick to high-browing. No false sentiment over Vale 1928 atque Ave 1929, either.

Alice Ruth Moore and Paul Laurence Dunbar *(photo courtesy of Schomburg Center, New York Public Library)* as they appeared about the time of their marriage, March 6, 1898.

D-N in the early 1900s, while living with Paul in Washington, D.C.

D-N (right) and Henry Arthur Callis (left), her long-concealed second husband whom she married on January 19, 1910 (probably the year this photograph was taken). Pictured among this St. Matthews P. E. Church Sunday School class, Wilmington, Delaware, are D-N's three nieces and nephew (second row, boy at left and girl at extreme right; last row, two girls at left).

Alice Dunbar-Nelson, about 1920.

Robert J. Nelson, D-N's third husband, as he looked about the time of their April 20, 1916 marriage.

Portrait of a distinguished-looking D-N.

D-N (standing, right) with a group of other prominent women (Geraldyn Dismond, standing, left; Daisy E. Lampkin, sitting) in New York City around the late 1920s.

D-N (front right, sitting) and Pauline A. Young, D-N's niece (back, left), during a visit in Cambridge, Massachusetts, about 1926 with Evelyn Johnson (behind D-N), one of Pauline's friends.

D-N (front, right) at May 22–23, 1931 conference, "Finding the Way in Race Relations," Pendle Hill, the Quaker Graduate Center for Religious and Social Study, Wallingford, Pennsylvania.

D-N with her nephew's wife, Rebecca, and their baby son, Laurence, Jr., in Chicago, August 1928.

(Left to right) D-N's mother Patricia Moore, D-N's older sister M. Leila Young, and Rebecca and Laurence, Jr., about 1930.

Robert J. Nelson as he looked about the time of his 1932 appointment to the Pennsylvania Athletic Commission.

Alice Dunbar-Nelson, late 1920s or early 1930s, a few years before her death in 1935.

# 1929

(January 1–November 27)

*To float on and on into sweet oblivion*

NINETEEN TWENTY-NINE SHOWS DUNBAR-NELSON's American Inter-Racial Peace Committee secretaryship becoming more hectic and demanding. In addition to her usual meetings, speeches, programs, and so on, the parent organization is pressuring her to raise money. Literarily, she begins syndicating her Washington *Eagle* columns for the Associated Negro Press, shrewdly deciding that there is no reason to bury her light in one "dinky" newspaper (which becomes a strictly fraternal organ this year, causing D-N to completely stop writing for it). On the personal front, Robert—who turned fifty-six in May—is growing more depressed about his work and becoming preoccupied with playing the numbers. Though she is still on the Industrial School Trustee Board and in club activities, Dunbar-Nelson believes she is losing friends and is feeling like an "out[sider]." Finally, her health—somewhat troublesome in the past—becomes more problematic, and she submits to periodic liver drainages.

The health of two other family members also begins to sound thematically through the diary. Dunbar-Nelson writes about her mother's ailments as if she thinks they are mostly hypochondriacal and/or manipulative. Nonetheless, it was true that Patricia Moore (1850?–1931) was growing old. Born a slave in Opelousas, Louisiana, she had united with Joseph Moore, a seaman, probably of white Creole extraction, with whom she had two children, Mary Leila and Alice Ruth. He disappeared when they were young, and she supported the family in New Orleans as a seamstress. "Mama" was very strict, always lived with her daughters, and exerted considerable influence in the home—her only major outside activity being membership in the Episcopalian church. During these last three years of the diary, Dunbar-Nelson, the entire family, and the reader feel her growing impact.

The other physically ill person in the household was Ethel Corinne Young, Dunbar-Nelson's second oldest niece, who was born in

West Medford in 1899. Because of a chronic and worsening asthmatic condition, she was delicate, always in poor health, and could not go to college. Characterized by her sister Pauline as pretty, loveable, well known, and "everybody's pet," Ethel spent a good deal of her time visiting friends and family, especially in Delaware and Pennsylvania. For example, she was a favorite of singer Marian Anderson, who, on one occasion, came down from her home in Philadelphia to cheer Ethel in the hospital. Dunbar-Nelson, however, was not so enthusiastic about her niece, who returned the comparative coolness. The diary does not reveal the source of their mutual distancing, but it may have been rooted in traits of Ethel's that her aunt (who was a morally adventurous woman) perceived as ethical squeamishness, prudery, and judgmentalness.

The high point of Dunbar-Nelson's journal this year occurs during the four weeks in July that she spent at Highland Beach, Maryland, on the Chesapeake Bay. Coming during a period when she had been responding in an intensely physical manner to a strange man on the Philadelphia streetcar and reading Radclyffe Hall's lesbian classic *The Well of Loneliness* (first published the year before), the emphasis is clearly on voluptuousness and sexuality. Overall, the edited diary— for which there are (again, unexplainably) no extant December entries— reads more novelistically, like the unfolding of an interesting situation moving to some dénouement.

---

*This* Christian Century *article, datelined "Philadelphia January 5," surveyed the interracial efforts of the Friends Service Committee under five subheadings: "Peace and Race Conflict," "Bringing Japanese Students to America," "Lessening Prejudice Against Negroes," "A Remarkable Response" (to Crystal Bird's work of "interpreting" Blacks to white audiences), and "Showing the Way to Others."*

## Thursday, January 3

This is a rushy busy day. Piles of letters to answer and have to get that *Christian Century* article in. I hope to be passed on by the Inter Racial Section which meets at 3:30. At five I fad out of the picture and get the 5:15. Have a lazy evening, reading papers and listening to radio. A thousand things to do, but too inert to do them. Must be getting fat-headed. F. F. [Frozen Face—Wilbur K. Thomas, executive secretary of the Service Committee] has invited us all to a dinner

and party at his house tomorrow. Shall cut the whist tournament . . .
to go. . . .

### Friday, January 4

We all dressed up today [at the Philadelphia office] for F. F.'s party
and he beamed approvingly upon us when he came in. So we all went
out to Landsowne [Pa.] on the 5:30 train, and were met at the train
by F. F. in a big car, who took as many as it would hold, and the men
folks walked. I was interested when we got to the house, a nice, ordinary family looking place, with a large lawn, and a huge "For sale"
sign on it—how he proposed to feed all that mob of twenty, which
with the family made twenty-five, at dinner. But the problem was
solved by the family appearing with trays, each individual, with his
own tray, on which was the plate, with minute steak, mushroom sauce,
petit pois, candied sweets. Then came hot rolls, butter, passed, and
water, and later olives, pickles, many jellies. A lovely nut sundae,
coffee, cakes, mints, nuts, and the dinner was over. No muss, no
tables, no nothing of a nuisance. Then we had music by the Thomas
family—[daughter] Jane plays and [daughter]Helen sings, and FF plays
and Mrs. W. K. T. [his wife] sings, and some recited limericks, and
jokes, etc., etc., . . . and finally we broke up. I was the only one going
into Philadelphia via the train, and someone drove me to the station
. . . and so caught the eleven o'clock from the Broad Street station.
Took taxi up, and found the family but just gone to their rooms, and
Edith [Fleetwood, their close friend from Washington, D.C.] in bed,
all snug and happy to be here. . . .

*According to a January 11 Washington* Eagle *article, this Research
Club was one of the oldest and most important in southern Pennsylvania. Mrs. George Johnson of Lincoln was the president.*

### Monday, January 7

Today finds me grinding like mad to get my speech ready for the
Research Club at Oxford [Pa.]. And I just about get it in shape before
it is time to make the 2:28. . . . The trip to Lincoln University is a
whang. Two hours and a half to go 45 miles! The last stage from
Wawa [Pa.], where we changed, made in a train run by gasoline, and

Advertisement in the Urban League's *Opportunity* magazine, October, November, December, January, 1928–29.

For her lecture on "The Relationship of the Negro to International Peace," D-N was paid $25, a fee which she did not often receive. She pasted this card for the series into her diary.

Program cover for D-N's very successful 1929 National Negro Music Festival, staged May 25 at the Philadelphia Academy of Music.

# American Interracial Peace Committee

❧

THE American Interracial Peace Committee, which is sponsoring the National Negro Music Festival, is the joint effort of representative American Negroes working in close co-operation with the American Friends' Service Committee, to develop and enlist the active support of the Negroes of America in the cause of Peace.

It aims to promote the spirit of understanding, good-will and co-operation between the races in America, as the basic principle of the Christ-way of life.

It presents to the Nation and to the world those talents and accomplishments of Negroes that may serve the cause of Peace.

It makes known and provides facilities for the expression of that increasing body of white citizens who are united in spirit with this cause.

It seeks for the Negro the open door of fraternal co-operation with all those agencies—industrial, social, religious and political—devoted to the cause of Peace.

It stimulates a public peace opinion in the press and on the platform.

It stresses loyalty to the fundamental ideals of the Declaration of Independence and the Constitution of the United States.

It teaches the fundamental equality of all races.

It joins hands with all those organization that are aiming to make war impossible.

Any American citizen who may be interested in furthering the cause of Peace, by the development of those right human relations which are the basis of Peace, is eligible for membership.

The American Interracial Peace Committee began active work in June, 1928, under the direction of the Peace Section of the American Friends' Service Committee. As the 1928 exposition of the talents and accomplishments of the Negroes in the cause of peace, there was presented at Broad Street Theatre, May 6, a program of speakers and music, in which the best of both races joined hands in the cause of Peace.

For the 1929 contribution, the National Negro Music Festival!

The program of the American Interracial Peace Committee is one of education; of reaching the youth of the race with the message of Peace and Interracial Good Will. The message has been brought before thousands, in churches, in schools, clubs, conferences, conventions, through literature, speeches, personal contact.

The war-weary world cries for peace now as never before. The Negro has made his greatest and most lasting contribution to America in the arts of peace, in the great gift of song. Youth cries not for death and hate and turmoil, but for life, and love and understanding.

This inside front cover of the program, which explains the AIPC and the Festival, was almost certainly written by D-N.

heated with a little coal stove in the corner.

It is bitterly cold. Professor Johnson met me, and to the house where I had a chance to get in a nap before dinner. This last is an important matter. Several guests—besides the family, and then we are ready to drive over to Oxford. It is now down to 17 degrees, and sharp and bitter.

The Research Club meets in the lecture room of the Presbyterian church. Good crowd out, in spite of the "flu" and the bitter weather. My talk on the "Negro's Literary Reaction to American life" apparently appreciated, but of course, they would want to hear dialect Dunbar [his poetry written in "Negro dialect"] at the end. Makes me sick. . . .

## Thursday, January 10

Pouring rain this a.m. Cold and mean. I put in a busy morning planning my itinerary. Then out to the University of Pennsylvania to meet Donald Young [head of sociology dept.] on the steps of College Hall at 11:55. His class at 12 in familiar old [room] 305 where I used to have Bible. . . . Talked for half hour—[fifty] case studies of juvenile delinquency—then the boys asked questions for 20 minutes. Enthusiastic applause marked the end of the discussion. Then Donald Young took me to luncheon. . . . Very interesting little lunch-room. . . .

## Friday, January 11

The morning mail at the office brings me a letter from [bank officer] Reiley with a flat refusal of the loan of $200. Reason—bank balance too small, payments on previous notes unsatisfactory. Well, that's that—and now for the next move.

Brought all my putter up and at five o'clock doll all up for the I.O.P. dinner to [A.] Philip Randolph [militant Black labor leader] at the Southern Grill. Very interesting dinner and Randolph speaks interestingly. . . .

It is late before we get away from there and we—Randolph, Lancaster [Randolph's associate], and I are driven by Helen [Bryan] to Germantown in her Maxwell coupe. Me seated on the knees of the gentlemen. . . . Home in Germantown—typical Quaker, beautiful. Plenty of folks there. Frogs and Quakers and highbrows. A violinist playing when we get there. Refreshments and we get back to Broad

Street by 11:30. . . . The Fireside Club (that was the meeting) asked me to be guest speaker in March. .Go to Helen's room at 304 Arch Street—Quaker Home and Meeting House. Lovely room. Take hot bath and into one of the double beds. . . .

## Monday, January 14

. . . Day started all wrong. Almost zero temperature, and the pipes are frozen. Because we went to bed too early, kitchen fire out. Did not know the blustering winds would subside into calm so did not drip the pipes.

Bobbo cross and hateful as the devil. Puts me in a bad humor which lasts half the day—near zero weather and all. . . .

## Thursday, January 17

. . . Leave on 5:50 for Baltimore to speak at "Y". . . . Bulletin says "obstruction on tracks at Short Lane." But go blithely on. Train stops at a point near Perryville [Md.], and then ensues a tedious wait, enlivened by all sorts of weird rumors of dead and dying, and weirder incidents. Eventually, I make friends with a fireman on a neighboring north-bound train—trains are piled up ten or more in both directions. Succeed in getting on the North-bound train about ten or thereabouts, and reach Wilmington a bit after eleven to the surprise of the family, which is still up, all but Edith and Mama. Borrowed a dollar . . . for fear I had not enough to see me through. And thus is another Baltimore speech ended before it begun by an accident in transit. . . .

Heavy, gummy, sticky fog possibly made the accident. Three trains involved and a whole crew killed.

## Friday, January 18

. . . The International Club meeting tonight; Chinese night; Amy and Chauncey [Wu, Friends' office secretary and her husband] entertaining. . . . Down on Race street, real local color, Chinese quarter and all. Never saw so much food in my life. About fourteen courses of Chinese food, and not one dish that I ever tasted or heard of before—except the rice and the lovely, lovely tea. The highbrows go to the Little Theatre on DeLancey Street to see three plays in French by Pennsylvania students. I go home on the nine something. . . .

## Tuesday, January 22

. . . Board meeting at three o'clock. . . . Very strenuous. Most of all is the putting the kibosh on my southern trip. And I get so tired of this howling for three thousand dollars that I am supposed to raise. I fairly cried with vexation! . . .

## Wednesday, January 23

. . . Have to get down to the National Benefit [Life Insurance Co.] office by 2:30. See both Rutherfords, and extract a check of twenty-five dollars from them, with the promise of twenty-five more on June first. I had hoped for two hundred. . . .

## Thursday, January 24

. . . I have an opportunity to read, bathe and get to bed early—fairly. Mama still enjoying poor health, although she has shed some of her head covering, and announces that her mump is better. Very gloomy, though.

Had funny experience on train. Little old man took a fancy to me, and had an ardent desire to borrow my paper, exchange addresses, give me tangerines from Florida. His ardor grew uncomfortable, so I got off at Wilmington, even though I had intended to go right through [to a speaking engagement]. . . .

## Saturday, January 26

. . . Got twenty dollars fee. Expenses about eight or nine, so the rest is mine. (Wonder what became of it?) To the office and put in quite some time. F. F. still in a state of blibber, so it is after one before I leave, as I have to listen to his fulminations. Out to Mrs. Ira Bird's for her luncheon. . . . We have a gorgeous mess of shrimp a la Creole, fruit salad, coffee, French pastry, wine, etc. And gossip ourselves pop-eyed. . . .

*Referred to here are* Jules Bledsoe, *a baritone who starred in* In Abraham's Bosom *and appeared on Broadway in other Black musicals and sang in private concerts, and* Bert Williams, *multitalented Black actor, famed for his "Negro comedy" routines.*

### Sunday, January 27

. . . After dinner to the Gallo Theatre [in New York City] to the very swank Jules Bledsoe concert. . . .

Bledsoe very good; the theatre crowded; everyone all swanked up in togs. Bledsoe gives the usual English and German songs, then for a scene from "Aida" in costume, wherein he is Amonasro in tiger skin and rusty knees, and throws pretty white lady, opera singer from the Metropolitan Opera Company, all over the stage. I held my breath, but the audience did not seem to mind. Time was he would have been shot. Shades of Bert Williams, who was not even allowed to come on the stage in the Follies when the white girls were on . . .

### Tuesday, January 29

. . . In a not too long time we are up in Harlem again, tired, and cold. Too far for me. I've gotten out of my metroplitan habits of journeying from town to town for a talk or a cup of tea. . . .

### Wednesday, January 30

. . . It was a relief to get home at a decent hour and not to have to go out. . . .

### Friday, February 1

. . . Edith and Pauline arrived at [her office in Philadelphia] 6:30, according to schedule, and after taking the car to a garage, and setting Edith's feet toward the Little Theatre, Pauline and I to Keith's [theater] to hear "Gotterdamerung." Had never heard it, and the music most beautiful, and the whole thing so well done, that it was a joy to the soul. Even the fatness of Brunhilda did not deter my enjoyment. That symphony orchestra was itself worth the price of admission ten times over.

Left the theatre at twenty minutes to twelve, got the car, picked up Edith at Broad street station according to agreement, left at exactly one minute to twelve, and opened the garage door in Wilmington at one minute to one. I had only a sandwich for dinner, so ate something before going to bed.

Edith did not get into the Little Theatre. They drew the [color] line [of segregation] on her. I shall not recommend any more theatres to her; every time I do, she has an uncomfortable experience. Poor kid! She does have the rottenest times!

### Saturday, February 2

Board of Directors meeting at eleven a.m. Uncomfortable, as usual. [Leslie Pinckney] Hill [chairman of the Inter-Racial Peace Committee] rushed, as usual. Has a dead teacher whom he is taking to New York for the funeral, and had to leave on a 12:15. Next time it will be something else. He's always too rushed to do anything but get HIS remarks out. My trip south squelched. Not sorry. I was feeling blue about it, anyhow. Everything now for the [National Negro] Music Festival [which she is planning].

Martha [her secretary] did not come in today for her last day. She told me some time ago that she was leaving. This knocked me into a cocked hat. Asked Blanche to assign me Henrietta [the Black secretary], and this was supposed to be all fixed. But F. F. called me into a conference, and said that he had never approved of Henrietta's working for me, as it made "compartments"—meaning segregation. Then, too, in the retrenchment, Miss Dunn is to go first, then Amelia, and then, unless she is indispensable to some one—Amy. Which would be hard on her and Chauncey and the baby. So I agreed to take Amy for my secretary. Everyone pitying me. . . .

### Sunday, February 3

. . . Somehow, I had the idea that the [speaking] engagement was at three o'clock in East Orange [N.J.]. It was not until I got on the train that I saw it was not until six. So, as I had had a fussy letter from Violet [Johnson, her good friend], decided that I would go over to Summit and see her. . . . I go on to Summit by way of Newark, first calling up. Find Vi lying down. . . . Buy a ticket to East Orange. We stop at Orange, and I look idly out of the window. And then that subconscious mind of mine, which keeps me from being an absolute ass, bade me look at my letter, and lo, the Oakwood Avenue Branch was in Orange. I literally FELL off the train, got a taxi and to the place. Skidding over the thick ice in the yard. So the three o'clock engagement at East Orange was a six o'clock one at Orange. . . .

## Monday, February 4

Begin with Amy today as my secretary. We'll get straight some day, I guess. Since I have to dictate two score letters breaking engagements, don't feel so good. Quiet evening at home. The *Christian Century* sent me a check for $5.40 for the article which I rewrote on the Quakers. . . .

## Wednesday, February 6

The weather all along has been clear, cool, crisp, frosty. Plenty of good skating. The ponds lovely with graceful figures. The air a delightful tang to the nostrils. Today is rainy, foggy, messy—flu weather. . . .

## Thursday, February 7

I had thought it was today that I was to go to Germantown [Pa.]. But got mixed up. However the Inter-Racial Section meets this p.m. and I turn over the $5.40 from the *Christian Century* article. Milton thought I should. It is promptly donated to the A.I.P.C. [American Inter-Racial Peace Committee]. Able to get home reasonably early and to bed by 9:30. . . .

## Saturday, February 9

Get the 1:17 home and to the [Wilmington] Playhouse. SRO but I buy the ticket and get in. Edith and Polly had succeeded in saving me a seat. "White Lilacs" is a lovely musical play based on the life of Chopin and George Sand as "Blossom Time" is based on the life of Schubert. It is very lovely and DeWolf Hopper supplies comedy in the character of DeBussy the publisher. A succession of lovely pictures, too, like the paintings we are used to. . . .

*D-N salvaged these two dates in Virginia from the more extensive "southern trip" that she had originally anticipated.*

## Sunday, February 10

. . . To the "Y" girls hour. Evening service in [Hampton Institute] Ogden Hall. I make a rotten speech. Felt it—coming after Jim [James Weldon Johnson]. . . .

## Monday, February 11

. . . A most fascinating hour poring over African curios—not much time for other nations. An interesting boy from Sierra Leone gives me hints. Acquire three carved amulets for good luck. . . .

## Tuesday, February 12

. . . Reached Richmond [Va.] at 11:33 and took taxi to Hartshorn College. A sorry sort of place. The principal—a white man—Baptist missionary school. About 400 girls. . . . The dean of women—Miss ——— is very pleasant, white. A mixed faculty. Speak to the girls and have dinner. . . .

## Friday, February 15

Writing this (and some of the preceding) in the Hotel McAlpin in New York [where she has come to make a radio talk]. Rank extravagance—but I'm reveling in it. . . .

For peace and comfort decide to come to the McAlpin. $5.50 a day—but worth it just to have a room and bath etc. etc. Good hot bath, rest, dress leisurely and to the Steinway Hall, up to the 17th floor to the studios of WABC [for Negro Achievement Hour]. Fascinating to see how radio is broadcast. The Clef Club [jazz band] and Geraldyn Dismond and a Lillian Galloway Stakeman and Mr. Boris and Mr. Brown the announcer. All very fascinating. Through at 12:04 and I taxi back to my sixteen story room. . . .

## Saturday, February 16

While I am luxuriating, I might as well be consistent, therefore I lie in bed and order my breakfast by telephone. Soon the man brings me a table and *service*. Only orange juice, coffee and rolls, but a multitude of plates and ice and silver, etc. Lovely. *Too* luxurious for words. So I smoke a cigarette, read the morning paper—slipped under my door—and telephone. . . . Bessye Bearden is cool. Someone has told her something and she is breaking with me. Sorry. I've lost both Geraldyn [Dismond] and her. Something wrong with me somewhere. Can't keep friends I want and can't get rid of friends I don't want. . . .

. . . Lo! Caspar Holstein [racially conscious NYC racketeer who provided the money for the *Opportunity* magazine literary contest prizes] is in! We have an interesting and illuminating interview, and though I do not get any money from him, I get hope that it will come later.

Feel more cheerful when I leave him. . . . [Back home in Wilmington] Leila and Edith in bed as per usual. Mama not as bad off as she'd like to be, but delighted at the doctor's coming to see her. Pauline said they got most of the [Negro Achievement] hour on the radio and delighted with my pronunciation, etc. . . .

### Sunday, February 17

Up early. Wash windows in Mama's room and the library and change curtains in former. Mama wants everything clean "in case anything happens." She keeps her teeth in for fear Leila and I wouldn't have him [the undertaker] to put them in. We have a lot of fun at her expense, as I assure her that the undertaker would get them in if he had to break her jaw.

Alain LeRoy Locke [Howard University professor and Harlem Renaissance cultural entrepreneur] is the speaker at the famous "Open Door Forum," and arrives early enough for dinner. We have an indifferent meal. Edith is happy. They have a good time together—a regular old home week. Have not seen her so excited and joyous for years. He makes a good speech at the Forum, comes home, and we have ice cream. Leaves for the Elberts' [a leading Black Wilmington family] on his way to the station. I get a chance to read the papers, and Edith goes to bed so excited that she almost has a chill. Mama thinks "Roy" is the cat's pajamas, because he put his arm around her as she lay in bed. . . .

### Friday, February 22

. . . To market, and home to cook me the kind of dinner I wanted. Beefsteak smothered in oysters, and queen of puddings. . . .

### Saturday, February 23

. . . To the office. Have date with [Leslie P.] Hill at eleven, and as usual he calls up to say something has happened and he can't get in, and will I just "run out" [to his school in Cheyney, Pa.], or spend the night, or come in the morning, or something. As usual, I am in tears, but we finally compromise by his agreeing to come in at 2:30, if I will wait for him. So I go to [her beautician] Marie's and get a wave and a manicure, and back to wait for him. He arrives at 2:30, and we have the most satisfactory interview yet. But he has DONE NOTHING about the festival of music, except write lovely essays on the Negro's contribution to music. Nothing concrete or definite. I see my work cut out for me. . . .

### Sunday, February 24

. . . Home, starved out. But before I can eat, I blow up and go to bed without food. Bobbo made me mad. Guess I was tired, irritated, hungry. He CAN irritate me. Edith brought me some dinner to my bed. I drank some of Bobbo's concoction, and smoked cigarettes. Bobbo and I made up, but I still felt mean. . . .

### Tuesday, February 26

What I am doing with a blank calendar, I know not. But I get my stuff ready for my column. Have begun to syndicate the *Eagle* column in the Associated Negro Press. No need hiding my light under the *Eagle* bushel, and since there is to be no money anyhow, might as well capitalize publicity. . . .

### Thursday, February 28

. . . When I get in the house, having eschewed taxi in spite of the lame knee, Mama informs me that Edith had a telegram from Garnet Wilkinson [Superintendent of Colored Schools, Washington, D.C.] and that she must report for duty next day—Friday, March 1. . . . Therefore I make ready to go with them. . . . She is partly happy at getting her job back, partly sorry to be leaving us. I am wholly sorry.

### Friday, March 1

. . . Over to the [Washington, D.C.] *Eagle* office. Bobbo out, so to Thurston's [restaurant], where I sneak up on him and kiss him on the back of his neck! . . .

### Tuesday, March 5

Such a storm! Where does all the rain come from? I noticed from the train that south Wilmington is under water, and our cellar is a mess again. Pretty soon we'll have to have hip boots to fire the furnace. . . . Had a bad attack of heart and insomnia and nerves last night and indigestion this a.m. Must ease up on the pituitrin [a trade medicine, aqueous extract from cattle pituitary gland]. . . .

### Saturday, March 9

Sleep until ten o'clock then have to hurry to get dressed by the time Mrs. Rose [the chairwoman] calls for me to go to [the Girls Industrial] school for the Board meeting. Good attendance—but what good? . . .

### Sunday, March 10

Bobbo leaves on the 11:49 for Baltimore and I have a lovely, busily peaceful day. Cleaning closets, gathering junk, reading papers, clearing out things. Gorgeous! I discover the perfidy of *The Chicago Whip*—publishing *my* ["As In A Looking Glass"] review of *Mamba's Daughters* under Georgia Douglas Johnson's name!

### Wednesday, March 13

. . . Since "The Scribblers" meet early—before the history class at the Y in fact—decide to go home, even though I may have to leave in the morning on the 7:22.

The Scribblers turns out to be a group of youngsters . . . who have the urge to write. Ugh! . . .

Much correspondence about the plagiarism of the *Whip*. Bobbo refuses to take it seriously. For me it is a very serious affair. [They subsequently printed an apology.] . . .

The Magic Island, *mentioned below, was considered by many people to be a commercially exploitative book based on Haitian voodoo, ouangas, charms, and the like. But D-N thought it good social and political history (Eagle, "As In A Looking Glass," March 1, 1929).*

### Friday, March 16

. . . New York by seven . . . to the [National Association for the Advancement of Colored People] ball. . . . I am to sit in [NAACP field secretary] Walter White's box, though I start out sitting in Inez Richardson's and dancing with Jack Nail [J. W. Johnson's brother-in-law]. Very colorful affair, with plenty of ofays [whites]. Carl Van Vechten and his Russian wife—he looking more like a white slug than ever. I meet [W. B.] Seabrook, who wrote *The Magic Island*, and find him very interesting. And Fannie Brice. And an interesting Russian. And some others. Find a curious selfishness on the part of the Jim Johnsons and the Walter Whites and have my usual loneliness in the crowd. Oh, so pitiful! . . .

## Tuesday, March 19

. . . I slip off [from work] at noon and go to see the new colored movie, "Hearts in Dixie." Good photography, singing and dancing and some good acting—particularly Clarence Muse and Stepin Fetchet. Had to write about *something* this week. . . .

## Thursday, March 21

. . . So hot. When I get home, all exhausted . . . found Mama and Leila all dressed to go to the Fashion Show. After the usual excitement of finding Pauline and getting her to get ready and go, they all got off and left me to a quiet, peaceful evening sprawled out in front of the radio, with the evening papers and mine [?]. I was dressing the brown-skin doll I had bought in New York last Saturday when they came home all agog and glee with the beauties of the Fashion Show and Anna Brodnax's glittering ensemble. So I dressed the doll—Octavie—in glittering lace—a fragment left from the dress I wore to [U.S. President] McKinley's second inauguration ball [when she lived in Washington, D.C. with Paul Dunbar]. . . .

## Thursday, March 28

. . . Mama and I upstairs early. But I sew until nearly one o'clock on a negligee made out of my old evening (blue georgette) gown. . . .

## Wednesday, April 3

. . . Reach Burris Mills [N.J.] and the old inn at 11:45. Lovely old place. Overcrowded with nearly 200 embryo ministers, women etc. for the [annual spring] conference [of the AFSC Peace Section]—

"The Challenge of War to Christianity." Somehow get my room, take a nap, walk, look around at the lovely place, dinner, go to lecture by Sherwood Eddy. Wonderfully fine. Bed by ten, thank goodness. Glad I could get a room alone. . . .

### Thursday, April 4

. . . Vincent Nicholson [of the AFSC] gives me a lesson in golf. Then another discussion group. The morning lecture—but before that I take a nice long walk, smoke a cigarette in the woods, and find some arbutus. *My first.* All my life I have hoped for arbutus—and now, right in the middle of the path!

After morning session . . . a gorgeous nap. Oh, how I am enjoying my naps. Except that I am eating too much—oh much too much—and not eliminating at all. The fly in the ointment. . . .

Dr. Stanley Jones was the night speaker. Very ladylike. Talked about India—on his way back now. And the difference between Nietzsche and Jesus. And after the lecture and bit of talk here and there I hurry to bed. But to dreams—lots and lots of dreams, caused by an overloaded system. . . . Such wierd dreams. . . .

### Saturday, April 6

. . . Home on the 5:15 and my marketing has not come, so I must out and up King Street before I can get any dinner. Mama half sick and Ethel tired and not well. Such a house, such a family! . . . Mama's gloom is like an enveloping pall. . . .

### Tuesday, April 9

. . . Peace section meeting at four. Hear lots of talk of budgets, and sat quietly while my pitiful $2000 [yearly salary] is discussed—and passed. . . .

### Thursday, April 11

Real cold today and I pile back into the fur coat gratefully. And I *can't* get warm. I drink things that scald my tongue and feel like ice in my stomach. I know I'm running a temperature. Feel "fierce." At four go to Marie's and submit to a shampoo and wave. Torture because my head aches. Drizzling when I leave to meet Pauline at Miss Nottingham's [a Black beautician who, apparently, used the more traditional hot oil-hot comb method for styling her customers' hair]. . . . I go in for warmth—even the smell of fried hair, being warm, is attractive. I sleep. . . .

### Friday, April 12

Was to speak at Howard School this a.m. Nothing doing. Had bought some tulle to beautify my dress for the Les Amis ball tonight. Nothing doing. I sleep and eat orange juice and cracked ice. And sleep. Pauline goes to party. I sleep. Misery. Guess [Dr.] Aldrich [Burton] doped me. Did write Bobbo.

### Sunday, April 14

Still miserable. . . . I stay in bed until nearly dinner time, then arise and eat with the family. Sit up a bit, then bathe and to bed. Sweat at night, cold, clammy, wretched. Feel like a squid. Or something dead and disintegrating. . . .

### Thursday, April 18

Take an early train for home. . . . Mrs. Whitten is pulling a Mother-Daughter banquet of the Alice Dunbar Nelson Girl Reserves. She had courage. But it went off very well, albeit late beginning. . . . All the big wigs on hand. Very fine. Really well done. Mrs. [Gertrude] Rose [of the Industrial School Board] looks like a mask of sorrow. Had to write her a note to turn up the corners of her mouth. Ten o'clock before I get home—very tired. . . .

### Saturday, April 20

Hard work getting awake. But then it's our [her and Bobbo's] *Thirteenth Wedding Anniversary,* and our 16th anniversary of meeting each other. . . . Pauline meets me on the 1:17 and with Ethel and Marjorie we go a dandelioning. It has grown hot again so we must stop by the house to shed the fur coat and get a lighter one. Showers gone and brilliant and hot sunshine. Get quite a mess of dandelion blossoms—14 quarts by actual measurement. . . .

## Monday, April 22

. . . Go to Auxiliary meeting . . . and have a heck of a time keeping the women straight. . . .

## Friday, April 26

Plenty of excitement over tickets etc. Hard work and nerve strain and L. P. Hill. Wonder if results will justify my struggles for this National Negro Music Festival. . . .

## Saturday, April 27

. . . Henrietta [the Black secretary in the Friends Service Committe office] and I met at 1:45 and go to Franklin Field [for the Penn Relay games]. A thrilling sight—those 50,000 people in the brilliant sunshine. And a thrilling lot of events—a colored fellow from New York University winning the javelin throw and various schools and teams starring in the track and jump. Saw [?] run on the one-half mile run. So glad I went. Been wanting to go for years and never could get anyone to go with. . . .

## Monday, May 6

A hectic week. Cold and rainy. Filled with hard, gruelling work. Thanklessness, tears and unhappiness. Tickets not going as well as Goldberg and Hill think they should go. Very hard, exacting grind at office. . . .

## Wednesday, May 8

Go to Chester [Pa.] in the a.m. and meet a reporter on the Chester *Times*. One Mullin by name. Fascinating second generation Irish Catholic. Agnostic. Communist, Bolshevik. Very interesting. Talk so long with him, late getting to Philadelphia. . . .

## Thursday, May 9

. . . Directors' meeting at four. . . . Mr. Hill presiding. A most unfortunate meeting. He maintains we are "headed straight for disaster." Somehow the thing reminded me of hammering on cold iron.

We break up at six, all irritable. Wilbur Thomas fallen down completely on his guarantee fund. Everything apparently at sixes and sev-
ens. In spite of my tears and heart-breaking work. . . .

### Sunday, May 12

. . . [Wilberforce University] meeting at 7:15. Very impressive.
Plenty of flowers—decorations. . . . Dresses of one color—"off white"
or sand. Very beautiful. Hallie Q. [Brown] on platform with me. Guess
"I spoke fine." Folks said so. Immediately following, the Alpha Phi
Alphas took charge. Changed banners etc. Also impressive program,
but I don't think Bishop Clair, their speaker did as well as I—for one
thing, he used a MS. . . .

### Monday, May 14

Hell and damnation! And I not home until after ten. This language the result of reading "Cradle of the Deep." Rats on Krusie—
and Negroes! Hot! Electric fans going. . . .

### Friday, May 17

. . . Back to office after meeting and finish up no end of work.
Then out to Mrs. Dickerson's for the dinner she is giving Mrs. John
Hope [wife of Atlanta University president] and Nannie Burroughs
[nationally known clubwoman, educator, activist]. Mrs. D's house is
perfectly *gorgeous*. All the things I'd like to have. And her dinner for
twelve quite elegant—all but the napkins, which should have been
large dinner were only tea madeira. . .

### Sunday, May 19

. . . Room gets drenched because I get a stubborn streak and won't
shut my windows—because Mama nagged me to shut them.

### Monday, May 20

Bobbo's 56th birthday! Bless his heart. The *Afro* [Baltimore *Afro-*
*American* newspaper] birthday-ed him last Friday and told his age. I
will not ha-ha. They may get me on July 19. . . .

### Wednesday, May 22

If Hill could be chloroformed or would break a leg—I could work. So much peskiness.

. . . The final meeting of the Woman's Committee at the Protective Association. Everyone serious and filled with sense of responsibility. . . .

### Thursday, May 23

Things seem to be moving so rapidly that my breath catches. Getting scared and jumpy [about the upcoming National Negro Music Festival] but keeping outwardly cool. Service Committee meeting. I speak on the spiritual significance of the festival and beat it immediately. . . .

### Friday, May 24

Feel dog-mean all day. Took calotabs to get the taste of Anna [Brodnax]'s too plethoric sandwich supper out of my mouth. Artists coming in—people phoning, sometimes I am wanted on *three* phones. Down at the [Philadelphia] Academy [of Music] getting last minute arrangements made and paying that $950 balance, and finding we will owe $84 more. People, people, people. Calls, talks, worries. [Violinist] Clarence White. Tickets wanted. Frantic calls. Details and big things. A hijjously and horrifically busy and hectic day. . . . At 5:25 I go home too exhausted to speak. . . .

*D-N described soprano* Florence Cole-Talbert *as "one of the few Negro vocalists achieving operatic roles abroad"* (Eagle, *"As In A Looking Glass" May 3, 1929). She and D-N wrote the official Delta Sigma Theta Sorority hymn.*

### Saturday, May 25

. . . Florence Cole-Talbert calls up and reassures me. Next I hit the ceiling about the Fisk singers, and soon the manager . . . telephones from the station—and all is well.

Bernice, whose boy friend has deserted her, parks on me, after weeping over her hard fate, and Elizabeth Stubbs, snubbed by Elizabeth Jones, becomes one of my attaches, and with Amy Wu [her office secretary], we form a Fourumvirate. We go to the Giles Hotel, and see how things are with the horde of Hamptonites. Find them all there, eighty of them, and happy. Then to the Academy, where I station Amy, Elizabeth [Stubbs] and Bernice with the door guard, and soon Elizabeth [Jones] and her batch come in chattering, and get into their caps, and their programs, and soon, lights up, people in, artists ready, theatre open—and the great show is on.

The afternoon house is not so good, but not so bad either, and the performance is thrilling, even to me. Especially the Hamptonites in their "Lord God Have Mercy." Clarence White plays after all the fuss, but I almost wish he had not. . . .

. . . When the crowd dies down and the congrats are over, I slip away. . . .

Time to go back to the Academy. I take Anna to the Star's dressing room, and she gets fixed up in great shape. Much to her delight. The night crowd comes pouring in. The Academy is crowded. A brilliant sight. I am here, there and everywhere. Calming this situation, and letting in old ladies who have the wrong tickets. And when I want to hear J. Rosamond Johnson and Taylor Gordon, I must be in the box office making up accounts with Mr. Haley. A wildly enthusiastic audience. A magnificent performance. Franklin Hoxter contorting over his chorus and band. Alfred Johnson winding up the program with not so much contorting over the "Lift Every Voice and Sing" and the band. A muchly commended performance. A historical event. People all enthusiastic and commendatory. Hill, acting like a congenital idiot all evening. And the program girls giving me . . . $292.00 in small change to take home. And Mr. Haley giving me a check for nearly three thousand dollars to take home. And all of us piling into the car and going home—because I am too tired to go anywhere else, and my feet hurt something hijjous.

Nearly cracked when I got home a wreck, and Bobbo asked me if there was anything to eat in the ice-box. It was too cruel. But when I got off my shoes, into nightie and bathrobe, and went down into the kitchen to eat the sandwiches he had cooked (fried egg) and a high ball, did not feel so near to tears. I might have bawled him out a plenty. And so to bed. The GREAT EVENT being all over—but the paying of bills. . . .

## Wednesday, May 29

Busy day, and I don't mean maybe. Luncheon at [a] Mrs. Clapham's [in N.J.] at two. Blanche [Stubbs, her Wilmington friend] comes for me looking like a million dollars in her green ensemble, lace, georgette and what not and picture hat in green, so that I feel quite dowdy. We go to Camden—it is hot, too, and finally find the house. Fifteen guests—Florence Cole-Talbert and Mrs. [John] Hope the honored ones. And such a luncheon! Such flowers! Such decorations! Alla-ma-gorgeous! Such food! Little Frenchy carved carrots and what nots on the breasts of the birds, butter molded into flower shapes, all kinds of do-daddles and what nots. . . .

### Thursday, May 30

. . . Nearly six [her nephew Laurence's wife] Beck arrives. . . .

The boy is adorable beyond description. A Murphy [Beck's family] at first glance, then Laurence in brown. All in rompers and sweater and sailor hat. Sweet and good and cheerful. . . . And Ethel is all one quiver of delight. Arleon [Bowse] and everyone else on hand to investigate. Excitement a plenty—and heap much joy. What a love of a fat, lusty boy. His "Big Anty" is all goggle-eyed with joy. . . .

### Tuesday, June 4

I go to Lincoln [University, Pa.] commencement. . . .

Went to the president's reception on the lawn, in honor of the graduates and his wife's birthday. Ate lots. Haven't been eating anything, trying to get off this too, too solid flesh. . . .

### Saturday, June 8

Awoke to a pouring rain. Felt sorry for Blanche Cuff [her successor as head of the public school department at the Industrial School], for I know what it is to have a commencement at the school in rain, when I had planned it for out of doors. Trustee meeting at the Harrison Street meeting house. More or less uncomfortable and acrimonious, as the meetings are apt to be. Undercurrents, more or less nasty, and all the rest of it. Very distressing. . . .

. . . Out to the school for the commencement. . . .

The exercises are very good, in spite of the handicap of weather. Mrs. Hargis [wife of the pastor of Ezion Methodist Episcopal Church], the commencement speaker, sweetly chirping about "li-yuf." I present certificates. . . .

## Tuesday, June 11

. . . Leave on the three o'clock, standard, train for Lewes [Del., where she is speaking]. Buy ticket to Georgetown. A hot, dusty, distressing ride. I can feel cinders around my waist. At Georgetown get the bus, which soon has us in Lewes—in about three quarters of an hour. No one to meet me at the bus terminal, and I have to walk quite a distance to get to [her hostess] Mrs. Miller's. Arrived and put them all in consternation, as they had intended to meet me.

Went up in that stuffy upstairs room to wash up. About two quarts of water in a tiny basin to wash and rinse. I am a mess of dirt, cinders, dust. Get clean with difficulty, and arrange my hair and face. By the time I have descended, my mind is made up not to stay in Lewes all night. Outdoor toilets, stuffy bed-rooms, wow! . . .

. . . It is daylight when I drive up to the house, the taxi man admiring my flowers, and take in the morning milk. But, oh, the joy of my own big bed and ventilated room!

*This entry anticipates D-N's June 21 "As In A Looking Glass" column, in which she wrote that she had vowed not to go to another picture after seeing "Joan of Arc," "the perfect film": "But I fell from grace, and after several such falls, in a moment of temporary mental aberration, allowed myself to be cajoled into seeing 'Noah's Ark.' Therefore I rise and unhesitatingly name it the world's worst."*

## Wednesday, June 12

. . . Leave at 4:20 to meet the Scribblers [writing club] at the Y.W. . . . We work industriously on a sonnet.

Afterwards do not feel like going home, so drop into the Stanley to see "Noah's Ark." Felt it my duty, although I knew I would not like it. Glad I went. It is undoubtedly the world's worst picture, and if I had not seen it, I would never have known how bad a huge picture ·can be. . . .

## Thursday, June 13

St. Anthony's birthday. I forgot to go to church today, and I believe my little St. Anthony is cross with me, although I gave him flowers and incense, in the shape of flower drops. . . .

### Friday, June 14

. . . Anna [Brodnax] had given me a card for [Howard High School] class night, and I feel in duty bound to go. It was a dreary mess. I got so jumpy and faint, had to slip out the door, near which I had prudently stationed myself—fire escape, rather—and sit outside to rest. And had to tell Anna the exercises were good. They were awful. . . .

### Sunday, June 16

. . . Very quiet day. . . . Now I am writing up this diary. I am going to put all this stuff together. And try to start the damn thing off again tomorrow and keep it up daily. Don't know why I am so dumb about it. . . .

### Monday, June 17

. . . Funny incident on South Street [Philadelphia] car. Awareness, physical awareness of huge shirt-sleeved man. Splendid arms. Hampton drifted hotly across my vision. We both got off at 20th Street and I looked at his face. Robert Russa [Moton, Tuskegee Institute president] as he looked 25 years ago. Same aura, I suppose. Disturbing. . . .

Home and glad to get into cool things. Lay on the roof in the moonlight and evolved a new cosmogony—each planet with its own particular God. Too huge a task for one God to look after both the spiral nebula in Orion and the plant lice that infested my poor little ivy plant that I brought home. . . .

### Thursday, June 20

. . . I lie on the couch in the living room—for the usual thunder storm cools the evening—and read [Radclyffe Hall's lesbian novel] "The Well of Loneliness" which Florence Baugh [Philadelphia elementary school teacher] loaned me, until the folks come home at eleven o'clock. . . .

### Saturday, June 22

. . . Don't think Bobbo is very well. Anyhow he is tired and discouraged with *The Eagle*—and well may he say so. He and Mrs. Wilson scrapping. He has a prospect. Hope he lands it. . . .

## Monday, June 24

. . . All dressed up in garden party togs for Mrs. [Addie] Hunton's dinner. . . . Everyone and his little sister there. . . . Addie Hunton speaks beautifully—but too long. She is fighting—not for the W.I.L. [Women's International League for Peace and Freedom] and their program (an imitation of ours) but for *her life*. I see that. . . .

Worked hard today to get the Club program together for conference with Olmstead tomorrow. *And* the column for the week. . . .

*Here D-N is attending the 16th Annual Meeting of the Ministers' Conference in Hampton, Virginia. This evening, she and President Moton are speaking to a combined session of ministers and teachers.*

## Thursday, June 27

. . . Later Moton and I have a "conference" in the living room of the house where we are both staying. Asked his help in raising money for the A.I.P.C. [her American Inter-Racial Peace Committee]. . . . To [Hampton University] Ogden Hall. Scared stiff at speaking before Moton comes on. But give good account of myself—as does Moton. . . .

## Saturday, June 29

. . . Sat around that dirty [Washington, D.C. *Eagle*] office with Bobbo alternately in dumps of blues or working out his numbers "system"—funny how it's in his blood—until Cap'n [Edith] rescues me at 2:30 and we go to the Republic. . . . Get off for Highland Beach [Md.].

A lovely drive and all too soon at Annozean's [proprietor of this beach resort for Blacks]. And now I'm homesick, in spite of an interrupted bridge game. . . . Genevieve Francis West is peevish and sulky because I turned her and her husband out of my room—as I refused to be moved around in a day or two. I wanted to be settled. So she got nasty. And the bedroom is crude, and *no* inside toilet. I doubt if I will stick it. Hope Bobbo comes down tomorrow—and brings my perfume and powder I left. . . . Hope he comes anyhow. Poor Bobbo. Poor, poor Bobbo. He's tired and discouraged and disheartened—I can tell that. . . .

Well, I'll get to bed and listen to the crickets and frogs and hope I won't have to get up in the night.

### Sunday, June 30

. . . Home and dress for the water and into the sparkling waves.
Ah, it was Heaven. We rowed over to the Curtis bungalow and at last
I got myself oriented. It had seemed wrong—the beach and I could
not revisualize myself, but as soon as I clambered over the boat that
Perry [Howard] Jr. was rowing and up the walk to Namah's loud voice,
I was straight. Here was the house, here the porch, here my old room
next door, there where the pier used to be, there the pavilion in ruins.
So I felt comfy and happy and reminiscent, and drank beer and taught
Laurence Smith how to eat cold, boiled hard shell crabs. . . .

Surely a lovely day and all homesickness and hurt gone. . . .

### Wednesday, July 3

. . . The next morning, Tuesday, July 2, I awoke early—due partly
to the birds and partly to the citrate I had taken at bed time. In smock
and nightie and slippers wander to the back. Was tempted to go in the
water only in my nightie. It was a sore temptation, to feel the water
on my [sunburned] back minus the bathing suit—and if it had not
been for the certain knowledge that Essie Tucker watches the sun rise
out of the Chesapeake each morning and might have been shocked at
seeing me arise from the bay clad in a dripping white silk nightie—I
might have gone in. So I contented myself with wading lots and then
back to bed to sleep until I was called for breakfast. . . .

### Thursday, July 11

. . . A Mrs. Butler of Baltimore whom I suspect is a strainer invited
Bobbo and me to a "party" after dinner. It was at Ware's and the
folks—well, a motley crew. In one of the bedrooms. Such a place is
Ware's—bedhouse and speakeasy. Ugh! Mrs. Butler said her husband
is a dentist or doctor and she has to "keep in" with his patients. Privately, I did not enjoy this induction to Ware's—but at least I can
speak by the card now. . . .

Blazing heat in the cities—temperatures ranging from 96 to 100.
People dying like flies. Hot and buggy even down here. Some bridge
games and nights Annozean and I going in after dinner—at dusk.
Lovely swimming in a sea of molten gold toward the setting sun. . . .

## Friday, July 19

My birthday! the 54th! And my pen is on the blink!

Does one have to record "thoughts"? The water! Luxurious, voluptuous, lovely. Lapping, caressing, loving my bare body—when I get way out and slip my bathing suit down and no one can see me naked. Yesterday, like the ocean, breakers, foaming over me. Day before yesterday when I had a touch of sun from crabbing too long in the creek, and so waited until evening, and Annozean and I went in— sunset glow, and the moon made a shimmering path and we went out and swam back to the sunset. And then Emily and I . . . sat on the sands in the moonlight and I told her to "get her man" which she does—and so she fled yesterday . . . and has not come back yet. . . .

But the water! I came here for it. Weeks I dreamed of it. Here it is. No inconvenience too great for the love of it—even these hot days when it was calm as a mill pond and none too clean—I could wait. Lovely, luxurious, voluptuous water. Howe was right when he spoke of drowning as "the gentlest death the gods gave to man." To float on and on and on into sweet oblivion. What a temptation.

Birthday thoughts? None. I am fifty-four, feel twenty-five, look forty. What will the New Year bring? Beauty and good fortune. . . .

I am lazily content today.

## Saturday, July 20

. . . Bluebirds in a nest in the telegraph pole. . . . Cardinals flying low in the bushes. The birds feeding shelf . . . where robins and grackles and cardinals and all come early and late. Whippoorwills calling at sunset and Bob Whites and humming birds hovering over the petunia boxes. Counted twenty-five varieties of birds. . . .

## Sunday, July 21

. . . Bobbo came Saturday night, the 20, and brought me a beautiful little diamond ring. Plain gold band but lovely stone, for my ring which I shall have made. ... .

## Saturday, July 27

My last day. Tomorrow Polly and Leila, Alice B.[anton, Conwell and Lizzie's daughter, and Pauline's friend] and Francine [Pauline's car] will come to drive me home. . . .

There was a "dance" at Ware's—to the tune of the Orthophonic. . . . It was good to dance again.

Betty Benjamin Gandy—a wildly attractive child, true daughter of my erstwhile friend Lyde—is a snappy addition. Life, which had flowed smoothly and evenly, now sparkles and ripples. . . . Dancing at Ware's—and then the glorious climax of my glorious four weeks—a midnight plunge in the stormy bay. Great, black, menacing clouds scurrying over a scared moon, blotting it out. Heavy, tormented waves, tossing in the rising tide and smashing on the beach in white surf and masses of phosphorous. The twilight of a dark night at sea. Vivid jags of lightening showing us to each other. Only five [of her resort friends] dared the midnight plunge Mac [Mae], Ruth, Albert Taylor, Weaver and I. Out—not so far—until up to our shoulders, the waves dashed over our heads. And we swam—matches of under water swimming, where the phosphorous made gleaming lights on the head—like miners' lamps. Swimming, swimming out to infinity—racing in under the pulsing water to the solitary light on shore. An experience worth having—a glorious, wonderful climax. Only equalled by the velvety luxuriousness of the times when swimming far out—we slipped off our bathing suits—Emily, Tea and I and let the water caress our naked forms.

—But the heavy waves swept us in—then we raced up and hurried into clothes—panting, flowing, breathless. Hungry. Four of us piled in Mac's [?] car, Ralph Weaver and I in the rumble seat, my wet hair flying out. So to Annapolis and hot dogs—Texas wieners with plenty of onions and coca cola and back. And so to bed at two thirty. . . .

The glorious month draws to a close. The voluptuous caresses of my lover—the Chesapeake Bay—will soon be mine no more. It has been a perfect time. . . .

### Monday, July 29

. . . Hot today and hard to cramp my feet into hot shoes and rush for the 8:28. But here we are—and all the oh's and ah's of the girls over my "sun-tan" over. Farewell vacation—hail work! . . .

### Thursday, August 1

Yesterday—July 31, was Ethel's birthday. Poor kid! She is *thirty* years old! It seems incredible. And she yet seems twelve. She has been substituting at the Babies' Hospital [a nursery]. But today it is all over—and she is resting. I gave her the goods for a dress. . . .

Took rings to Wanamaker's to have *one* good one made. Can only use three rings and will have the new ring placed in the green gold mount. The cost for the ring with the three stones will be $35.00 and the replacing of the other $5.00.

Left the order and wondered when I would get the money to pay for it—when lo! the morning mail brought me a check for $35.00 from the Methodist Book Concern for the story "The Revenge of James Brown" which Katherine Gardner placed for me. Hope I won't fritter it away before I have to pay for the rings. . . .

## Monday, August 5

. . . Took parlor car to Harrisburg. Reported at church. Went to Cramp's [Dr. Crampton, an old M.D. friend] office and flirted properly with him. . . . Abstracted a cigar lighter from his desk.

The meeting the same as usual. Same fat women, hot church, reception afterwards, warm chicken salad and runny ice-cream and synthetic fruit punch. . . .

## Wednesday, August 7

One day last week dropped in the Palace and saw an underworld thriller, "Alibi." My taste is very low. I love underworld movies and detective stories. Have gone S. S. Van Dine crazy now.

Today dropped in my little 20¢ movie and saw Dolores Costello in "The Glad Rag Doll"—thankfully silent. Every time I go to see trash like that I suspect that I am an imbecile. . . .

This morning decided I wanted an oil burner in the cellar, a Pittsburgh water heater in the kitchen, the range done away with and a big radiator put in the kitchen. Don't know how it will work out. Nor where the money is coming from—but I have hopes. I don't feel like dumbly going through another dumb winter—slave to a coal bin and ash can. . . .

## Friday, August 9

. . . I inaugurated my new policy of taking time off in compensation for the time spent in attending night meetings. And collecting for dinners. . . .

### Wednesday, August 14

. . . I've been working and digging in the yard and watering it every night to try to make it look half decent—but it got too far a headway while I was away to do much about it. Some lazy folks I have in my house. Leila's a wonderful cleaner—she *says*—but I can always find cobwebs and dust *up high*. Never on the floor. Queer psychological study—sees everything under her feet; never anything above the level of her waist. Well—as Bobbo says: I'm loading myself down with five or six hundred dollars of debt—for what? Mythical comforts of home. We shall see. . . .

### Monday, August 19

I am so flat broke that it is funny. An epidemic of poverty seems to have struck us all. For Polly had a penniless time in New York— telling us a woeful tale on her return Friday night, and her birthday Saturday was quite a meagre affair. We had a good dinner, and I bought her a piece of chocolate layer cake—and while the three of us—Leila, she and I were playing "500" Ethel came in (she is substituting again at the Babies' Hospital) and gave Polly 50¢, which bought ice cream enough for a treat.

Of course, Leila always lies about money. She never has any and always short changes. Her way of holding on to what she has. And according to Leila, poor Pauline gets so little salary (more than anyone in the house, including Robert and I) and has so many heavy responsibilities (payments on her car and her garage rent) that of course, even though she taught summer school—she has no money. Somehow both mother and daughter seem to feel that it is my duty to carry Pauline board and room rent free, pay her long distance telephone calls, entertain her guests, use up all electricity, wine etc. etc.—and get nothing for six months in the year and a pittance the other six months—and be tickled to death. The exasperating thing about it is the absolute impossibilty of argument. All attempts at a rational discussion are shut off absolutely by a sullen silence. In other words to put it baldly—my niece intends that I shall support her partially—and there's nothing for one to do but to grin and bear it. Some more post war stuff. "Youth must be served." Therefore shall I grow stingy and mean too. . . .

*Clearly, this litany of her vacationing friends rouses some good-natured envy in D-N.*

### Thursday, August 22

. . . Cards from Anna [Brodnax] and Alice [Stubbs] out in Chicago, from Connie [Murphy] in Florence and Laura [Fleetwood] in Chartres, France, and Eva [Bowles] in London and Maudelle Bousefield in Norway. Ugh! . . .

### Monday, August 26

. . . Pauline and Mitch [her boyfriend] went to the Bordentown ball. Now there's where I would have liked to go. Not that messy stuff Thursday. I would have preferred going up Friday for the finals, stayed to the ball, and all night, home Saturday a.m. Hereafter I'll make my own pleasures and stop being the purse for a bunch of sponging nitwits. . . .

### Wednesday, August 28

The bottom has dropped out of my world. . . . Yesterday (Tuesday, the 27th) after I had eaten Mama said, "Now we'll tell you the bad news about Arleon." Annie Mabry [Bowse's landlady] had received a letter . . . saying that Arleon was in a hospital, would be there indefinitely, would not return to Wilmington this winter, "will not be with you good people," and wanted Arleon's winter clothes and some information from her safety deposit box concerning payments on the car. It pointed to the one thing we have dreaded and whispered about—complete nervous breakdown and mental collapse.

Called up Anna B[rodnax] and we mourned together. Later, Annie Mabry came over and we sat and wailed for an hour or more before I had courage to wash my hair. This a.m. found a card at the office from Polly saying same. . . .

### Wednesday, September 3

. . . Dropped into the Little Theatre and saw a weird Russian picture, "The Revolt of the Robots"—supposed to be laid on Mars. A thrilling combination of R.A.R., Metropolis and the Cabinet of Dr. Caligari. Unfinished—but it was only a fragment—said the screed.

I liked best a fantastic story with Will Rogers and Lila Lee in the leads called "One Glorious Day"—where Ek, an adventurous unborn sprite, gets possession of a mild professor's body. Very charming. . . .

*About this lecture of D-N's, the Philadelphia* Tribune *for September 19 reported: "The lecture was well received by an enthusiastic audience who enjoyed especially Mrs. Nelson's own brand of humor."*

*The Arleon Bowser story continues for some time.* William *was a Howard High School student of Bowse's who chauffered her to her home in Cohasset, Massachusetts, dove into too-shallow water, and broke his neck—but he eventually recovered.* Isaacs *is the minister whom she did not marry because her family objected to his dark complexion.* Pat *is Pat Harris,* Wilmington *pharmacist who was also associated with local racketeering.* De *is DeLancey Hamilton, who was a truck driver–deliveryman for a wholesale grocer.* Marguerite *was his wife.*

## Wednesday, September 12

. . . We go to Arden [liberal, arty, northern Wilmington community]—Bobbo, Leila, Jean, Polly and I. I am to speak on "The Relationship of the Negro to International Peace." Get away with it, but do not provoke as long a discussion as did [W. E. B.] DuBois [who had spoken earlier in the lecture series]. Finklestein [the organizer] slips me a check for $25, but I'm not advertising it. Learning to be secretive about money matters. It will be taken from me nevertheless. . . .

Sitting down in the dining room looking over the evening papers. Leila sat down portentously. "Must tell you this"—but I must swear not even to tell Bobbo. Some nurse, or member of a commission, interviewed her about Bowse. To make a long story short, the alienists [?] believe she is hopelessly insane and an institutional case for life. And the state of Massachusetts does not feel she is its problem. But that rather Delaware, where Bowse worked for 19 years, earning over $20,000 and voted for nine years, should maintain her in its state insane asylum.

Horrible! I could not sleep, though it was after two when I got to bed. Poor Bowse! A hopeless lunatic. Visions of our 19 years companionship, days and incidents and pleasant times together. God! how terrible. Again that empty, *lost* feeling that overcame me when I first heard she was not coming back. So much that I fixed in the house was for Bowse. So many plans for *her*. So many things for *her* approval. And Bowse, sunshine loving Bowse—in an asylum for the rest of her life. Ye gods, I am sick all over.

What caused it? Sex frustration? Hair dye? Family feuds? Wil-

liam's accident? Mabel's death? All together. She has been heading
for collapse for two years. Far better had she married Isaacs, or committed fornication with Pat or De.

What changes! Krusie an animal. Bowse insane. De fled. Marguerite lone and pathetic. But Bowse. Her loss is like a knife-thrust in
my side. . . .

### Saturday, September 21

Went to office—but home early. Pretty exhausted. My internal
complications are most uncomfortable. Stomach, liver, intestines—
misbehaving. . . .

### Monday, September 23

My internal arrangements continued to bother so cruelly, decided
to go to see Virginia Alexander [Delta Sigma Theta soror and Philadelphia physician]. She's young, modern, and still in hospital practice. She went over me with a fine tooth comb. Found hyperacidity
due to congested liver (as I knew), jaundice threatened. Set Wednesday a.m. for date to wash out stomach and drain gall bladder. . . .

*Letters to Robert such as this one were included among the pages
of the diary as if D-N intended them to form a part of the record.*

### Wednesday afternoon
### September 25

Well, I'm back in the office, after spending three hours on Virginia's operating table. Went to her office direct from the station this
morning. First she washed out my stomach. If you have never had
your stomach washed out, you have a great experience coming to you.
I had not eaten anything since last night's dinner, nor drunken water,
nor even brushed my teeth, for fear of getting a drop of water in my
tummy. This washing process, which took in several kinds of waters,
apparently pleased her for she decided there were no signs of gastric
ulcers, etc. Then she moved her operations into the liver. You evidently thought because I sald GALL BLADDER that it had something to do with the kidneys, thinking of GALL STONES. But the
Gall Bladder is the what-you-may-call-em that feeds the bile to the

liver, which bile digests food and keeps you well. When the bile doesn't percolate, you get "Bilious." When it backs up and gets congested, etc. you get jaundice, colitis, cirrhosis of the liver, and other disagreeable and fatal diseases. My bile supply had ceased, utterly. My stool was as white as this paper, and all kinds of hyperacidity were going on in my tummy.

So—having moved operations down liverwards, the draining began. I drained, and drained, and drained. All kinds of terrible things came out of my liver through that little tube. Then she washed and washed with various kinds of stimulants. And still I drained. Viginia said I drained much more than most of her patients because I am so active, take lots of exercise, swimming, etc., and this morning when I got up, I did all kinds of setting up exercises to make the liver softer. Then she poured olive oil into my liver through this long tube, and it came back out bringing all kinds of stuff with it. She said this was just the beginning of a perfect time. That when she gets through she will have the accumulated dirt secretions of years out of me and in bottles. I am to go back next Thursday morning.

Then she made me drink a cup of tea, eat some crackers, and come to work. I stopped at the drug store and got a glass of malted milk and egg—not that I wanted it, but knew I needed nourishment. Feel rather battered, but able to go to the Peace Section meeting, I think at four o'clock.

Yes. I have a rigid diet list—no liquor, no candy, no fruit, no nothing that anyone would want, but lots of milk, eggs, etc. No coffee, of course, but weak tea. I can do it, if I have to. . . .

I hardly expected money from you Elks. But what I can't understand is why that ass Houston ignores my letters? Now, all I'm trying to get him to do is to say yes or no that he will use one or two subjects for his constitutional contest, and that coon won't pay me any more mind than if I were a lunatic. I'd like to choke him until his eye balls burst. I'd never write if it didn't come in the order of my work. I get so mad when I think of his bad manners that I'd have a stroke if I didn't have low blood pressure. Told Finley [Wilson] about it; he said let HIM have the subjects, and he'd think it over. Wrote him a polite note—after he left Wilmington, sending it to Washington, putting the three items on a piece of paper. Silence from HIM. I never saw such an aggregation of low-bred morons. Niggers haven't an idea in their heads but convention and election.

Well, that's enough quarreling for one day. See you some more.

Your own adoring, and much becleansed.

P.S. Instead of going to the Peace Section meeting I pled a headache and went instead to the Palace to see Greta Garbo and Nils Aster
in "The Single Standard." Much more edifying and enjoyable. Home
on the usual train. And to bed early after recounting my adventures
to the family. Letter from Lydia, mostly about herself. But she did say
that Arleon is down to 120 pounds. But is better—which is vague
enough to mean anything. . . .

### Monday, September 30

. . . Around to Emma's [Emma Sykes, her illegal numbers agent].
Bought a Pemlico sweepstakes. Put in some numbers. Mama's dream
numbers. But Bobbo all on fire over his 844.

Today two of Mama's dream numbers came out. How dumb of
me not to have played the .01 for 0 instead of *one*. . . .

### Wednesday, October 2

. . . Bobbo writes me that the Board of Directors of the *Eagle* met
and decided to make it a strictly fraternal [IBPOE] journal, instead of
a combination—which I think is wise. It was neither one thing nor
the other. I did not get any issue last week. Understand it was a make-
shift and Bob did not want me to see it. . . .

### Saturday, October 5

. . . Arrived home about eleven, and found Mama and Leila sitting each at a window guarding the open garage. Charles Overall brought
up the flivver, and probably forgot to lock the garage. Taking Jack and
a stout stick, I went over, looked all through, found no burglars, and
locked it up. . . .

### Thursday, October 10

Virginia kept me draining until three o'clock. Very trying. That
was caused probably by the fact that she had three other females
a draining at the same time. Looked like a hop joint, all those women
lying around with tubes hanging out of their mouths. . . .

### Friday, October 18

Took one o'clock bus from Philadelphia for Salem, New Jersey. Lovely two and a half hour ride. Such autumnal glories! New Jersey State Federation [of Colored Women's Clubs] in usual conclave at an A.M.E. church. . . . My subject—"What Can" is "how can" white and colored clubwomen work together. A white clubwoman spoke after me. And these colored women showed their teeth and bared their fangs. A mean exhibition—and I said so. . . .

### Wednesday, October 23

Up in the gorgeous Poconos [Pa. mountains, for a peace conference]. Chilly sunshine, but gorgeous view. Sitting in group discussion. All about cruisers, battleships, etc. No one gets down to fundamentals. If we ever decide in our hearts—*why* fight—we won't have to waste a beautiful day in a beautiful baywindow looking out on the magnificent Pocono range talking about tonnage etc.

*Peace people talking about killing.*

*Five and Ten*—Fannie Hurst [noted American writer]—Harper Brothers. A scathing, searching novel of the new rich.

*Our Trip to Sky top.* . . .

At 2:30 everyone started on a hike. . . . First the cottage. Then a skiddy tramp to the Falls. A climb to the upper reaches. A rarely lovely experience. The Falls and all a beautiful sight—spray and all. A five mile tramp. Janet leading us with a wild tale about seeing deer in their native lair about two miles beyond Skytop. Our tramp in the lovely sunshine up and up and up was lovely. Only my thin shoes made me foot conscious. And we got very hot and perspiring.

Skytop Lodge a gorgeous hostelry, making the beautiful Buck Hill hotel small fry by comparison. A huge living room—a fire place where quarter trees were burning. Music by a violin and piano—lovely and lilting. Tea served by a pretty maid and lovely little cakes. We rested on a huge divan and a winged chair. Janet raving like wild to go hunt deer and all of us tired. . . .

Janet begging to go further into the woods to find deer. Dusk in an impenetrable forest. But we did see deer. Two lovely young ones— who stood close together, our lamps shining in their eyes. Then turned and ran, their pretty white, upturned tails flashing in the dusk. We saw them leaping high over bushes and little trees. . . .

## Thursday, October 24

. . . The conference, even to the last group discussion and forum, was horribly disappointing. Seems to me everyone is preparing for war and temporizing with the thought of it. Sickening it was to me. . . .

## [Chicago, Illinois]
## Tuesday, October 29

. . . Someone gets Barbeque. Never tasted barbeque. Roasted spare ribs doused with tabasco. Drank the high balls which I had refused to wash it down. . . .

*"Mae B." below is* May Belcher, *executive secretary of the Phillis Wheatley YWCA. She arranged D-N's Indianapolis itinerary, which included a talk, "Trends of Peace in Interracial Understanding," sponsored by the Y's interracial committee, a committee "made up of both white and colored women who meet alternately at the homes of both to study the problems and literature of each and discuss matters which will bring about a greater understanding between the races." D-N stressed the proper teaching of children as the foundation for world peace.*

## [Indianapolis, Indiana]
## Saturday, November 2

. . . Took taxi up. The Phyllis Wheatley [YWCA] quite imposing. Not as tall as the one in Cleveland, but more beautifully appointed. Mae B. gushed over me. Wasted most the afternoon waiting for her at one time or another. My fate. Always waiting for some one. . . . After supper (and waiting) went to the Walker Theatre in the Walker Auditorium. Beautiful theatre—all Egyptian is everything. Good movie and rotten vaudeville. Good enough—but I'm fed up on Negro shows of that type. . . .

## Tuesday, November 5

. . . Arrived 9:50. Looked longingly at Philadelphia as we passed through [enroute to New York City]. To the "Y," bath, dressed and up to the Grand Central Palace where the sessions of the National Council of Women are held. The auditorium the most atrocious room I was ever in. Lot of literature about the designer. He should be shot at midnight. No unity. No focal point.

Sessions interesting enough but slimly attended. . . .

Up town to "Y" for supper conference Council of Women of Darker Races. DuBois speaking about Pan African. . . . Quite a meeting. . . .

## Wednesday, November 6

. . . To the banquet hall. . . . Such gowns! The fashions are definite. Stewart's fashion show confirmed the awful news from Paris that had seeped through. Long-goshawful long skirts! High-goshawful high waists! I felt like my own country cousin though I had on my tan lace. Oh, well! . . .

Sallie Stewart [president of the National Federation of Colored Women] is a fine woman. But she offends my aesthetics. Fine woman in the sense of achievement—but hopelessly, frightfully, commonplace, provincial, middle class. . . .

## Sunday, November 10

. . . Bobbo told me some good news. He had an interview . . . and it looks as if with [Josiah] Marvel's entering the senatorial race, there will be some work, and Bobbo may have his heart's desire—to head up a national Negro Democratic office in Washington. . . .

## Monday, November 11
## Armistice Day

. . . When I entered the house, found the family at dinner. Pauline and Leila shouted, "You have a letter from Arleon."

Sure enough, from old Bowse, in her own writing. Not much, just a note, but a sign that she is in her right mind at least. I was hysterically glad. It was a tonic for my tiredness. . . .

*The commitment to the Garrick mentioned here is apparently a reference to the Garrick Theatre, Philadelphia, where the AIPC held a "Popular Assembly" on December 8 featuring addresses by R. R.*

Moton; Thomas E. Jones; *AFSC chairman* Dr. Henry J. Cadbury, *head of the Department of Biblical Literature at Bryn Mawr College;* *and others.*

## Tuesday, November 12

To the office in good time. A.I.P.C. meeting at two. Hill over-powering us all. Helen Bryan making an impassioned plea, that actually moved me to tears, for better support of my efforts, Mrs. Dickerson incisively putting her finger on sore spots, Ray Newton stunned beneath the impact of Helen's blows, Rachel Davis DuBois agreeing with Helen, and Hill brushing aside all of our talk and making long sermons about things that are never going to happen. And so we are still committed to Garrick.

Amy [her secretary] and I stumble out headachey and dazed. Thank Heavens, there was tea being served upstairs, and we were refreshed.

At home I fixed the morris chair, made some cushions, and puttered generally, while Leila and Pauline went to the hospital to see Ethel. . . .

## Thursday, November 14

Mama being more so than ever, I gladdened her heart by not going down to Dover [Del.] until the 1:45 train, when I was able to wait on her a bit. Afraid I am a cold creature towards her at best. Leila, for all her talk of bitterness, is much more apt to wait and do things.

Went down on the train with Carter Woodson [the Black historian], who gave me lots of help in giving me names of prospective contributors to our cause. He is the first person whom I have met who has a cause for which to collect, who is willing to share his experiences, names, addresses and prospects. All others are polite, vague, profuse with good wishes, but gorgeously generalizing. I wrote on bits of paper all the way down, and ate some chocolate ice cream which he insisted on buying, and spilled it down the front of my white blouse, so that when Dr. Henry [Dover M.D., husband of her pharmacist friend Cecie] called my attention to it, had to pin the coat scarf end over it.

Dr. Henry scared me almost into a faint by suggesting that Virginia's treatment is but a palliative, and that after all there might have to be an operation, and there might also be a cancer of the gall bladder, and it had better be out. Almost keeled over.

But recovered, ate luncheon, spoke after Woodson—ten minutes to his fifty, and sold all the booklets I had, and collected about nine dollars more. I guess the Youth Peace Contests will go over big in Rural Delaware.

Home on the five something, and in the house at the usual time, and made more cushions, etc. . . .

*There are no extant December 1929 diary entries.*

# 1930

(January 1–December 31)

*One glorious fling—freedom, anyhow*

NINETEEN THIRTY WAS REALLY, IN DUNBAR-NELSON'S WORDS, "one glorious fling," and the diary—full of intense, moody, introspective flashes—mirrors the exhilarating as well as some calamitous times. She began the year with a "much heralded Southern trip," which in ten weeks, took her not only through the South (and a host of small, Black colleges), but as far west as California, then back through the midwest. According to a Friends Service Committee Newsletter (No. 23, April 1930), she traveled ten thousand miles, visited thirty-seven different schools and colleges, and spoke to twelve YW- or YMCA's, seven churches, and ten clubs or teachers' organizations, reaching a total of about twenty-three thousand persons. A February 10 article in the Savannah, Georgia, *Morning News* typifies the general publicity given her appearances. Her tour and local schedule are announced, and then this statement follows: "Owing to her relationship with Paul Laurence Dunbar, famous American poet, and her reputation as a forcible speaker, it is expected that her message today on world peace will be of special interest." Yet despite this triumphal journey, Dunbar-Nelson is forced to admit defeat in her Inter-Racial Peace Committee position. When the work starts to end this year, she finds herself in the same straits as she was two and a half years before. This time, however, she is "tramping for jobs" with the rest of the five million Depression unemployed.

California provided the initial setting for one of the major stories in the diary. In her April 5 "So It Seems" column, Dunbar-Nelson wrote that after she settled in the Los Angeles Dunbar Hotel, "life became a fascinating melody, with all sorts of tunes played to the accompaniment of California climate and sunshine and rain and hospitality." This happy statement is a publicly veiled reference to a romantic fling that she had with Fay Jackson Robinson, a younger newspaperwoman and socialite whom she met on the trip. Fay, whom

Dunbar-Nelson calls her "little blue dream of loveliness," was a member of the executive council of the Los Angeles Civic League. The mother of at least one daughter, she eventually separated from her husband John (under scandalous circumstances) and secured a job as a journalist with the California *Eagle.*

Another woman, Helene Ricks London, an artist (especially a watercolorist), also figures prominently in the story. She and her husband had two children and, after leaving Iowa, she lived in Chicago. In 1931, Dunbar-Nelson vacationed with her and the children in Bermuda. Untangling the triangular relationship which existed between her, Dunbar-Nelson, and Fay is difficult. It appears that Helene and Fay were involved with each other before Dunbar-Nelson entered the picture and that both of them were passionately interested in her. This intrigue accounts for many letters, sonnets, domestic scenes, arguments, heartaches, and tears during the months following Dunbar-Nelson's return home.

This situation, of course, raises many questions about the nature and extent of Dunbar-Nelson's lesbianism—the answers to which are speculative. Nevertheless, this unequivocal documentation gives additional meaning to other things—said and unsaid—in the diary. Certainly, it casts a more telling light upon her earlier attention to homosexuality and lesbianism. And, this same year, when Edwina Kruse dies and Dunbar-Nelson eulogizes their friendship as "closer than sisters" until their "Eden" was broken up by other relationships, the emotional resonance is stronger. "Twenty years ago," she says, "her death would have wrecked my life."

Professionally, Dunbar-Nelson is becoming discouraged about her literary ability. Practically everything extracurricular she writes—a satirical novel, a fictional piece for *True Story,* and six sketches—is rejected. Other events, large and small, further try her. At fifty-five, she attempts to learn to drive, but fails her road test (calling herself "hopelessly dumb"). Her niece Ethel dies, while her mother continues to disintegrate, her husband discovers that he has uremic poisoning, and she herself suffers health problems and liver drainages. Though money shortages are aided somewhat by Robert's bandwagoning with the unsuccessful Delaware Democratic campaign in a corrupt election, this is not enough to hearten Dunbar-Nelson. She is beset by strange urges and preoccupied with suicide. At the end of the year, she is thankful for Robert, writing on Christmas Day, "At least Bob was *here.*" And, looking backward on December 31, she decides that the only good thing she can say about 1930 is that it "brought me California. I shall bless you for that."

---

## Wednesday, January 1

. . . Mama [is] 80 years old today. . . .

## Friday, January 3

. . . L. P. H. [Leslie Pinckney Hill, chairman of the American Inter-Racial Peace Committee of which she is executive secretary] came in popping mad. . . . Did my heart good to hear him rave. So much better than love and Jesus stuff. We parted mightily cheered. . . .

Played some "Nullo" tonight. We were bored to tears with each other. Must get a girl to stay with Mama [because of her failing health]. . . .

## Monday, January 6

The meeting at the College Club [Philadelphia] was at three. . . . I "spoke fine" on Negro poetry from Dunbar to Cullen. Drank tea and hurried to . . . the . . . bus. . . . The darn thing burned—I sat on a burning seat, put paper between the seat and my legs, and it caught fire. On and out the bus we piled while the driver plied a fire extinguisher like an ear syringe. Finally as a fire department in some Jersey village chugged up, all of us passengers piled into another bus. Reached Mt. Holly [N.J.] at seven instead of six. My gentle spinsters . . . were concerned and had put up dinner. Lovely ladies, quaint and charming as their lovely home.

The Fortnightly Club—mixed male and female, about 70 odd, met in their drawing room. Very congenial. Made same speech and was made to read [Dunbar's Negro] dialect [poetry]. Funny. . . .

## Tuesday, January 7

. . . Had spoken to Helen Hill [their next-door neighbor] about looking after Mama yesterday. She came in tonight to close deal. Wants $5.00 per week. I'll pay. Anything to ensure Mama a hot meal and some care. . . .

## Thursday, January 9

. . . Mama full of complaints. The weather is hot. Nearly 70° today and most enervating. Leila [her sister] says Ethel [her niece] has had a nerve specialist examine her, but from the description, I think it must have been a psychiatrist—which is what she needed years ago. . . .

## Saturday, January 11

. . . Met Mrs. Rose [of the Girls Industrial School] and her usual car load and all to the school. Tedious board meet [on which D-N still serves] and luncheon and fear the oxtail soup had tomatoes in it, for my mouth is a mess of blisters inside. . . .

## Thursday, January 16

. . . Bobbo met me [in Washington, D.C.] . . . and we taxied up to his [new] room. Pleasant place. And so I start out on my much heralded Southern trip broke and with a rotten cough. . . .

## Washington, D.C.
## Sunday, January 19

Twenty years ago today on a Wednesday did Arthur [Callis] and I make fools of ourselves [get secretly married] at Old Swedes Church. How vivid it still seems. . . .

Very pleasant at the Ellis household—Mother Wilson all patchwork quilts and Daughter Ellis grown to good meals and plump cheeks. Bobbo, Harry Jones and one named Johnson are the boarders. . . .

*The following entries give the flavor of D-N's fast-paced trip through the South, where she spoke to a variety of audiences—predominantly at Black colleges—about her Inter-Racial Peace Committee work.*

## Petersburg[, Virginia]
## Tuesday, January 21

*Petersburg Normal and Industrial School*

A strangely futile and disappointing day. Up early and to breakfast, almost falling down in the sleet and icy roads. . . .

**Deltas Pose For Courier Photographer**

D-N stands fourth from right, front row, in this photograph of the officers and delegates to the Delta Sigma Theta Sorority biennial convention, the Pittsburgh *Courier*, January 11, 1930. Note that she has begun wearing glasses.

The most impressive engagement of D-N's 10,000-mile, cross-country speaking tour. She addressed a "large" and "enthusiastic" audience about "World Peace and the Negro," and was personally enthralled by being in California.

Los Angeles

CIVIC LEAGUE

PRESENTS

Alice Dunbar-Nelson

Second Baptist Church Twenty-Fourth at Griffith Avenue

Tuesday, March 11 1930, 8:15 p. m.

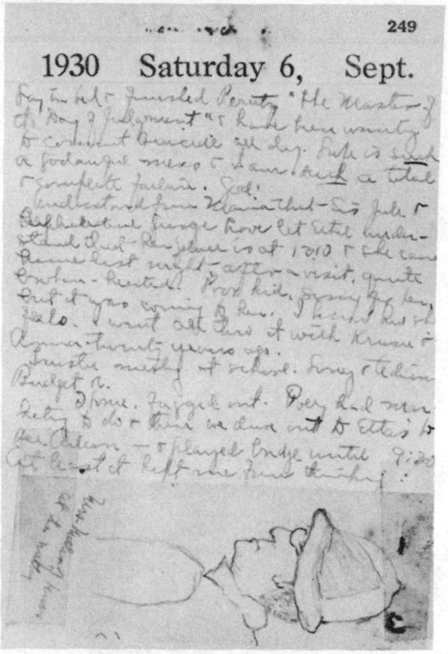
249

1930 Saturday 6, Sept.

D-N's sketch of this "Mrs. Miller of Lewes [Delaware]" who also attended the "long and tedious" Girls Industrial School Trustee meeting suggests D-N's artistic (and perhaps satirical) bent.

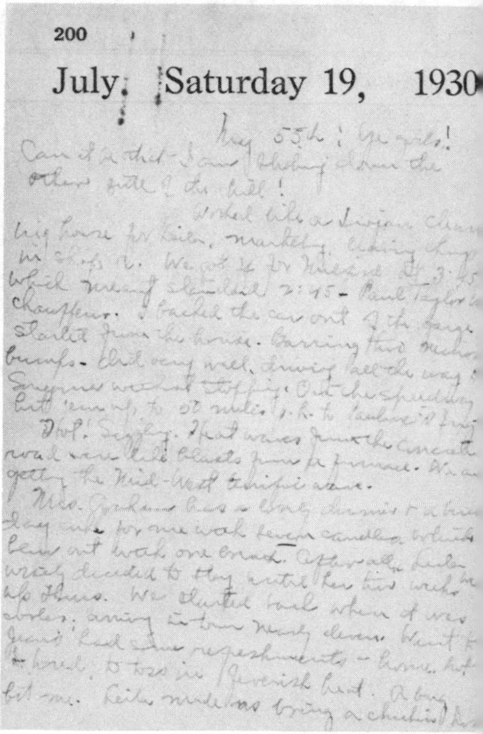
200

July Saturday 19, 1930

D-N's fifty-fifth birthday—a relatively low-keyed enlivened by a dinner party in Smyrna, Delawa and drinks later at a friend's home back in W mington.

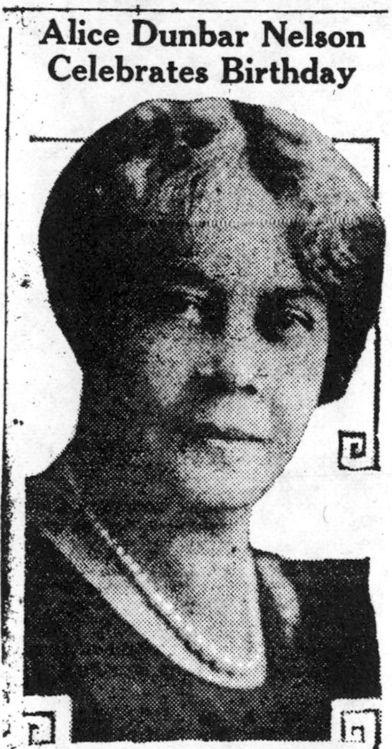
Alice Dunbar Nelson Celebrates Birthday

MRS. ALICE DUNBAR NELSON formerly the wife of Paul Laurence Dunbar, poet, who will celebrate another birthday Saturday, July 19th. Mrs. Nelson is executive secretary of the American Interracial Peace Committee and author of several books. Mr. Nelson is editor of the Washington Eagle.

The Baltimore *Afro-American* newspaper, July 19, 1930.

# THE EAGLE

### National News of the I. B. P. O. ELKS of the WORLD

#### Published Weekly by the Washington Eagle Publishing Co., Inc.

Office: 930 U St., N. W.,
Washington, D. C.

J. FINLEY WILSON
Founder and President
ROBT. J. NELSON, Editor.

Entered as Second Class Matter, Post Office, Washington, D. C.

RATES:

Single Copy ......................5c | 3 Months................ ..........75c
Month .........................25c | 6 Months ..............  .........$1.25
2 Months ......................50c | 1 Year ...............  .......$2.00

MEMBER
NATIONAL NEGRO PRESS
ASSOCIATION

## EDITORIAL

### FRIDAY, AUGUST 8, 1930

### A POLITICAL OPPORTUNITY

One of the important news breaks of the latte   art of last week was the announcement in Delaware tha   mer Senator Thomas F. Bayard would be a candidate for the Democratic nomination for the United States Se  .te. It will be recalled that Senator Bayard was elected to  ie Senate in 1922 and his election was due to the support 1 received from the colored electorate of the State.

It is very pleasing to the colored voters of   elaware that Senator Bayard has entered the lists for th   Democratic nomination for he is one of the few Democrats in Delaware who can command support of the colored people with whom he is very popular. He is popular with  .hem for the reason that he is honest, fair and st       in   in his dealing with them. When, he was in       to enate serving from 1922 to 1928, he served all the       that

## NOT WITHOUT LAUGHTER
By Langston Hughes
(Alfred A. Knopf, New York $2.50)
Reviewed by Alice Dunbar Nelson.

It was a foregone conclusion that when Langston Hughes decided to write prose it would be good prose, and that when he turned his attention to the novel it would be well-constructed, compact and evenly banlanced. It would not have been enough to have written such a striking story about this poor group of mid-west Negroes, without doing it so well that it is possible to enjoy the story, feel its pathos, recognize the types presented and throb with poignant sympathy at their pathetic lives. To be judged by the strict standard of the novel, the story must be well-balanced, the climax led up to by perfect graduation, the characterizations sharply etched against an adequately described background. The day has past when any book about Negroes is hailed as a masterpiece. The time, Thank Heaven, has gone when any Negro writer is acclaimed as a genius. The writer must do well, and the Negroes in the story he writes must be worth writing about. For this, lovers of literature are devoutly grateful.

Mr. Hughes has done well. If his book is more objective than subjective, as some have asserted, the objectivity is of a high order, holding the interest, and containing within it the appeal of the individual, not the race. We cannot but wonder how much of the book is autobiographical. Remembering his unforgettable poem about Brass Spittoons, we feel that Sandy's experiences in the cheap hotel, and in Chicago are some of Langston Hughes' own life, set down as Dickens set down his own story in David Copperfield.

Editorial page of the August 8, 1930 Washington *Eagle*, with D-N's husband "Bobbo" as Editor and her review of Hughes' *Not Without Laughter*, which she originally wrote for the Washington *Tribune*.

Some futile going to classes. An ineffectual beating of wings at
chapel 12:30. Some uninteresting classes. A rest. Dinner. Went for
the conference—no one came, at least very few. Sorry for this, for
Eleanor Hill came and I hate to have her report to her father [Leslie
P.] my failure. The Delta [Sigma Theta Sorority] card party—also
ineffectual and just over. I must be bilious. It is all such a failure.

Batch of mail today. . . . A letter from Hill forwarded. He bawled
me out in fine shape. He even said "in sooth" at me.

### Wednesday, January 22

Much better day. Plenty mud, slush, fog, rain, but better results.
Breakfast . . . very delightful. . . . To *The Training School* and a very
*pleasant time with Miss Hamilton, the principal* and all over the school
and she promised to put on a Youth Peace Contest. . . . After lunch
made a corking good speech in chapel . . . class to which I read *Ange-
line*—it was so *dull*, from 3 to 5:35 in the parlor talked to groups and
then to . . . dinner. Very pleasant. . . . To my room in the rain by a
quarter to eight—and peacefully to stretch out and read [Oscar Wilde's
*The Picture of Dorian Gray*]. . . . Well, it has not been a complete
failure. . . . Perhaps the visit will bear fruit.

### Bricks, North Carolina
### Sunday, January 26

*Bricks, North Carolina, Junior College*

Left Greensboro [N.C.] at 7:55. Mrs. Bluford [wife of Greensboro
A & T College president] drove me down and I ate breakfast before
leaving, which was fortunate, as it was hours before more food was
forthcoming. Left coats and one bag at Mrs. Bluford's. Such a trip!
And such a funny J. C. [Jim Crow] coach—like an antiquated parlor
car, but very comfy chairs. Selma, North Carolina, by 11:58 and waited
until 1:40. A God-forsaken place. I walked a bit in the crisp sunshine,
then sat in the stinking J.C. room and wrote letters. Bought some
crackers and ate. Finally aboard the Atlantic Coast line and Bricks by
4:09—eight hours to go 200 miles! . . .

Met . . . and to a forlorn-looking dormitory and a faded would-be
pretty matron. . . . Poor living room—and down at heels bathroom—
but hot water and I took a bath (standing) in the dubious tub. Felt
better and to supper—which was nice in a nice hall, but little I could
eat. Then chapel at 6:30, where I spoke. Then a group meeting of the

Christian World Education, who study International questions with
the students of the Atlantic Christian College at Wilson (white).
[Dunbar-Nelson called this arrangment "an unique interracial experiment."] Just colored students tonight. Very stimulating. . . .

### Thursday, January 30

*On board Pullman in Greensboro, N.C.*

I broke a side tooth Sunday at Bricks. One of those Juice was to
pull and didn't. So made a date yesterday wth Alex Rivera to file it
down so it would stop cutting my jaw. And my mouth was beginning
to look like the Luray caverns. Said he could fill and save it and I told
him to shoot. Upshot was that he put my mouth in condition, something I've been begging that lazy nigger Juice [her Wilmington dentist]
to do for two years. Filed both of those uncrowned teeth, crowned
both, bridged one, cleaned my teeth thoroughly. The dead front tooth
which Juice ruined . . . will have to go of course, but for the present
it will do. Now I can smile without embarrassment. . . .

### Asheville, North Carolina
### Monday, February 3

. . . Reached Marion at 5:08 [P.M.] Hugh Moore and Miss Wildman met me. Drove me all over Marion. Showed the Relief Station
(huts). Told me the situation with the strikers etc. Drove 40 miles over
the Blue Ridge Mountains in the little Chevrolet. Dizzy curves. Got
to Asheville about 8. No train to Knoxville until 6:40 tomorrow. So
they left me and my bags standing in the middle of the station and I
had had no supper. Left me politely and I wouldn't have that on my
conscience for anything. However, I applied to the Travelers' Aid who
sent me to a weird (but respectable) hotel in the neighborhood and
here I came. Room and bath, however, and had some kind of a scram-
bled egg supper and brown lye in a sarcophagus for tea. Better than
nothing. Lots of nuts. Been writing post cards—and I'm sorry for Hugh
Moore and Miss Wildman. . . .

### Thursday, February 6

*Letter to Bobbo*

Well, here I am in sunny South Carolina, and it is living up to its
reputation, although I am told it has been very cold and snowy down

here also. Today is lovely, so that I had to discard my fur coat at last, and even am uncomfortable in my lighter coat. Had to buy a straw hat also, for the little felt one was dilapidated and greasy and black past all endurance, and the one with the lace too dressy. So I was taken down town, and got me a dark blue straw, too pretty for words for the small sum of $3.50. It was $3.95, but I told the clerk that I was a stranger from Philadelphia, and having come all the way to South Carolina to buy a hat she must make special concessions. Which she did. . . .

I left Knoxville. . . . It was a doggone trip, and I hate upper berths, but I had the satisfaction of knowing that there were at least three *other* white women in uppers. . . .

I know I am in South Carolina with the pretty girls and handsome boys. There is a joke about this school [South Carolina State College] (700 students and a great institution) to the effect that applicants for the freshman class have to send their photographs with their application, and if they are not good looking they are rejected, and have to go elsewhere. That is a joke, but from the looks of the student body it looks like a reality. . . .

### *Orangeburg, South Carolina*
### *Thursday, February 6*

. . . So *many* folks. And beautiful. Either lovely octoroons or wirey black Geechies. With the quaint foreign accent I always noted in Sallie Arnett [Rev. Arnett's wife]. And spring at *last!* Saw mistletoe growing for the first time. Huge bunches of it . . .

### *Orangeburg, South Carolina, State College*
### *Friday, February 7*

Such a lovely day. And spring! . . . Lay in bed late and had my breakfast brought me about nine o'clock. Spoke in chapel at eleven. Good attention and the response in yells. I have been cheered in so many schools. After dinner, Mrs. Wilkinson [Pres. R. L. Wilkinson's wife] took me . . . out in the country to see their log cabin. A "log cabin de luxe" I named it. With all modern conveniences in as lovely a rustic setting as I have ever seen. Tall pines and oaks with their silver draperies of Spanish moss. The lovely sad banners that take me back home [to New Orleans]. And pecan trees! We ate nuts and oranges before a roaring fire—there were *two* fireplaces. Every quaint antiquity in the world. With the radio and electric light and perfect plumbing. Then a sightseeing drive. Daffodils blooming in the streets.

Home and washed my filthy hair and put in a "home made wave" which is horrible.

Telegram this a.m. from Leila, saying that Ethel had been operated on yesterday and was doing well. Poor Leila. Wrote Laurence [her nephew in Chicago] a scorcher today about wanting our "pocketbooks open." Addressed some valentines. Went to a whist party at Mrs. Wilkinson's and made usual mediocre score.

## Saturday, February 8

Charleston! Proud city by the sea! . . . As we paused at the entrance to the bridge . . . a scene from "Porgy" was enacted before our eyes— a street fight between two black women, a mushroom growth of spectators, crates on heads, passersby gave attention, a woman balancing a washtub filled with everything, bottles too passed, arms akimbo, speaking choicest Gullah. A boy walking backwards on his hands. "Porgy" true to life. Perfect. South Carolina Negroes either ebony or ivory. No intermediate shades. No intermarriage.

Supper and a perfect drive home in the soft moonlight. . . .

*D-N began writing a weekly column for the Pittsburgh* Courier *"So It Seems—to Alice Dunbar-Nelson" in late January of this year. These articles are not as lively and engaging as the "As In A Looking Glass" pieces that she produced for the Washington* Eagle. *Perhaps their quality was affected by the general turbulence of this period (January–May 1930).*

## Paine College
## Augusta, Georgia
## Sunday, February 9

. . . Borrowed a typewriter and improvised a table of suit case on rush bottomed chair and sat on bed. Got *Courier* article done between my three speeches and conferences. . . .

*Daytona Beach, Florida*
*Tuesday, February 11*

. . . Bad start. The boy was late who was to drive. . . . So we hurried. So—we sideswiped a car going at right angles to us and the two boys were scared to death. A white boy was driving the car—and they were afraid of trouble in court, trouble at school [Georgia State Industrial College] etc. The policeman (motorcycle) was very nice. Subpoenaed the two colored and white boys and let me off. Gave the boys $10.000 to help them out. Which cleaned me out. . . .                    ·

*Daytona Beach, Florida*
*Wednesday, February 12*

. . . I had been longing to see the ocean in the moonlight, and then came Mrs. Mason to take me for a drive. We crossed the Halifax river . . . and then were down on the famous beach where the world auto races are run. Hard, close, dazzling sand, brilliantly white under a wondrous moon—great waves piling in, for the tide was coming in with a great rush. A never-to-be-forgotten sight.

At home later tried to do something to this homemade head, while Mrs. [Mary McLeod] Bethune [founder and president of Bethune-Cookman College, Daytona Beach] had her feet pedicured and we gossiped in her room. . . .

*Friday, February 14*

*Florida Normal and Industrial School*
. . . Letter from Leila at home saying Ethel improving. She had appendix, ovary, and a dozen adhesions removed. And so to bed. . . .

*Sunday, February 16*

*Bethune-Cookman College*
. . . In spite of rain and wind and storm a big meeting. Outside of school, mostly white. From about 20 states and Canada. Winter hotel visitors. The program was interesting, the music intensely so. . . .

*My first appeal to a white or almost white audience.* I hope it went over. I think it did. Mary [McLeod Bethune] in her glory and rightly so. She's built up something of which to be justly proud. Takes up a collection that I judge is pretty generous. Must get name of Mrs.

Dreyfus, the German Jewess who is so wealthy. . . .

It's been a very restful, charming, pleasant time. Mary is like all self made women, like Krusie [her old principal, Edwina B. Kruse] and the rest. Well, why not? When you have wrought, you should be proud of the result. I know the visit has pepped me up and stiffened *my backbone* on the A.I.P.C. [American Inter-Racial Peace Committee]. . . .

### Fort Valley, Georgia
### Tuesday, February 18

*Fort Valley Industrial School*

. . . Rebecca and Laurence wrote—rather pitifully—so that I am ashamed of my outburst. Laurence has had whooping cough—caught it from the baby, since before December. It wrung my heart. Leila had whooping cough. Caught it from Mary Ross's child—and had it to her death. I've worried all evening. . . .

### Thursday, February 20

. . . Tonight we drove to Macon [Ga.]—three carloads. . . . Frank Horne [a noted dramatist] is putting on "The No 'Count Boy" and wanted the students in the cast to see the Carolina Players who were at the Macon auditorium under auspices of some Macon College. The Carolina Players—one of the best of the amateur Little Theatre groups—were good in three short one-act plays. Very good. Enjoyed them. Fair house. Afterwards sandwiches and tea at the station restaurant and home on that lonesome road between the red clay hills, smelling some of that Georgia soil for 30 miles until one o'clock.

### Friday, February 21

*Farmers Conference*

The too-hoosing continues. More farmers. . . . Clubs, marching around the campus with the school band, brilliant sunshine, excitement. By eleven o'clock auditorium packed, farmers and their wives, children and leaders of the county. Government agents cutting up hogs to show how etc. etc. I spoke at 12. Here was an audience to challenge one; young, old, unlettered and school children, teachers, college people, people of the soil. Made good. Mr. Hunt broke into song, "Lord I want to be a Christian," and the great audience swung into the rocking chorus. As it was the first time he had ever sung, I must have fired him. . . .

*Talladega, Alabama*
*Wednesday, February 26*

*Talladega College*

Rain pouring on the roof—lovely, lazy sounds, awoke me. . . . Rain ceased. Drove to station in an old fashioned *victoria* drawn by two gray unmatched horses and a student driver who flourished the whip and tucked Miss Blair and me in. It was funny—but nothing else could endure that road of slippery red clay—as a wrecked auto testified.

Left Calhoun [Ala.] 9:40. . . . No train for Talladega until two. . . .

I did not go J.C. [Jim Crow, which means that she indulged in this bit of occasional "passing" for white for the traveling convenience. . . .

*Birmingham, Alabama*
*Saturday, March 1*

Did get up at five and [Melvin]Chisum came on time. . . . We get off in a pouring rain, with his big Nash filled with our bags, and I on the back seat ready to doze in a comfy fashion. Alas! a more miserable ride I've never had. The road from Tuskegee to Montgomery [Ala.] soon became thick red mud. We struck a stretch of new road, which the dumb roadmakers had forgotten to label impassable, skidded horribly and careened over a four foot embankment. Fortunately, Chisum held the wheel steady. So we neither turned turtle nor on our sides. But there we were down in a gully.

It took a half hour, eight or ten men, four dollars and herculean driving to get us up to the road again. The Negroes guarded us to the detour and soon we were on our way. No harm done, save to my bag, which was badly split.

The rest of the ride was torture to me. I needed a rest room and Chisum drove too slow—over cautious. Good road Montgomery to Brimingham. Reached there five minutes after a train for Jackson [Miss.] had gone. We *could* have made it. So bidding him good-bye, proceeded to bum for nine or ten hours. . . .

Now sitting in station until I can get in my berth. . . .

### New Orleans, Louisiana
### Monday, March 3

. . . I am in Stone Hall at Straight [College] [her alma mater]—
the dream of my childhood realized. 38 [years] this coming May since
I graduated and I believe there is some of the same furniture here that
was here then. Such queer mixed emotions! . . .

### Tuesday, March 4

Awoke this morning saying, "I am in New Orleans and this is
Mardi Gras."
. . . I wonder and wonder. Was I satisfied or disappointed? . . .

### Wednesday, March 5

It's been such a lovely day that I can't write about it. And yet I
have done nothing extraordinary. . . .
But the old friends, the streets, the houses . . .—and just everything. I can't describe—only feel. Every inch of ground seems
sacred. . . .

### Thursday, March 6

. . . It has been so lovely [in New Orleans]. . . . And there was
Emile Maspess [?]! Think of seeing him after all these years! That
stocky, grumpy, little second grader . . . who resisted my blandish-
ments with all the strength of his seven year old Creole body, now a
stocky, grumpy, bald-headed pharmacist, still resisting my blandish-
ments with all the strength of his 43 year old body! . . .

### Sunset Limited
### New Orleans to Los Angeles
### Sunday, March 9

All day crossing Texas. At 7:30 reach El Paso . . . the Rio Grande,
and Mexico—Juarez—on just across the border. I longed to go over,
but we have only fifteen minutes. All day, cattle and ranches, cowboys
with lariats and herds and mesos and mesquite, sagebrush and cactus,
plains and mountains and still Texas. I do an article for the Courier.

They don't deserve my punctuality—but if I stop they will have an excuse for non-payment. . . .

Scenery is thrilling in its barrenness and aridity. Passengers as usual. Snippy and suspicious. Consumptive girl coughing her life away, pretty and hateful; grouchy porter, inquisitive maid and Creole porter, urbane and suave. . . .

### Los Angeles, California
### Monday, March 10

Awoke this a.m. in Phoenix, Arizona, the hottest place in the U.S. . . .

We crossed the Continental Divide in the night. San Marino range at breakfast. Desert, desert, desert. Oasis of stations. Then orange and lemon groves, snow-capped mountains; the Salton sea. A quaint couple trying to be friendly and then, like all the rest, cooling off. Manicure by the maid and not well done. Heat. Terrific and no surcease. Desert dust, Indian squaws at Yuma. Cattle, cowboys. And then— Los Angeles! . . .

To the Dunbar Hotel. A lovely place, unbelievably so, where I have a *suite*, a sitting room *as is*, bedroom and bath. I stretch out in joy. Hooray! . . .

*This appearance here was her largest and most important. The Los Angeles Civic League, which sponsored her, was considered a "bunch of young radicals." Her audience was described as "large" and "enthusiastic" by the California* Eagle *(March 14), which reported the event under this headline: "Alice Dunbar Nelson Thrills Great Los Angeles Audience on World Peace and the Negro." The report continues: "Mrs. Nelson has a pleasing personality and her lecture on World Peace and the Negro was easily a masterpiece in oratorical elegance and logic." The slightly shortened text of her entire speech then follows.*

### Tuesday, March 11

Los Angeles Civic League
"I spoke fine." It was a good audience, far better than I had expected at 50¢ per. And I did my darndest. . . .

## Wednesday, March 12

To Pasadena to speak at the "Y" for the Council [of Presidents of the California Federation of Women's Clubs] (Executive). Usual type of uplifting dames. But Pasadena is *so* lovely. Asparagus ferns climbing to roofs, geraniums climbing way up palm trees, sweet peas as big as orchids, roses everywhere. . . .

## Friday, March 14

Rain, rain, rain. How disappointing, a devastating cloudburst. Flooded streets. Dismal skies. I could cry.

To the University of Southern California. Two history classes. The first dumb, the second interesting. . . . The rain depresses me. Tried to get a nap, telephone ringing all the time—would like to see some of the people who call, but a fool program, which gets me nowhere. . . .

## Saturday, March 15

I know now where I shall want to spend the end of my life—here in California. The Spanish lure—the call of the blood. I have come home—home—home. My heart is singing, my pulses pounding, I am home. New Orleans did not feel this way, even though it be my birthplace. But *here*— . . .

*One of D-N's speeches below occasioned a slightly strange article about her in the Pasadena press: "She pleaded particularly with the Negroes, whom she calls 'my people,' although she possesses a marked degree of English and Spanish blood, to advance the education of the young people of the race in order that they might understand history and become aware of the futility and inequity of war" (The Pasadena Star-News, March 14).*

*Felix is Reverend J. Benjamin St. Felix Isaacs, with whom Arleon Bowser had her thwarted romance in Wilmington.*

## Sunday, March 16

. . . Strange that eight of us who were together in Seattle in 1919 are here in Los Angeles. . . . To Pasadena where I spoke at Reverend

Carter's [Friendship Baptist] church. Took up a collection and made me stand by the table. Collected $14.06. Later I turned it over. . . .

Back in a cloudburst to the Y and the Civic League nearly an hour late. Here another speech. Another collection. A hectic rush with a wild group of young Nordics to Hollywood, to the [Hollywood] Congregational Church—an unsettled and uncomfortable five minutes with a group of youngsters, a hectic fifteen minutes with the congregation. A wild and furious eight mile drive back to Felix's [Los Angeles First A.M.E.] church, me with two of the young Nordics in a coupe, the driver a leader of the Young Students Group—(whose visiting card is printed on one side in Japanese). Here I speak fine again—another collection—then bid . . . good-bye. . . .

## Monday, March 17

My last day in Los Angeles and a most eventful one. . . . To the Paramount Lucky Studios. Saw a picture being filmed, "True to the Navy," where Clara Bow is to be, and another [picture] "Gone Native." Fascinating to see some of the sets I recognized. . . .

*This airplane ride—D-N's first—was the most widely reported happening of her national tour, appearing in a score of newspapers with catchy headlines (such as "Alice Takes to the Air"). The articles closely followed the American Inter-Racial Peace Committee Press Service News Release, which read:*

> *Word comes from Mrs. Alice Dunbar-Nelson, Executive Secretary of the American Interracial Peace Committee, that in order to keep engagements in Los Angeles and San Francisco within a few hours of each other, she had recourse to an airplane on the T.A.T. route. San Francisco is 12 to 14 hours by rail, but a passenger airplane makes the 471 miles in a bit over three hours. The Los Angeles Civic Club and a delegation of its friends were at the Glendale Airport to bid Mrs. Nelson bon voyage as she stepped aboard the plane. The flight was made on schedule time, and the San Franciscan engagement kept.*

*Julian is Julian Bagley, who was raised in San Francisco and became a city institution in his role as "impresario" of the San Francisco (War Memorial) Opera House. He also wrote and traveled widely.*

*D-N's reticence in these early entries about the precise nature of her interaction with Fay Jackson Robinson, a Los Angeles civic League*

*Executive Council member, is notable—though not altogether sur-*
*prising. Only gradually does she later reveal clearly that they became*
*lovers.*

## Tuesday, March 18

*Writing this Wednesday on Overland Limited*
San Francisco—*A Perfect Day*
God, what a marvelous day? Emotions of beauty too profound to
describe. One just doesn't. You feel and thrill and surge—but you
can't write it. Fay's husband [John] drove me to Glendale Airport.
Took off at ten. That indescribable moment when the plane rises in
the air. Above the snow-capped San Gabriel mountains. What a thrill!
At the Alameda airport by 1:30 and Polly's Julian awaiting me. Ensues
a perfect day. In San Francisco, we collect Gene [Carcanelli], the
Italian youth with the liquid eyes and lengthy name. To my hotel—
the Springer, pretty, little, quaint. Collect Fay—marvelous Fay. Lovely
San Francisco—cliffs and hills, the ocean, seal rock, Nobb Hill, winding
drives, Spreckles Museum, Rodin art, The Golden Gate at Sunset
. . . sunbathing in the cliff tea garden. The Fox Theatre and a lovely
show . . . the States restaurant and abalone steaks and to the little
hotel and Fay stays all night with me. Julian, the prince of enter-
tainers, pays our bills. A most marvelous day. A day ever to be remembered. . . .

## Overland Limited
## San Francisco–Omaha
## Wednesday, March 19

Fay and I were awakened early. . . . So we arose. And were soon
dressed. No hot water in our private bath. Put our queer folding bed—
attached to the door—up. It was all very lovely. I put the two bunches
of violets on my coat, Fay took the red roses. . . . At 11:45 I bade
good-bye to my lovely new-found California friends—Julian Bagley,
Prince of Hosts, Gene Carcanelli, Italian of the lovely eyes, and Fay-
Fay, Little Blue Pigeon with Velvet Eyes.
    All day climbing the snow-capped mountains of California, from
golden poppies to snow-covered ranges. Again I cross the Bay of San
Francisco and bid goodbye to the Pacific Ocean. All day I dream of
the eight perfect days—of the romance, the beauty, the loveliness—
and register anew a vow to return to California to end my days. . . .

*Overland Limited*
*Somewhere in Utah*
*Thursday, March 20*

. . . Wrote a sonnet to Fay, "I had not thought to ope that secret room."

*Omaha, Nebraska*
*Friday, March 21*

Well, here we are and how standardized is the world. Everywhere, same kind of people, same clothes, homes, jokes, bridge games, Amos n' Andy radios, etc. I must be pessimistic or something. Too much emotional upheaval those two days on the train—thinking of California, and Fay. Consequent depression. . . .

Perhaps it is the return to winter since yesterday—bare trees, drab lawns, ice, snow, bitter winds—winter, which I have not seen since February first, for though the winds may have been cold, there have been daffodils since North Carolina. And these low gray and brown plains of all day today! . . .

*Des Moines, Iowa*
*Sunday, March 23*

Dear God, what a day! Arriving seven. Mrs. S. Joe [Brown, black civic leader who had sponsored D-N's trip to Iowa nine years before] met me and after getting a taxi—lo there were Helene [London, her artist friend] and her husband. So we got out and away. Helene all radiant. To Mrs. B's home, which is no more of a home now than it was in 1921. . . .

*Monday, March 24*

. . . Helene finally left at four promising to see me in my berth at 9:30. But Mrs. S. Joe dragged me out anyhow, to an organ recital and dedication at the First Federated Church way out somewhere and to the newspaper office anyhow for *that* interview. Had her way. Crazy about newspaper write-ups. If I were, I'd be better off, I suppose.

Nearly half past ten before I finally got to my berth. Poor Helene had waited for me for an hour and was wild with rage and disappointment. So we both cussed and were cross and catty with each other.

She gave me some lovely thank you cards.

Snowing now. A wind all day.

### Chicago, Illinois
### Tuesday, March 25

"The worst blizzard of the worst season." A 60 mile gale, drifts six feet high, stalled cars and engines. Paralyzed traffic. Crashing "L" cars. Score of lives lost. Terrific. . . .

Laurence and I left [his apartment] at 6:30. We had to walk blocks, or rather fight blocks to the "L." It stalled several times. Then we had to walk blocks and blocks to the B & O. No other means of transportation. Got my berth at 8. Worried about his getting back up-town.

Have written this up since Saturday on the B & O train going East. First time this year I have lapsed. Never again!

### Wednesday, March 26

*Going home!* The snowstorm following us. Dreary day. Dreary thoughts. Half sick all day.

*At home.*

The train . . . 35 minutes late . . . at Washington. Had wired Bobbo. Got off expecting five or ten minutes chat. He was there in new suit, hat, brief-case ready to come to Wilmington with me. Pleasant surprise. We dined together on the train. Smoked in the club car . . . Home. Pauline and Leila at the station.

Patsy [Mama] combed and in her pink jacket; Jack [the dog], big, fat, noisy and wild to see me. We drank some cognac and made mild whoopee. My room dirty and messy, but everything about the same.

### Thursday, March 27

God, what a hell of a day! I think if I could have had a letter from Fay when I came in at eleven tonight, it would have been better. . . .

I'm rotten bilious—that's why life does not seem worth living. . . . I'd *better* have a drainage.

### Friday, March 28

. . . Forgot to mention yesterday was [American Friends] Service Committee [her parent committee] meeting and I spoke briefly touching high lights of my report. Somehow it didn't seem to go over—so *that* helped make me miserable. . . .

Gifford Pinchot, *mentioned below, was former governor of Pennsylvania (1923–27), who was running again for the position. From this point on, the campaign, Pinchot's election, and Robert's (and D-N's) hope for a political appointment from him are major themes of the diary.*

## Saturday, March 29

Another gosh-awful day. The worst of the three that have passed since I came home. Bilious as a dog. Took the 7:45 for Philadelphia and at work by 9:15. Hustling some details anent Music Festival. Bobbo came in office—came up to Wilmington last night after all. Trying to get into the Pinchot campaign. . . .

Letter from Helene. It *was* pretty raw. But enclosed a mutilated scrap of a letter from Fay to her, showing that Fay had made certain promises to Helene about me—not to get friendly, I judge. God it hurt! I must have dropped Helene's envelope and all in my blind rage. Bobbo got it, read it—he *will* read my things, diary and all—God, he *pufformed.* Called Helene and Fay horrible names. I don't know how I assumed an air of nonchalance and cool indifference—which threw him off. Inwardly I raged—at Fay's deceit, at Helene's asininity—hurting of me with Fay's letter, at Bobbo's meddlesomeness and coarseness. It nearly wrecked me. Got through somehow. . . . Went to market with Bobbo. Came back and deliberately tried to get drunk—and played poker. Succeeded in getting drunk. Maudlin tears and satisfied Bobbo. Tears of rage and pent-up emotion. God, that my little blue dream of loveliness should end thus. I could commit murder.

## Sunday, March 30

. . . I re-read those poems of Paul [Laurence Dunbar]'s, "Lyrics of Love and Sorrow." Exquisite things. Shall copy them tomorrow and send them to Fay. Deceitful hussy.

## Monday, March 31

. . . Stayed [at Women's International League mass meeting] to hear Nannie Burroughs [famous educator, activist, speaker from

Washington, D.C.] She was all full of impassioned eloquence. Wish I could talk like that, God knows. But I can't. . . .

Sent Fay a Farewell to the Little Blue Pigeon with Violet eyes, The Lyrics of Love and Sorrow, and the mutilated letter Helene sent. And that's that. Another chapter ended [or so D-N thinks. However, the repercussions of this affair continue for some time]. . . .

/ . . Scholley [Alexander, Virginia's brother] came in the room [at Dr. Virginia Alexander's] after I had a bath and was in bed to talk. His voice has . . . [a] dreary hopelessness. . . . He is discouraged and has a chance to go to California. I told him to go. Who wouldn't want to go to California?

## Wednesday, April 2

. . . *Strange Interlude* is even stranger as a play than reading it. Glad I had a good seat, so I could hear all those strange "asides." Saps one's emotional vitality. I was perfectly exhausted when I got home at midnight. A wreck. What with the trip to New York, the play, the emotional dam in me. Found wild letter from Helene enclosing a lock of her hair, scented. Destroyed all. Seemed like a lock of Medusa's hair. That curl actually seemed poisonously alive. Wretched night.

*The "you" of this sonnetlike poem is obviously Fay. During this period, D-N writes numerous other poems to her. Unfortunately, copies of them do not exist among D-N's extant papers.*

## Thursday, April 3

Damn wretched tummy. Going on a strictly milk diet. Wired Helene today not to send me any more letters to the house. With Bobbo running up every weekend during this Pinchot campaign, can't take any chances. Another outburst like that from him and I won't be responsible. . . .

You did not need to creep into my heart
The way you did. You could have smiled
And knowing what you did, have kept apart
From all my inner soul. But you beguiled
Deliberately. Then flung my poor love by,
A priceless orange now. Without a sigh
Of pity at the wreck you made. Smashed
The golden dream I'd reared. Then unabashed

Impaled the episode upon a stupid epigram,
Blowing my soul thro' smoke wreaths as you sneered a "Damn!"

## Friday, April 4

Poor dumb Negroes! They don't know what it's all about. I went down to the Settlement [House] tonight as I had promised Dr. Stubbs [her friend and Wilmington physician]. . . . Went into [Dr. Stubbs' wife] Blanche's part where she had an audience of about 75 or 80 in the room with not a breath of air and a stench that clutched your throat, giving a *Health* play, with about fifteen children—she all messed up on the stage with them. It was a scream. I told about the Youth Peace Contest and fled to the other room—the Citizens' Independent League. I know them—dumb, heavy. Ready to "appoint a committee" to "investigate" the case of Saunders, who was fired as a [?] enumerator. Fortunately, Juice [Jamison, her dentist] and Blanche protested Dr. Stubbs' motion, as did by me, and we got a committee to act. Guess I was the Moses, for while Juice drew up the letter to the governor, I got the *Morning News* on the phone and the story. After the meeting, brought Juice and George [Anderson] down while I typed the letter to the Governor, found envelope and stamp. The reporter came and we filled him up. I think George Anderson was scared. Poor one cylinder folks and, as the man named Cooper [at the meeting] said, that cylinder knocking. . . .

Wrote a sonnet—"Pale April, decking her hair with daffodils."

## Saturday, April 5

. . . Georgia Douglas Johnson [important poet, writer, literary person from Washington, D.C.] called from the station and soon *she* came. . . . Put *her* feet in the right path of the stairs and stayed in blissful quiet getting out cards etc. . . . On to . . . Germantown for the Association of Negro Life and History. Quite a large meeting and much talk. Georgia quite a hit. . . .

## Sunday, April 6

. . . I enjoyed the ride on the train going up [to Philadelphia] for I did not read, just sat and enjoyed my soul. And when we got to Lansdowne [Pa.] in time for the end of the Quaker meeting, and there were some more minutes of peace and quiet—it was like a spiritual bath.

Well, it was a quiet, lovely, low-keyed day. We four, the Foggs, Georgia [D. Johnson] and I. Reading a quaint book of verses about dogs, talking around an open fire, eating dinner and finally driving through a pelting chill rain to Wilmington. . . .

## Monday, April 7

. . . Hill at the office when I got back and we clashed as usual. Bobbo put his finger on the crux of the whole matter of my failure with the A.I.P.C.: "Subconsciously you have a contempt for Quakers and a contempt for Hill and that's why you don't put it over."

And as soon as he said that, I knew that I would *never* put it over, for I *do not* believe in the A.I.P.C. Horrible to admit it, to admit defeat and failure. But better to face the truth. I do not believe in it. And Leslie's only ideal is for his own aggrandizement. Principles mean nothing to him. We are doomed to failure. And I don't believe in him. . . .

## Tuesday, April 8

Waked up feeling wretched. This damn cold has got me. The very marrow of my bones seem ice. It is so cold and raw and bleak and I feel as if I shall never be warm again. . . . Amy [Wu, her office secretary] . . . gave me a personal telegram from Fay. "I defy her to show all my letters to you." A week ago, this would have made me so tremulously happy the world would have rocked. But in the three weeks which have elapsed since I set foot in San Francisco, I have gone through the whole gamut of emotion. Nothing left. All dried. Empty. . . .

Got letter from Fay. I could not appreciate it. Read it perfunctorily. Too late. Too late. . . .

But I shall [re]read . . . [it] ere I go to sleep.

## Wednesday, April 9

. . . Dropped in to see Mrs. [Addie W.] Dickerson [head of the Republican Council of Colored Women] today [in Philadelphia]. She's going out after that legislative nomination. . . . But she looked tattered, unmended, and ungroomed today. *Why* will women do that?

Walked around in the sun so much that I got warmed up and felt almost human.

At home found another letter from Fay. Just a little poem about

me and orchids. Bless her heart. Life seems more interesting. Even
though I am doped by the chloroform in the cough medicine. . . .

## Thursday, April 10

. . . Wrote a sonnet, "I could not even dream—"

## Friday, April 11

. . . Don't remember much else what happened during the day,
as I am writing this on April 18. Probably hopped up and down over
the Music Festival [which she is again planning for this spring]. Feeling pretty rotten. . . .
Wrote a sonnet on the girls in the office and their chatter.

## Saturday, April 12

. . . Raging fever all day. Wrote a sonnet on my feverous condition, likening Fay to a cool lake, a cool flower. Wrote it in the [Girls
Industrial School Trustee] meeting.

## Sunday, April 13

. . . I wrote a sonnet, "Lest I should worry you if day by day"—
while he [W. E. B. DuBois] was speaking. . . .

## Monday, April 14

. . . Damn bad luck I have with my pen. Some fate has decreed I
shall never make money by it. Alternately cussed, cried and shivered
myself to sleep. . . .

## Tuesday, April 15

. . . Wrote a sonnet, "I knew I'd suffer if I let love come," and
sent the last four or five to Fay. Helene deluging me with wild letters,
even having her nurse write. . . .
[After Virginia Alexander, her doctor, left] I broke down and cried.
Tired from the exhausting draining. *And* miserable. Sobbed for an
hour and couldn't stop. Ira Lewis, Hill, the A.I.P.C., Fay, Helene—
oh hell, I wanted to die. Cried myself to sleep in Virginia's bed.

## Wednesday, April 16

. . . I sat outside in the car and read reams of Helene's vapor-ings. . . .

Found letter from Fay. All steamed up over Helene's sending me that mutilated letter and my bitter reaction. Helene is a first class mischief-maker. She writes a lot of innuendo about Fay's letters to her.

## Thursday, April 17

. . . Took 5:13 . . . for New York for this was the day of my ticket for [the famous play] "Green Pastures." . . . Stupendous. Wonderful. Majestic. Beggars description. And Richard Harrison, [in his leading role as] "De Lawd," doing the finest piece of acting Broadway has seen for an age, just because it isn't acting. A marvelous thing, funny and yet not funny. Tears come because of its very ludicrous pathos.

And got the 11:35 home and in the house by 2:30. Feeling better too. Needed a tonic. Felt too low-down.

## Friday, April 18

. . . Told Helen [Bryan, with whom she worked] I was unhappy in my job and put in my bid for a place in the new inter-racial com-mission. . . .

And now I've written up this damn diary since April 11. Thought I wasn't going to let it pile up again! No will power.

## Saturday, April 19

. . . Tonight was a family affair. Laurence and Beck and the baby [from Chicago] and Bobbo vying with each other for noise. Very pleasant. . . .

All admiring the Frigidaire. Bobbo's anniversay present to me.

Daily letters from Helene. Wild and incriminating to the office. God! How well Jessie Fauset [Black female poet and novelist] wrote in "La Vie C'est la Vie." I'd welcome a daily letter from Fay. Helene loves me.

Ethel [her niece] at the house today. First time I have seen her since I came home and her operation. . . .

## Tuesday, April 22

. . . Tonight Anna [Brodnax] had the old Bridgets [bridge club] in honor of Bowse's home-coming. . . . Bowse [who had suffered a nervous breakdown] looks lovely, hair almost white, but bobbed and tremendously effective. It was quite like old times, playing bridge for the "pot" and eating good supper and later . . . telling rotten stories. After one when we came home. . . .

I believe I'm going to get over that Fay trouble. Hope so.

## Wednesday, April 23

Ye Gods! What a day. Up early. Washed windows and wiped walls, dusted, cleaned, picked up, watered flowers, pressed linen. Downtown marketing. . . . Struggling to get things moving . . . tables set up. Wanamaker's box unpacked etc. etc. etc. A ghastly mess of work. All Wilmington's elite out. A *big* party. Six tables—two extras. . . . Leon [Anderson, their congenial family friend] to the rescue with spike for the dandelion cocktails. Very lovely. But once I thought I just *couldn't* do the dishes. But I did. Leila worked like a Trojan. And now . . . I am going to take a bath and go to bed after pulling the prettiest party of the season. . . .

## Thursday, April 24

. . . Interested in a new book "The Prophet" by a Persian writer of whom I've never heard, but who seems to be quite a favorite, Kahlil Gibran. Very appealing in its Oriental mysticism. . . .

## Friday, April 25

. . . Getting the [Youth Peace Contest] essays fixed up for judges— and a thick letter from Fay. Typed, cool, suave and amusing. (Helene's letters are still almost a daily nuisance.) . . .

## Monday, April 28

. . . Lovely little letter from Fay—not formal—enclosing one of California's huge violets and a little white flower, a "what not" Fay called it, that tiny Joan [Fay's daughter] had plucked. . . .

## Tuesday, April 29

. . . Pauline and I have decided that life is too rushy and complex for words. Can't ever get to bed early and sleepy as dogs in the morning. It's long past one now.

Definitely decided to write that novel, "Uplift," finish it by February and enter it in the *Harper* contest. Feel somehow that I'll win, too. . . . That is, if I ever get to it. But go, go, go—so busy, so futilely busy. As I wrote Fay today, like an old horse hopping up and down in one place, or like Alice in Wonderland running with the Red Queen. . . .

## Wednesday, April 30

. . . It is growing warmer and spring shows in the trees at last. It's been miserable waiting for it. But I can't dig up a thrill—such as I had a month ago. Even Fay's letters, sane and witty, fail to stir me. Wonder *now* what's the matter? . . . I insist upon feeling sardonic. . . .

## Thursday, May 1

It occurs to me with a feeling as if the bottom of my tummy had dropped out that the National Negro Music Festival is going to be a financial flop. Sales not as good as this time last year and bills mounting by the minute and Helen [Bryan] always wiping out any surplus with some "overhead." I feel faint over it. . . .

## Friday, May 2

Home is getting to be a novelty. It was nearly ten before I got to the office from Virginia [Alexander]'s. Another futile interview with a "too busy" woman. . . .

## Saturday, May 3

. . . I go to the Walnut Theater [Philadelphia] to see "Lysistrata," Aristophane's uproarious comedy. Norman Bel Geddes did the theatre over to look like the Acropolis and Fay Banister as Lysistrata was rare. The whole performance was rare, screamingly funny and gorgeously beautiful, deliciously frank and unashamed. Bobbo [who is probably passing through the city on business] meets me after theatre and we come home to a cold dinner—but then it is a warm day. . . .

### Norfolk, Virginia
### Sunday, May 4

. . . Eating breakfast, chanced to look at my hand, and to my disgust and horror saw one of the stones out of my three diamond ring. Rushed back to the train [on which she had traveled to this Norfolk engagement], and the porter and I tore the bed to pieces. No diamond. I felt it had been washed down in the basin. Felt sick over that empty ring—looked like a pretty woman with a tooth out. . . .

### Tuesday, May 6

. . . Chauncey [Wu, her secretary's husband] told me today that he had gone into the matter of the cigarette lighter [which she was hoping to design and patent] with the professor of physics. Due to my imperfect knowledge of electricity, I could not know the natural laws which make it impracticable. So there go my dreams of wealth. . . .

### Wednesday, May 7

. . . I never win anything [at bridge]. Augurs bad for the Festival. My luck at cards usually points the way to my general luck. . . .

### Sunday, May 11

Instead of being able to stay in bed and rest, must get out . . . and race all over Philadelphia making slushy Mother's Day speeches. . . .

The folks had driven down to Cecilton, Maryland, to visit Ethel on Dr. Mullin's estate [Dr. Mullin is one of Ethel's doctors]. I fixed my dinner, fed Jack, and was writing to Fay when they came whooping in, all gleeful over the good time they had had. Scotch and rye and dandelion n' everything. And a day of such gorgeousness! Clear and lovely out and cool. How I would have enjoyed the trip. Ethel well and happy. I sent her the chocolate straw she wrote for. . . .

### Friday, May 16

As the time draws nigh for the Festival I grow colder and emptier. Took all my clothes in a suitcase down to the Citizens' Hotel. Put

them in my room—a very pleasant one on the third floor front. . . .
Bobbo comes in on the 6:41. . . . [He is] delighted with our intimate
little home. . . .

## Saturday, May 17

A gray day, cool and pleasant that turns to sunshine and the
[National Negro Music] Festival is on. . . . Afternoon performance
lovely—to almost empty seats. In between . . . I drink some good
liquor and cuss Hill. . . .

Night performance lovely. Better crowd. But I was heartsick when
the Academy [of Music, where the festival is staged] check . . . was
seventeen hundred instead of three thousand as last year. And programs three hundred instead of five. I see I am sunk. It makes me sick
and I am rude to Hill, horribly rude. But I pay off . . . [people] and
Tibbs makes me horribly tired. I am cross, cross, cross. Pack bag at
the hotel and we . . . fliv home, get some sandwiches and drink some
whiskey. Two letters from Fay today. She has dyed her hair blonde.
That made life seem more better. . . .

## Thursday, May 22

. . . Went down to [American Friends] Service Committee meeting and allowed myself to be bored for an hour or so. Smug Quakers
prattling about infinitesimal sentimental nothings. Skirting the edge
of reality. . . .

## Friday, May 23

Awoke early, having slept well and dreamed of a huge check of
$99.81, wherefore I shall probably waste a lot of money playing those
numbers! . . .

## Monday, May 26

. . . Went down to Unity [a religious/spiritual practice] Center
and stayed for noon meditation. My belief in that sort of thing always
shaken by the mediocre hypocrites who expound it.

[AIPC] Board meeting fully attended and stormy. Hill [AIPC
chairman] jumped out first and laid the failure of the festival to every-

thing I did. Politely and subtly said I was inefficient, inept etc. I almost burst with rage. However, he did not go scot free and the session was bitter. We've got to raise that $500, and let the $1,000 go. I came out a nervous wreck, sick and shaken. Wish I had another job. . . .

### Tuesday, May 27

. . . Home, puttered in the garden, and beat Jack for digging up my Japanese dwarf pine. . . .

### International House, New York
### Friday, May 30

"In sooth" I don't know why I came to New York. No compelling business until Sunday and Monday—but I just went on planning, engaged room here and here I am. A strange urge against reason, commonsense and economy. For I can ill afford to spend money now. But—after a lazily pleasant day at home, from which I tore myself reluctantly, here I am. . . . I need rest, change from home chatter, a chance to get a perspective—to think. Maybe I'll meet someone interesting. . . .

### International House, New York
### Saturday, May 31

. . . Uptown and to see George Schuyler [conservative Harlem Renaissance satirical writer]. He has a white wife and she *is* from Texas. And their apartment is the last word in all that is exotic. To [her friend] Martha Arnold's. And had a dinner prepared for me. . . . Then to the Roscoe Bruce's [her bureaucratic friends] and played bridge and . . . ate homemade ice-cream until 1:30. Took a taxi back here and found both beds occupied. So piled up in the other room with the Russian girl. It is all so incidental and casual. But amusing.

### Tuesday, June 3

. . . [At night back in Wilmington] Took down curtains etc. Conflict within me still raging. Good God, how long!

## Wednesday, June 4

. . . Felt today for the first time as I came along the street—"Oh, I can't, can't stand it"—the heat and all.

I'm tired. This conflict [which can only be inferred from what the diary suggests about her outer and inner life] is wearing me down. . . .

## Haverford College
## Haverford, Pennsylvania
## Tuesday, June 10

. . . Met the little Pauline Myers that I've heard so much about. Poor kid, she's in for a lot of disillusionment. Far be it from me to be the one to tell her there's no Santa Claus. . . .

## Haverford College
## Thursday, June 12

. . . Made breakfast, devotions and all six classes today. . . .

Started definitely on [her projected novel] "Uplift" today. Did 1700 words or more. I'm 10,000 words behind. Must catch up. . . .

## Friday, June 13

. . . Worked a bit on the novel. Did less than a thousand words. This won't do at all. . . .

## Saturday, June 14

. . . Finished chapter I of the Great American Novel—no, not quite finished. . . . Found Ethel home and the usual air of unrest and nerve-strain when she is about. . . .

## Monday, June 16

Started Chapter II. Dick wanted to hear Chapter I. Read it to him after luncheon. Sounded flat, meaningless. But when I read the two pages of Chapter II, I burned with mortification. Such inane, sophomoric, amateurish puerility—! I could not sleep at night for being ashamed of it. . . .

### Haverford[, Pennsylvania]
### Tuesday, June 17

. . . Found letter from Fay enclosing picture of herself and snap of me belonging to Bobbo. She has left her husband and it looks like a hell of a mess to me. Privately, I think they were both after Tesse and John won. . . .

### Haverford[, Pennsylvania]
### Thursday, June 19

. . . Met the gang at Chestnut Street Opera House to see the picture "All Quiet on the Western Front." Horrible war picture. 41 of us pacifists from the college went in. . . . A terrific indictment against war—that picture. Wish I had a glass of milk.

### Friday, June 20

. . . Had a lovely time exploring today—a rabbit in the sunken garden, squirrels in the big grove, thrush and [?] in the secret path in the deep grove, four leaf clover in the field—a lovely time alone. Suddenly grew tired of being talked at—and very tired of old man F[?] who comes every day and bores me with much talk and atrocious table manners. Finished "The House of Mirth"—was it only 16 years ago I read it first? It shall be the model of "Uplift." I need a model.

Home—explanations. . . .

And now for the dreary certainties of an uncertain life. The interim at Haverford was restful and lovely— . . . It is 2:30. I am not sleepy. . . .

### Monday, June 23

*Krusie* [Edwina B. Kruse] *died tonight* at nine o'clock [of double pneumonia]. Poor dear old Ned-Odduwumuss. My mind goes back over the years from 1902 to 1909 [when D-N first came to Wilmington] when we were closer than sisters—till first Arthur [Callis], then Anna [Brodnax] broke up our Eden—and then to 1920 with our semi-friendship. Those first seven years! Well, she passed away. . . . When Baldy [Gertrude Baldwin, at Kruse's house] called over the phone . . .

I went down at once and I did the last thing I could for her—did articles for the papers and . . . drove around after midnight putting them in. And sent wires and letters.

Krusie—her life spelled more romance than will ever be told. A friend she was—and paradox of paradoxes—one of my worst enemies. Let her soul rest in peace. I loved her once. Twenty years ago, her death would have wrecked my life. . . .

### Thursday, June 26

. . . Krusie was buried today. Such a funeral with the kind of quiet pomp and elegance as would have pleased her. She had sloughed off these evil years and looked as she did 20 years ago. . . .

### Springfield, Massachusetts
### Hotel Charles
### Friday, June 27

. . . Arrived in a down-pour this A.M. and to the Municipal Auditorium. . . . Smallest [NAACP] conference I've seen in years. Financial depression. Interesting program, but the people don't seem to know what to do when it is over—they stand around and talk anxiously to each other—it's pathetic. . . .

It's a dry sort of affair, somehow. I'm sorry I paid up for four days. Maybe it will get better. . . .

### Springfield[, Massachusetts]
### Sunday, June 29

. . . Richard Harrison [the white actor] and I scandalized everyone by going into an embrace in the hotel lobby. . . .

### Wednesday, July 2

. . . Did about 12 or 1300 words on "Uplift" and went out to the Allen Auto School for a driving lesson. It's costing me ten dollars—but it's the only way I'll ever learn—to have to go and be compelled to take a lesson. If I wait for amateur help, I'll be just as I was last year, putting off—And I just can't have Polly's flivver standing in the garage all summer while she's [going to school] at Columbia. Got on pretty well, though I sweat bucketsful. . . .

### Thursday, July 3

. . . Pauline met me at the train, and we went out on the road and practised a bit. She yells at me of course. . . .

### Saturday, July 5

Polly had a bright idea about driving to Cecilton [Md.] to see Ethel—the whole damn family, with me doing most of the driving. Went . . . and applied for license. Not ready until Tuesday. However, after much travail and packing of luncheon . . . we got off. Mama and Leila and Bobbo on the back seat.

I drove about 22 miles—after we passed the state highway police station. Did some reprehensible things, calling for ejaculations from the back seat. . . .

### Monday, July 7

. . . Cried all morning because I thought I had also lost the notebook with "Uplift" in it. Amy phoned home and Pauline said it was there. Didn't remember taking it home. . . .

### Wednesday, July 9

. . . Some people—Warrens, market people—here to see what Bobbo can do for the boy [a young Black man] Theodore Russ, who is to be hanged July 25 on insufficient evidence of rape [of raping a lower-class white woman who sold bootleg liquor and was friendly with him in downstate Delaware]. Wrote Bobbo and Walter White [who handled such cases for his NAACP job]. . . .

### Saturday, July 12

. . . Went to [first Black Wilmington lawyer] Louis Redding's office to get data about the Russ case and sent it to both Bobbo and Walter White as they had asked. . . .

### Monday, July 14

Bastille Day. And more or less interesting to me. Started out telephoning and telephoning and writing letters, interviewing people and getting more or less het up over the Russ boy—so that it was quite like old times, getting under way. Louis Redding being professionally "ethical," George Anderson being slow, Dr. Stubbs—but going pussy-footing and everyone milling around busy doing nothing—while time for the boy's hanging—July 25—draws nigh. . . .

### Tuesday, July 17

. . . Took a driving lesson from William [Lewis] and was super-normally dumb. . . .

### Thursday, July 17

. . . Louis [Redding] came over tonight and we talked hours. Everyone has backed out now but [Howard High School principal George] Johnson, Louis, Polly and I. Couldn't locate Stubbs—Juice too busy, others all indifferent. Well, we'll go to court tomorrow at Dover and see what the outcome of a motion for a new trial will be.

### Friday, July 18

. . . Got through a tedious trial [in Dover] with perjuring witness and a brace of foolish lawyers. Frame was a sorry sight. When recess was called, we knew the jig was up. Went to the Henrys [her friends] for rest and refreshment, for it was a *hot* day. Back to hear the curt negative of the judge's on the motion for a new trial. . . .

### Saturday, July 19

My 55th! Ye gods! Can it be that I am sliding down the other side of the hill!

. . . I backed the car out of the garage and started from the house. Barring two minor bumps—did very well, driving all the way to Smyrna [Del., site of the state prison] without stopping. On the speedway, hit 'em up to 50 m.p.h. to Pauline's fright. . . .

### Sunday, July 20

Hot! 90° early in the day. . . . Faced three disagreeable tasks. 1. Clean and dress that chicken; 2. Fumigate my bed—a bug bit me; 3. Bathe Jack—heat breeds flies.

Gave the chicken to Mrs. Murray [her neighbor] and did the other tasks. . . .

## Monday, July 21

. . . Eddie Chippey [brother of Edna, who worked in the *Advocate* newspaper office] wanted to do something on the Russ case, so Louis got up a petition and he hustled around and got signatures—all "prominent citizens." We got the petition off to the governor. And my letter too. Andrews of the New York N.A.A.C.P. writes that he has wired and written Frame and no reply. . . .

## Tuesday, July 22

. . . Went out to take a night lesson with William and drove around the dark and skeersome curves of the Brandywine [River], and home through traffic. Scared—but getting the hang of it better. . . .

## Wednesday, July 23

. . . We [D-N and Pauline] drove Reverend Holland to the Workhouse (his daily trip) to see Theodore Russ. Handsome, stalwart fellow, too handsome and too young to die. He calmly accepted Reverend Holland's book and knelt in prayer. Poor fellow.

At night, Eddie [Chippey]'s mass meeting at Ezion [Church]. . . .

Meeting milled along, [Charlie] Colburn [Black Wilmington politician], resenting Eddie's implication of inaction, said they had been "meeting" at the Settlement [House] for three months. It took "Boots" Evans to crystallize the thing. He had been talking with the Governor over the phone. The Governor leaving in the morning for Camp. No use of going to Dover. But he had promised Boots he'd see a delegation if it came before midnight. I said "Let's Go!" In 20 minutes, delegation arranged and a line of about 30 or more cars filled and on the road to the Governor's farm down the State Road about ten miles. Paul Revere's ride was tame. We piled into his yard, his porch. We talked, argued, expostulated. Poor Governor [C. Douglass] Buck! We left with a half promise. Back to Ezion and on the sidewalks talked more.

## Thursday, July 24

An anxious day. The *Morning News* carried a well-written and exciting story of the appeal to the governor last night. Rumors flew thick and fast all day. Elbert and Banton [Black community leaders] called in hasty conference with the governor. Hastings [white Wilmington lawyer, judge, senator] and Colburn in conference. The governor and Hastings. . . .

I decided I'd rather remain home and wait for news. It came while Aaron was here—25 days respite. Well, that's something. Louis came and we went into deep conference over the legal aspects of the case. Leila and Pauline came home in the midst and soon Juice and Jean [Jamison]—and we had a "kitchen conference" with me re-enacting the scenes of last night. Louis stayed until one o'clock—going over the case and some other things. . . .

### Friday, July 25

Went up to [Dr.] Virginia [Alexander]'s today to "drain." Much evil-looking black stuff out of my gall bladder and evil-looking bile out of my stomach accounted for my headaches. . . .

### Sunday, July 27

. . . We all get off—me muchly dressed—to the National [Theater] for the mass meeting. Well attended and considerable enthusiasm. Russ' mother and two sisters there and on the platform. Not so much oratory—but potent. Collect $190—not so bad. . . .

### Monday, July 28

. . . To George Sykes [Emma's dentist husband] at nine for Executive Committee meeting on Russ Defense. [Conwell] Banton again, swelling and strutting. All the "big" lawyers seen today by Sykes and Johnson refuse the case, so that leaves Louis to hold the bag. Best, I suppose. . . .

### Tuesday, July 29

. . . All bright and early to take my driver's examination. Passed the oral with flying colors. Couldn't park my car the way the examiner—a cynical highway state cop—thought right. Smashed the parking sign and messed up things generally. Was sent home in disgrace. . . .

### Wednesday, July 30

Did a review of Langston Hughes' [novel] *Not Without Laughter* for the Washington *Tribune*. Took a lesson in parking on a drive at

the Auto School. Then came home, ate dinner, and took another
lesson . . . I am hopelessly dumb. God ought not to make any one as
dumb as I am. . . .


## Saturday, August 2

"Life is such a Godawful mess I don't blame anyone for getting
out of it." Wrote this tonight to Bobbo anent Douglass Wetmon's
suicide. Poor fellow just said he was tired and shot himself to freedom.
And the famous [Black] Binga bank failed in Chicago.
Life *is* a mess. I am profoundly in the D's—discouraged, depressed,
disheartened, disgusted.
Why does one *want* to live? . . .


## Thursday, August 14

. . . Home on the 5:15 expecting some [driving] practice. Polly
and Louis [Redding] gone to Dover. Did not return until after eight—
Polly cross and hungry. Louis *is* a mess. Mr. [George] Johnson's
description of him as a physician who tells his patient he will die
unless radium treatment is given and all the radium is in Siberia is a
good one.
If Russ gets free, I will be surprised. . . .


## Friday, August 15

. . . My extension on my beginner's license expires today. . . .
Guess I am fated not to drive. . . .


## Monday, August 18

. . . Had a bright idea of taking my road test in Dover . . . borrowing [Black businessman] John [Hopkins]'s Cadillac from his chauffeur,
proceeded to go out and fail my test again. Couldn't manage that big
Cadillac.
So into the Supreme Court room to the hearing, being ushered in
over everyone else. Hearing had been going on an hour and a half.
But I heard enough. Linwood Gray's perjuries. Frame's excitement
and [white Wilmington lawyer] Tunnell's masterly arraignment.
Wonderful. Told him so. . . .

[Pardon]Board went into Executive session when all was over. . . .
We waited outside. They disagreed and decided to meet later. So came
home. . . . Cleared desk. Mailed a pile of checks, after eating. Waited
for some word. None came. Puttered, cleared, cleaned, bathed—bed.

### Tuesday, August 19

Arose early, bought *Morning News*. Glaring headlines—Pardon
Board refused plea for clemency. Good God. Those dirty, white-liv-
ered cowards. They knew what their decision was when they sent us
home. They were afraid to face the crowd. I saw red—furious, angry
red. All day I hated white people. Stormed about my broken watch
bracelet in Wanamaker's, and I fear gave Gladys [white office secre-
tary] a poor wedding farewell, ere I went to have my hair shampooed
and waved.

The night's papers said the lawyers were trying to get a new trial.
Talked with no one. Played solitaire and went to bed. . . .

### Wednesday, August 20

. . . Talked with Louis before I left home. The lawyers still busy,
though everyone realizes their efforts are like blood transfusions in
pernicious anemia. Went to Pocahontas [Daughter Elks] Temple
meeting. Had promised . . . I would to clear up that "Honorary Past
Daughter Ruler stuff." It was such frightful boredom, I thought I must
throw myself out of the third story room. . . .

### Thursday, August 21

. . . Ike Howard called to say that the Court had refused a new
trial. Evening paper said gallows is up and Russ resigned. Saw John,
still full of foolish talk about Grantland's political maneuvers. Howard
in, bitter and filled with poisonous propaganda. Louis called and I
made him come over. He was pitifully tired, but we talked and smoked,
and I got the truth out of him as to Hasting's "helpfulness." An I.L.D.
meeting which had been advertised by handbills, I was told by a *Morning
News* reporter, was broken up by the police at Odd Fellows' Temple,
and a street meeting was likewise dispensed. Well—"they're hanging
Dancey Diever in the morning," as a baritone sang over the radio.

## Friday, August 22

The baby [Laurence Jr.]'s birthday. Two years old today. And the end of Theodore Russ. Poor chap. Life snuffed out at the end of a noose. I felt cross and bitter all day. . . . Went home feeling depressed to read how calmly Russ met his fate protesting his innocence. How I wish all those who sent him to his fate could swing alongside of him.

Went to wind-up of Russ Defense Committee. And [Conwell] Banton all filled up with the [Daniel] Hastings alibi—campaigning all ready. . . .

Rain set in and Bobbo . . . came for me. . . . We talked and drank highballs in the kitchen as usual. Jean [Jamison] was pulling a party, but I was in no mood to go. . . .

## Sunday, August 31

. . . Big Quarterly [an old Black after-harvest holiday]. Ethel out all morning. Reported it was a fizzle. Hope so. Slave institutions ought to be abolished by supposed freedom. . . .

## Monday, September 1

One day [Labor Day] that I take life easy. outside of giving Bobbo some breakfast, making some gelatin and custard, I take life easy. Reading *Moby Dick* all day and finally finishing it. Did not go out of the house all day. At night, Jean and Juice [Jamison] and Alice [Banton] troop in—and Louis [Redding] comes like the skeleton at the feast. Yes—did go driving as far as the Scotts' with Alice and Bobbo and Polly to turn up a bootlegger.

Play some bum bridge—and Bobbo does some efficient bar-tending so that Alice waxes philosophical and even custard doesn't sober her. Louis blackly reading and saying nothing.

Hot as Hades and humidity about 200 per cent. We gasp for breath.

Bobbo saw Mealy at Bayard headquarters today. Big talk about large monies in Bayard's [Democratic senatorial] campaign. Hope some comes my way. . . .

## Wednesday, September 3

. . . To the Garrick [Theater, Philadelphia]—late—to see Luaua. Fair. Not as good as the play "Bird of Paradise" from which it is taken, or is it that what was beautifully romantic 14 years ago is now bore-some? . . .

### Thursday, September 4

. . . Bought cord to glasses. Looks very swank. But it's a nuisance. . . .

### Saturday, September 6

Lay in bed and finished Perutz' "The Master of the Day of Judgement" and have been wanting to commit suicide all day. Life is *such* a Godawful mess and I am *such* a total and complete failure. God!

Understand from Mama that Sis Julia and Alphabetical George [Anderson] have let Ethel understand that her place is at 1310 [French Street] and she came home last night after a visit, quite broken-hearted. Poor kid, sorry for her, but it was coming to her. I know how she feels—I went all through it [exactly what is not clear] with Krusie and Anna [Brodnax] twenty years ago.

Trustee meeting at [Girls Industrial] school. Long and tedious. Budget etc. [See D-N's sketch on page 346.]

Home, fagged out. Polly had marketing to do and then we drove out to Etta's to see Arleon [Bowse]—and played bridge until 9:30. At least it kept me from thinking. . . .

### Tuesday, September 9

Meetings! Bah!

But first went out to Virginia's [Dr. Alexander] . . . and had Gertrude [the nurse] launder my nasty stomach. Then that delayed [AIPC] Board meeting. . . .

Ten present. All harmony and blah. They seemed pleased at me for once. Hill talked a lot about everything but the Russ report. And *talked*—

Swamped with envelopes for the Teachers' Conference *and* preparations for Sunday's recital.

Tonight [in Wilmington] Parole meeting at "Cousin Bessie's" [Mrs. Tatnall of the Industrial School]. More Blah! Gertrude Henry [another committee member] and I walked home together—it is a perfect moonlight night—and complained to each other about being rubber stamps.

### Wednesday, September 10

. . . Interviewed our (Helen [Bryan]'s and mine) new prospective secretary. I shall probably like her. But Helen will gobble her up—we talked together—and I shall be a subsidiary. But if she does the work— I don't care. . . .

### Friday, September 12

. . . Went to the Royal [Theatre]—ostensibly to see about Sunday's meeting. . . . Really to see Lon Chaney in the "Unholy Three"— his first and last talking picture. Wonderfully thrilling. I've been chasing after that picture all over Philadelphia. . . . Goodness, what a pity Lon Chaney had to die. . . .

### Sunday, September 14

Hot, humid, muggy, sticky today and I had devilish internal pains all morning. . . . Drove up to the theatre. [Richard] Harrison [famous actor] was there. . . . Smaller crowd than I expected. Disappointed. [Rev. Henry] Arnett presided—but not much money in the house. Harrison was *wonderful*. I enjoyed him as much as I did in Springfield—almost. Hill was conspicuous by his absence. Spoiled child. The dinner at the Golden Dawn was a fizzle. Harrison had to hurry back to New York on the six o'clock train, and half the folks who promised to go didn't show up. . . .

Came home tired out and wondering how much longer my job will last. Not long I fear. . . .

Collection less than $75. Not enough for expenses.

### Monday, September 15

I'd like to wring Polly's neck. Mulcted me out of my last dollar. Some girls giving a dance at the National. . . . She roped me in as a "sponsor," but in spite of exhaustion from the blazing heat, dressed to go, as did Leila. And when we were ready—lo, no one had the requisite 50¢, so I had to pay that dollar for Leila and me. I was so bored that I went to sleep in spite of a ten piece orchestra blaring in my ears—so bade Leila and Annie Murdah goodnight and walked home. And had to comb my room with a fine tooth comb to find 15 pennies for carfare tomorrow. . . .

Electric light man got a predated check for . . . the frigidaire today. Hoch [the banker] writing bitter denunciations in the day's mail. I've had a hell of a time financially. Don't know where the leak is. If Bayard isn't nominated tomorrow [which will give Bobbo some additional income], I'm sunk beyond redemption. . . .

### Tuesday, September 16

Gave the conductor on Car 33 this a.m. the 15 pennies. He gave me a very dirty look and I smiled. . . .

Jim Sewell [Black Wilmington politician] called up tonight with the glad news that Bayard was nominated. . . . Praise be!

Had to borrow a dollar from Henrietta [Black secretary] for lunch tomorrow.

### Wednesday, September 17

And couldn't pay her back today. Seems as if I get in these financial ruts ever so often. The worst of it is, they go on and on, and there is no apparent end. . . .

### Thursday, September 18

Did not get up early today as today was the day that Hoch was going to boil me in oil if I didn't pay the Industrial Trust loan up to date. . . . Such a vicious letter I never read. So after cooking breakfast . . . went to the bank, saw "Miss Mary" who deplored Hoch's lack of tact, took my pre-dated check for $128.25 and suggested a way to get rid of Hoch and his peevish letters by having some kind of a bond or something. I gladly agreed and thanked her and we'll get that fixed up. . . .

### Friday, September 19

. . . Bobbo avers something has gone wrong with the Democratic situation in spite of Bayard's victory. . . .

### Monday, September 22

Five months of this beastly hot weather has done my nerves in. . . . Went to Marie's . . . for shampoo and wave, for my hair is a crime. So is my face—these masks I've been making of peroxide and almond meal have made me look like a sieve. Took a facial and a manicure, shampoo, wave—all of which set me back about $6.25. The price of beauty! . . .

## Tuesday, September 23

I've spent an hour this morning writing up this darn diary. Haven't touched it since last Monday night. No need of making resolutions about it either. . . .

## Wednesday, September 24

Things are funny with me. I get the strangest urges. All the week it's been Green's Hotel, the historic old building of convivial fame at 8th and Chestnut [Philadelphia]. I knew it must be terribly expensive, but I could not resist going—and so lunched there as inexpensively as at Hanscomb's—at the lunch counter, of course. And now I've seen Green's about which I have heard for 30 years. . . .

## Thursday, September 25

Today bored to tears by the general committee meeting of the Friends' Service Committee. . . . Spoke of the history conference and coughed at every word. Anyone who would have hay fever, bronchitis and prickly heat all at one and the same time deserves lynching. . . .

Reservations for the conference coming in very slowly. Gosh, if *this* is a failure, I'll hang up.

## Friday, September 26

Still hot. Still slow reservations. Still broke and worried. Finished up that bum story, "No Sacrifice." Would have sent it in to the True Story contest, but concluded to wait for it to get into the October contest. Certainly is rotten.

Polly and I were playing pinochle when in came Lorraine [Hamilton] with Langston Hughes [popular and prolific Harlem Renaissance writer]. We talked and then tried some bridge—and then Edwin Anderson came. Next came "the judge" [Louis]. Then Juice and Jean and lastly Bobbo—with pep for the party in the shape of liquots. Waffles, bacon, punch with my apple jack etc. The "party" lasted until one a.m.

I've never seen Bobbo so genial with a litterateur as he is with Langston.

He "saw" Mealy and Mooney [Democratic politicians] during the evening. Men have to "see" each other so much before they get anything started. . . .

## Sunday, September 28

My last peaceful Sunday until after election, I guess. Tried to take it easy and let Bobbo get breakfast, but the result was so disastrous, i.e. about ten slices of burnt toast, burnt to a crisping, that I resolved anew always to get out of bed when he is home.

Bobbo has to "see" more people, and bums and bootleggers begin tramping to the house to "see" him. . . .

*It is hard to understand how D-N could have doubted the reality of Ethel's illness—especially after the radical surgery (appendix, ovary, a dozen adhesions) that the thirty-year-old Ethel had undergone in February. Her skepticism on this point is yet another indication of the ambivalence she had toward this particular niece.*

## Tuesday, October 7

Ethel died tonight about 8:50. Leila [Ethel's mother and D-N's older sister] went to the hospital about a quarter to seven. After leaving her there, Polly [her niece] came back and we went to . . . the Bridget meeting. Leila called about 8:45 to say she was home from the hospital. In less than five minutes, Robert called to say Polly and I were to come at once to take Leila to the hospital. We dashed out—picked up Leila at home and to the child's bedside. She was dead. Sitting up in the bed, a ghastly stare of surprise. That's all.

Ensued the sordid dictates of death. Robert over, Gunby [the mortician] to take the body, telephoning, telegrams, people swarming in the house etc. etc. Poor kid. I misjudged her. I never thought she was really ill. Ought to teach me a lesson never to be so harsh in my judgements. She's better off, infinitely so. . . .

## Wednesday, October 8

. . . Busy all day with the thousand and one affairs of funerals. Mama quite pitiful and Leila a scurry of talk, talk, talk. People coming and going. Insurance policies. Undertaker—Mr. Gunby early and picking out coffin, making lists of cars, pall-bearers, and all. What seemed at first a pitiful strain on Leila turns out better than we thought, for Mama, with admirable foresight, had insured Ethel again and again, so that all her little policies total over five hundred dollars. I am chief cook, William Lewis constitutes himself doorman and errand boy. Julia [Robinson] on hand in habiliments of woe, and Helen Murray [both friendly neighbors] in and out—also others. . . .

Bought white kid slippers for Ethel to be buried in. . . .

## Thursday, October 9

Edith [Fleetwood, their close friend from Washington, D.C.] specialled a letter saying she would come and help and I specialled back a "come." I have cooked and washed dishes until my spirit is swathed in suds. . . . Talk of black clothes, dresses, hats and veils and gloves. People and people. . . . Liquor, lots of it. . . . Excitement. Confusion. People. Julia [Robinson] holding up things because Agatha [Lawson] had to make Ethel's dress and Julia had to go to Philadelphia to bring it down. Polly and I to Gunby's to see if the hair was right. Ethel brought home in the white velvet coffin and breaking the plants in the window box to get it in. Flowers and flowers. . . . People, people—streams. Talk, talk. From Leila—the story of Ethel's last five days' illness over and over. Ethel very lovely with her pink silk dress and white kid slippers and rouge and lip-stick (mine) and watch and necklace and fluffed hair. People, people, people. Mrs. Johnson with potato salad and lemon pie. The Grahams from Maryland [where Ethel stayed] with a new story of her last illness.

## Friday, October 10

Up early and dressed in black and the house made tidy and breakfast cooked and eaten . . . and the day crashes to two o'clock. Mrs. Turner with cakes and biscuits. Flowers. Flowers. There is no room in the house. Cars. Cars. Cars. People. People. Surely Ethel had not lived in vain. Scores and scores of friends—more than I had.

And then two o'clock. . . . The family swathed in veils in the library. Mama went downstairs to the kitchen early and stayed all day— for the last of the coffin borne from the window. All the young boy pall-bearers. . . .

To the grave and Ethel is lowered to the ground. All over, a gorgeous October day, brilliant skies and clear warm air. A string of fifteen or 16 cars. . . .

Dinner of ten or eleven, Edith in the kitchen. I washed dishes for she was swamped while Polly tended Mama. I could have dropped from sheer weariness of spirit—but I soaked in a tub of hot water.

Ethel left. Her spirit never returned to the house. She has completely gone—no trace. Only her material things remained.

### Saturday, October 11

. . . My story back from *True Stories* and all six of my sketches from the *Ledgers, Record, Inquirer, Daily News.* . . .

How tired and wretched I feel. . . .

*This entry reveals the difficulty D-N often had in accurately and firmly judging people.*

### Tuesday, October 14

Dr. [Wilbur K.] Thomas [former executive secretary of the Friends' Service Committee] has been for some time "getting in touch with me." Went to his office today and we talked for an hour and a half. I don't understand him. Professes great friendship for me [despite his not being helpful to her when he was her boss]. Wants the A.I.P.C. scrapped—(it will be anyhow in January) before the Friends' Service Committee [the parent body] scraps it for us. Peeved still about being eased out of the treasurership. . . . Clever trick. Wants to start something new, radical, startling—with me shouting red outcries against smug complacency and Quaker cant. We talked and talked. I'm to "think it over," but not discuss it with Helen [Bryan]. We agreed as to her superficiality. I am puzzled. Thomas is unhappy—wrapped in cotton-wool of "vested interests."

Bobbo has his "headquarters" [with the Delaware Democratic campaign]. Some place to go nights.

### Wednesday, October 15

. . . To the W.I.L. [Women's International League of Peace and Freedom] meeting and I promised to write a Christmas play to go to Haiti next January. Decided that I can't go on in this docile rut. Dr.

Thomas and I both said—we have at best but a few years left, let's adventure through them, not rot through.

But I saw an old Quaker woman, pitiful, almost blind, in the meeting house today. God—I don't want to live like that. One glorious fling—freedom, anyhow. Went to Bobbo's headquarters tonight. Very pathetic. . . .

## Saturday, October 18

. . . Bobbo and I went to finish marketing and "shop." He bought me ½ dozen pairs of stockings. Prosperity on our door step [from his political work]. He deposited $300 to my account today. . . .

*The protracted demise of D-N's job as executive secretary of the American Inter-Racial Peace Committee continues with such periodic developments as the following, although—despite her fearful predictions—the position does not actually end until next April. However, at this point, D-N begins searching for other employment.*

## Monday, October 20

Last night's bitter cold awakened me before six with the thought that the window boxes would be ruined if I did not get in the flowers. So arose early and worked in getting in the flowers, and re-potting them for the winter. . . . Did not finish before eight, ate, and Polly's car being on the blink, had to hoof it to the station. . . .

Went to Allied Social Agencies luncheon meeting, and a lot of time taken up with having the photograph of the chattering, gabbling group taken. Got back to the office in time for tea, and found a letter from Anna Griscom. It was her resignation from the Board of Directors of the A.I.P.C. with reasons, chiefly that—well the letter is so significant that it is best kept here on file.

This is a definite notice that no more money, room, interest or what not is to be expected from the Friends' Service Committee. Good. Wilbur Thomas was right. He knew whereof he spoke.

Wrote Hill, enclosing letter, and asking if we should go on with the mass meeting. Held up payment of check to Broad Street Theatre. Wrote to Raskob Foundation, asking for $2000 [for herself] for research and travel in the West Indies.

Have been expecting the blow to fall, but at that, it has me worried. . . .

Laid awake most of the night celebrating the fact that on January 1, I shall be one of the 5,000,000 unemployed in the United States—unless the Raskob Foundation comes across.

### Tuesday, October 21

. . . Good meeting [Democratic political rally] in Pychion Hall [Middletown, Del.]—which was locked by the good Republicans, but got opened. Yapped. But in the last analysis, it's who has the most money to give these thugs. . . .

### Wednesday, October 22

Finally, after frantic and often telephoning, got Hill to come in and discuss . . . the bomb Anna Griscom threw in the camp and the futility of having a meeting at the Broad Street Theatre. . . . It didn't occur to anyone to say, "Go on with the A.I.P.C." Its demise was taken for granted. The ethics of holding a public funeral was all discussed. It was finally abandoned—not without a struggle on the part of Hill. Check up on finances revealed not enough to pay my November salary [$166.66]. I shall be on the bricks after Thanksgiving. Good God!

When I came home late . . . found letter from [Secretary] Gary of the Raskob Foundation. Nothing doing. Wow! Right between the eyes. . . .

### Thursday, October 23

. . . Service Committee meeting. I reported on the Historical Conference. It was received in stony silence quite different from the discussion which Lucy Meachan Thurston's report elicited.

Sweet Quakers!

Tonight's *Every Evening* [Wilmington newspaper] carried a laudatory editorial on Bobbo!

The Communist folks came to see me tonight to ask my help in getting a hall for their meeting November 2. I! . . .

### Saturday, October 25

. . . Went to see the Raskob Foundation sectetary, Gary, to try to argue with him. No avail. . . .

## Monday, October 27

Talked with Mrs. Olmstead for an hour about W.I.L., Haiti etc.
She was aghast when I told her—in strict confidence—about the proposed dissolution of the A.I.P.C. How the W.I.L. would love to have
me—but no money.

So said DuBois [editor of the NAACP's official journal, the *Crisis*]
in today's letter about the N.A.A.C.P. Poor me! Tramping for jobs!

Schuyler's proposition out. Raskob's out. *Crisis* out. Now remains
only [Wilbur K.] Thomas [for the prospect of a job]. . . .

## Tuesday, October 28

. . . Finley [J. Finley Wilson, Elk leader] called from Philadelphia. He and Bobbo had a long talk, the gist of which I could not
gather. . . . Afterwards . . . Bobbo told me that Ike Nutter of Atlantic
City was coming to see him at the request of Keene of New Jersey who
is interested in Hastings' [Bobbo's candidate Bayard's Republican
opponent] election. The idea is to see how much Bobbo will take to
be conveniently ill on election day. He said ten "grand," then decided
it was worth 25 "grand" to stultify his soul. I was horror-struck. When
we came home from the meeting, he argued with me—though I knew
he was arguing with himself—that all the damage that we could do to
Hastings has been done. That even if he were ill, he could give the
names of his workers to Mealy etc. etc.

He was terribly tired and slept wretchedly. Tossing and moaning.
I am afraid. They might dispose of him. . . .

## Thursday, October 30

Dark faces lowering, arms tossing and brandishing, cries and curses,
threats, jeers, applause, a mob milling to and fro threatening to break
and toss us on the platform, music roaring monotonously. Bobbo on
the platform shouting defiance above the music at the mob of about
350 men, women and children. Leila brave and white faced, me,
laughing and exulting. Thus—[their Democratic political rally in
downstate] Milford. . . . Had been . . . weak when I got home, but
game. The meeting enthusiastic. . . . A note saying the Republicans
were going to steal the meeting at ten o'clock. And sure enough here
came [Black Republican loyalists] Colburn, Jeff Coage, Louis Redding and Holland, the Reverend of Russ [the Theodore Russ case]

fame. Bobbo said he had hired the hall and paid for the music and would not allow any more speaking. Rioting—almost. Colburn told me they had been sent for and told to be there at ten o'clock.

We left at 11:45 and . . . drove home through a pelting, blinding thunder and rain storm. My indigestion grows by leaps and bounds. The Sussex Countians have been "forbidden to talk about the Russ case" [in which a young Black man was hanged on a very flimsy charge of raping a lower-class white woman in Sussex County].

Home by two. Ate some hot soup and drank apple brandy and to bed—exhausted beyond measure.

## Saturday, November 1

. . . To Varick Temple [Philadelphia], for a large Democratic campaign meeting featuring local and national Black leaders by 8:30. Monster outpouring of humanity and oratory. Mary McLeod Bethune, Finley [Wilson] . . . Perry Howard, Mrs. Pinchot [white wife of the Pennsylvania governor], Me, Ed Henry—Wow! So much oratory some of the sisters shouted. . . .

## Sunday, November 2

. . . Life is one continual procession of visitors, one unending routine of collecting and washing glasses and emptying ash-trays. . . .

*Though D-N is silent about the outcome of the proposed bribing of Bobbo by the Republicans, there is apparently still sufficient illegality for her to be concerned about his possible Election Day arrest.*

## Tuesday, November 4

. . . Stayed home "to bail Bobbo out" should he be arrested. Early in the day, we conceded Bayard's election—for he absolutely refused to put out any money [for bribes]. Bobbo could have swung the election but he was hamstrung—no funds. A hectic day of gloomy men in a constant procession of frantic telephone calls, of plenty of liquor of various sorts. I took it easy. . . . Returns until midnight. Very thrilling, mixed with bridge, cocktails and crackers.

Hastings over [i.e., elected], of course. . . .

"The Nelsons" have failed again in Delaware.

*D-N unfailingly commemorates this day every year by mentioning it in her diary, but never discloses any further information about the "friendship."*

## Wednesday, November 5

"To my friend of November 5, 1892."

And in 1892, November 5 came the day after election day—and there at my place every day on the table for 38 years is the little silver Harrison spoon to commemorate a beautiful friendship. . . .

Looks like a Democratic Senate and if Bayard had used sense, he would have been in. However, I "put a bad mouth" on Hastings. He'll never serve out his term. [He in fact, served until 1937.]

## Thursday, November 6

Bobbo went away today [back to his regular job routine in Washington, D.C.]. Kissed him goodbye and then had the blues. . . .

## Friday, November 7

. . . Rollo Wilson came in and stayed to talk over the campaign and to ask me what job I wanted under Pinchot [newly elected Democratic governor of Pennsylvania, whose patronage was expected to extend to the Nelsons]. Suggested I look in Sewell [?] and pick one out. Dumb girl at the Mercantile Library never heard of Sewell, so I went out on the Parkway and picked out seven jobs, which I tabulated and sent to Rollo by mail.

Dropped in to see Eddie Cantor in "Whoopee." Pretty picture—Eddie good, but same old sap about Indian being white after all so the white girl can marry him. . . . Sickening. . . .

## Monday, November 10

"The thing that hurt most," said I to myself, "was the fact that in my three years here, I haven't really made a single staunch friend on the board. They don't really care that I'm out of a job, before Christmas, with no possible chance of another."

That's feeling sorry for myself. The board of the A.I.P.C. met. My elaborate report commented upon. I think Mr. Hill would have pushed us to a few months more of trial, but Anna Griscom [who had recently resigned] came . . . and the cold, wet clamminess of that Quaker wet blanket came down heavily upon us. We "suspended indefinitely" December 1. One more check—then I join the vast army of the 5,000,000 unemployed. God knows what then. No word from Dr. Thomas [with whom she is hoping to launch some new venture]. . . .

### Wednesday, November 12

. . . I've been wondering for several days if I am through. Because if I am, why stay here [on earth]—except for Bobbo. I wonder if I have done all my work? I wonder. . . .

### Saturday, November 15

. . . We [D-N and Hill] agreed to continue to run the A.I.P.C. as best we can—I shall probably get no money—but that's better than lying down on the job. . . .

### Sunday, November 16

. . . Mrs. Harrison and Mrs. Ferguson [of the Industrial School] in with a tale of woe about Arneta [one of the school girls]. Sorry for the kid and, since she is a senior, I advocated some strenuous birth control [probably abortion]. . . .

### Tuesday, November 18

Busy getting out a lot of doo-dads and giggleisms trying to make a stab at resuscitating the A.I.P.C.

Tonight was [one of the office secretaries] Gladys' dinner and out to her house. Traipsed—all seven of us—on the bus. Her little apartment is cute—in a development that is all Spanish n' everything, but congested— as all newly wed apartments are. No wonder there are so many divorces. No privacy. All piled up on each other. Terrible. . . .

### Thursday, November 20

Went out to Rita [Dix Burton]'s after office hours to have a heart to heart talk with her. . . . Was aghast to learn that she had not the slightest idea what the A.I.P.C. is about, or peace or our ideals or anything. As ignorant as a child in the backwoods, which she assures me is the state of mind of 99.9% of all the women and most of the people of Philadelphia on the A.I.P.C. and the W.I.L. It made me pretty thoughtful and I decided that hereafter I would always talk to people on all subjects as if they were kindergarteners. . . .

*New York[, N.Y.]*
*Hotel New Yorker*
*Friday, November 21*

Drive like a slave under the whip all day. . . . Rachel and I lunched at the Golden Gate. She is all fired up over my traveling for the National Child Welfare Association and putting over a program for them similar to the one I did in the schools for the A.I.P.C. Said I'd see her folks tomorrow. . . .

*New York[, N.Y.]*
*Saturday, November 22*

Had our [D-N and Leila, who are indulging in a weekend excursion] breakfast served in our room. Packed leisurely and forth and to the National Child Welfare Association as Rachel had asked. More or less futile—except for "contact" with the female secretary person—the males all being away. . . .

*Sunday, November 23*

. . . Ends our Big Adventure. Cost more than I can afford. But it was nice for Leila. Came home and got panicky at once over A.I.P.C. money etc.

Patricia [Mama] quite interested in the "big boarding house" at which we stopped.

*Tuesday, November 25*

. . . Glad I've lost two pounds since last week. 156 now, 4 pounds too many.

. . . The Bridgets . . . came and I fed them on pickled lamb tongues, liverwurst, ham, pickles, cheese, celery, lettuce, olives, crackers, toast, macaroons, tea, dandelion wine, etc. Then washed up dishes . . . and now packing to go [to Washington, D.C.] tomorrow. . . .

## Thanksgiving Day
## Thursday, November 27

. . . Last night's dull evening warned me that there is not much to be expected here except Bobbo, so I just settled myself to anything that might happen, be it bad or good, dull or lively. Best thing to do, especially in Washington.

. . . By and by all out to the [Finley] Wilsons' where was a mess of Elks and Daughters. All tanked up against the cold, but I feared discomfort, so did not. To the ball park finally, and seated. . . . Punk [football] game. . . .

Dressed and went to the Finley Wilsons' for dinner. . . . Then we went to Narka [Lee Rayford]'s to call on her and Lottie Cooper. . . . Home by midnight. I washed out my offending intestines, and curled up and ached all night. And so endeth Thanksgiving 1930. And yet I have a lot to be thankful for. Bobbo, first, last and always, the best of all.

## Friday, November 28

. . . Slept until time to dress for the famous Bachelor-Benedict [ball].

Wore my egg-shell satin, and looked very nice. Danced with several. Notably Arthur [Callis, to whom she had been secretly and briefly married in 1910]. He has not forgotten. Rather intense. Promised him and Myra [Arthur's wife] to dine with them Sunday. He was as eager and breathless about it as when he was a kid in Wilmington. The party, or rather ball, very pleasant. Left at three. Felt as if I'd give my hope of heaven for a hot malted milk, and got one at the Masonic Temple drug store.

## Saturday, November 29

. . . To Narka's, and she, Tessa and Lottie filled me with the latest dirt—and I mean DIRT. Then Bobbo and I down to see his aged spinster cousins, and the elder, "Cousin Lizzie," fascinating in her tracing of the Nelson family tree to Horatio and his sojourn in the West Indies. . . .

## Sunday, November 30

. . . We got over to Arthur's [who is now a Washington, D.C. physician]. . . . Pretty home, and Arthur all dressed in correct afternoon attire. Good dinner. . . . Later Hallie Queen [Brown] and some boy friend came in, and we enjoyed her delightful lies. She says she has to tell something amusing every morning at school, and we wondered, Bobbo and I, when we got home, if any of her vivid lies could approach the truth of the situation in which she was participating (unwittingly) of the gentleman and his wife entertaining his divorced wife and her husband. . . .

## Monday, December 1

. . . Must begin to think of curtains and house cleaning, and cushions on the sofa, and new dresses for the dolls and Christmas presents.

## Tuesday, December 2

. . . Been worrying about Minnie [Stevens, who is growing old and senile] in this cold. I know she has neither food nor fire—Polly took her a Thanksgiving basket—but couldn't get in. . . . Leila said that . . . the next door neighbor . . . had called up saying something should be done, as she knows Minnie is freezing and starving. And the thermometer down to 19 today! Leila called up Dr. Stubbs and Roland [Milburn] to tell them something must be done. I shall wire [Fred] Butler in the morning. . . .

## Wednesday, December 3

A big envelope from Lichtnauer dismayed me this a.m. Returned "No Sacrifice" with four pages of criticism. I paid $8.00 for the worst panning I ever got. I can't write—no use trying. Can't even do a "True Story." No money this a.m. No letter from Bobbo. Piles of letters to get out. Henrietta [her secretary] slow as time. . . . Rita as dumbly uninterested as ever and now reports that Elizabeth and her girls didn't want to serve Sunday and Rita said it was the last for all. I never really gave up hope until then. What's the use of fighting for the A.I.P.C.? Nobody wants it. . . . A pall of black discouragement envelops me. I have little heart for anything. . . .

## Thursday, December 4

Today all excitement at the office. At last we were to be allowed to see Rabindranath Tagore [Hindu poet]. . . .

Tagore came into the meeting shortly after we convened. . . . In his heavy dark brown gown, with his thin white beard. Looked as Dr. Stevens [Minnie's deceased M.D. husband] might have looked had he lived to grow a white beard and hair. Was disappointed in his talk, for he said practically nothing worth straining to listen to. But his spirituality emanated even to touch my gross soul. . . .

## Sunday, December 7

. . . Good day, clear and crisp. Good audience out [for her and Hill's A.I.P.C. benefit program], I thought, for the Union Baptist Church is a big church to fill, and the auditorium was filled. . . .

Collection, counting the fifteen dollars in subscriptions from the Cheyney [State College] teachers which Hill [who was Cheyney president] brought in, amounted to $81.75, which will net us about fifty dollars, when expenses are paid. . . .

Well, that means enough money for my December salary, anyhow. . . .

## Monday, December 8

. . . I went on down to 937 Christian Street. My first day at the volunteer job that I have picked for myself—two half days a week at the Southwark Branch of the Family Society [whose work is critical because of the Depression]. I'm an office assistant. Job to interview applicants, write them up, telephone in to main office, record in book, etc., etc.

Got all harrowed up. Too much of a strain on my nerves and sensibilities. Nearly five thirty before I left, and I was a wreck from the Italians and Negroes who impacted on my soul. Many harried and worried-looking workers. . . .

## Tuesday, December 9

"Snuck off" this a.m. to Keith's and saw a new film star, Marlene Dietrich, with Gary Cooper and Adolph Menjou in "Morocco." A strange play, a strangely exotic and provocative actress. Thoroughly enjoyable. . . .

## Wednesday, December 10

. . . Mama growing more and more feeble by the minute. Absolute disintegration. Yet her mind is clear and active, and her sight and hearing good. . . .

## Monday, December 15

. . . Down to my place at Christian Street. Usual rush. New volunteer worker in the person of a Mrs. Wharton, colored. Bitter cold as it is—and the cold is biting, piercing to the marrow, suffering is frightful, and urgent cases predominate.

Got a 6:23 home, and pretty fagged out. Called up Polly, and glad of the warmth of the house. Could not help but think of the people whom I had registered who have no warmth, no food, nothing, but cold and hungry children. Oh, the pitiful patience of the poor! . . .

## Wednesday, December 17

. . . Had told Polly not to come to the station until I called her. She forgot that, of course, and met oodles of trains, so when I called her she was out and Leila nasty, as usual, whenever a suggestion is made that Pauline meet a train. Then Polly came in, and went to the station, and I came on up anyhow, and by the time we met, both of us were mad and cold and tired. She blazed at me in Mama's room about thinking I was the only person who works and is tired, and I snapped at her, and Mama jawed at both of us and said there was never any peace in the house, and she is the cause of it all, as she has us all edgy and cross, what with Josephine's dirt and inefficiency, and of course, but for Mama's helplessness, we wouldn't have to have Josephine [who takes care of Mama Patricia], and there you are. So we were all cross. I fled to my room . . . but Foster Brown [insurance man] came in . . . to make out the final blank in my insurance claim,

and we three [D-N, Pauline, Brown] played pinochle after the important document was mailed, and so I bathed and got to bed about one
o'clock.

## Thursday, December 18

Still feeling hurt and sorry for myself, and mad at Pauline, not for
snapping towards me the way she did, but for the underlying reality of
her feelings which makes such anger flare forth whenever she is cross
or tired. Showing on what slight foundation her esteem of me is built.
So I fared to work rather glum, and said little to the family, except to
say to Pauline that I would not be home early.

Feeling so sorry for myself that I couldn't do much. Tried to sing
in the carols at Wanamaker's in the morning, and got all teary over
"Silent Night." So left the other hundreds in the grand concourse
yowling to the organ and tried to find gifts. As was to be expected
could find nothing, but bought a tea-pot and some wreaths—the latter
for the cemetery.

Went to the Palace to see William Haines in "Remote Control,"
such a thriller that I forgot my sorrows. . . .

We've decided to fire Josephine.

## Friday, December 19

. . . Went . . . to Helen [Bryan]'s tea at the Friends' Select School.
. . . Crystal [Bird, young Black woman who also did racially related
work for the Society of Friends] began speaking just as we got to the
parlor—Mary Jones adoring her. My cynical amusement must have
shown in my eyes for Crystal gave me her left hand when I spoke to
her and was distinctly aloof. She *was* amusing. The meaningless,
insincere patter of words, words—*how* could those Quakers *not* see
through her? The pose of deep contemplation (Leslie [P. Hill] does it
too) when Ida Brown sang spirituals—I could have gargled with delight
at *my* heroine of "Uplift"—"in person." . . .

## Sunday, December 21

. . . I had a gorgeous day. From 3 to 5, the New York Symphony
with Toscanini conducting. Schubert's "Unfinished Symphony," the
Venusberg from "Tannhauser," Beethoven's "Eroica." We ate to it,

washed dishes to it, and then I settled down to enjoy it to the fullest before the horde came home. . . .

It was oh so worthwhile—the day's music.

## Wednesday, December 24

. . . I told Bobbo . . . to await me at the [Wilmington train] station. Thought he seemed queer going up [French Street to their house], but thought he was vexed because I was late. Home—one good look at him, and crash! My world came tumbling, crashing about my ears! Jaundice! Uremic poison! Ill for two weeks and hadn't told me. And Algernon Jackson [Washington, D.C. physician] giving him all kinds of wrong medicine, mostly palliatives and a funny diet list—when what he needs is to have the bile drained out of him. The irony of my giving him a flask.

I trimmed the Christmas tree tearfully. . . .

Bobbo gave me a gorgeous diamond ring.

## Thursday, December 25

Leila's birthday—she is 61 today. Jack and I gave her cards. . . . Ended Christmas, 1930.

Pretty punk—but it might have been worse. Suppose, like Neonta [Howard High School secretary, who had dropped in to visit], I had had no dinner and my husband gone somewhere! At least Bobbo was *here*. . . .

## Friday, December 26

Called Virginia [Alexander, D-N's Philadelphia M.D.] . . . and made a date for Bobbo. . . . He's in rotten shape. . . . Uremic coma threatened. . . . Why in the name of patience Bobbo didn't come home two weeks ago! . . .

## Tuesday, December 30

. . . Home. To coddle Bobbo who is beginning to look like a human being again.

### Wednesday, December 31

Here I sit at the close of the year—farewell 1930. And thank God you're going, for a disastrous year you have been. . . . Did not go down to Christian Street [for her volunteer labor with the Family Society]. . . . Shall resign—in fact did—from the work there. Too much to do. . . .

And now as Polly dresses to go to the Bantons', and Bobbo reads, and the radio rants, and Leila in bed watches Polly, and Mama sleeps, I bid farewell 1930. Farewell!

May 1931 bring good fortune. 1930 you brought me California. I shall bless you for that.

# 1931

(January 1–December 31)

*This damn waiting, waiting, waiting*

ASSESSING HER LIFE ON HER BIRTHDAY (July 19), Dunbar-Nelson characterized 1930–31 as "a year of marking time," and four months later she would cry, "I'll go crazy with this damn waiting, waiting, waiting." For this is precisely what she was doing these months, while the themes of 1930 were continuing, modulating. She was waiting for her Inter-Racial Peace Committee job to finally drag itself out—which it did in April, with her tired of the "whole damn mess." She and the rest of the family were waiting for "Mama" to die—a yearlong process that was so enervating and protracted that one day during the summer Dunbar-Nelson stole into the room to see if "Mama" was still breathing. She and Robert were waiting for his quest for a political sinecure to be realized, their hopes being raised and deferred so often that she said, bitterly, that the power brokers were playing politics with human misery.

Dunbar-Nelson herself could not secure a position though she searched hard and even tried to originate paying projects. She maintained her speaking engagements and writing and began working on educational books with Carter G. Woodson, meanwhile quietly allowing her "Great American Novel" to die a silent death. Psychologically, her self-doubts of the previous year remained with her. More than ever before, she felt tired, burdened, pessimistic, bored, fearful, useless, and blue. On the positive side, she bobbed her hair, changed her signature to Aliceruth to numerologically correspond with her life number, and visited Helene London in Bermuda, a trip she pinched out from her Depression-reduced Dodd, Mead royalty check. All of this Dunbar-Nelson chronicles in a strikingly ruminative style as the drama of her life approaches closure. After finally being driven to a Chester, Pennsylvania, loan-shark for two hundred dollars to ease an acute money shortage in December, she ends the diary at her optimistic best, hoping for universal prosperity and joy.

---

### Thursday, January 1

Hail 1931! And may you be gracious to me. A pleasant New Year's Day. . . . Ministered to Mama. It's her birthday. 81 years I guess. . . . Arleon [Bowser, her dear friend, a Wilmington schoolteacher] came in, saying she was bored at the quietness at home. . . . So I had her take off her dress, put on a smock and spend the day. . . .

### Friday, January 2

Tragedy came through the telephone this a.m. Bobbo answered the bell and from the gravity of his remarks, I feared trouble. It was Emma saying that Minnie [Stevens] had burned to death this morning about three o'clock. Polly told Mama; Leila and I moralized over her horrible end. Polly and I drove to the house. The third floor burned, the house wrecked. . . .

Mrs. Griffith received us in her dingy parlor next door [to Minnie's] and wept her nervousness upon us. Then to the hospital and found Mary Waters [a Black woman who did domestic nursing work] and broke the news to her and left her in despair. She was with Minnie up to 7:30 last night. Papers filled with it. And when I came home from the office tonight, more and still more horrible details from various sources. Body just a charred and hideous lump of flesh that could only be wrapped in a sheet and hidden in the coffin for the funeral tomorrow. So is the horrible end of Minnie the Magnificent. And all day today, Shelley's [poem] "Ozymandias of Egypt" has haunted me. . . .

Miss Mary Waters *nursed Mama Patricia for the year. Because she attended nightschool and dressed in a youthful, jaunty style, the family dubbed her "Collegiate."*

### Saturday, January 3

. . . Miss Waters came today to look after Mama. She is charging $15.00 a week. Polly and Bobbo think we are foolish to pay that much—

but it is a comfort to know that she can do the thousand and one things Mama needs.

## Sunday, January 4

. . . To the [Wilmington Open Door] Forum. I spoke—radically—and no one liked my speech which was refreshing. Too much truth. I enjoyed shocking—even Pauline. . . . Bobbo was silently disgusted, Louis [Redding, her young Black lawyer friend] the picture of black disapproval.

## Monday, January 5

. . . Did 1400 words on the neglected Great American novel and home—to a muddling sort of kitchen full of a nervous overwrought Leila and Pauline, a diddling Miss Waters and a glum Robert. I sometimes wonder why I come home at all. . . .

## Monday, January 12

. . . Went over to see Wilbur Thomas [formerly her AIPC boss, with whom she is discussing a new venture]. He is still for a separate organization—so we planned one. Hope something comes of it. . . .

## Tuesday, January 13

. . . Couldn't bear the thought of going home and not finding Bobbo here. . . . Stayed at the office and finished [George S.] Schuyler's screamingly funny [novel] *Black No More*, as racy a piece of satire as ever Swift did at his best. Then . . . to the Forrest [Theatre]. . . .

Ethel Barrymore and her young daughter Ethel Colt in "Scarlet Sister Mary." Why would Ethel go Negro, and Gullah Negro? Well done, but as Dr. Johnson said of a woman preaching and a dog walking on its hind legs, "Who do it at all!"

A good production, a fine piece of acting—but oh, how [famous Black actress] Rose McClendon and a colored company would have gotten away with it! When Ethel labored and struggled and achieved effects, Rose would have swept through the scenes with terrible abandon. Well—a worthy experiment anyhow, if Nordic refinement did persist in breaking through the brown make-up of the cast. . . .

# Heaven Bound

### A NEGRO MIRACLE PLAY—WITH CHORUS OF 500 VOICES

METROPOLITAN OPERA HOUSE

September 30,  October 1 and 2, 1931

R. R. WRIGHT, Jr. Chairman
NELLIE L. DAVIS, Author-Director
ALICE DUNBAR-NELSON, Publicity

HEADQUARTERS—1500 SO. COLLEGE AVE
PHILADELPHIA

THURSDAY, SEPT. 17.
Been working on HEAVEN BOUND a month to-day. Well, even if I don't make anything but expenses coming up, it has been a god-send--to get away from the house, to be in Phila., to feel useful again, to keep from brooding on my condition. And I'm working hard. To-day and yesterday afternoon telephoned, telephoned, telephoned. Fortunately, it is colder decently cool so I can shut the office windows and so be heard partially. For this is the noisiest corner in the world, what with three lines of trolleyes, five streets, trucks, cars and whatnot converging at the building, so you can't hear yourself think.

D-N typed her September 17, 1931 diary entry on this "Heaven Bound" letterhead while working at production headquarters.

## ROMANCES OF THE NEGRO IN AMERICAN HISTORY
### DRAMATIC EPISODES IN OUR HISTORY

Told by

ALICERUTH DUNBAR-NELSON

1. The Seven Fabled Cities of Cibola
2  Creole
3. Thomas Jefferson     and     Benjamin Banneker
4. The North Star
5. The Golden Gate

A Series of Five Lectures telling some of the romantic stories of our history in which the Negro played a compelling part.

Lectures may be given singly.

Address

ALICERUTH DUNBAR-NELSON

1310 French Street

Wilmington, Delaware

D-N's brochure for advertising herself as a "raconteur" of Black history.

PRO BONO PUBLICO

# The Recorder

Price 3d.                                    Published Weekly

HAMILTON, BERMUDA, SATURDAY, OCTOBER 17th, 1931.

# DISTINGUISHED VISITORS.

## Mrs. Dunbar-Nelson and Mrs. Sadie Harrison.

Two or three weeks back we mentioned in these columns that soon Bermuda would be honoured by a visit from no less distinguished a person than Mrs. Alice Dunbar-Nelson, relict of t h e late Paul Laurence Dunbar, America's foremost lyrical Negro poet. It was then mentioned that Mrs. Dunbar-Nelson was herself distinguished in poetry and prose, was an international journalist, and was Secretary of the Inter-racial Peace League of the United States, an organization that was doing immense good in fostering a better feeling between the different Races.

At the time we wrote we did not know that Mrs. Dunbar had been honoured by the greatest of purveyors of knowledge and general information---the British Encyclopedia. The latest edition of that work describes her as a writer. We may say that in that work pettifogging scribblers are not heralded to the world as writers. They must be persons whose writings contain unmistakable signs of t h e divine afflatus---talent.

"An Evening with Paul Laurence Dunbar"
BY
Alice Dunbar-Nelson
AT THE
ALEXANDRINA HALL, Court Street
ON
Wednesday, October 14, 1931
AT 8.30 P.M.
Patron

A Social Dance

FOLLOWING THE DUNBAR LECTURE
will be held
AT THE ALEXANDRINA HALL

Wednesday, October 14, 1931

DANCING FROM 10.30 P.M. TO 1.30 A.M.
Foster's Windsor Hotel Orchestra in attendance

Gentlemen 4-

Local newspaper announcement of D-N's October 12–24 visit to Bermuda, and cards for her "An Evening with Paul Laurence Dunbar."

## Friday, January 16

. . . Mrs. Charlotte Smith ate with me. We had much talk about Federation etc. She's anxious to use me—and I her, so that makes it unanimous. . . .

## Sunday, January 18

. . . To St. Simon's . . . The foundation Episcopal service was pleasant to participate in. I took the sermon time. Only got nine members [for the American Inter-Racial Peace Committee] and only three of them cash. Guess I haven't got any C.A. (cash appeal). . . .

. . . Over to Tindley Temple [for her program] . . . Hill came and was difficult—perhaps ashamed to come to the platform. As I was presiding, I made him come up. But Becton made such a cracker-jack speech—a speech so restrained and dignified and well-informed that Hill—and I—were captivated. He got members too. Wish I knew how he does it. . . .

## Monday, January 19

. . . Arthur [Callis] and I were married twenty-one years ago today— 1910. Ye gods! And here I'm getting ready to have my hair bobbed!

## Wednesday, January 21

. . . Got a ticket for "Strictly Dishonorable" at the Broad [Theater]. . . . Enjoyed the play immensely, light, frothy comedy, well done, a bit risque, but maintaining the moralities nicely. . . .

*Here is the first time this year that D-N mentions the convoluted romance/friendship that existed between her, Fay Jackson Robinson in California, and Helene London in Iowa.*

## Thursday, January 22

. . . To the office, and wrote Fay. She and Helene seem to have made up. Fay wrote that she called up Helene one night when she was drunk. Helene wrote that she had received two letters from Fay.

Both are probably lying to me, so I sedulously avoided mentioning either to each in the letters I wrote them. . . .

## Friday, January 23

Not having heard from Bobbo was naturally anxious to know . . . what luck he had[in securing a position from Pennsylvania Governor Pinchot]. . . . So many conflicting tales. . . . Bobbo saying he is going to play the "Lone Wolf" act, which is sensible. But I wonder how far he'll get. [Philadelphia magistrate] Ed Henry told Cramp [Dr. Crampton] Bobbo had more influence with [Governor] Pinchot than any other Negro. Will that mean him good? I am worried. If Bobbo does not get something from Pinchot in the nature of a good position, it will kill him. He'll die of a broken heart, and the doctors will diagnose it as pneumonia or heart disease. . . .

And then—the most hideous and shocking experience of all! The New England Mutal Agent came to see me. . . . I knew my policy fell due—endowment. That's why I began thinking of Europe. Oh, I knew I had borrowed, but figured there'd be about five or six hundred left. Had it all figured out—one hundred to Miss [Alice G.] Baldwin [loan repayment]. A theatre and dinner party to Leila and Polly—and the rest on the trip to Europe. So comes the agent to try to sell me additonal life insurance and shows the balance sheet—$91 and some cents! I have borrowed $900—and spent it! Ye gods! And interest! It made me sick. . . . And that's that. . . .

## Sunday, January 25

. . . Tired. Dispirited. Disappointed.

Well, you can't eat your cake and have it too—and I've been eating mine for years. . . .

## Thursday, January 29

This afternoon went on a quiet little war-path over [secretary] Henrietta's slow motion activities. Helen [Bryan], of course, keeps her jammed to the hilt. I do so much of my own work that I spoil my secretaries. However, I got some action out of Hennie and an apology from Helen.

In the morning slipped into the Karlton and saw "Litttle Caesar."

Enjoyed it too. Edward Robinson looks for all the world like Senator Hastings.

Helen Anderson has been trying all evening to get in touch with me. She's run afoul of a traffic law and Polly blabbed that I had so much influence with Coleman and had gotten him twice to let her off. So Helen has discovered my phone number. Nothing doing. Let her pay her fine. I said jokingly that she didn't invite me to her pajama party (I wouldn't go anyhow), so I wouldn't help her.

Mary Nichols, too, has been trying to get in touch with me and got me at home at last. Wants me to train some Ezion Dramatic Club in a minstrel show. Again, nothing doing. I've had my mess of helping Negro females and getting a swift kick for my pains. . . .

*Pauline A. Young (Polly) remembers that the acronym of this exclusive club of two meant "Not on the Shelf Yet."*

## Saturday, January 31

Today was my day for entertaining the "Notsy Club" with Polly as special guest. Said Notsy Club being Leila and me. . . .

Leila and Polly up [to Philadelphia] in due time. [Actress] Jane Cowl was lovely. "Art and Mrs. Bottle" a delightful, brittle, well-done modern comedy. Then to Broad Street Station where we had a good dinner. Feeling good, we then went to the Royal Theatre to see "The Cat Creeps," one of those mystery plays. And so home. . . . My treat set me back $9.50. . . . But it was worth it. . . .

## Wednesday, February 4

. . . To the [Philadelphia] Academy of Music. . . . The temperamental L'Argentina. . . . Her dancing exquisite. . . . All fire and grace and Spanish abandon, castanets and bells making unheard of rhythms, eyes, teeth, arms—all vocal. Yet I thought of lovely Pavlova, the incomparable swan, so lately dead of the flu! The old conflict in my soul of the classic and the Gothic. . . .

## Thursday, February 5

Was awake by 6:30. Something portentous on my mind! *The* day had come. My hair to be bobbed!

Mildred [her beautician] gravely concerned lest I should welsh at the last minute. But to Wanamaker's I went and went through it all—cutting, shampooing, waving. . . .

The finished product delighted the office and the folks at home too. I certainly look trimmer, better groomed—but I don't like the creases showing in my neck. Too fat. Very dignified—strange to say. Going to be a lot of trouble, I see now, keeping these long ends in place.

Well, it's done—after all these 50 odd years, and coming through the craze of six years ago. . . .

[Read novelist] Fannie Hurst's *Back Street*—until 4 A.M.

## Friday, February 6

And of course, felt punk all day from insufficient sleep, and bilious, too. This day Mrs. [Gertrude] Rose [one of the founder-administrators of the Girls Industrial School] wanted me to go with her to see Dr. Candee about this prevention work of hers. . . .

Rosie all eager hanging on the subject. Candee full of orotund Methodist evasion and trite generalities. I thought of Bishop Cannon, William Jennings Bryan—all the M.E. [Methodist Episcopal] hypocrites I ever heard of. Nothing was accomplished by the interview. . . .

Louis [Redding] . . . presiding [at Industrial School committee] with heap much dignity. . . . Me, he ignored utterly, after asking if I had brought his bill . . . Addressed remarks through Mrs. Tatnall or Mr. Richard [also committee members]. Felt important, I guess. Such an ass. . . .

## Monday, February 9

. . . Paul [Laurence Dunbar] died twenty-five years ago today. Great guns, how time flies!

## Tuesday, February 10

. . . Called Dr. Atkins. Couldn't connect with him. Disappointment No. 1. Then went to see W. K. T. [Wilbur K. Thomas]. As I had foreseen, his ardor had cooled on his new peace project and he gently let me down. I was not surprised. I spoke of the W.I.L. [Women's International League for Peace and Freedom] thought that seems to be hovering in everyone's mind. . . . He saw difficulties, as I do, was all negative, no constructive suggestion. Disappointment No. 2.

Went down to see John Gibson . . . "Too busy." I was escorted to a box seat to see . . . a new "Snake Hips." . . . Gibson waved at me, but refused to talk. Disappointment No. 3. My calendar said—WATCH THIS DAY. . . .

### Friday, February 13

No black cats or jinxes today. Took my luncheon hour to go to the Academy of Fine Arts to see the Annual exhibit which has been going on since the second week in January. Awfully stupid to be in a town with an event of national importance on hand—and not see it.

Did the exhibit thoroughly with a catalog. Glad to see a swinging away from the crude brutality of the so-called modern stuff—(I call it Russian barbarity) and an insistence on good drawing, clear colors, low tones. Particularly impressed with the portrait of a Japanese artist, and two Negro heads—a man's and a girl's. And of course, Eve, in wood and Tagore and the lovely head of Mrs. Lessing Rosenwald. . . .

. . . To the [Darby, Pa., Methodist Episcopal] church for the Elk Temple Educational meeting. . . . Superintendent of Schools—Doultren—whom I had met before, talked about 50 minutes which was 45 minutes too long. I slept, but my subconscious self registered his plea for segregated schools. In the bustle caused by the entrance of a glee club, . . . he escaped. . . . I was quite furious, and made a nasty "radical" speech, which seemed to enliven the poor high school youngsters. There was much talk from them afterwards and I heard all the talk about the segregated operatta etc. . . .

### Monday, February 16

Strangely hectic day. Rushed to get things done and out to the A.M.E. [African Methodist Episcopal] minister's meeting [in Philadelphia]. . . . Gertrude Waters there with her plea for the outdoor camp. She is Field Secretary and made a telling talk. I came on with my verbal invitation to the Ministers' Council. And R. R. [Richard Robert] Wright [A.M.E. Church minister and bishop] backed it up. But oh, the parsons seemed so dumb and faintly hostile. I couldn't evoke the hearty applause vouchsafed the missionary lady from Georgia. . . .

. . . To the Baptist meeting. A stringy, cluttered, packed in, heterogeneous collection of divines and visitors. Noisy, disorderly. Goodall hostile as soon as he saw me. The usual difficulty with the hearing committee, the usual dumb slowness. Why do ministers *have* to walk slow? When—after delays and obstructions, I got a chance to talk—I railed at them for not answering my letters and a brother from the back piped up, "Sister, we didn't know how you look!" . . .

### Thursday, February 19

. . . To the [Philadelphia] Fashion Show. Had intended coming home to get the evening gown, but too late, and I was too tired and it was too rainy. So decided to be the "well-dressed business-woman" or something. . . .

. . . And my "practical business woman," one dress for all occasions, was a success. . . . Oodles of dresses and models. . . .

### Friday, February 20

. . . A.I.P.C. [American Inter-Racial Peace Committee] Board at 2:30. W. K. Thomas came in. Much clarifying of issues, attitudes and Thomas' plan for a *new* organization discussed pro and con. After 2–½ hours, we were left as at the beginning—no plans, nothing decided, but considerable "illumination" as Hill put it. . . .

### Thursday, February 26

I'm getting panicky about this Ministers' Conference [which she has planned]. Suppose no one comes?

[American Friends] Service Committee meeting this p.m. And I ducked that too. These damn Quakers make me tired. Here's Harry Timbres and his wife, Rebecca, spending three thousand dollars running over to Europe and India and back every few weeks, and he's done nothing yet that he started out to do—help [Hindu poet] Tagore, and do preventive medicine in India, and Rebecca has never left England. And they begrudge spending 2,000 dollars [her yearly salary] for work among 12,000,000 Negroes!

Began my Negro History Course [which she is teaching] in six lessons over a period of 12 weeks out at the Germantown [Pennsylvania] "Y." Like going to San Francisco to get out there. . . .

## Friday, February 27

A rarely beautiful day. Spring-like. Like late March. I bought some red tulips for the piano in the lecture-room of the church where the Council [of Ministers and Laymen, her program] was held. . . . My fears were founded in fact. Few came—less than a hundred in the afternoon—less than that at night. Pitiful. And such a wealth to offer in speeches and discussions. Such a wealth! Dr. Gulick said I am a "wonderful organizer." . . . *Not a single representative from our office* . . . nor an excuse. Contemptible. Logan's choir did not show up at night and he made no excuse. So the evening was musicless. But the Cheyney Singers were good in the afternoon. . . . And such good speeches! . . . Bobbo was home when I got in and stupidly sleepy. I was hurt, heartsick, cross, needing comfort. Sat with my hat on on the couch for a half hour, too wounded to move—and he snored!

Another failure!

And so well planned and all. It was a perfect party, but the guests didn't come. Why? . . .

## Saturday, February 28

Bobbo and I talked late this a.m. . . . At last I got a chance to tell him of my desperate state. Debts. No money. Bottom dropped out of my job. Confusion. Bafflement. Embarrassment. It got over to him. He was very quiet—but going up on the train he went over his hopes again for the A & P Automobile Association [another of his fruitless money-making schemes]. I think he felt his impotence to help me. . . .

Made up expense account. Expenses 65.00. Recipts 15.00. . . . Deficit 50.00. Out of the balance toward my salary. I *would* have a conference! Well, I paid $50 for it. . . .

And something is buzzing in me just below the horizon of consciousness. . . .

## Sunday, March 1

. . . Took the 7:05 at night for West Philadelphia and the Mt. Olivet [Baptist] Church. Some kind of Woman's Day on. Shepard [the pastor] graciously gave me ten minutes *before* him. The rain kept the usual thousand away.

I spoke. Polite, earnest, careful attention. That's all. I struck no spark of fire. And I wanted so to practice on this congregation. What was wrong?

Shepard spoke. I listened carefully. Analytically. The intellectual content of his sermon (brief and to the point) was clear, well-rounded, logical. He's a seminary man. But it was *not* the intellectual content that stirred his hearers—that made the woman on the platform go delirious and the Amen corners rock. It was his voice, inflections, thunderings. His hearers could not analyze his logic as I did, but they *could* feel emotion at his outpour.

Now why can't I do that? Because I can't feel? But I do. Because I am cold? But I am not. I sympathize with the least of them. Too intellectual? Too cynical? Too scornful of bunk-hokum? Must be that. Now there's Nannie Burroughs, for instance, and Mrs. [Mary McLeod] Bethune. But I've got more brains than either—or have I? Probably not—if I had, I'd be where they are instead of wondering at 55 where in God's name I'm going to turn next? . . .

The bubbles are coming to the surface. Thought is emerging, taking form. I may not have to sell apples on the street with the other unemployed millions after all.

### Monday, March 2

. . . I wanted to walk. It was a spring day that made you want to laugh and throw away all the fears and [?] of winter. And as I walked to and fro and hither and yon on errands, I grasped the ideas which came to the surface at last and crystallized. My "Temple of Peace" which I dreamed of last year in California. I will begin to build it now—soon. If I can get a foothold in New York—and why not? Then I will build it—a haven.

But I must learn how to arouse emotion. I must get that electric thrill back. Inspiration—I need. Must have. I *can* do it. I must. I cannot go coldly to win the shekels necessary. I must pay off the A.I.P.C. debts—including my own salary. Try to find a good manager. . . . Dreams. Why not come true? I have started so many things and they are near-successes. Bobbo says I've never gotten my stride yet. No. It's time. 55. Time is flying. I can. I must. I can learn. I will yet start my "new religion." Christianity. Meditation upon a theme. . . . Milling over my schemes. . . . I wonder why I can't hold success. . . .

Can I do it? I must learn how to "emote." . . .

### Tuesday, March 3

Emotionally exhausted this a.m. from ruminating over my fate until after 2:30 a.m. . . .

. . . Home on the eleven o'clock [p.m.] . . . to find a check . . .
from Dodd and Mead. The depression hit my royalties! . . .

## Wednesday, March 4

. . . To St. Philips [Episcopal Church] to see Shelton Bishop [the
pastor]. He, like every other minister in New York, can talk and think
in terms of nothing but unemployment, starvation. The situation in
New York is not only more acute than it is in Philadelphia, it is more
terrifying. The resources of charity have failed. There is no more money
available. And there is frightful need among the 200,000 poor Negroes
of Harlem. Shelton all but put me out in disgust. . . .

## Thursday, March 5

. . . The A.I.P.C. weighed heavily on me—so I went to see
W. K. T. [Wilbur K. Thomas] again. We conferred and considered
for an hour or more. At parting, we had agreed: 1) To scrap the A.I.P.C.
by April; 2) To make up a new board of new folks; 3) To include
L. P. H. [Leslie Pinckney Hill] on the new board. This last I had to
fight for—but it was the only decent—and expedient thing to do. I
was exhausted by the interview. . . .

I felt like a motherless child all day. Guess I let my blueness and
misery out to Bobbo in my letter. Sometimes I get *so* tired of the
burden. If only I had a *strong* pair of shoulders to shift it upon. . . .

## Friday, March 6

. . . Helen [Bryan] and I conferred. I suggested transferring the
budget account to the Transit fund to pay outstanding bills and my
salary provided I clear out by April 1. Helen talked with Clarence
Pickett. He agreed. So she said. Now to break the news to Leslie [P.
Hill] so he'll think *he* suggested it. And to clear out. Not sorry to go
now. It's getting stale and messy in the office now. Better be salary-
less than stultified. *And* there's just nothing to *do*, nowhere to turn. I
hate to come home and confess I'm out of a job—but maybe [Pitts-
burgh *Courier* editor] Vann's project will eventuate. Let us hope. . . .

## Monday, March 9

Sometimes I don't wonder men and women go wailing about their
spouses "not understanding" them. I marvel at Bobbo's obtuseness.

But I have been marveling for 18 years and continue with a cheerful hope that only a congenital idiot could possess. I hope he will *see* and understand and say the helpful word, the sympathetic phrase. I wonder if I disappoint him as much as he does me? I guess I *have* whined a lot in my letters lately, for his reactions are the queerest imaginable. Deep down inside of him I'll bet he's as scared as I am, but he's not admitting it to himself. To me it seems that in all our years, our combined fortunes have never been as precarious as now. Maybe I'm bilious or pessimistic—but fate is hard on the unestablished middle-aged. And that's us. . . .

A new "Our Gang" comedy. Farina [one of the characters] getting leggy and doing heavy acting and a little new pickaninny with wonderful eyes. Sweet voice and undoubted talent. . . .

## Monday, March 16

Snowing, blowing, raining, mean. A nasty day. The conductor called me to tune on the 8:24 about my 50 trip ticket and its replaced punches. He's no gentleman and I shall ride on his train no more.

Long and delightful letter from Fay [Jackson Robinson]. She has her divorce at last and a job on the California *Eagle*.

Another (the 4th) Bermuda letter from Helene [London].

Long interview with W. K. T. Now he's not so keen on my closing out April 1. I am. I'm tired of the whole damn mess.

Did not go to Allied Social Agencies luncheon. Felt mean and crotchety and the weather was too vile to go battling down in South Philadelphia. . . .

## Tuesday, March 17

. . . The Flower Show was glorious. It seemed miles of gorgeous blooms, lovely little gardens, rock gardens, oh plenty of them, confirming my intention to have one in that central plot. Azaleas and orchids and everything but violets. Such a few wild ones in an exhibition, called "The Outdoor Living Room"—but I would have welcomed a profusion, as there was of tulips and hyacinth and roses. . . .

## Wednesday, March 18

The Anniversary of My One Perfect Day. My day last year in San Francisco and my ride in the plane from Los Angeles to San Francisco, and all the perfection of that day. . . . And Fay, lovely little

Fay. One day we saw each other, *one day*, and a year has passed. And still we cannot meet again. . . .

## Thursday, March 19

. . . Viciously bilious. Will not take any more calomel. So tried some force of mind on my recalcitrant stomach, gall bladder, and liver.

## Friday, March 20

Felt better. But got in touch with [Dr.] Virginia [Alexander]. She opines nervous indigestion. Told her I was neither worried nor nervous [obviously a proud lie]. Insists that there is a sub-conscious condition which is affecting the weakest parts of me.

Bored! I don't think I have ever been so completely bored in all my life. Wrote Bobbo I was afraid I'd get into mischief. Bored to tears. Or is it biliousness? . . .

Still I'm bored! Tired of doing nothing, of being nobody, of being shunted to the shelf.

But I have nothing. Fay says if you have an idea, it will be heard. My mind is a blank. Ye gods! Must I always be at the lower middle of the ladder? . . .

## Wednesday, March 25

. . . Helen [Bryan]'s treachery *was* made whole at last. Like the unrelated pieces of a picture puzzle, her queer attitude and actings have annoyed and mystified me. W. K. T.'s showing me the minutes of the Service Committee Board of Directors was the key piece and the whole thing fell into a complete pattern. For months she has been subtly undermining the A.I.P.C. so as to take advantage of its failure for the Service Committee to take over *her* work. It appears that they will. Selah.

After the Peace Section meeting . . . I learned that Hill had neither cringed nor begged, but had been finely loyal (as he always is) to me. . . . I learned of appreciation from [Chairman] Cadbury and [committee member] William I. Hull and all.—But that's not a job.— So, the recommendation to pay our indebtedness and clear us out.

Hill saw me to the 6:23. I am ashamed of the way I rail at him. He is so loyal and fine to me always. . . .

## Thursday, March 26

. . . Decided not to go to the Service Committee [meeting]. Couldn't. Choked me. Bought a new dress this a.m. at Finkel's. Bought seeds, [?] etc. at Wanamaker's. Go right on piling up bills. No money. No job. Plenty debts. Plenty responsibilities. And as cheerful as an idiot. . . .

## Friday, March 27

. . . Fairly fell in bed. Miserably collapsed. Don't know why. Hope I'm not getting so two speeches a day is too much. . . .

## Saturday, March 28

. . . Enjoyed being at home today for a novelty—but wouldn't want it always. Hope I won't have to.

## Sunday, March 29

. . . I am tired, however, emotionally more than anything else, with sudden panicky fits that shake me from head to foot and leave me weak with apprehension. With Bobbo's whole concentration on beating the number game, he can offer me no help but what he will do for me when he makes that big killing. A real gambler, so I must resign myself to the fate of a gambler's wife.

Was reading over my diary for this time last year. What a turmoil and pother I was in, what with Helene and Fay and the Music Festival coming on!

Must to bed and pray for inspiration. . . .

## Tuesday, March 31

I'll go ga-ga . . . if I don't get out of 20 South 12th [the Friends office]. The girls are getting mournful and long-eyed and saying the most doleful things! Juliet regretted that she hadn't had time to know me better; Mildred's eyes filling with tears everytime she looks at me— even Elizabeth Marsh . . . regretting that she will miss my "Good morning, Merry Sunshine" cach day. I believe they planned some kind of affair for me at staff meeting today. . . .

Did the Bulletin. Wrote what I thought a cracker-jack editorial.

Ray [Newton] *would* find fault, of course. . . .

Gone crazy on numerology. Lapped up one book. Found it elementary, so went . . . and acquired a more advanced work. Thought I'd change my name to Aliceruth Dunbar-Nelson to harmonize with my life number. But *that* may be wrong. . . .

Fear, fear, fear—it haunts me, pursues, dries my mouth, parches my lips and shakes my knees, nauseates me. Fear! And no money—yet. . . .

### Thursday, April 2

I was dreaming that I had to rescue Marie Antoinette when everyone yelled at me to know if I proposed sleeping all day. . . . In the office by nine.

I was clearing out and throwing away when my News Bureau idea crystallized and took clear form in every detail. So I promptly wrote Hannah Clothier Gull all about it and suggested the W.I.L. [Women's International League] use it for a consideration. Talked with Helen [probably Bryan]. Went down to Hartman's, went over newspaper list, asked for estimate on work. Changed address at P.O. Took trolley down to Citizen's Bank to cash check, saw Major [R. R.] Wright and went in to see him. When I got past his barrage of words, asked him what he thought of it. *Said* it was fine idea and promised business. . . .

### Friday, April 3

Good Friday. So I do penance. Clean my room. Do the garden. And I mean worked, spreading humus, etc. until my bones ached and my back cracked. Everett [who helped with heavy work] washed windows. Made trips downtown in [Pauline's] Belinda [Buick]. Out to the cemetery with tulips and hyacinths and helped Leila putter on the graves. And—gathered some rocks for the rock garden—a whole goods box of them. And had Everett lug them in the yard. And when I had immured the only dish pan in the house in the top of the mound for a lily pond and disposed the rocks, there was a respectable beginning of the famous (to be) rock garden. We had to wash dishes in big pots and kettles.

Then I dyed eggs—and Robert came unexpectedly early, in time for dinner in fact.

So, in spite of Good Friday, we played some bridge. Leila pathetically blue, brooding over Ethel [Leila's daughter who had died six months earlier].

Bobbo brought me a lovely little bottle of [?] Paris—the gorgeous perfume I love. . . .

### Monday, April 6

. . . I did finally get to the bank and changed my signature to Aliceruth Dunbar-Nelson. . . .

### Friday, April 10

. . . Back to [Friends] office and all of us—twelve—to the Blue Lantern, to eat [as a farewell] in my honor!

Funny quaint "Cheerful Cherub" place cards. Lovely roses for me. A scrapbook that is just darling. Funny quips and cranks and a quaint biography. Characterization of me, lovely compliments, funny pictures, poems. Each one contributed a page. All very lovely. Best of all, Clarence [Pickett] made a speech—and lo, a Parker pen and pencil set. I could not make a fitting response, for fear I'd cry. I'm afraid I fell down horribly. . . .

### Monday, April 13

. . . Reached Philadelphia. Went at once to see Gideon. He makes me nervous and irritable. Seems dumb and ignorant to me and half the time we aren't talking about the same thing. Any man who has to be told a dozen times each interview what Moton's name is and his position as principal of Tuskegee certainly isn't the man to make an appeal to Negroes to sell books. I left him limp with rage, disgust and irritation. . . .

### Friday, April 17

. . . Up town [in Washington, D.C.] and saw Carter Woodson [noted Black historian]. We talked of the books he wants me to write—Bobbo's "Romances of the Negro in American History," and another book he had in mind. He loaded me with heavy volumes, and many injunctions. . . .

*"Bobby" below is* Robert Clash Nelson, *who was D-N's stepson. Born in 1905, he does not appear in the diary, having died of "pneumonia"—probably influenza—April 18, 1918.*

## Monday, April 20

*Our Fifteenth Anniversary.* Awake early to celebrate our fifteenth anniversary, and then to Philadelphia to Virginia [Alexander]'s. Here we lay all day on operating tables in the same room, and so we celebrated our fifteen years of married life! Home on the 8:38, ate some dinner, which I prepared, and in bed before nine o'clock.

And I had planned for years the kind of party I was going to give on my fifteenth anniversary.

Bobbo gave me three pairs of stockings. I did not give him anything. For the first time in our married life—except when Bobby [Nelson] was buried on our second anniversary.

## Tuesday, April 21

. . . And now today begins my real experience with staying at home. . . .

## Friday, April 24

. . . Met Polly . . . and to the Earle for dinner. Jean [Jamison] had gotten tickets for the new colored show, "Singin' the Blues." It is a melodrama and Frank Wilson as the protagonist is excellent. But the play does not live up to its possibilities. Too much old stuff— ostrich ballet, waving hands in air, Eubie Blake [stage pianist] in the spotlight etc. Too bad there is never an original idea in a Negro play. . . .

## Saturday, April 25

. . . Bunch of Howardites drove from Washington [to the Bryn Mawr Liberal Club Conference]. . . . Virginia Alexander parked next to DuBois and the two inseparable and horribly obvious all day. Walter White a little throaty bunch of absolute conceit—"I-I-when I—as I said—"all day. . . .

## Monday, April 27

Cleaned room. Did test K-A-D-N column [her news bureau idea]. . . .

Blanche [Stubbs] is taking Minnie [Stevens]'s place at wandering and parking. Had her on my hands until 11:30 when I walked home with her. . . . And she talks incessantly of Dr. Stubbs [her husband] and his "mental cruelty" to her. She'll go blooie some day—if the rest of us don't first.

## Tuesday, April 28

Between Pauline and Neonta [Jones, Howard High School secretary] got enough stencil paper to cut my own stencils for the News Bureau Station KADN [actually a column that she hoped to syndicate]. Neonta ran off the sheets for me. . . .

## Wednesday, April 29

. . . Went to the City Hall to see Mrs. Moore about the case-working job. . . . I *may* get in. Pays only a hundred dollars a month—but that's a hundred more than I'm making now and I'm feeling desperate. . . .

Sat late in the library meditating—and dreading lest the oil tank is empty and the furnace out.

*About the enterprise here, D-N's cards augured correctly. This column was not successful and later this year, she enumerates it among her failures.*

*The article referred to is "Women in Politics with an Emphasis on Negro Participation," The Journal of the College Alumnae Club of Washington (April 1932).*

## Thursday, April 30

. . . The first issue of "Station KADN" in the mails by one o'clock. Hope it will go. My cards say not—and they *never lie*. My nightly trials very disconcerting.

And—did the article for Hope Lyen's College Alumnae Magazine on women and politics. . . .

### On Train Enroute to Cincinnati
### Saturday, May 2

. . . I played two hands [of bridge in Newark, New Jersey] with
Fannie Holland and against Jessie Fauset [well-known Black female
novelist]. . . . Jessie seems cheerful over the description of her marital
adventures. . . .

### Cincinnati, Ohio, or
### Covington, Kentucky
### Sunday, May 3

. . . So we drove across the Ohio River to Covington, Kentucky,
where I am to park at the home of one "Mabel," a soror. . . .

"Mabel" is "Old Miss Young," but very nice. There is a thin husband, "Will," and a thinner daughter, Wilma, an adolescent, pleasant and gently cynical of her flapperish mother. . . .

### Monday, May 4

Up, took a shower and breakfast over by 7:50 and all started out as
befits teachers. All the "set" in Cinti, whether Deltas or A.K.A. [Black
sororities], teach and husbands go on too. We put Mabel at her school—
the famous Harriet Beecher Stowe and on out to the kid Wilma's
school—the school for superior children on the hill. Then Will drove
me around to see the homes of the rich. . . . Then back to Stowe
school.

The principal, Jennie Porter, is another Krusie—save that she fought
for all her degrees, B.A., M.A., and Ph.D., the latter grudgingly given
by the University of Cincinnati. But she shows signs of the tremendous blood pressure of 235—thickness of speech, difficulty in talking.

But—a gracious hostess. . . .

### Sunday, May 10

. . . The [New York Abyssinian Baptist] church was nearly full
when I got there and nearly every seat taken when services began by
8. Young Powell—Adam [Clayton]—in charge since Senior Powell
just convalescing. The boy is handsome, graceful and his [sic] marvelous personality and control of the massive congregation. Only 22

or 23. Ordained without any divinity training. But he can handle the people.

"I spoke fine." Mother's Day and all. . . .

### Monday, May 11

. . . Polly and I went for a drive—raining as usual. . . . We explored "little roads." Lovely roads. Hunted for the new "Old Mill Dam" and found it after some adventurous explorings and backings and fellings. It is a magnificent piece of engineering. And best of all, a sheer rock, a veritable mountainous precipice across the stream—such grandeur I did not know so near home.

Then home where, after pinochle, gave myself up to the blues. No job in sight. That $25 the last I'm likely to see for a long while. Lester [Walton, first Black columnist on the New York *World* news-paper] will have nothing to do with me. Floyd Snelson [a newspaper-man with the Associated Negro Press] ignored my letter to come and see me at Abyssinia last night. K-A-D-N is a failure. No paper used it. Only the [Pittsburgh] *Courier* and that I know only because they owe me. [?] writes from [North Carolina] A. & T. that it is too late to get on the summer schedule. The circulars which Bolden did strike me (and Bobbo) as unconvincing. No one wants me, for anything. A sudden drop in temperature has made the house chill and there is no oil in the tank. Rain. Rain. I could howl out my heart. . . .

### Wednesday, May 13

. . . Marketed on the way home and hurried to cook a good din-ner—pigs in blankets with brown gravy of mushrooms, carrots and onions and a monstrous lemon meringue pie.

Still depressed. Weather gloomy and cold. Did not feel like going near my desk—all day. Played cards and . . . made an evening of it. Bath. Bed. Cussing inwardly all the time—Oh hell, what's the use. No good. Nobody wants my stuff. Might as well kick out. Never thought I'd get so low that nigger papers would refuse to print my pennings. I *must* be punk. . . .

### Friday, May 15

. . . Went to the [Philadelphia City] Hall. . . . Jean Ritchie said the $3,000,000 which Pinchot is holding up had curtailed their work, so they might have to close down. Called up Dr. Thomas. He has a new strafe. Now it's Ray Newton who, he says, has induced the Service Committee to hire Malcolm Dade to do peace work among Negroes. If that be the case, then Thomas' committee falls flat. So that was disappointment No. 2. . . .

["Strangers May Kiss"] being my second movie today, it was no wonder I was tired and jaded in the flesh. Took off all my clothes when I came home and stayed naked, walking around my room to let my body breathe. . . .

### Saturday, May 16

. . . [Then] followed the [Lincoln University] prom in the gym. So dark you couldn't see what anyone wore and quite atavistic as to music. Tom-tom jungle stuff. Still I danced every dance but one and enjoyed being made love to. . . .

### Monday, May 18

. . . Had the blues all day. Wrote letters until one thirty and then told my fortune [with cards], which made me bluer than ever.

Decided to go back to Washington with Bobbo next week and stay two weeks. I shall certainly kill Collegiate [Mary Waters] if I have to have her under my feet all the time in the kitchen. . . .

### Friday, May 22

. . . I had made engagement to have my hair waved at a beauty parlor at Ninth and King [Wilmington]. Didn't know whether I'd "get by" [not be challenged because of her race], but evidently did. Nice wave. Nice place. Nice girls. Beauty problem solved. Gave me as good a cut as Wanamaker's. . . .

### Monday, May 25

. . . Bobbo—for no good reason—had one of his fainty, not fainting, spells, and I had to snap into it with ammonia and aromatic spirits etc. Very weak and cold. So he slept three hours and we postponed going to Washington. . . .

I wonder if my insisting on his getting tickets for the drill and the prospects of having me to entertain and look out for while I am in Washington could have depressed him! . . .

*Washington, D.C.*
*Tuesday, May 26*

Bobbo got off on the ten something. Said mournfully as he left, "I'll try to make it as pleasant as I can, but I'm awfully broke." Poor fellow! I'm just as sorry as I can be for him. It's this poverty, uncertainty of the Pinchot job and hideous waiting, waiting that is lowering his vitality, blood pressure, resistance, weight, everything. Then there came back the check of $10.50 he had given me, with $2.21 protest charges. Foolishly I told him before he ate breakfast and it made him *sick*.

Finally got packed and off myself.

Bobbo easier in his mind since a belated salary check from the Elks for $100 came through today. He began at once poking money at me and buying me things.

*Wednesday, May 27*

Got under way reasonably early. After breakfast, to Carter Woodson's office. He had just gotten in from Oklahoma the night before, and was swamped with mail. However, he gave me three, nearly four hours, while we sat, I taking notes, he haranguing, collecting books and getting the new book planned out. I fear it won't have any too much to do with the proposed lectures, however. . . .

*Washington, D.C.*
*Thursday, May 28*

Tried to do some work, such as collating notes, etc., but the day got away, and here it was time to dress for the drill. . . . The great thrill came when the whole regiment of 13 companies were drawn up for inspection and parade. One could not help but feel the martial thrill, and that audience of 30,000 Negroes cheering and yelling themselves hoarse—well it does not look much like a pacifist race. I marvel at the white man's obtuseness, and when I think of Ray Newton, I feel like leading a militaristic parade. We were tired, sitting two hours, but it was well worth it. . . .

### Friday, May 29

. . . [The ball] closed out at three. A very tame affair. Music lacked
pep, people middle aged for the most part, and dowdy. Supposed to
be extra elegant, but it was queer to me. Washington is getting to be
like Baltimore used to be—looking like an Old Folks Home. Still, it
was a diversion. . . .

### Tuesday, June 2

Having finished up the text-book research, turned my attention to
the Library of Congress today, and had a very pleasant day there,
although the building was uncomfortably cold. But it was nice to sit
at the desk, and have books brought, and to go up to the cafeteria and
have a dainty luncheon and a smoke, and back down stairs in silence
and cleanliness. Got a lot of reading done too. . . .

Had a crying spell this morning, what I call the "Useless Blues." . . .

### Thursday, June 4

. . . When we were driving down to the office to get Robert . . .
Arthur [Callis, her secret exhusband] said—well, it was not much, the
four years of our romance, the jewel around which his whole life was
built—and a bit more and I haltingly replied that it was a beautiful
thing that I hated to destroy. Yet I knew that destroy it I must—to save
him. Ruthless I was—but it was best for him. And he told me again
something of his desperation in Chicago, and how he never hated
Robert—how could he help loving me!

So we arrived at the office, picked up Robert and so to the Jack-
sons' apartment, bade Arthur good-bye and a lovely little dinner and
Robert had to leave. . . . I . . . walked slowly home through the beautiful streets thinking after all, love and beautiful love has been mine
from many men, but the great passion of at least four or five whose
love for me transcended that for other women—and what more can
any woman want? . . .

### Friday, June 5

Arthur joined us [her and Bobbo] at breakfast . . . this morning
and I asked him to drive me to the library which he agreed with alac-
rity to do. . . . He announced that he had some time to kill until he

met Myra [his wife] coming in from Nashville at 11:35—so we drove
around the river drive and the tide water basin. It was lovely, the water
all ruffled up in whitecapped wavelets and we drove slowly and talked
about the Brandywine [a Wilmington river] and held each other's hands
and grew wistfully silent while I took off my hat and let the breeze
blow my hair away. But all things must end. So to the library and
bade him adieu. . . .

### Sunday, June 7

. . . Over to Edith [Fleetwood]'s—looked over papers, yellowed
with age and worth their weight in gold—from her father's collection,
which I want to give to Woodson for the Library of Congress. We
went then to [Howard University Professor] Alain Locke's—a surprise
party because he is sailing for Europe next week. An interestingly heterogeneous collection of folks of all races and sexes. [Locke was homo-
sexual.] Much talk—some music. . . . Refreshments and I enjoyed
hobnobbing with Georgia [D. Johnson, her poet friend] and a Quaker
woman I met at Pocono Manor four years ago.

### Monday, June 8

. . . Down to [Woodson's] Associated Publishers. Woodson was
in and hurried . . . but took time to go over the yellowed papers I had
brought him, to gloat over the signatures, to bark at me because I had
not brought more and to order me to get additional letters and data.
Then gave me some notes on which to work. . . . Went out to the
Franciscan monastery. The loveliest experience I've had since I left
California. A most beautiful place, profusion of roses, flowers of all
kinds, rock gardens de luxe, chapels, grottos, replica of the catacombs
of shrines in the holy land, music, barefoot friars—oh a veritable dream
of beauty. I was happy beyond words, hills and sunset in the distance—the Missions of California. . . .

Met Bobbo. He was full of joy—Stahlnecker and the Governor
[Pinchot] made much of him before the Elk delegation and Stahlnecker privately assured him that he was trying to get his appointment
to the Athletic Commission by July 4. . . .

### Tuesday, June 9

Bobbo a new man today. The prospect of a five thousand dollar a
year job has straightened his shoulders, put spring in his step and

forgotten cadences in his voice. . . .

Did one story—"How Robert Smalls saved the Planter."

*The hostess below, Jennie Maguire, was the wife of a well-to-do mortician; she was active in club affairs and was a member of the Washington, D.C. Board of Education.*

### Wednesday, June 10

. . . It was after twelve before I got to Woodson's dusty place. And I was inert until about three when words leapt at me from somewhere and I began and finished "Harlem John Henry Views the Airmada," a poem in blank verse, with spirituals running through. A weird thing, five pages long, which left me in two hours' time as limp as a rag. . . .

Jennie Maguire had invited me in to play bridge. There were seven other women. Jennie doesn't play, but draped herself picturesquely on the couch in a flame chiffon while the maid did the work—very excellent highballs etc. Talk ran to books before all had arrived and Narka [Lee-Rayford] boasted that she had the original unexpurgated edition of D. H. Lawrence's *Lady Chatterley's Lover.* Our frank accusation of lying sent her to her apartment and back with the book in battered brown paper covers. We read aloud delicious bits of pornography until time to play bridge. I won by the highest score—and by being a guest. Lovely bracelet. Bobbo in for eats—and I brought Lady Chatterley home.

### Thursday, June 11

. . . Stayed in in the morning and finished *Lady Chatterley's Lover. Some* book. Beautifully written, but quite gorgeously frank.

See my picture advertising Black and White [skin cream] in all the [Black news] papers—*Courier, Afro, Tribune* etc. . . .

### Friday, June 12

. . . Got home, found it much cooler. . . . Everything seemed lovely at home. Window boxes flourishing. Awnings up. Screens in. Bookcase moved in the library. Garden and lawn lovely. Hedge tree filling house and yard with fragrance. Drapes and curtains down. Home never seemed so attractive. . . .

## Monday, June 15

. . . Leila took by breath away by saying she has applied for retirement. I judge it was suggested to her. . . . She will get $50 a month—and peace. And that's more complications. . . .

## Wednesday, June 17

Was awakened about 6:30 by a chill next my flesh. Bobbo feeling like a live glacier crawling under me to get warm. . . . He finally got warm, and we both off to sleep. Awakened at eight by Polly whispering to know of my decision on the teachers' gift [for Leila's retirement]. I had thought of a pretty arm-chair from the beginning, and it seemed to have been unanimous.

## Thursday, June 18

. . . The problem Pauline had today was to get Leila down to School to get her presentation of her present. Maneuvers finally did it, and she went down, and was properly overcome.

Checked up on my research reading while in Washington. Went through 70 books. Not half bad. I'm lazy though. Should have that book finished by now. . . .

. . . Up to bed and rushed down to change a preposition in a line [in "Harlem John Henry"]—"And that wild wonder *of* a soundless world" to "And that wild wonder *at* a soundless world." Now which is better?

## Friday, June 19

. . . Sent out "Harlem John Henry" to four places, *The Bookman,* *Atlantic Monthly, Harper's, Mercury.* . . .

## Sunday, June 21

. . . I bought myself a suit of vivid red cotton house pajamas and, arrayed in these, disported myself all day. . . .

### Monday, June 22

Persuaded Bobbo to stay over today. While he's waiting for word as to his appointment, he may as well be here. And comfy. "Harlem John Henry" came back from the *Bookman* disgustingly prompt. . . .

### Wednesday, June 24

My morning task now is urging Bobbo to stay one more day [from his job in Washington]. And I loaf with him, play cards, read papers etc. etc. . . .

### Friday, June 26

Got Bobbo straight for this week now. . . . Pinchot will be . . . back Monday to begin appointments for the beginning of the fiscal year, July 1. And I pray God Bobbo will be among the first. To ease the carping care that must be his. And mine own. For my affairs are in a most parlous state. I have come to the center of a stagnant pool where I drift aimlessly around a slow oozy backwash of putrid nothingness. And Bobbo's appointment is the only thing that can wash me out of the slimy mess. If it fails—there is no future for either of us. Blank nothingness. . . .

### Saturday, June 27

The last of "John Henry" letters came in today. Now I have rejection slips from all. . . . Shall send him forth again. . . .

### Sunday, June 28

Got the habit now of waking up early in the mornings. Conscience troubling me about my work, I guess. So this morning to the tune of what seemed like a flock of robins came downstairs and sat by the open window enjoying a gorgeous breeze and writing up a nine days' diary—drinking tea in the meanwhile. . . .

### Monday, June 29

Seven years ago today, or was it tomorrow? we moved in this house. Gracious, doesn't tempus fugit? . . .

Sent "John Henry" out again—the *Nation* and *Poet Lore*. Cleaned out a lot of mail. Played bridge because it was too hot not to.

Gorgeous moonlight nights, huge red moon and sultry red skies. . . .

## Wednesday, July 1

. . . Papers full of interesting stuff about the Athletic Commission in Pennsylvania [to which Bobbo was waiting to be appointed], Governor Pinchot and what not. The event draws nigh. I pray with bated breath for it to come true. I am nervous, irritable, jumpy and miserable from the suspense. I wreak my nerves on Collegiate and the unfortunate white-wash man whose slowness drives me to desperation. Time seems to stand still.

And if I am suffering, how much more must Bobbo be in the awful Washington heat and the intolerable suspense of it all. I could scream for him.

## Thursday, July 2

. . . I arose, cooked breakfast. . . . Waved them [Polly and Leila] goodbye and stood on the sidewalk smiling with the realization that I had just one dime to see me through until Bobbo (who is even as broke as I) comes. . . .

## Friday, July 3

Had a busy and rather happy day, preparing for Bobbo, and his weekend. In a way, made me think of preparing for Christmas—and it eventuated the same. Went to market, and bought and bought and bought food [with money raised at the pawnshop]. . . . Bought melon, honey balls, flowers, oodles of black-eyed Susans and baby's breath to decorate the house. Came home and cleaned and cleaned and cleaned. Cooked leg of lamb, made big bowl of Bobbo's corn-starch custard. Got dinner. . . . Then bathed, took a bit of a nap, just a few winks, and awaited Bobbo's arrival. . . .

He came, kissed me, asked if I had seen the evening papers, and then said, "Don't faint now, Pinchot has appointed the Athletic Commission, and he didn't appoint me."

Things went black. I took the paper and read for myself. . . . Such a doleful end to my happy preparations. Like the Christmas Eve sadness. Somehow, in spite of my common sense, I had prepared for a happy celebration of Bobbo's good fortune. And this let down. . . .

### Saturday, July 4

. . . Late in the evening [Howard High School] Principal [George] Johnson came to call, having first called up. I knew he had something on his mind. . . . So I went downstairs and out on the sidewalk to Johnson's car with him. We stood and talked for an hour. In a round-about and shamefaced way he let me know that he wished to have me in his school as a teacher, and wanted me to apply for one of the vacant positions in his school.

Came in and talked with Bobbo about it. Felt all sick, and things went black before me at the thought of teaching in Howard School or anywhere. . . .

### Sunday, July 5

Another day of gloom, conjectures, hopeful surmises, building up of alibis for the governor and Stahlnecker, scanning the papers for light on the subject, pitiful clinging together. Good God, that any man could make human beings so miserable. For political expediency Pinchot and Stahlnecker had failed in their promise to Bobbo. But how about him? No one could ever guess the anguish of spirit when we stood and saw our very life gone down like a house of cards. For it is no secret between us that we have come to the end of our resources, the end of our rope, and unless Bobbo lands some kind of a paying job, God only knows what will become of us. . . .

### Tuesday, July 7

. . . Dressed early and went over to Howard School, ostensibly to get Laurence Jr.'s picture for Polly in her library, really to talk to Johnson. . . . We went into the situation carefully, and then I called [Wilmington Superintendent of Public Schools] Stouffer's office from Johnson's desk. The girl at the phone said he was out, or engaged, and would be tied up probably all afternoon, and was my business about an appointment? It was. And what school? Howard. I could overhear a conversation on the side for every one of my answers. And what name? Nelson. Well, she would call back in a few minutes. I gave the number, and sat chatting with Johnson until the call came back in fifteen minutes. Was I the Mrs. Nelson who had formerly taught in Howard? I was. Well, to save me any trouble she would tell me that it had been decided at a board meeting that no positions were to be given to married women, and all vacancies to be filled from the single applicants. Thanked her. And said I'd call to see Stouffer in the morning. I suspected that . . . I was being forestalled. . . .

### Wednesday, July 8

. . . At a quarter to two back at Stouffer's office. Miss Devine at her desk in the outer room. Called my name loudly—so that I knew she was signalling Stouffer. Waited until he was through dictating. Went in. Effusively cordial. Ingenuous. Open-eyed, a child's blue stare. Too candid; too cordial. From his first sentence I knew he knew my biography from a to z, so I was not surprised at his real sorrow at having to tell me that the old board had made a ruling that no married teachers were to be employed where there was a vacancy for which there are single applicants. He was full of Who Struck John, but I knew that I was on the black list for ever and ever amen. So I came home, ready to kick holes in the atmosphere that I had been let in for this new humiliation. And wished I was dead and buried. Just think, if Stahlnecker had kept his promise to Bobbo and had seen that he got a job by July fourth, I would not have considered trying for a job here. I wished I was dead and buried.

So ate dinner. Though it choked me. And played bridge. Though I did not know the cards half the time. . . .

### Thursday, July 9

. . . Patricia [Mama] pleased and glad to see Laurence [Mama's grandson]. She chirked up a bit at his coming. Though for the past few days in the intense and devastating heat, which had me gasping, she was frail and pathetic, and I thought she would succumb.

### Friday, July 10

. . . Went to Howard . . . and poured out my tale to Johnson, whose jaw dropped in amazement. He said Stouffer was lying, there had been no such ruling made by the Board, or he had never heard of it. I said I knew Stouffer was lying, and he knew I knew he was lying, but it was a pleasant way of telling me I was permanently black-

listed, and there was no hope, though he DID say that if ever there
was an abrogation of that rule to come and see him and he would be
glad to consider my application. Johnson was stunned, and I grew sick
again at the memory of the thing. . . .

. . . Went to Jo Hopkins [her friend] and sat on her porch. She
came out. We talked. . . . Jo was embarrassed, and I knew she was
full of something. Then she began. If I wanted a position at Howard
School—and I knew it was all over town that I had applied and been
turned down. Jo was all for a fight, and was full of complimentary
things about my worth to the community, etc., etc. etc. She was kind
and lovely and bitter and hot, and all—and I wanted to cry, so I hurried away. When I got in the house something broke, and I burst into
anathema of Lizzie [Banton, her old enemy]. It seemed to me that
she was the cause of all my woes, my troubles, my miseries. And here
she had kept Laurence from me for nearly two hours, while I sat waiting on Jo's porch, and she always had done it, always putting me in
embarrassing and humiliating positions, and I raved and cursed and
swore, while Leila looked worried, and tried to shut me up. All the
ten years of miseries came over me. It was she who was responsible
for the [1920] school fiasco [which cost D-N her Howard High School
position]. It was she who had hung over and tormented my whole life.
I could have sobbed in rage, but thought better, and cooled off. . . .
I guess I was plain hysterical from worry. . . .

### Sunday, July 12

. . . Leila is talking about money. I don't blame her. She is paying
Miss Waters [Mama's nurse] entirely. I have given her nothing since
March . . . and it must be an awful drain on her. She is getting worried, but Lord, she doesn't know what worry is. I have been almost
frantic, for I don't see any hope, any opening, any rift in the darkness.
Got some kind of stuff from . . . the Boston chap who does the Applied
Self Improvement stuff. It DID lighten me a bit as I read it. For suicide seemed to me the only hope, and as my life insurance has lapsed,
that was hardly a solution—and then I do believe it would crush Bobbo
horribly. But I seem so useless, so done for.

Maybe not. Old man Warbucks, blind and destitute, in Little
Orphan Annie, seems about ready to stage a comeback. When he flew
into a rage and smashed the chair Thursday and Flop-House John
recognized him, and they made plans, and he dressed up by Saturday,

it seemed as if my own fortunes grew better. But it's those checks, those constant bad checks. . . . I need a Hoover to declare a permanent moratorium for me.

Leila said she had no idea Mama would be so ill so long. Now if Mama were ill that would be something. But she is merely old, and deliberately helpless, and there you are. And she may be in this condition for another year, and by that time, as Leila says, we will all be out in Farnhurst, either in the lunatic asylum or in the poor-house. . . .

Been putting off doing up this diary for days. Tonight I got at it. I could not write before when the misery and wretchedness and disappointment and worry were so close to me that to write it out was impossible, and not to write it out, foolish. But even though I may not get that money tomorrow [a loan], and will then be worse than penniless, I haven't felt the wretchedness of the past week. Just dumb volatility, I suppose. . . .

## Wednesday, July 15

. . . Mowed and tended the lawn this afternoon. Took me nearly two hours, what with mowing again and again, raking, clipping edges and watering. Afraid I did not do any constructive thinking while I was doing it. Embittered me somehow, though I know it's the best of exercise for me. . . . Why I should hate to do it, I don't know. Not the actual work, but what it symbolizes. . . .

## Thursday, July 16

. . . Blazing heat continues. I'm all in in the mornings—as ever from a child—and don't gather momentum until afternoon. . . .

## Saturday, July 18

. . . Lolled around all evening until bed-time. Too feeble to move out of my own way. . . .

## Sunday, July 19

Just finished reading over my diary of last year's birthday celebration. At least I *did* something. Not today. . . .

Shall next year be like this?

Thinking back [over] 1930–31, I cannot see that I have advanced *one* step or done one thing. It has been a year of marking time. Let us pray that 31–32 will not be like unto it. . . .

### Tuesday, July 21

Felt industrious. Washed clothes, lots of them. Gathered data and whipped in shape speech for Pittsburgh. Quite a job. Vilely hot. Mama very feeble. Almost collapsed. Felt apprehensive for her. Slept most of the time, and there were moments when I leaned over her to see if she were breathing. . . .

### Wednesday, July 22

Cooler today and Mama pepped up. Became whimsical, petulant, insulting—quite herself. . . .

*Here D-N is obviously telling interesting biographical narratives about successful Blacks—for instance, Estevanico, the western explorer; Norbert R. de Rillieux, New Orleans Creole, who gained international recognition for inventing a vacuum pan used in sugar refining; and Austin Dabney, a freed slave who served as a substitute for his master in the American Revolutionary War.*

### Friday, July 24

. . . Studied my "piece." A new line and I am "trying it on the dog." For luncheon, donned the new white silk and afterwards to the Assembly with Allston and Dr. Gandy. The former introduced me—rather fulsomely. My natural nervousness wore off soon, and soon I was telling my stories—a "Raconteur" am I? Got through three—Estevanico, Norman de Rillieux and Sugar Austin Dabney. Went over big. The school sat silent, spell-bound. Gandy was charmed—delighted. Said it was the best assembly of the season and warmly invited me back to the winter season and next summer. And considering that [Nathaniel] Dett [the composer], Harry Burleigh [singer and composer] and [Oscar] DePriest [Chicago politician who was elected to Congress in 1929] have been there—I felt flattered.

Now—I've got a line none of these other nigger women have! . . .

## Tuesday, July 28

. . . Mrs. McMillan of the corset company caught me at last and talked to me for an hour. I promised to go to work for her next week. Must do something. . . .

## Friday, July 31

. . . Bobbo fussing about my wanting to sell Spencer [under] garments. Asked me to be patient and hold off. It will be easy to be patient with $260 [newly acquired]. But if I had not—I should certainly disregard his admonitions. . . .

Went to the Queen today to see Sir Carillo in "Hell Bound." An interesting enough picture, but pernicious. Glorifying gangsters as heroes must be unsalutary to youngsters. . . .

## Sunday, August 2

Delightfully pleasant all day. Did nothing but put a tan bleach on my face. . . .

## Thursday, August 6

. . . Reached Wanamaker's . . . and found [R. R.] Wright awaiting me. We conferred about three quarters of an hour. He is planning to bring "Heaven Bound," that much talked of Negro morality play which has so excited Birmingham and the South—to Philadelphia and wants me to manage the executive end of it. We sparred for a while, and finally decided on a conference Thursday a.m. at the Citizens Bank with the author-producer. Felt a burden lifting from my heart—work to do, an interest in life, a job, money to make. Philadelphia!

Leila and I lunched in Wanamaker's. I bought a hat—one of the new Empress Eugenie affairs, in brown felt. . . .

## Tuesday, August 11

. . . Had to wait a bit to see Wright at the bank as he was in the Bank Directors' meeting. Funny. I had planned such a swell costume for the day—my black georgette done over with frills and the Eugenie hat. And—it was down to 60° and I had to get into my silk suit—and needed a fur—though didn't wear it.

Wright and I sparred, as usual. The author of "Heaven Bound," Miss Davis, was not present. This week's *Time* has quite an account of the play with Miss Davis' picture and the announcement that it will be given in Philadelphia in September. Wright has selected September 28, 29, 30. . . . He's doing most of the groundwork. My job to get *at least* 500 patrons at $5.00 each. "Ofays and dictys" [Whites and upper-crust Blacks]. Percentage basis. 20% up to $500—25% over that. Guess he thinks I'll hustle harder. Advance payment to be deducted from commissions. I had thought of flat salary—but, oh well, guess I'm lazy. To go to work Monday the 17th at the A.M.E. Book Concern. . . .

### Friday, August 14

. . . To the Ambassador [in New York] . . . to see Katherine Cornell in the Barretts of Wimpole Street. . . . . The play was finished, perfect. The big scene between Elizabeth and her father—when his incestuous love becomes evident, was awe-ful. I felt as if I should draw a curtain. It was too terrible to be looked in on. Wonderful play. . . .

### Monday, August 17

. . . Wright was not in his office at the Book Concern building. Neither was Ruth. Waited. Ministers came and went. . . . Ruth came and put me in her father's office with my brief case filled with mailing lists. Said I was to have a nice office which she showed—but she wouldn't do anything until "Dad" came. Waited. He phoned apologies—would be up soon. Waited. Read. Walked the floor. At 2:40, I told Ruth to tell him I had waited five hours—which was 4½ hours longer than I had ever waited for *any* man. And went to Virginia's, too lazy and inert to get indignant. . . .

### Tuesday, August 18

Hot! Ye gods. Well, I only had to wait an hour or so until "Dr. Brown" came and allowed me to move in his office. Wright profuse in his apologies for yesterday's dereliction. Finally settled. But the heat and the noise from the pavement wrecking machines had me almost distracted. Came home fairly early, exhausted. . . .

Emma [Sykes] throwing a party . . . Polly not invited. Dressed up and she suggested I dress even more, so wore the white dress and the white costume jewelry. Rotten bore—the party. Either I'm out of kilter or I've outgrown the crowd. Didn't even get a good game of bridge. . . . Tired of the gang. Tired of their stale dirty stories. . . .

## Friday, August 21

. . . We [D-N and Polly] went to Rita [Dix]'s, there for the three to plan the details of this wild-goose trip to Maine. Rita irritated me more than ever with her laziness and listlessness. The episode of the tea just about finished her with me. The family was eating dinner and the usual perfunctory offer was made. I was half sick and wholly starved and said I *would* relish a cup of tea. So Rita told me to go out in the kitchen and make it myself. And wanting the tea, I did—but I got mad afterwards and the more I thought of it, the madder I got. I wouldn't have done that to Leila or Polly coming in when I was eating. Such lazy lack of hospitality. So we catted at each other about the Maine trip. . . .

## Sunday, August 23

Cold, damp, rainy [in Princeton, New Jersey]. Our quoits and brookside supper picnic gone flooey. But we did drive over to the Walker-Gordon huge dairy farm to see the roto-lacter in use. A wonderful sight—the huge "merry-go-round" with its constant procession of 50 cows every 15 minutes, being bathed, groomed, sterilized, milked by machinery on the revolving affair. I thoroughly enjoyed it—and visiting the thousands of cows in their stalls and drinking milk and buying caramels. It was fun. . . .

## Monday, August 24

Rose early . . . Exercised vigorously, as per usual—oh, I'm most meticulous about this morning and evening exercising. . . . Tindley Temple [Philadelphia] was packed and jammed, and I got a seat by Leslie Hill, who was all ready for a lot of dissertation. I listened to Abbie Johnson, too badly dressed for words, and to Emma Kelley, who was putting the rousement on. I said to Hill that I had always longed to be able to do that sort of thing, and he averred he hoped never to see the day when I did. . . .

### Thursday, August 27

. . . Raining cats and dogs [in Philadelphia, where they are attending the national IBPOE, the Black Elks convention] when we [D-N,
Polly, Leila, and friends] came out, but we cruised around Elk-dom
awhile, and everyone being dry, cold and blue, said I'd find Bobbo
and Elk's milk. No one believed I could, but I dug him out of the
convention hall, and he drove with us to his room, and set us up in
fine shape, giving us the rest of the quart to bring home. Alice clapped
her hands and sang about how beutiful is life all the way home, while
Jean grew morose. . . .

### Saturday, August 29

The printing for "Heaven Bound" came up, after I had stayed at
the office until after five, and Wright had moved heaven and earth to
get the folder cut, and then when I saw it, I could have cried from
sheer vexation and disappointment. It seemed so cheap and cheesy to
me, I couldn't speak of it to Bobbo until next morning when he assured
me it was quite all right. . . .

Bobbo and I came home about midnight and made our own party
in the kitchen, being both hungry and thirsty. As a celebration from
the week's strenuosity he broke his eight month's abstinence, and drank
some liquor for the first time since December [when he discovered his
uremic condition]. . . .

### Thursday, September 3

. . . Check from Dodd and Mead came today. . . .

Helene [London, in Bermuda] writes that I must get my reservation on the Franconia sailing October 10. Now I shall be able to do
so. Hooray! . . .

### Friday, September 4

. . . I had my seance with [beautician] Margaret. Quick work.
Only fifty minutes to get a wave, a manicure, and eyebrows plucked.
Never had that done before, and it is irritating in the extreme. But the
shapeliness of my amber brows (ahem!) compensated me for the
inconvenience. . . .

## Wednesday, September 9

. . . Went down to the Furness-Bermuda line this a.m. and paid deposit of twenty-five dollars on my passage. They called up yesterday saying the reservation was ready. . . . Now all I have to do is to raise fifty-five dollars for the first of October. Virginia [Alexander] can't go. Her little Dr. Winston failed his state board exam so she can't leave him in charge of her practice as she had intended doing. Well, I said there would be one other, and I'll trust to luck for someone going. Leila absolutely refuses. . . .

## Saturday, September 12

. . . Happened to say casually to Mrs. [Sadie] Harrison [at an Industrial School meeting], "You'd better come and go to Bermuda with me," when she spoke of being tired. She jumped at the proposition, saying all her life she had yearned for Bermuda, from hearing of her grandfather, Bishop [Benjamin T.] Tanner [Reconstruction-era A.M.E. Church theologian and author], speak of it. So we were soon inspecting her wardrobe, and she had given me her check for twenty-five dollars to pay on her passage.

And so home, too exhausted to do much. Horrible weather. Even the electric fan hardly helps. Sleep was a nightmare.

## Sunday, September 13

. . . Best of all heard MAHATMA GANDHI over the radio. He has reached England with his goat's milk and loincloth and unexpectedly spoke over the radio from England, an international hook-up. Reception was unusually clear and satisfactory. Could hear him as clearly as if he were in Philadelphia. Spoke for over twenty minutes, most marvelously. It was a thrilling experience. . . .

## Tuesday, September 15

. . . Telephoned far and wide frantically today, rounding up "patrons" [for "Heaven Bound"]. Went down town and "mingled with the proletariat," meaning saw Mrs. Rhodes, Mrs. Dickerson and hated to find the elusive Marquesa-es. Seems to be an impression that Wright and I are making a fortune out of this. Ye Gods! And considerable snobbery about it. . . .

Special from [newsman] Floyd Snelson with tentative plans for a lecture tour from October 14–November 12. Now I'll have to wire him I'm going to Bermuda. Hell! If I could only make some money *before*. And such an enthusiastic letter from Helene! All sorts of lovely plans she's making. . . .

### Thursday, September 17

Been working on HEAVEN BOUND a month to-day. Well, even if I don't make anything but expenses coming up, it has been a god-send—to get away from the house, to be in Philadelphia, to feel useful again, to keep from brooding on my condition. And I'm working hard. . . .

### Wednesday, September 23

. . . Before going to bed, had a desperate struggle with Mr. [George] Johnson [Howard High School principal]. He's been calling me, and we had a struggle over the phone from the Philadelphia end. Wants me to take the Academic work of the Howard High School night school. That means two nights a week, $5.00 per night, forty dollars a month for about seven months. I suppose I was a fool to refuse it, and Leila and Pauline felt so, but in the first place I'm too sore on Wilmington to want to teach in its system; second, I *might* do much better doing the lecture stuff, if Snelson puts over his plans; third, I'd have to give up Bermuda—might have to anyhow; fourth, I couldn't go to Washington in January, and help Emmett [Scott] with HEAVEN BOUND; and fifth, I don't want to be doing the same thing Emma [Sykes] and Big Liz [Lizzie Banton] are doing—just too proud, that's all. If Bobbo's job would come along I could thumb my nose at all the misguided folk who are trying to give me bread to eat. Johnson was hurt, too, at my refusal, temper it though I did. . . .

### Thursday, September 24

. . . So went on home [from Philadelphia] on usual train. Leila and Polly went out to the latter's dressmaker, and Collegiate [Miss Waters], of course, to night school. Mama and I alone, and she needed ministrations. I tended her—and it was unsavory—and put things where Collegiate could clean up when she returned. But Mama did not like this, and made the remark that if she had known it was C's night school night, she "would not have let Leila go out." Then something snapped in my head, and I wanted to know if Leila was working for Miss Waters, or Miss Waters for Leila, and a lot of words passed between us, so that Mama took refuge in her usual classification of me as "Fussy."

When Leila and Polly came in we played bridge. I repeated the fuss, and saw that Leila was taking sides with Mama at once. She and Polly still sore at me for passing up the night school, so that I feel like a whipped child.

### Friday, September 25

Mama stopped speaking to me last night, and returned no greetings nor goodbyes this a.m. Mention of this fact to Leila elicited the reply that Mama had said she had shed some tears, and that she (Leila) felt that the matter of Miss Waters was a "one-sided affair." "When she was hired last January I thought the understanding was—" and then she stopped and I knew she meant that I had not done my share towards paying her wages, and therefore had nothing to say about her discipline. So I kissed her perfunctorily good-bye, and left in a blind rage which stayed with me all day, making me feel whipped, chastised, beaten, miserable. So always did Mama make fusses, stir up strife, and the worst passions in the family. . . .

### Tuesday, September 29

. . . Had a long talk with Dr. [Harvey] Murray [their family physician]. Assures me that Mama will probably outlive both of us, and said Bermuda trip okeh. Also [her] neuritis largely mental.

### Wednesday, September 30

. . . Called up the Bermuda Line, and impersonating Mrs. Nelson's secretary, asked if she could delay paying her final payment until Monday, as she was away and would not be back until Sunday. Was assured it was okeh. . . .

### Thursday, October 1

. . . [Polly and Leila] dropped me at the MET [for a performance of *Heaven Bound*] and went on home.

[Leslie P.] Hill came buzzing in, making more noise than a brass band, with fifteen of his faculty and students [from Cheyney State College, Pa.]. But he didn't put it over at all with me. I knew just what happened. He and his faculty ignored my appeals, until they or rather he, read the morning papers, and all—*Ledger, Record, Inquirer, Bulletin, Daily News,* all carried most flattering reviews and criticisms. Then he hastened to climb on the band wagon—probably induced by having heard that Biddles, Yarnalls, et als. were helping me. But he did not put it over with me, for I very coldly told him just what I thought of him.

The performance was good, but there was no spot light for the devil. [*Heaven Bound* was a black musical morality play.] Maybe I was tired, it seemed to me the chorus lacked spirit. However, I enjoyed it, saw lots of folks. A good house, not quite as full as Wednesday, and a lot of "paper," I think. . . .

## Friday, October 2

. . . Decided to get luncheon and dinner in one. . . . Found a little Italian place on 16th street, "The Caruso." Lovely like all Italian places. The only fly in the ointment was flies now and then. . . .

But such a luncheon! Antipasto. Soup. Spaghetti. Broiled live lobster, with potato. French bread. Spumoni. Coffee. For fifty cents! I felt like a million dollars when I had finished. And grew reckless and tipped the waiter fifteen cents! . . .

## Saturday, October 3

. . . Went out driving with Leila and Polly. Former very nervous and tired. Mama will see her out yet. . . .

## Monday, October 5

So went to Philadelphia as usual. Found some mail and some checks and Bobbo's Friday letter saying the Elks couldn't pay him any salary until November. Great grief! I believe Bobbo *invented* bad luck.

Collected some money from Mrs. Taylor, went to the Bermuda line and paid for my passage and Mrs. Harrison's (now I have to hustle to cover Bobbo's check). . . .

## Tuesday, October 6

. . . Virginia drove me back to Wright's. He . . . and I checked up. My receipts . . . gave me commission of $129.00 [for her *Heaven*

*Bound* work]. . . . That eased my mind a lot. It will enable me to pay my October obligations nicely, thanks be, and meet that $55.00 check I gave Bobbo. We made touching farewells and so home. . . .

## Thursday, October 8

. . . At night had another severe gas attack. Thoroughly frightened at pressure on heart. Thought I'd croak once. Bobbo attentive nurse. Quiet about four after two hours of agony.

## Friday, October 9

. . . Back [to Maison Marie's] and was in Margaret's hands for nearly three hours. She darkened my hair, which I didn't like. It's red now. . . .
We leave at 5 a.m. tomorrow.

## On Board the Cunard RMS Franconia
## Saturday, October 10

It was very exciting this a.m. I began waking at 1:30 and awoke every hour but three. Promptly at four my eyes were propped and I stirred. . . . For once there was unanimous and concerted movement on the part of the familee. The news had to be broken to Mama and a picture of the ship left her. . . . Goodbyes said. Bags and us packed in the car . . . and at five minutes past five, we were on our way. . . .

Arrived at the Furness line pier No. 95 [New York] at a quarter to nine . . . and had to wait until nine for the boat to let us on.

Once on, the stateroom found, bags stored, and we started on a voyage of exploration. Lounges, card rooms, salons, writing rooms, bar, etc. etc. until Polly flatly said she was not going home, but stay on the boat. Flowers came. . . . Eventually Mrs. Harrison [her traveling mate] appeared. The crowds surged and roared and turgided on decks. . . . Ribbon streamers over everything, and me all tangled in it. All ashore! The gangplank in. Waving and farewells. Two tugs pushing the great vessel out. Bobbo looking as if he were going to cry over his smile. . . .—the pier just a blur of faces—and we pass the Statue of Liberty, as I hurriedly pen Bobbo a special to go back to Wilmington.

Arrange for deck chairs; for dining table. Luncheon—ate too much. . . . A sheaf of cards and letters from [friends]. . . . Lie on deck and

read and doze. Have afternoon tea. Go upstairs for life-boat drill. Go
to Deck A for the horse races. . . .

Dress for dinner and I put on the lovely blue and white polka dot
dress Fannie Hamilton brought me last night—a whole lovely dress! . . .

And on deck in the lovely starlight. The boat gently swaying—not
too much. Warmer. A romantic night. Boat full of hilarious youths
of both sexes—full of the joy of having passed the twelve mile limit.
A beautiful time thus far. . . .

And my heart aches at the memory of Bobbo's pitiful smile. Poor
fellow! I know how he feels—could not help at all, and I had to give
him five dollars for change. He has had no check since August and
none likely till November. And when he did try to help—I had to pay
$2.33 on his protested check.

Poor Bobbo. *He* needs to cross water.


### On Board the Franconia
### Sunday, October 11

. . . While we were dressing for breakfast, Mrs. Harrison broke
loose with a bona fide sea sickness. . . . The sea *was* rough. Portholes
in the dining room had to be closed. Great lovely waves. White caps.
Blue sky with white cumulus clouds. And *such* a blue, blue sea. I
didn't know water could be so beautifully blue. . . .

The air warm, soft, languorous. And I'm wondering why, after five
months' torture from the hottest of summers, I would come south to
prolong the summer season. Langorous breezes are blowing. The stars
eerily brilliant in a black velvet sky. And I long for someone to walk
the deck with me and feel romantic.

We arrive tomorrow morning.


### Sea Spray—Pembroke West
### Hamilton, Bermuda
### Monday, October 12

. . . And there was land! Barren cliffs, white and brown, gleaming
chalk white, stark rocks. For all the world like the islands in the Casco
bay [Maine]. Nothing tropical about them. New England rather. And
even now, in spite of blooming oleanders, double hibiscus, gorgeous
bougainvillea, and the bluest water imaginable, it does not seem tropical. . . .

Mrs. Harrison and I strain our eyes for a friendly face—I watching for Helene, she for some Misses Eve. She saw them first and waved—though she knew none and soon I waved at Helene—my toes curling in excitement. . . .

Such a quaint place! Roads cut in the solid rock. Up and down. Narrow rocky roads, filled with bicyclists. A world on bicycles. And such lovely bougainvillea and oleander. And now over a hill, a wide sweep of blue. Up another hill—Helene's bungalow, white, quaint, oleander embowered. . . .

A lovely afternoon and evening. . . . And I slipped away down to the sea to a cliff—which I named Prospero's Precipice, and down below are Caliban's Coves. And sea, blue, and the Franconia riding at anchor—oh lovely! Then back.

We saw the tender go out and so I must go and show Sadie [Mrs. Harrison] the way down and we lay on the edge of the cliff and waved good-bye to our ship that had been such a generous home to us as she steamed away to St. Georges. . . .

### Sea Spray
### Tuesday, October 13

. . . We were to go to St. Georges today but decided to wait until Friday when my "show" [her lecture] is over. . . .

I must set down that queer half-fright, half-remembered constriction of breast and throat that assails me when I pass between the high white walled lanes and streets. As of a terror once experienced in such a situation. Dream? The cemeteries in N.O. [New Orleans]? Which?

### Hamilton, Bermuda
### Wednesday, October 14

. . . Surprised to find such evidence of interest in things Negroid and American—dialect etc. Quite a good program, well given. English thoroughness. . . .

Strange to say the ball which followed was exclusive—being limited to holders of patron's tickets. I had to open with a married gentleman—it being Bermuda convention for a married lady to do the formal dance with one in her own matrimonial state. My escort—a little gentleman with a fierce mustache . . . hopped me valiantly through an interminable waltz. Music good. Floor divine. . . . Courtesy. "May I have the honor and the pleasure of the next dance?" Got along nicely—

except for waltzes. Danced my fool self simple. Feet like pin-cushions. But enjoyed it. The scene—might have been anywhere in the United States—anywhere. Same satin dresses, same everything. But *no* bumps. And a passionate sign on the walls proclaimed that anyone dancing the Lindy hop would not only be ejected but refused future admission.

So home in our romantic Victoria in the lush dark night. A wonderful success, said the Bermudians—a brilliant affair and only Mrs. London could have engineered it.

All of us tired, cross and sleepy when we got in—and my feet! . . .

### Sunday, October 18

. . . To St. Paul's Church. All introduced. Sadie [Harrison] speaks. How we kidded her about "My sainted grandfather, Bishop Tanner." She admitted that she might be talking to some of her cousins. Who knew what the tie between the Bishop and the "gentle Bermudians" was? . . .

### Monday, October 19

. . . Back to L'Esperance on the ocean front. A lovely home—radio and all—in which seen the Vancrossans and her sister, Miss Boland—Trinidadians. He's tremendously interesting—and handsome. Tiring of his affair with Effie DaCosta, wife of the principal of the high school—an elderly Jamaican. An interesting tangle. The women folk handsome, after a fashion, with unstraightened hair—what a field for a *good* hairdresser!

We play bridge—drink "West Indian punch," salad etc. Interesting evening. . . .

*The implication of this passage seems to be that D-N and Helene did more than simply converse with each other. Ted appears to be a gentleman friend and intimate companion of Helen's, while Jean is one of her two children.*

### Thursday, October 22

. . . After a night of intermittent sleeplessness—room doubtless too close—rise early for walk on Prospero's precipice—and took Helen with me. Our *talk* clarified things. She was walking on air when we returned with Ted and Jean who came and found us there. . . .

### Friday, October 23

. . . Helene gave me $5.00 more—$74.00 in all.

*Below, D-N alludes to the biblical story in which Mrs. Potiphar (the wife of Joseph's guard) unsuccessfully attempts to seduce Joseph (Genesis 39).*

### S. S. Veendam
### Saturday, October 24

It was well nigh perfect moonlight last night, so Helene and I walked down the road, now and then going out on the cliffs to enjoy the moonlight on the spray tossing high in air. It was gorgeous. Tried to feel romantic—couldn't.

By the time we were all in our pajamas, Ted returned with liquor, cigarettes, and a box of rum chocolates, which I shall give Leila. We had a funny seance, Ted playing the role of Joseph to Helene's Mrs. Potiphar.

Then Helene insisted on sleeping three to a bed. Embarrassing. Uncomfortable. So I arise at 6:40 a.m. and started things going—having packed last night. Was rewarded by seeing the most beautiful rainbow I have ever seen. Raining as usual—Bermuda gusts and sunshine. Helene cried out suddenly and we rushed to the window. A magnificent arch—one end in the ocean at the foot of the cliff, one far distant, the arch reaching high over sea and landing—clear, distinct, gorgeous. It was the thrilling sight of a lifetime. . . .

Crowd down to see us off. . . .

Saw Sea Spray as we passed and waved wildly.

Good-bye Bermuda. With mingled feelings of relief and pleasure, we say it. A lovely time—but it is good to set faces home—even though it may be unpleasant. . . .

### On board the S. S. Veendam
### Sunday, October 25

. . . All my Bermuda pictures spoiled. Had them developed on board and all blank. I could cry, for there were some lovely views I wanted. Sadie's more successful—but ugly choices. Mostly people—while I had spray of ocean, Prospero's precipice, the blind donkey, etc. Sickening.

### Monday, October 26

. . . Slowly we came up the river and docked. I was hurt not to see one welcoming face on the pier. Had hoped for Bobbo—hoped he would meet me radiant with good news. Had written Floyd Snelson— and that round-faced fool was not there. Went through customs so easily . . . that I regretted the glass bottle of Scotch tucked in my waist and hurting me all day—and all the good liquor I left in Bermuda. . . .

### Tuesday, October 27

That let down feeling of a holiday over and no future. . . .

### Wednesday, October 28

Early today decided that out of this mess I must evolve some workable philosophy. No use running to Washington. No use running away. Must stay and face issue, money or no money. Job or no job.

And here's the issue:

Mama's expensive illness. Collegiate's wages which Leila is paying alone. And buying all the food. And so I owe her two hundred or more. And Wanamaker's [a fine department store] and the [newly purchased] frigidaire, and last winter's fuel oil bill, and everyone else [she owes money].

And about thirty dollars between me and jail. And no job. And Snelson keeps a glum silence, and Lawson hasn't vouchsafed a word, and Bobbo is worse than broke. Borrowing from me. No salary paid him by the Elks since August. And Pinchot and Stahlnecker [from whom they are expecting to hear about Bobbo's appointment] worse than useless. And there we are.

Flatly—where? What? How?

I don't know. I can only hope. Look. Try again. Well—that's that. . . .

### Thursday, October 29

. . . To bed early. To read "Five Handsome Negresses." Wrote Helene today—sent her the poem [probably about Helene and the Bermuda trip] I did on Monday night. . . .

## Saturday, October 31

. . . Ed Henry's story was that he had been in Harrisburg [Pa. capital] to see Pinchot and endorse Bill Ramsay for the Athletic Commissionership. But the Governor said, "I am going to appoint Bob Nelson to that job." At which Ed expressed his pleasure and withdrew his endorsement for Ramsay.

Fine. But WHEN? That's the question! Most of my little money is gone, financing Bobbo! . . .

## Sunday, November 1

All Saints' Day. Went to the Unitarian church and heard a Dr. Westwood on the Sub-Conscious Mind. He said nothing beautifully. . . .

## Monday, November 2

. . . Sent "Harlem John Henry" [which had been rejected by seven other magazines] to the *Crisis* today. . . .

## Wednesday, November 4

Mama was conscious a little while this morning and asked—thickly—for a peach. I said, "Canned peaches. No fresh ones." To my suggestion that it might be difficult to get fresh peaches now, she insisted that she had seen fresh ones on the tree. And lapsed into indifference. Collegiate has difficulty getting even a tablespoon of wine or broth or coffee down her throat. She is perfectly helpless at last. But each progressive stage of deterioration is a long drawn-out and tedious one. This—her crying and moaning—is terribly distressing to us all. The house is sinking more and more under the pall. . . .

## Thursday, November 5

But Leila called me excitedly at a quarter to five saying that Mama was breathing her last. Went down stairs, but could not see that she was dangerously sinking. So—as I dressed, decided to keep awake by work. So cleaned house. Leila vacuuming the floors, but I doing windows, paints, pictures, electric fixtures, putting up curtains and drapes all over the house—in short, "digging in" for the winter—a thing I never expected to do. I had thought Mama would be gone, Bobbo appointed, the home broken up, and all of us settled in Philadelphia. How strangely different things turn out.

By two, had finished—after a day's strenuous toil—which ordinarily would have taken several days.

Had intended going to Virginia's today and had so phoned. Now had to phone cancelling engagement.

Dr. Murray said it was a question of *days* with Mama now. Seems hours to me.

I slept on the library couch to be near her room. Leila and Collegiate in and out all night.

## Friday, November 6

Mama able to talk feebly this a.m.—asked "Who was that lady?" meaning me. But lapsed into unconsciousness by noon. Such a tiny flicker of life. And such a horrible disfigurement of face as she fades away before our eyes. . . .

Dr. Murray today said Mama might live through the night. Hardly seems that she can.

Polly off to Baltimore with her and [Principal] Johnson's car full of football heroes for a game. Glad she got a respite from this House of Gloom.

God! Are we always to live in the shadow of gloom and misery? Killed time by reading [George] Schuyler's "Slaves of Today." Couldn't work.

*Mama died at 9:40 or 9:39-½.*

Leila and I were in the Library playing honeymoon [bridge] listlessly because we could not read. Collegiate went up to lie down until midnight. So I would go to her room every five minutes to look. Mama slept–breathing heavily. At nine I went again. The breathing growing shallow. Called Leila. She sat by the bed. I put away cards and table. Went back and stood. At 9:39, Bobbo's footsteps on the steps. His key in the door. A long last sigh from Mama. The end of Patricia Moore. Bobbo stepped in the room. All over. He called Collegiate. Polly came in at ten. We were through telegraphing and telephoning and Mr. Gray was in. . . .

## Monday, November 9

. . . Jack [their dog] refuses to eat. Mopes and pines. Leila opened Mama's room today. He keeps going in looking for her—or cakes that she used to give him.

## Tuesday, November 10

. . . How strange to come home to an empty house! . . .

## Thursday, November 12

. . . We all seem frightfully tired and want to go to bed early.

*This clipping from a Reading (Bobbo's hometown), Pennsylvania, newspaper gave premature notice of Governor Pinchot's intent to appoint Bobbo to the Athletic Commission.*

## Friday, November 13

. . . Leila gave me a letter from Bobbo with this clipping from the Reading *Eagle*. Too bad this has gotten out. Now opposition will develop and only give Pinchot another excuse for delay. I told Leila and Polly. The latter had heard from Lorraine [Hamilton] of the gossip. Too bad. I hate a lot of talk. Usually makes trouble. . . .

## Wednesday, November 18

For days and nights the fog horns and sirens on the [Delaware] river proclaim murk and danger. For days the weather reports scream 16 or 17 or 20 degrees above normal. Well—it's good for the poor and down and out [among whom she clearly—and interestingly—does not include herself]. . . .

## Thursday, November 19

Bobbo's letter today said he . . . might stay over [in Harrisburg] and prod up Stahlnecker. I'm growing more and more bitter each day.

Pinchot's playing politics with human misery—*my* misery—is devastating.

Morning mail brought a letter from Harris the pawnbroker saying the time limit had expired on my rings and they would be sold. Made me sick. Called up and he promised to hold on until Saturday. Amount has crawled to $18.00. Now where am I going to get $18.00?

The [Pittsburgh] *Courier* came and Bobbo's supposed appointment to be is all over the front page, screamer and all, in [editor] Vann's most scurrilous style. *Now*, Pinchot will have an excuse for not making the appointment.

God! I wish I could find a job! . . .

### Friday, November 20

. . . Well—if Vann's dirty article in the *Courier* is the cause of Bobbo's loss of that appointment, I shall calmly kill him. The earth has been cluttered up with that skunk too long anyhow. Wish to God I hadn't gone to Bermuda, but had stayed home and taken that night school job. I've *got* to find work. I'll go crazy with this damn waiting, waiting, waiting. Wait even for these damn Elks to pay Bobbo's salary. God! Wait! . . .

### Sunday, November 22

. . . Leila invited the whole Jamison family to dinner. I was quite aghast. Such a muchness! So I helped her after we came home. It was fun having them, after all, in spite of trouble and dishes. . . .

### Monday, November 23

Had the house to myself most of the day. . . . Whipped myself to do a story—Austin Dabney. Really *whipped* myself, in between reading Edna St. Vincent Millay and listening to the Atwater Kent audition, and getting dinner. . . .

Bobbo calls me everything but a Child of God in his letters because I said I didn't believe those wily old politicians in Harrisburg. Says I'm a quitter, yellow, and what not. He's peevish and might as well take it out on me. I'm tough. . . .

## Monday, November 30

. . . In the morning mail received an invitation from "The President of the United States" to a conference on Home Building and Home Ownership. Fired with a desire to go to Washington, but no money, either from Bob or me. Raining. But walk to station with Bobbo. For exercise. We talk of possibilities. I want so to attend that mess of [nationally prominent Black Chicago politician] Oscar DePriest's [also]. . . .

## Washington, D.C.
## Wednesday, December 2

Bobbo not apparently pleased when I arrived at 9:55 last night. Definitely grouchy. "Hated to see me mixed up with all these pussy-footers." I know better. His pride is hurt because he was not able to bring me here himself. That I had to maneuver, borrow Leila's coat (in which I look swelegant) and get here myself. And so he took out his self-grouch on me. And took me by the office, where I sat quietly while he read and gave a Christmas check for $1.00. The fund he had failed to keep up. "If I had just put in each week what I have played on numbers, you'd have a big check."

Numbers! . . .

## Washington, D.C.
## Thursday, December 3

. . . Then dressed for the DePriest reception, and went to the church to hear [W.E.B.] DuBois. He put us to sleep, while Nannie Burroughs woke us up, magnificently. So we gassed around awhile, talking to the "Big Niggers" and all the she-cats of the country, and to the Y.W. to this knock down and drag out reception. Poor Mrs. DePriest didn't have a chance to show who was hostess, for the shemales took off their hats and coats and stood on the receiving line willy-nilly. It was amusing. Gassed around awhile, and then followed Jeannette Carter's instructions to go to Howard Manor to the apartment of some Miss Dellinger, where was being pulled a "hot party," which I had suggested last night.

Nice apartment. Plenty men, few women, Chicago and Detroit

furnishing most of the males. Very much interested in a Mahoney from Detroit, lawyer, handsome, fascinating, married, pleasant. Others with whom I made impossible dates in Chicago, I've forgotten. Plenty liquid refreshments, and [at] about 2:30, broiled dogs, spaghetti, slaw, hot biscuits. We brought Mrs. Billboard Jackson . . . home about 3:30, and to bed ourselves.

### Friday, December 4

. . . Got in a long line of taxis at the east entrance to the White House, and dragged along, but arrived just as the clock was striking five [for the reception of the Home Building and Home Ownership conference]. Ensued all the long waits, the crowding, the standing, the slow process through innumerable rooms and past innumberable officials and secret service men, and at ten minutes to six had finally progressed to the room where stood President and Mrs. Hoover. We had wondered if [he] was shaking hands with everyone, and he was, and so was she. With a pleasant word and smile and handshake for everyone. Never have I felt my heart go out so to anyone as I looked on that tired face, that lined, careworn face. Good God, he can have his job! And she, much stouter even than she seemed on the stage, but pleasant, though seemingly weary too. But then there must have been over 2000 of us! . . .

We went to the John Wesley Church, where I had spared myself the pain of hearing the women pule all day about their greatness, and Blanche Beatty must have me on the platform, where all the "gang" was perched. [Philadelphia magistrate] Ed Henry presiding, and Clarence Darrow [the famous lawyer and writer] spoke. I had been excited about hearing him, and was horribly disappointed. Poor speech, and when he said that Paul [Dunbar] was so unappreciated that the only job he could get was running an elevator, and so died of tuberculosis from confinement, I almost blew up. So sent him a note, and afterwards we had an interesting conversation—he was sitting almost in front of me. . . .

### Tuesday, December 8

. . . Called up finance company in Chester [Pa.]. [They] said I'd have to have Pauline go on my note. Broached it to her tonight saying I'd pay her the twenty I owe her. Said she would. . . .

## Wednesday, December 9

. . . Miss [Alice G.] Baldwin [Wilmington schoolteacher] called a round table discussion of the N.A.A.C.P. with [Philadelphia minister] Robert Bagnall tonight. Twelve or thirteen responded. Roused the old fighting spirit and re-organized the ancient group. Young Reverend Jones, the new minister of Shiloh Baptist Church, made president. I nominated him. Somehow I got elected vice-president, Pauline secretary, Gertrude Henry treasurer. Looks as if we might come alive again. . . .

## Saturday, December 12

When I was thinking of getting ready to make a dash to Chester with Polly, she said that Leila said one of the Chester men had been at the house yesterday while I was in Philadelphia and that he would return at nine. I felt that was queer, but went on getting breakfast. At nine, Anderson, the boy friend of the other day came, and put Pauline through the third degree. It was humiliating, horrible to see someone else have to go through what I had suffered earlier in the week. Made my breakfast taste awful. Later he called and said it was ok for us to go to Chester, as I had said it was the only day—Saturday—that I could get the two together. Leila ready to go to Dover, and we three dashed out without a word. Rushed to Chester. The Personal Finance a horrible place of newness, raw and uncompromising looking. And such a horde of miserable people, furtive, downcast, sordid. We waited nearly an hour for our turn, finally into one of the "consulting rooms"— to be told, after Polly and Bob had signed innumerable papers—that I could not get the money until Monday. Disappointment profound and crushing. I complained of the expense—these signatures must go before a board, etc. So dash back to Wilmington, very cross and silent— and I thought I would faint from shame and misery at the whole thing. . . .

## Monday, December 14

Took the 8:24 to Chester this morning. Arrived, and waited my turn . . . only to be told by the urbane young man that he had bad news for me—the Board of Directors could not lend me the money, as Polly's credit was too strained, Bobbo too far away, me out of a job,

etc. I was wild. Thought of the checks I had out, and almost collapsed. The young fellow said maybe I could get a loan at the Globe
across the street—the place whose flamboyant advertisement on the
window had made us laugh Saturday. Stumbled over there, put in
application, etc., and the young fellow promised he'd be at the house
to see me about two.

Walked up from the [Wilmington train] station because I had taken
my last dollar to pay railroad fare to and from, and had no carfare.
Pouring rain, and was tired and wet when I came in with the bad
news. Bobbo looked as crushed as I felt. He had expected me to return
with cash, and he would take a train to Washington. He had his brief
case packed down stairs. Nothing to do now but wait this new affair. . . .

Bowse, Leila and Polly going up to the Royal to see Tallulah
Bankhead in "My Sin." Had invited Bowse to dinner, and cooked a
lovely little rabbit and mushrooms, etc. They were indignant that Bobbo
and I would not go, and Polly threatened not to go—I had told her
the loan fell through, and that the signatures had been returned. Also
had to call up Jim Sewell [a Wilmington friend and supporter] and
tell him not to put in that ten dollar check I had loaned him yesterday.
But neither Bobbo nor I was in the mood or had the money for movies. So they went and we stayed home alone, and read and tried not
to seem concerned about each other.

### Tuesday, December 15

Ten days before Christmas! Whew! Far from Christmas to me. Of
course, poor Bobbo couldn't get away today, waiting for the Mr. Miles
[of the Globe finance company] to come from Chester. I called yesterday to see why he was delayed. They said he was on his way. Called
twice today. He finally came, and was very pleasant in his appraisal. I
was wiser than with the Personal [finance company]—said I had a job,
told of my royalties, etc., made me seem more dependable. Job with
the Associated Publishers [Carter G. Woodson's press]. Writing. Bank
called me up twice about the stream of worthless checks of mine which
began coming in. About 5:30, called to know if loan had gone through.
Miles out, but he called me later, and said it had gone through for
$200, instead of $300—which was something. And I could get it
tomorrow a.m. Great relief. Could play family bridge with a lighter
heart. . . .

Miserable! Flowing like a river from leucorrhea—pure nervousness. . . .

### Friday, December 18

Did a wee bit of shopping, and tonight tied up packages, etc. Not many, but enough to make me feel less like a Mohammedan [who would not celebrate Christmas]. Cards piling in. Weather warm, spring-like, making heavy coats unbearable, but a blessing to the poor. God knows what the [Depression-racked] country would do if we were having one of our hard winters.

Tied up parcels—we were tired and went upstairs early, and read in "Years of Grace"—a fascinating book.

### Saturday, December 19

. . . Had my hair done tonight, and my nails manicured. Not manicured, dirt and stain dug out—a terrible job, what with the gas-range grease, and the permanganate of potash I've been using as a douche. Bought rubber gloves for future use. . . .

### Wednesday, December 30

Christmas Day at Virginia's, we saw the January *Crisis*. "Harlem John Henry" was featured. "An epic of Negro Peace to which we give the whole of our poetry page." . . .

### Thursday, December 31

The last night of the disastrous year of 1931, and I am, as usual, ten days behind in my diary. So I am going to do a "blanket" entry, and call it a year. . . .

Somehow the little Christmas preparations did not irk, nor was I as blue and miscrable as last year. I would not pin high hopes on Christmas, but as the time drew nigh, and the warm, spring-like weather gave way to crisp sharp, frosty nights, I could not help it, and all the old childish love of Christmas came back—and it was not in vain. For this year, though there were but three of us here together, we were all three well and cheerful, and Bobbo had heard good news that he was positively to be appointed when the legislature adjourned. . . .

It was a surprisingly lovely Christmas. When you think of how unpromising it seemed. No money, no way to give things, no job, Mama deceased so short a while, and Leila gone to Chicago—it looked pitiful. But—the Christmas tree was trimmed, and we were very happy, we three, Polly, Bobbo and I.

Anna [Brodnax] had a bridge party Saturday evening, and Bobbo and I went to that, and from there to Leon [Anderson]'s where Polly and the "gang" were, and stayed until three or thereabouts. But I find that the responsibility of bringing in that darn milk wakes me at seven, even as it wakes Leila, and I'm up and down stairs, feeding Jack, drawing curtains, starting up the furnace, and generally acting like Leila—even to being careful of garbage and floors, and cleaning a lot. . . .

Leila wrote an enthusiastic letter of her good time in Chicago, and I'm so glad she could go and be happy away from us. Polly and I improved her absence by getting twin Simmons beds for those two rooms, and I worked like a dog yesterday cleaning and doing over Mama's room, putting in the new bed and all. It's better now, for that room had me as nervous as a witch. Every time I passed it, I expected to see Mama's face reflected in the mirror as it used to be. The room is quite pretty now, but I suppose Leila will raise hell, for she did not want it touched—just left as a memorial, I guess. I couldn't stand it.

So now it is December 31. Bobbo has come. . . . We are preparing to sit up and welcome the new year with a quiet bang.

Good-bye 1931—you were a whang of a year. But if you did lose my job for me, you sent me to Bermuda, and that's something. And I wax fat, like Jeshurun [poetic biblical word for Israel, meaning "The Upright One"] and the end is not yet. The Pennsylvania legislature has adjourned in disgrace—the special session costing more than it was worth, and doubtless [Governor] Pinchot has gone to Milford to recuperate, and maybe early in 1932 he will give Bobbo the coveted job. Let us hope. And hope, too—for prosperity for all, and happiness distributed everywhere.

*This time, D-N's hopes were realized. In January 1932, Governor Pinchot appointed Robert to the Pennsylvania Athletic (Boxing) Commission. The entire household moved to Philadelphia, where D-N continued to busy herself with civic, social, and literary activities. Three years later, on September 18, 1935, she died of heart trouble at the age of sixty in the University of Pennsylvania Hospital. She was brought back to Delaware for cremation when no establishment in Philadelphia would perform that service for a Black person. D-N's last wish, eventually executed by her husband at the Delaware River, was to have her ashes strewn to "the four winds, either over land or sea."*

# Alice Dunbar-Nelson

## A Chronology*

| | |
|---|---|
| 1875 | July 19, born in New Orleans, Louisiana. |
| 1892 | Graduated from Straight College, New Orleans; subsequently studied at Cornell, Columbia, the Pennsylvania School of Industrial Art, and the University of Pennsylvania, specializing in English educational measurements and psychology. |
| 1892–96 | Taught school in New Orleans. |
| 1895 | Published *Violets and Other Tales* (Boston: The Monthly Review Press)—short stories and poems. |
| 1897–98 | Taught in Brooklyn, New York; helped to found the White Rose Mission, which became the White Rose Home for Girls in Harlem. |
| 1898 | March 8, married poet Paul Laurence Dunbar and began living in Washington, D.C. |
| 1899 | Published *The Goodness of St. Rocque and Other Stories* (New York: Dodd, Mead, and Co.)—short stories. |
| 1902 | Separated from Paul Laurence Dunbar and moved to Wilmington, Delaware (he died February 6, 1906). |
| 1902–20 | Taught and administered at the Howard High School, Wilmington; for seven of these years, also directed the summer sessions for in-service teachers at State College for Colored Students (now Delaware State College), Dover; and taught two years in the summer session at Hampton Institute. |
| 1909 | April, published "Wordsworth's Use of Milton's Description of Pandemonium" in *Modern Language Notes*. |

*For a fuller listing and bibliographical details of Dunbar-Nelson's publications, see Ora Williams, "Works By and About Alice Ruth (Moore) Dunbar-Nelson: A Bibliography," *CLA Journal* XIX (March 1976), 322–26.

| | |
|---|---|
| 1910 | January 19, married teacher Henry Arthur Callis secretly in Wilmington. He left the next year for medical school in Chicago. (They were later divorced at some unknown time.) |
| 1913–14 | Wrote for and helped edit the *A.M.E. Church Review.* |
| 1914 | Edited and published *Masterpieces of Negro Eloquence* (Harrisburg, Pennsylvania: The Douglass Publishing Company). |
| 1915 | Was field organizer for the Middle Atlantic States in the campaign for women's suffrage. |
| 1916 | April 20, married Robert J. Nelson, a journalist. |
| 1916–17 | Published a two-part article, "People of Color in Louisiana," in *The Journal of Negro History.* |
| 1917–28 | Published poems in *Crisis, Ebony and Topaz, Opportunity, Negro Poets and Their Poems, Caroling Dusk, The Dunbar Speaker and Entertainer, Harlem: A Forum of Negro Life,* etc. |
| 1918 | Toured the South as a field representative of the Woman's Committee of the Council of National Defense. |
| 1920 | Served on the State Republican Committee of Delaware and directed political activities among Black women; edited and published *The Dunbar Speaker and Entertainer* (Naperville, Illinois: J. L. Nichols and Co.); drawing on her interests in juvenile delinquency and "abnormal psychology," worked with women from the State Federation of Colored Women to found the Industrial School for Colored Girls in Marshalltown, Delaware. |
| 1920–22 | Coedited and published the Wilmington *Advocate* newspaper. |
| 1921 | August, began her *Diary* and kept an extant portion of it for the remainder of the year. |
| 1922 | Headed the Anti-Lynching Crusaders in Delaware fighting for the Dyer Anti-Lynching Bill. |
| 1924 | Directed the Democratic political campaign among Black women from New York headquarters; August and September, published a two-part article on Delaware in "These 'Colored' United States" in *The Messenger.* |
| 1924–28 | Was teacher and parole officer at the Industrial School for Colored Girls. |
| 1926 | January 2–September 18, wrote column "From the Woman's Point of View" (later changed to "Une Femme Dit") in the Pittsburgh *Courier.* |
| 1926–30 | Wrote column "As In A Looking Glass" in the Washington *Eagle* (her columns and/or versions of them were also syndicated for the Associated Negro Press). |
| 1926–31 | Resumed and kept the remaining extant portions of her *Diary.* |
| 1928–31 | Was executive secretary of the American Friends Inter-Racial |

Peace Committee, which entailed much travel and public
speaking.

1930  January—May, wrote column "So It Seems to Alice Dunbar-
Nelson" in the Pittsburgh *Courier*.

1931  Included in James Weldon Johnson's *The Book of American
Negro Poetry*.

1932  Moved to Philadelphia, after Robert was appointed to the
Pennsylvania Athletic (Boxing) Commission in January.

1935  September 18, died of heart trouble at the University of Pennsylvania Hospital. She was cremated in Wilmington and
her ashes eventually scattered over the Delaware River.

# Index

# Index

479